Longevity Industry 1.0

Dmitry Kaminskiy | Margaretta Colangelo

LONGEVITY INDUSTRY 1.0

Defining the Biggest and Most Complex Industry in Human History

Contributors:

Sergey Balasanyan | Kate Batz | Franco Cortese
Robin Farmanfarmaian | Stefan Hascoet
Eric Kihlstrom | Richard Siow

DKG | NTZ

2020

Longevity Industry 1.0: defining the biggest and most complex industry in human history.

Deep Knowledge Group
https://www.dkv.global/

NTZ
https://ntzpublicacoes.com/
contact@ntzpublicacoes.com

ISBN 978-1-9163917-1-0

First Edition

Table of Contents

Quotes and Advance Reviews 8

Preface by Margaretta Colangelo 11

Preface by Dmitry Kaminskiy 14

Facts vs. Fiction 19

PART I - Longevity Mega-Complexity: Challenges, Issues, Opportunities 25

1. The Biggest and Most Complex Industry in Human History 26
2. Formulating the Longevity Industry Framework 40
3. From BioTech Stagnation to Longevity Prosperity: Forecasting on the Future of Longevity Biomedicine 56
4. Longevity Investing 1.0: Disproportions in the Current Longevity Investment Landscape 64
5. Longevity Investing 2.0: Why Traditional BioTech Analytics Fails Against the Longevity Industry's Extreme Complexity 71
6. Longevity Analytics 2.0 - Modern Analytical and IT Solutions to Manage Longevity Complexity 81
7. Longevity.Capital: Specialized Hybrid Investment Fund for Longevity Industry, De-Risking and Diversification 103

PART II - Longevity Policy and Governance 113

8. The Rise of Longevity Technocracies and MegaHubs: Governance and Policy as the Next Great Longevity Frontier *(Contributor: Eric Kihlstrom)* 114
9. Longevity Progressive and Regressive Nations: Israel, Singapore and the USA 140
10. The Swiss Longevity Valley: How Switzerland May Become a Global Longevity Financial Industry MegaHub by 2025 *(Contributor: Stefan Hascoet)* 153
11. The Longevity Leadership Role of the UK: The Emergence of Longevity-Focused Parliamentary Groups and Government Bodies *(Contributor: Eric Kihlstrom* 170

12. California - Longevity Hype in Silicon Valley: Will the Traditional Approach to BioTech Investment Lead to a Longevity Boom, Bubble or Bust? *(Contributor: Kate Batz)* 188

13. The Future of Longevity Governance: How Longevity Will Become a Major Priority Item for the National Agendas of Progressive Countries by 2025 198

PART III - Longevity Financial Industry 200

14. The Longevity Financial Industry and Novel Financial System 201

15. Major Longevity Financial Industry Trends, Predictions and Insights 218

16. Longevity FinTech *(Contributor: Sergey Balasanyan)* 242

17. Longevity Finance and the Shift from FinTech 1.0 to FinTech 2.0 257

18. FinTech 2.0 and the Rise of Longevity Banks: Where Healthspan Meets Wealthspan 261

PART IV - Longevity Industry (Science, Technology & Biomedicine) 279

19. The Birth and Rise of Geroscience (The Science of Longevity) 280

20. Most Developed Domains of Longevity R&D and Top Longevity Scientists 286

21. The Current State of Longevity Clinical (Human) Trials 303

22. Precision Medicine and the Patient as CEO *(Contributor: Robin Farmanfarmaian)* 309

23. AI for Longevity and Precision Health *(Contributor: Richard Siow)* 321

24. The Effect of Diet and Exercise on Biological Aging: From Hype to Reality 331

25. Longevity FemTech *(Contributor: Robin Farmanfarmaian)* 336

26. Biomarkers of Longevity 2.0: The Shift Toward Actionable, AI-Empowered Biomarkers of Aging, Health and Longevity *(Contributor: Franco Cortese)* 343

27. The Crucial and Fundamental Role of AI in Longevity R&D and Practical Implementation 358

28. What if Geroscience Fails? - Pragmatic Optimism in the Longevity Industry and Defining Hype vs. Reality 373

Longevity Industry 2.0 Summary - DeepTech Engineering The Accelerated Trajectory of Human Longevity: The Blueprint and Pathway from 1.0 to 2.0 383

PART V - Longevity Industry Navigator 386

1. Longevity Industry in UK Landscape Overview 2018 387
2. Longevity Industry in Singapore Landscape Overview 2019 388
3. Longevity Industry in Israel Landscape Overview 2019 388
4. FemTech Healthcare Landscape Overview 2019 389
5. Longevity Industry in California Landscape Overview 2019 390
6. Top-100 Longevity Leaders 391
7. Top-100 Journalists Covering Advanced Biomedicine and Longevity 392
8. Top-50 Women Longevity Leaders 393
9. Top-30 Longevity Conferences 394
10. Advancing Financial Industry Longevity / AgeTech / WealthTech 395
11. Longevity Industry in Switzerland Landscape Overview 2019 396
12. Top-100 Supercentenarians Landscape Overview: 100 Longest-Lived, 100 Currently Living, 25 Socially and Professionally Active 397
13. 1000 Longevity Leaders IT-Platform 398

About Deep Knowledge Group 399

About the Authors 444

About the Contributors 446

Online Resources 448

Quotes and Advance Reviews

"Longevity is the most complex, important and impactful field, and the biggest business opportunity of this century! The problem is that there is so much information about longevity that even beginning a quest for answers can be overwhelming. Thankfully, Margaretta Colangelo and Dmitry Kaminskiy, the ideal people to distill this information to its essence, have done so in their new book Longevity Industry 1.0: Defining the Biggest and Most Complex Industry in Human History. *Colangelo and Kaminskiy are experts and thought leaders in this massive field. They have conducted extensive research and formed partnerships with commercial, academic and non-profit organizations. They understand that now is the time to open the gates and help everyone understand the importance and the possibilities that await us all to have longer, healthier, and higher-quality lives."*

Andrew Bogle, Managing Director, Reva Capital Markets, USA

"The new book Longevity Industry 1.0: Defining the Biggest and Most Complex Industry in Human History, *by Dmitry Kaminskiy and Margaretta Colangelo, is a highly topical, comprehensive and insightful explanation of the potential opportunities and threats of longevity research and how the convergence of AI, advanced data science and longevity research will accelerate important medical breakthroughs that will benefit us all. By sharing their in-depth understanding of this burgeoning industry, including the different roles of the multiple stakeholders, the authors have enabled all of us to gain a better understanding and consider how we might contribute to this exciting field of research."*

Karen Taylor, Research Director, Deloitte Centre for Health Solutions, UK

"I am delighted to see this latest of Dmitry Kaminskiy's many important contributions to the emerging, and exploding, longevity industry. He and his co-author Margaretta Colangelo have composed a volume that will serve as a great source for investors contemplating entering this space but intimidated by the required learning curve. I am sure it will also be hugely valuable to all those interested in monitoring and contributing to this foremost crusade in the history of mankind – the escape from our historical certainty that we will get sick when we get old."

Aubrey de Grey, biomedical gerontologist, Chief Science Officer of the SENS Research Foundation, USA

"We can all be grateful to Dmitry Kaminskiy and Margaretta Colangelo for producing this book. The depth of research involved is clear and the content will be of interest to many people whether they are medical researchers, policy-makers, healthcare providers, insurers, investors, etc. The authors have captured the enormity of this emerging industry and its likely positive impact on human (and animal) health and happiness. It's very striking to read 'The Longevity Industry will be the biggest and most complex industry of all time'. Then on reflection, I had to agree! It makes sense that it will be larger than the current pharmaceutical market.

Dr. David Brown, PhD, Co-Founder, Healx, Sponsor of the Global Sepsis Challenge, Former Global Head of Drug Discovery at Roche, Co-Inventor of Viagra, UK

"Longevity Industry 1.0: Defining the Biggest and Most Complex Industry in Human History, *by Dmitry Kaminskiy and Margaretta Colangelo, promises to be immensely useful — I greatly look forward to using it!"*

Christine Peterson, Co-founder and Senior Fellow, Foresight Institute, USA

"Longevity Industry 1.0 *is a stupendous resource for understanding one of the most significant and underappreciated developments of the modern era. The title* — Defining the Biggest and Most Complex Industry in Human History — *is not exaggerating. Longevity, like the weather, has been an age-old subject for speculation. However, longevity is no longer a topic for idle chatter. Now, longevity is happening in various ways and in many spheres. Multi-disciplinary science, machine learning, big data, social networking, Googlization of knowledge, Amazonizing of commerce, and an awakening political resolve are converging to put humankind on the precipice of achieving what has only been a pipe dream!"*

G. Alexander Fleming, MD, Endocrinologist, Founder of the Metabesity Conference and Executive Chairman of Kinexum, USA

"In their new book Longevity Industry 1.0: Defining the Biggest and Most Complex Industry in Human History, *Dmitry Kaminskiy and Margaretta Colangelo provide an extensive look into the many areas that make up the Global Longevity Industry. If you're interested in the current state of Longevity Science, Longevity Politics and Longevity Financial Instruments including AgeTech, WealthTech and FinTech, then this is the book for you."*

Zoltan Istvan, United States former Presidential Candidate, journalist, entrepreneur and futurist, USA

"15 years ago the longevity industry was non-existent, and today we see entire books dedicated to it. Insilico Medicine powers most of the credible groups and start-ups in this emerging industry and I am very happy to see many of these partners abundantly covered in Longevity Industry 1.0: Defining the Biggest and Most Complex Industry in Human History, *an important book by Dmitry Kaminskiy and Margaretta Colangelo, authors deeply entrenched in the business of longevity."*

Alex Zhavoronkov, PhD, CEO, Insilico Medicine, Hong Kong

"The longevity industry is one of the most exciting and complex, filled with potential for innovation that can change the course of human health and thus of humanity. To take the right steps in the right direction, it's important that we understand market forces, the challenges and the opportunities. There's no better book to ground us in the fundamentals and to set the foundation for the future than Longevity Industry 1.0: Defining the Biggest and Most Complex Industry in Human History. *Well done, Margaretta and Dmitry, for stepping up and providing the industry with what it needs: a framework from which we can build."*

Naheed Kurji, President & CEO at Cyclica and Executive Officer, Alliance for Artificial Intelligence in Healthcare, Canada

"I'm very much looking forward to reading the new book Longevity Industry 1.0: Defining the Biggest and Most Complex Industry in Human History, *by Dmitry Kaminskiy and Margaretta Colangelo, especially the chapters where the authors describe the convergence of AI, advanced data science, biology of aging and longevity research which will accelerate important medical discoveries that will benefit all of humanity."*

Gopal Karemore, PhD, Principal Data Scientist, Novo Nordisk, Denmark

"As we enter the Age of Longevity, it is clear that aging is becoming one of the biggest economic opportunities of the century. The field of longevity is growing exponentially, together with the most advanced technologies in early diagnostics and treatments for slowing down aging, extending healthy lifespans, and fighting killer monsters like cancer and heart disease. Longevity Industry 1.0: Defining the Biggest and Most Complex Industry in Human History, *by Dmitry Kaminskiy and Margaretta Colangelo, analyzes the current trends, companies and initiatives united by one mission: helping people live longer and healthier lives."*

Sergey Young, Founder & CEO, Longevity Vision Fund, USA

Preface by Margaretta Colangelo

Every cause of death is, in principle, preventable. I became aware of this in the 1990s and since then I have been following aging research very closely. There are two main aspects of aging research that appeal to me. The first is that scientists who work in this area regard aging as a disease and therefore, a problem to be solved. When I realized that biological aging is malleable and that some of the world's most respected scientists are researching ways to intervene in the aging process, I read extensively about the science of Longevity.

The second is the amount of suffering that could be alleviated by curing age-related diseases. Aging is the biggest risk factor for developing many diseases including Alzheimer's, osteoporosis, cardiovascular disease and cancer. Few breakthroughs would make as profound an impact on humanity as curing aging. If we could cure age-related diseases and eliminate the suffering that they cause, it would benefit our grandparents, our parents, our children and all future generations.

Longevity science is far more advanced than other areas of science. In fact, it's considered next generation. Longevity research focuses on prevention rather than treatment. It is the most complex area in science because Longevity requires the complete optimization of health at the deepest level targeting biological systems that control disease. Longevity researchers are using the most advanced technologies including AI to exploit the full value of research data to discover new interventions and diagnostic tools to slow aging, extend healthspan, and perhaps even reverse aging.

Scientists have demonstrated that it is possible to extend lifespan. Now that they know some of the pathways that are the primary drivers of aging, they are developing novel strategies to treat the diseases of aging. A number of companies are working on developing drugs that target aging and some of these drugs are currently in clinical trials. This is why there is so much excitement and interest. Although no Longevity drugs have received regulatory approval yet, a number of Longevity therapies have passed phase I and phase II clinical trials, and a few are in phase III clinical trials.

Two Possible Scenarios of Longevity MegaTrends

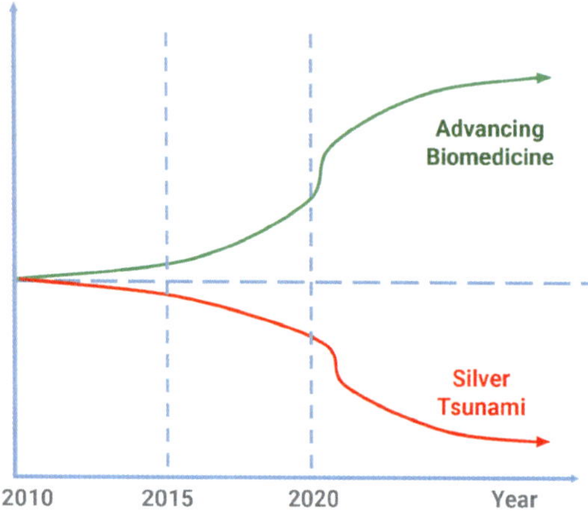

The acceleration of biomedicine has been mainly spurred by advances in the collection, gathering and analysis of data. The industry is poised to witness a quantum leap in the near future, particularly because of the impact of Artificial Intelligence in biomedicine R&D and in light of the upcoming paradigm shift from treatment to prevention.

At the same time, the inevitable Silver Tsunami (demographic aging) poses major economic burdens not just for the healthcare systems of developing nations, but also for major financial institutions, including pension funds, insurance companies, asset management firms and retail / private wealth banks. It is expected to increase the costs associated with old age.

I have been working in the software industry in Silicon Valley for over 30 years. In the 1990s I was a core member of the team that developed the first Java-based secure messaging software used by the world's top multinational investment banks at the core of large-scale stock trading applications. After three decades working in the software industry, I developed a deep and multifaceted understanding of business, science and technology. Although I became adept at forecasting innovation in technology, it was clear to me that making realistic assessments about aging research was much more difficult. From a technical perspective, extending the number of years that humans live in good health is possible; however, it requires deep knowledge, assessment, and strategic foresight.

A turning point for me occurred when I met Dmitry Kaminskiy, my co-author. Through Dmitry I became aware that the Global Longevity Industry extends way beyond aging research and medicine and into all areas including government and the financial industry. When confronted with the extreme complexity in the Longevity Industry, Dmitry's response was to establish a dedicated analytical entity, Aging Analytics Agency, to educate himself and to provide actionable expertise to our company Deep Knowledge Group. Dmitry is the most capable and knowledgeable person I have ever worked with. Although he believes that Longevity is the greatest business opportunity of all time, he is driven more by ethical motives than by mere profit. Dmitry and I have developed a synergetic union of mission and vision.

Today, change occurs at the intersection of two or more scientific and technological domains. We are at the beginning of a trend where the degree of complexity and the number of convergence points will increase exponentially. The convergence of AI, advanced Data Science, and Longevity research will accelerate important medical breakthroughs that will benefit all humans. I know that advanced technologies can save lives. I know this because advanced technologies saved my life. I'm actually an early adopter of life extension technology.

In the next decade, the Longevity Industry will impact many areas of our lives. Longevity policies enacted by governments and changes in the financial industry will transform society. Longevity companies that prove capable of achieving tangible results will become the next Googles, and investment firms that invest in those companies will become the SoftBanks and Vision Funds of tomorrow.

Achieving small but practical results in Longevity distributed at scale will have enormous and multiplicative effects on society. Extending the functional lifespan of humans by just one year will decrease suffering for tens of millions of people and will improve the quality of life for billions of people.

This type of ROI is much more valuable than money.

This is the real type of return that Deep Knowledge Group seeks.

Preface by Dmitry Kaminskiy

Approximately seven years ago I became acquainted with a number of scientists working in the field of aging research. The more I learned from them, the prospect of successfully intervening in aging in the next few years seemed less a mystery like time travel and more a challenge like space exploration. At the beginning of the 20th century, the sciences necessary for space travel – rocketry, Newtonian physics, mathematics and basic astronomy – were already centuries old. It was the additional powers of foresight and precision, brought about by digitization, alongside government initiatives and funding, which opened the door to another world. So it was with space travel last century, and so it is with Longevity this century.

This realisation brought with it my personal eureka moment: I understood that the extension of Healthy Longevity is scientifically feasible, and that it just requires an engineering mindset to structure, formulate

Aging Analytics Agency was established in 2013 as a Longevity-focused analytical subsidiary of Deep Knowledge Group, and began producing analytics before the Longevity Industry itself emerged. The company is exclusively focused on Longevity, Geroscience, AgeTech and Preventive Medicine, has been developing its methodology since 2015, and is the main source of market intelligence in the field.

NeuroTech Analytics was established in 2020 by Deep Knowledge Group to serve as the world's premier source of NeuroTech Industry Intelligence, Forecasting and Benchmarking and the central repository of market insights and trends and news for the NeuroTech space, including sectors, influences, investors, technologies, R&D centres, Hubs, companies and more.

Deep Knowledge Analytics focuses on DeepTech and frontier technology industries using sophisticated multidimensional analytical frameworks and algorithmic methods that combine hundreds of specially designed metrics to deliver sophisticated market intelligence, pragmatic forecasting and tangible industry benchmarking.

and format its practical realization — that all necessary components are in place, and that these components just need to be assembled, integrated and synthesized in an optimal way.

Having understood this, I also realized that the tangible and practical implementation of Longevity technologies could create value and generate wealth far beyond any profit and wealth itself, outperforming the opportunities and impact existing in any other sector and industry, and at the same time delivering the most valuable thing that you could provide for humanity, for your family and for yourself.

In 2013, I founded Aging Analytics Agency in order to keep track of relevant technological, social and political developments as they unfolded, which I now can proudly claim has since evolved into the undoubtable leader in the Longevity Industry analytics sphere, producing a great quantity of open access and proprietary analytical reports, and being capable to monitor, analyze, forecast and ultimately understand, on the deepest level, the entire scope of the current state of Longevity science, technology, business and policy, and to predict the future trajectory of the industry, taking into account its unprecedentedly diverse scope and extreme levels of complexity, multidimensionality and intersectionality.

The Longevity sphere attracts some of the brightest, most innovative and most committed talents in the world, being on the very forefront of human progress. As a result of this, it was natural and logical that during my journey along this pathway I met Margaretta Colangelo, who has since become my closest friend, business partner and confidant. Deep Knowledge Group's activities in the Longevity field became a magnet for the talented and forward-thinking experts and specialists, and we found ourselves blessed with a stellar team of like-minded people with

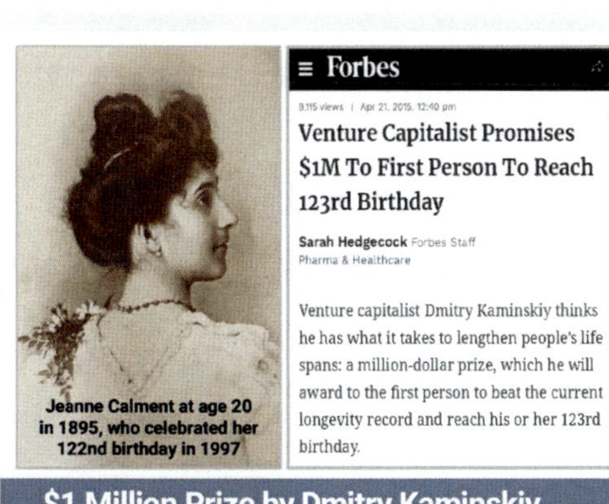
Forbes

8,115 views | Apr 21, 2015, 12:40 pm

Venture Capitalist Promises $1M To First Person To Reach 123rd Birthday

Sarah Hedgecock Forbes Staff
Pharma & Healthcare

Venture capitalist Dmitry Kaminskiy thinks he has what it takes to lengthen people's life spans: a million-dollar prize, which he will award to the first person to beat the current longevity record and reach his or her 123rd birthday.

$1 Million Prize by Dmitry Kaminskiy for Human Life Record

In 2015, Dmitry Kaminskiy created his $1 million prize for the first person to beat the current lifespan record and reach their 123rd birthday in an effort to motivate the acceleration of Longevity Industry progress and to incentivize individuals to apply the practical applications of Longevity and P4 (Precision, Preventive, Personalised and Participatory) Medicine to their own lives and healthspans.

us, including Eric Kihlstrom, Stefan Hascoet, Kate Batz, Richard Siow, Franco Cortese, Sergey Balasanyan and Robin Farmanfarmaian, each of whom is a bright star in our constellation, and each of whom contributed a wealth of valuable content and specific chapters to this book.

This brings us to a quick note I must make on the structure of this book. The science behind the industry is highly advanced and involves a great many technical concepts, many of which are already quite well documented in other relevant books. Our concern here is presenting a broad, industry-level conceptual framework in order to provide a general overview of the industry with the degree of understanding of specific domains necessary to discern threats versus opportunities, fiction versus facts, hype versus reality, and realistically predict future scenarios. As such, in this first edition we have restricted the science to fifty pages. But as true participation in Longevity sphere will inevitably require some mastery of advanced scientific concepts, interested readers of the first edition can request a free of charge second edition after January 2021, which will contain hundreds of additional pages on science and technology. We are confident that most readers would be interested to read about the science, technology and advanced biomedicine no less than they would about the investment, financial and governance sides of the Longevity Industry.

The science and technology of Longevity are much more multifaceted than in the current biotechnology industry in general, requiring much more sophisticated analytics. This is due to the highly complex and cross-sector nature of the technologies, which range from advanced biomedicine, Data Science and Artificial Intelligence to finance, investment, governance, policy, socioeconomic domains and others, and this intercomplexity requires much more sophisticated multi-tier analytical frameworks, the integrated synthesis and assembly of many frontier domains of knowledge, and novel de-risking techniques because of the wide scope for risk and failure, much higher compared with the current BioTech industry.

We at Deep Knowledge Group value knowledge as the most precious of all assets, and knowledge in the Longevity space as double precious deep knowledge. Deep Knowledge Group has an analytical GigaFactory, comprised of two major analytical arms (Aging Analytics Agency and Deep Knowledge Analytics), and seven analytical divisions within them, each focused on specific domains (AI-Pharma, e-GovTech, NeuroTech, Longevity-GovTech, Longevity-FinTech, Systemic Risk Forecaster, and InvestTech Laboratory).

We also are in possession of a specific strategy, involving first acquiring an extreme breadth of knowledge in particular domains, producing tens of thousands of pages of open-access and proprietary analytics on specific sectors, created with the primary purpose of gaining a broad understanding of the entire scope of such industries, in order to lay the groundwork for identifying all relevant players in the field, their activities and progress. We then utilize this extreme breadth of knowledge to cultivate an equally extreme depth of knowledge, sufficient to hone our strategic business agenda in each specific sector. Acquiring sufficient knowledge of the Longevity Industry was the greatest challenge, but we can feel safe to say that we have now accomplished the first level of it. And as such, we will work proactively in the following domains within the scope of Longevity Industry: Biomarkers of Longevity, Geroscience R&D, P4 Medicine, Regenerative Medicine,

Advanced Cosmetics, Longevity FinTech, Longevity NeuroTech, Longevity FemTech, AgeTech and first of all AI for Preventive Medicine, Precision Health and Longevity.

Two looming global changes, one demographic, one technological, are about to shake up the global financial system. One is the "Silver Tsunami", the economic devastation resulting from the global aging demographic. The other is the advancing Longevity Industry, the complex interplay of intersecting technologies which together will give healthy productive life back to this population.

The nations who succeed to thrive rather than decline in the face of the tsunami will have reformed themselves beyond recognition, having been forced to adapt and refashion around novel business models, new types of financial institutions and entire national financial systems, supported by progressive initiatives of technocratic governments.

Government will be responsible for driving forward the development of many facets of the Longevity Industry, ranging from social care to financial reforms, and also for developing and supporting the missing technological synergies, such as the integration of Big Data and healthcare with the focus on AI for Preventive Medicine, the current lack of which further slows down industry growth. As such, Aging Analytics Agency is systematically producing Longevity Policy Proposals for a number of international and government entities, including the World Health Organization and the United Nations.

The Longevity Industry will be the biggest and most complex industry of all time, generating enormous wealth, and representing the most ethical way to conduct business, and its end product will be the most valuable and real asset ever conceived — Healthy Longevity. But it also inevitably carries an unprecedented number of risks. As such, Margaretta, myself and our team feel that it is our duty to demystify this sphere and to inform all future participants in this industry of potential benefits and pitfalls in equal measure.

Indeed, we would like to see a greater number of participants in the industry, an industry so big and diverse, calling upon so many forms of talent from so many sectors, from so many world regions, that there is enough space for unlimited cooperation, and zero competition, unlike any other industry before.

We want to welcome as many people as possible into this industry, which is why we decided to publish this book, bringing the actual deep knowledge of the Longevity Industry to the public.

Facts vs. Fiction

Top 10 Myths

1. Practical implementation of life extension is a long way off. Many people believe that the technology needed to extend human life will be developed in the distant future and that the clinical trials needed to validate such science are decades away. Some of these technologies are already here and others are only several years away. The pace of practical implementations in Longevity therapeutics will increase until we achieve the Longevity Escape Velocity, where advancements in Longevity will be sufficient to maintain health and the rate of addressing damage will be higher than the rate of accumulating it.

2. Extending life means prolonging illness and suffering. On the contrary, life can only be radically extended as a consequence of illness being radically postponed. Extending people's healthy later years is the most promising aspect of technologically increased Longevity.

3. Extending life will increase overpopulation and pollution. It is anticipated that slowing down aging will result in lowering the birth rate. Furthermore, it's estimated that the planet's capacity for humans is around 25 billion. Technologies such as drones, robots, nanotechnologies and biochemistry for cleaning the oceans and the soil (such as genetically engineering bacteria to decompose waste much quicker) point to the fact that we should be able to add 15 billion extra humans to the planet without the danger of overpopulation.

4. Longevity benefits will only be available to the wealthy. Initially, the wealthiest people may have more access to these technologies; however, over time, the price of these technologies is expected to decrease exponentially, and in 10 - 15 years they will be affordable to the majority of individuals.

5. Sports and fitness can extend life. Some exercises have been shown to improve strength, muscle mass, flexibility and other functions, and seem to be capable of improving quality of life and physical and psychological well-being. However, there is not yet sufficient evidence to suggest that exercise can prolong lifespan. A more detailed summary on our specific thoughts and insights on myths vs. reality on Fitness and Longevity can be read at **www.longevity-book.com/practical-longevity** .

6. Vitamin supplements promote Longevity. Research has not determined that vitamin supplements promote Longevity. Some ingredients in multivitamins may even be dangerous in some cases and some bio-supplements may cause side effects. Myths around the health effects of vitamins are mostly driven by the food supplement industry, and many effects of vitamins and supplements require larger scale and more personalized scientific validation to determine their effectiveness in practice.

7. Organic food and diets promote Longevity. Although there is no conclusive scientific evidence that organic food and certain diets promote Longevity, scientists are researching the effects of methods such as intermittent fasting, veganism, and gluten-free diets on Longevity. While some diets can improve an individual's health, science has not determined that any one diet increases Healthy Longevity. More of our thoughts on this matter can be read at **www.longevity-book.com/practical-longevity** .

8. Doctors know how to prolong Longevity. Only recently has medicine started to aggregate actual data which could lead to tangible recommendations for Healthy Longevity. Some doctors have been trained to ease the suffering of elderly patients, but only recently have more advanced and progressive doctors started to recommend techniques and products backed by data science that are practically validated and relevant to the realities of Healthy Longevity. This specific field is still in its inception, and much more work remains to be done to make it practically applicable to most people.

9. Life extension alone is adequate. If science and medicine aim to merely extend lifespan without extension of healthspan (Healthy Longevity), it will result in billions of people suffering from disease. Of course, extension of lifespan without corresponding extension for healthspan (healthy and active period of life) is inadequate.

10. Animal experiments are sufficient for human treatments. New approaches to clinical trials are needed. A decade ago, testing on model organisms such as mice seemed comparatively efficient, but Longevity requires more sophisticated methods focused on human testing.

Top 10 Facts

1. Life expectancy is longer than we assume. On average, young and middle-aged people today can expect to live to 120 years; the elderly can expect to live to 100.

2. You are the CEO of your own health. The most effective manager for your own health is yourself. As the number of Personalised and Precision

Medicine practical applications increase, individuals will take a direct participatory role in managing their own health. Patients should also own their own health data, and be able to lease it out to third parties at their own discretion.

3. You can manage your own financial, psychological and overall wellness. Each individual can manage their own money, time, priorities and physical health to realistically plan for increased life expectancy and quality of health. Advances in Precision Medicine and financial wellness technologies (FinTech, AgeTech and WealthTech for Longevity) can enable financial security over extended periods of Healthy Longevity.

4. The Longevity Industry is already one of the largest industries in the world. Currently, the Longevity Industry is already worth US$17 trillion and it is on track to become the biggest industry by capitalization, and will dwarf all other industries including the carbon economy and real estate.

5. Many countries will decline and become bankrupt because of the Silver Tsunami. This will cause multiple political crises and defaults of national financial systems. This will be due to short term thinking and a lack of implementation of the technologies capable of extending the healthy period of life, from the government's part.

6. New innovations in human-centric testing are needed. Experiments should be conducted on humans using very sophisticated technologies and new approaches, such as integrations with embedded sensors, *in silico* testing, Big Data analysis and AI.

7. Many BioTech companies will switch their business model to Longevity. As Longevity becomes a multitrillion dollar opportunity for start-ups and corporations, many big IT, Tech, Healthcare and Pharma corporations will prioritise Longevity in their business models.

8. Limited, controlled stresses can repair age-related damage. Hormesis refers to the body's increased repair potential following microstresses such as fasting, sauna, cryosauna, short intense exercise and even short psychological stress and others. It works by training the immune system, thereby repairing some of the incurred damages.

9. Rejuvenated organs will pave the way for ultimate Longevity. The first organ to be rejuvenated will be the biggest organ — the skin. In the coming years, sufficient progress will have been made to allow for the healthy maintenance and rejuvenation of the skin, covering both aesthetic and functional concerns. This will be followed by muscle function restoration.

10. The synergetic convergence of many technologies will drive Longevity. The major engine of actual, practical life extension solutions will be the combination of AI, Data Science, mathematics and advanced sensor technologies capable of monitoring, testing and diagnosing in real time from within the body. Many of these technologies are already on the market, and there will be very substantial progress in the coming years.

Top 10 Opportunities

1. The first head of government elected with an agenda of Healthy Longevity. In the political arena, the opportunity for the first president or prime minister to be elected with a mandate that heavily prioritises Longevity would create incentives to accelerate Longevity across the globe.

2. The first country to become a Longevity Hub. While multiple contenders are qualified for this amazing opportunity to lead the world in Longevity, one country or world city could become a leader in this mission.

3. The first Longevity corporation to truly capitalize on the market potential of Longevity. The first Longevity start-up to achieve true success in creating fully-integrated Longevity technological ecosystems has the potential to evolve into the first Longevity corporation, becoming a US$10 trillion company.

4. The first AI-driven Longevity centre. By bringing together the disparate arms of AI in AgeTech, rejuvenation biotechnologies and diagnostics as part of P4 Medicine, there is a huge opportunity to establish the first global AI centre for Longevity.

5. The first Longevity Finance Hub. By leveraging the new developments in Longevity finance, a new centre for Longevity connected funds, for new financial derivatives tied to Longevity, and for modern analytical systems could bring unprecedented wealth to investors while accelerating Longevity technologies and making them more available.

6. The arrival of the first Longevity drug on the market. While the past several years have seen incredible surges of growth in Longevity Industry activity and financing, the rise in investments that will occur after the first Longevity drug hits the market and is available for public use will be even more significant.

7. The first multicountry Longevity-focused healthcare system. Longevity-progressive countries have enormous opportunities to accelerate the extension of their National Healthy Longevity by focusing on synergistic cooperation with other countries, establishing Longevity-focused initiatives that leverage the unique strengths of different regions, including joint Longevity Industrial Strategies, and pooling health and life data to vastly increase the volume of data available for AI-empowered Longevity biomarker development.

8. Redefining insurance and work. As people's Longevity and health expand, their lifestyle transforms to accommodate more work, more spending power and more opportunities later in life. Workplaces, banks and financial products will reinvent themselves to cater for a new makeup of the population, and this presents many opportunities for those ready to take them on.

9. Continuing education. As older people gain extra health and lifespan, the previous model of retiring with a pension for 10-30 extra years of life will no longer be appropriate. People will be able to keep working, and therefore will change careers multiple times, and require retraining. Education catered for adults and older people will be a great opportunity for the future.

10. Planning longer term. As the number of people 65 years or older increases, many opportunities will present themselves across the board for longer term planning. Governments may spend longer implementing changes, policies will concern themselves with a bigger picture of 10-20 years ahead rather than the current 4-5 years ahead, because the longer term future will impact everyone, not just the young.

Top 10 Paradigm Shifts

1. The shift from treatment to prevention. We can already expect conventional healthcare to become substantially more focused on prevention over treatment by the year 2025.

2. Prevention will be followed by Precision Health. As prevention overtakes treatment as a paradigm shift, it will be followed even further by a shift towards Precision Health. People will be able to monitor their health long before an illness has had the opportunity to develop, and to maintain their health in a precise way.

3. People will be able to purchase Longevity. Longevity and health, rather than wealth, will be embraced as the most important asset. People will be able to purchase it like any other good, and Healthy Life Extension will become preferable above traditional assets such as luxury real estate among the wealthy.

4. Medicine and healthcare will become driven by Data Science, mathematical technologies and AI. Digital medicine powered by Data Science will become a major component of how medicine is practised. Outdated medical approaches will be replaced. AI currently has a supporting role in healthcare, but in the near future it will become absolutely central.

5. Longevity hubs will overtake tax havens. Instead of seeking tax havens to protect assets, people will be searching for Longevity hubs and the countries that can offer the most advanced Longevity. Switzerland's Longevity valley might become one of the first hubs.

6. Aging countries and national economies will decline. Without tackling the threats posed by the Silver Tsunami and collapsing pension funds, some ill-prepared countries will see their economies suffer.

7. BioTech and Pharma outside of Longevity will decline. Any companies operating outside the greater purpose of Longevity will eventually see their business model failing, and will themselves shrink or collapse.

8. Big Tech corporations will morph into healthcare corporations. The current wealthiest companies are IT and Tech corporations. These, notably Google, Amazon, Baidu, Samsung, etc., will very likely evolve into healthcare corporations, potentially boosting their market cap 10-fold from US$1 trillion to US$10 trillion.

9. Wealth management will include health in an integrated manner. As health and Longevity become measurable, wealth management companies will shift towards managing health as well. There will be many synergies between AgeTech, WealthTech and Longevity.

10. Surge of financial derivatives tied to Longevity. The coming years will see the launch of a number of novel types of financial derivatives tied to the Longevity Industry as health becomes measurable and investors turn to Longevity over traditional assets (i.e., to health rather than wealth). These will include derivatives whose value is tied to specific composites of Longevity companies (i.e., to the value of the Longevity Industry itself), as well as to specific Longevity technologies, and even to the current Longevity state of entire nations and economies (i.e., to the positive Longevity standing and the negative aging standing of whole countries).

PART I

Longevity Industry Mega-Complexity

Challenges, Issues, Opportunities

- **The Unprecedented Complexity, Intersectionality and Multidimensionality of the Longevity Industry**
- **Longevity as the Biggest and Most Complex Industry in Human History**
- **From BioTech Stagnation to Longevity Prosperity**
- **Forecasting the Future of Longevity Biomedicine**
- **Defining and Formulating the Longevity Industry Framework (Biomedicine, Technology, Finance, Governance)**
- **Why Traditional Methods of BioTech Analytics, Forecasting, Benchmarking and Investment Strategy Will Fail For Longevity**
- **The Need for New Analytical Methodologies and Frameworks Equal to the Complexity of the Longevity Industry**
- **Disproportions, Challenges and Opportunities in the Current Longevity Investment Landscape**
- **Longevity.Capital: Specialized Hybrid Investment Fund for Longevity-Industry, De-Risking and Diversification**

Chapter 1: The Biggest and Most Complex Industry In Human History

"The future Longevity Industry not only has the logical potential of becoming the wealthiest in all history, but also represents the most ethical way of doing business."

Dmitry Kaminskiy in *Longevity Industry Landscape Overview Volume II: The Business of Longevity* (Aging Analytics Agency, 2018)

Key Points:

- The Longevity Industry is set to become the biggest industry in human history.
- Besides having immense opportunities for ethical profit, it will also deliver an entirely new kind of ROI more valuable than money: health as wealth, and additional years of healthy, functional, productive life for both citizens and national economies.
- Developed nations now face the oncoming collision of two opposed Longevity MegaTrends: aging population and advancing biomedicine.
- Whether they stagnate or prosper when this collision hits depends entirely on how proactively and progressively they act today.
- The Longevity Industry has the potential to transform the challenge and deficit of aging into the opportunity and asset of Healthy Longevity, turning a source of stagnation into a thriving wellspring of growth, prosperity and stability.
- However, as it is located at the intersection of the most advanced domains of **science, technology, medicine, finance and governance in human history**, it possesses unprecedented levels of complexity and multidimensionality, necessitating entirely new methods of industry analytics, benchmarking, forecasting and investing in order to leverage and manifest its opportunities and neutralize its risks.

Longevity Industrialization: Unprecedented Challenge and Revolutionary Opportunity

The demographic challenge of an aging population, though unavoidable, is not insurmountable. And, more importantly, if addressed in a strategic and proactive manner, this challenge can be transformed into the greatest opportunity humanity has ever faced.

Governments, health services, businesses, technology, medicine and financial institutions can and must adapt in order to create an opportunity for growth and prosperity **(Healthy Longevity)** out of the possibility of stagnation and loss (aging population). And there are already signs that this is happening.

In medicine, partly in response to the growing gap between life expectancy and Health-Adjusted Life Expectancy, a paradigm shift is slowly occurring, from a treatment-focused system to a personalised, precise, patient-participatory and prevention-based system (known as "P4"). Artificial Intelligence will play a major role in obtaining this degree of precision.

Then there is the development of the AgeTech market: personal devices designed to help the elderly to improve their health and quality of life; the various possible innovations in finance to make life easier and more financially secure for the elderly; and various government initiatives around the world, ranging from investment in biotechnologies to continued education for the elderly and WHO-certified "Age-Friendly Cities".

But what is required is coordinated action. Governments, health services, businesses and financial institutions must respond in a coordinated manner to the Silver Tsunami. Furthermore, the nation that coordinates this response will be capable of bringing more benefit to humanity than any other in history.

Ultimately it is the public, governments and active industry participants who will decide whether population growth and increases in life expectancy impact the world in a positive or negative manner.

This book seeks to offer a brief overview of the technological, political and financial means of taking control of this situation, on an industrial scale.

The Collision of Two Opposed MegaTrends: Aging Population and Advancing Biomedicine

This book explores the current state and prospects of the highly complex, multidimensional, nascent but rapidly expanding industry that has the power to transform a source of stagnation and economic loss into a source of new health, wealth and prosperity. It also explains how and why the Longevity Industry will be the biggest and most complex industry of all time, as well as the most ethical, with more potential to benefit society in all of human history.

At its core, this book is about the looming opposition of two opposed MegaTrends: population aging and advancing biomedicine. So, it's worthy to analyse again the following figure.

Two Possible Scenarios of Longevity MegaTrends

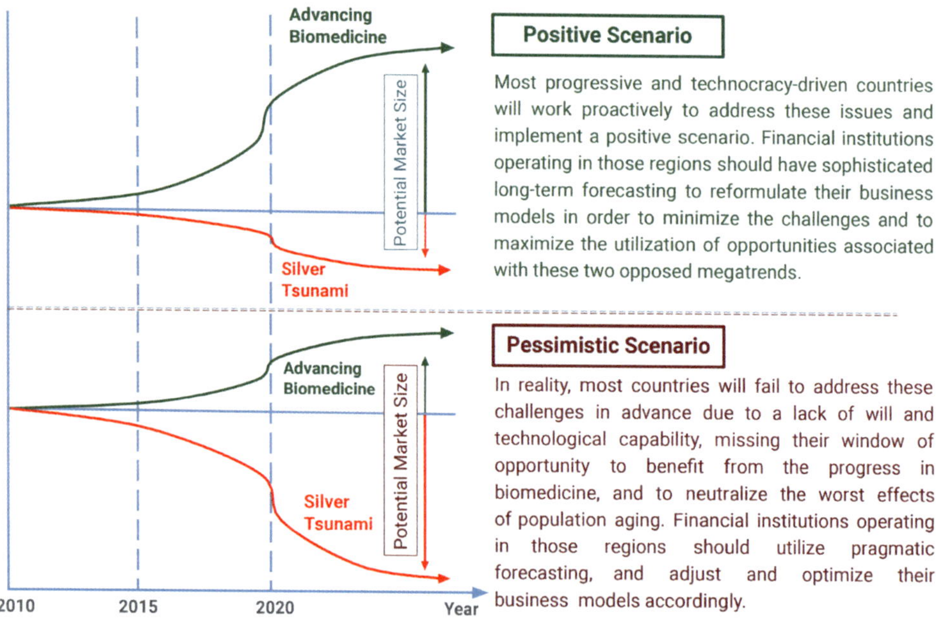

It is no secret that for some time the median age of populations of many countries in the world are rising, in some cases slowly, in many cases rapidly.

This phenomenon has been taking place over the past century or so to varying degrees, in nearly every country in the developed world, including Western and Eastern Europe, North America, Australia and

New Zealand, and Japan and South Korea, and some in the developing world, including China, India, and most countries in South America.

This phenomenon is known as the Silver Tsunami. It brings with it many serious societal and economic challenges, but, as this book argues, human will and ingenuity can refashion these challenges into opportunities.

The social and economic ill consequences of an aging population can only be remedied in the long term by ensuring that while the numbers of elderly people increase, there is a corresponding increase in the age at which people remain healthy and productive.

In other words, the increase in **Health-Adjusted Life Expectancy (HALE)**, the age up to which people are able to live relatively healthy lives, has to keep pace with the increase in life expectancy, to avoid the widening of the age bracket in which people are alive but unable to work productively, relying on the taxes and economic outputs of others in order to maintain their health and livelihood.

Developed nations are set to either sink or swim in the face of the oncoming Silver Tsunami, and their success depends on how proactively they deploy broad, well-funded national plans to extend Healthy Longevity and financial reform to neutralize the economic pressures of their aging populations.

They have the opportunity to transform the deficit-model of aging into the opportunity and asset-model of Healthy Longevity.

There is no great need for the further development of many experimental new technologies or therapies any time soon.

Most developed nations already have the technological means to increase Health-Adjusted Life Expectancy through Preventive Medicine, advanced biomedicine, socioeconomic policies and lifestyle changes.

What governments really need to do at this stage is simply perform the necessary initial diagnostic analysis via the use of panels of biomarkers of aging, executed on a scale at least in the millions.

The missing element is not biomedicine or biotechnology, but the aggregation and analysis of huge amounts of health data. It is not a medical or BioTech problem, but a Big Data analytics problem.

Such government-led projects, if properly implemented, would be the greatest source of developed nation's health and wealth, and should be considered a matter of the highest national importance, implemented with the urgency and rigour of the Manhattan Project (the 1939 American nuclear weapons program completed in 6 years) or the Apollo Program (the program for the world's first lunar landing completed in 8 years). With the current pace of development of science and technology, these projects could be completed in 5 to 7 years.

Initiatives in Several Countries

National Master Plans

- BIRAX Ageing
- Society 5.0
- Seoul Metropolitan Government, South Korea ministry of Health and Welfare
- China Health and Retirement Longitudinal Study led by Peking University
- National Population and Talent Division, Modern ageing Incubator, Silver Infocomm Junctions

Industrial Strategy

- UK Research and Innovation, UK Industrial Strategy, Industrial Strategy Challenge Fund

Independent or Municipal Government Programs

- Older Americans Act, The Building Our Largest Dementia, Affordable Care Act
- Swiss Personalized Health Network
- Department of Health, Labour Department, The Hong Kong Council of Social Service
- Durango, Age-Friendly City
- Groningen Active Ageing Strategy, HANNN, Deltaplan for Dementia

90% of the digitized data globally was collected during just the last 2 years and this rate is only going to increase, and increasing HALE can be largely considered data collection.

In most instances, the technologies pushing forward the Longevity frontier have reached roadblocks which can only be cleared by government coordination. So realistically, the roadblocks to progress are not scientific or technological, but political.

In Switzerland, for example, the state of research into Precision Medicine procedures is very advanced and yet the fragmented healthcare system makes nationwide coordination and harmonisation of biobanks, electronic clinical information systems and clinical data management infrastructures difficult.

Yet government initiatives are appearing up all over the globe that will not only better coordinate technological progress and overcome such barriers to progress, but also directly influence Healthy Longevity, and the probability of living long enough to benefit from advances such as P4 and regenerative medicine.

These range from the industrial strategies of Britain and Japan, to the elderly care banks of Switzerland, to the places of continued learning for the elderly in China, and to the WHO-certified "Age-Friendly Cities" cropping up on every continent.

This situation will only be turned around when Longevity can safely be regarded as an asset again, just as it was historically, back when innovations such as the ability to make it through middle age in good health (with one's job, health and teeth all intact) was regarded as a self-evident good from a ***social, economic and ethic*** point of view.

Achieving this scenario will require serious advances and paradigm shifts in medicine and technology. In fact, it will require a whole new industry, remarkably different than any sector in the history of humanity — the rising Longevity Industry.

The Two Opposed MegaTrends of Progress and Conservatism

Throughout human history, we can see a trend of the seeds of progress attempting to rise to the surface, and the overwhelming weight of human ignorance trying to hold that back and slow it down. Any new strand of progress due to a great technological innovation is at first only recognized and accepted by a small handful of individuals, with 99% of the rest of society resisting either because of a lack of understanding, or a willing state of disbelief and comfort with the modes and patterns of yesterday.

In fact, the great majority of humanity, about 90% of the people, would rather die than face and accept the real potentials of progress in Longevity. This is why societies have invented artificial wealth-holders such as money, power, fame and nationalism, instead of applying their greatest energies toward realizing the only true form of value and wealth — life, health and Longevity.

As most of the wealthy cannot face this prospect, they are still trying to anchor their values to trivial pursuits such as big mansions, overvalued luxuries, cars, yachts and private jets, and other superficial values that belong to past centuries. For most of history the technical capacity to extend healthy Longevity has not been within reach. Now that it is within reach, they face the same psychological barrier as a horseman at the beginning of the Space Age.

There is comfort in continuing to ride that horse, even when the knowledge and reality of everything from space rockets to autonomous cars, and then to efficient AI systems, not to mention the technological reality of extending the healthy period of life, have emerged and can be witnessed firsthand. But it all happened so suddenly! Instead of desiring to fill their gap in knowledge, they would prefer to stay in their comfort zone, and to remain unaware of actual, tangible opportunities to extend their lives.

This is the predicament we currently find ourselves in with regard to the industrialization of Longevity. With all our old enemies largely defeated — disease, poverty, ignorance — our oldest and ultimate enemy, which perhaps always had something to do with all of these, still awaits us. However, there are psychological barriers standing in the way of intelligent coordination and investment in this nascent industry. Those are the barriers which this book attempts to tear down.

While we consider it's our duty to share this knowledge and our life-changing understanding of the Longevity Industry with the public, and to help ever-greater numbers of people realize the feasibility of extending Healthy Human Longevity and the many opportunities it can bring, it is also our duty to do it safely and realistically. Once increasing numbers of people accept the idea, they may accept it too much, and fall into the traps of players selling scientifically-unfounded hype, either via active fraud, or passive, well-meaning but harmful negligence, and risk spending their money on false promises — just as the aerospace industry in its first few years saw many rockets fall, before technology had matured to the level where the majority of launches were successful.

It will be an industry presenting equal levels of opportunity and risk, and it is critical that the public is armed with knowledge neither too conservative nor too optimistic, but rather with deep knowledge that is reasonable, pragmatic and realistic, to enable them to realize and take advantage of the opportunities of the **Longevity Industry's future growth from stage 1.0 (low-Earth orbit) to 2.0 (the Moon), 3.0 (Mars) and beyond,** which is similar to initially treating age-related diseases, then systemically delaying aging, and finally achieving Longevity Escape Velocity, efficient rejuvenation and the continual maintenance of a state of Precision Health.

The Industrialization of Longevity: The Transition from Advanced Science to Frontier Technology

The Longevity Industry defined and described in this book began with basic research into the biology of aging in the 20th century, expanded with the emergence of advanced aging biomedicine at the turn of the 21st century, and then blossomed with involvement of financial and digital technologies.

With these developments underway, in 2014 **Aging Analytics Agency correctly predicted the 2018 boom in Longevity Industry investments and activity, four years in advance**, believing its runaway growth to be inevitable, having considered its extreme prospects for profitability and its potential to deliver substantial ROIs while providing a greater benefit to humanity than any other industry in history.

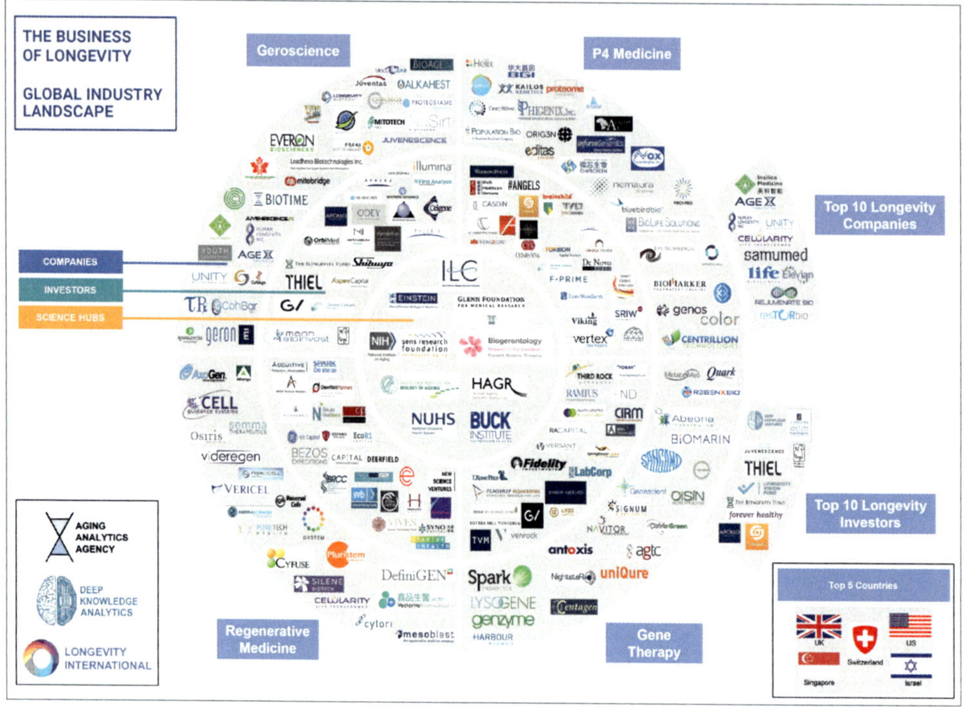

In more recent years, the reality of this industry's emergence has been acknowledged by even the most conservative entities, including top-tier business and finance media brands like **The Economist**, **Financial Times**, **Bloomberg**, and by large financial institutions and investment banks (who now regularly host conferences and release analytical reports on the topic of Longevity for politicians, such as parliamentarians, as well as their own institutional and HNWI clients).

Today, the momentum and diversification continues, with thousands of Longevity companies and dozens of Longevity-focused investment firms active around the globe.

The Longevity Industry is a Multitrillion Opportunity

Older people are the fastest growing demographic group (with around 2.5% annual population growth vs. 0.7% for the entire population).

With growing numbers, older adults represent a dynamic emerging market and human capital resource. The multitrillion market of 1 billion people currently on retirement can be thought of as the world's 7th continent. The Longevity Industry includes the products and services satisfying the needs of the cohort aged 50+. The substantial increase in the population of this group is the main driver of the industry.

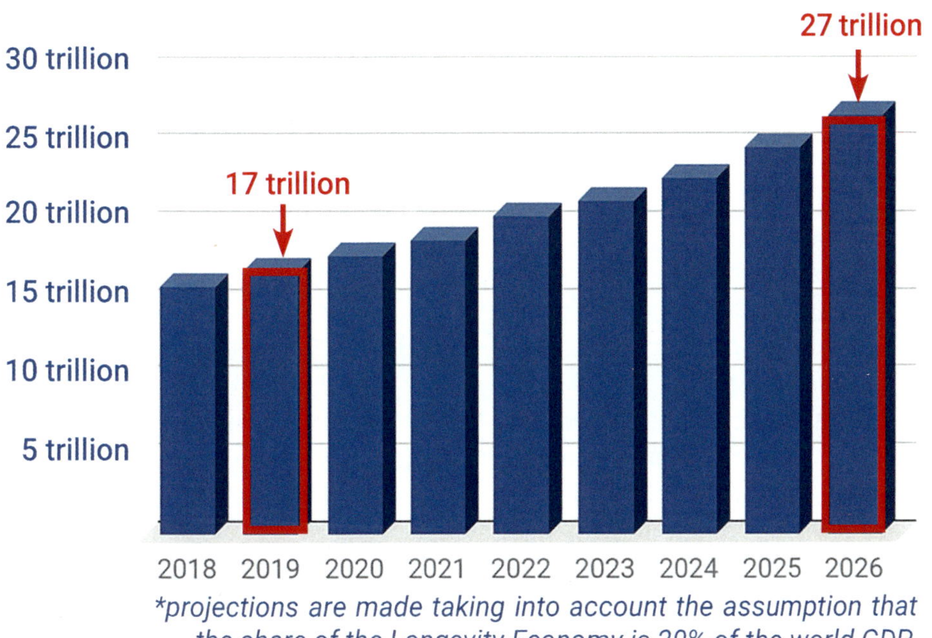

*projections are made taking into account the assumption that the share of the Longevity Economy is 20% of the world GDP

The global Longevity Economy reached US$17 trillion in 2019 and is showing a stable growth, and thus it will reach US$27 trillion in 2026. **According to the most conservative estimates, it takes 20% of the global GDP.** While the global Longevity Economy is projected to reach US$27 trillion in 2026, the AgeTech segment alone will reach US$2.7 trillion by 2025. This would imply a 21% annual growth in the global AgeTech market.

This growth is driven by the general development of the elderly care sector enhanced by advancing IT, FinTech and other digital technologies and solutions.

This creates both opportunities and threats for the economy as a whole and for the financial industry in particular. As for the last one, we believe aging is going to have a positive rather than negative impact on the global financial industry as there will be a greater need of new types of financial products over the longer term — new asset classes, new investment strategies, and longer-dated bonds/securities will have to be developed.

This will require participation and collaboration across both the public and private sectors to have a positive effect for all long-livers.

Longevity Mega-Complexity Equally Multiplies and Magnifies Challenges and Opportunities

While many analysts and investors consider the Longevity Industry to be of a much more limited scope, consisting of core anti-aging therapies at the forefront of advanced biomedicine, Deep Knowledge Group has been working for the past 5+ years to landscape, and understand, the global multifaceted Longevity Industry, through the work of its analytical subsidiary Aging Analytics Agency, which has gained such an understanding through tens of thousands of pages worth of public and proprietary Longevity Industry analytical reports.

The perception of the Longevity Industry, in both its scope and its main trends, in the USA in general and in Silicon Valley in particular, most often is conflated with biomedical moonshots — very advanced biomedicine not yet on the stage of human clinical trials — and this is an angle that severely underestimates technologies which we consider to be within the scope of the Longevity Industry, those that are actionable and closer to market readiness.

Our work in this area has led us to define the industry much more broadly, and to include sectors that lie completely outside of biomedicine such as AgeTech, WealthTech, FinTech and the emerging Longevity Financial Industry, which are also much closer to market readiness and market capitalization than the anti-aging biomedicine sector.

However, importantly, the uniquely intersectional nature of the Longevity Industry, and the fact that it is emerging at the centre of a complex web of advanced domains of science, technology, finance and governance, mean that the task of actually understanding the industry presents more challenges than in the case of any other industry in history.

The interaction and exchange of so many fields of frontier human activity into a single concentrated inflection point creates extreme levels of industry complexity. As a result of this unprecedented complexity and multidimensionality, the typical approaches used for analytics, investment target identification and due diligence that worked for the BioTech industry are destined to fail when applied to the Longevity Industry.

While the challenges of making a reliable assessment, benchmarking and forecasting posed by this increasingly complex and multi-faceted industry are daunting, they are not insurmountable. It simply requires the rapid development of sophisticated, quantitative methods of analysis, and this is exactly what Deep Knowledge Ventures and its Longevity-focused analytical subsidiary, Aging Analytics Agency, have set out to do over the past five years. More recently, these organizations have been analysing not only the biomedical aspects of Longevity but also novel Longevity-related financial frameworks, instruments and derivatives, novel InvestTech for forecasting and due diligence within Longevity, and the proactivity, strength and relevance of various nation's government-led national Longevity development plans.

Analytics that can withstand Longevity Mega-Complexity has been a major part of Deep Knowledge Group's mission — to create a robust and sophisticated market intelligence and analytics basement that can survive under the enormous weight of the Longevity Industry complexity.

Longevity has stronger prospects for growth than any industry in history, but its high degree of complexity poses substantial challenges and risks. Specifically, the risk of fraud, such as that experienced in gene therapy, for example, the effects of which could be drastic, and set the industry's progress back substantially.

This is why we urgently need analytical frameworks that can enable assessment and optimization now, rather than later.

Similarly, if national governments intend to progress rather than stagnate under the pressures of the oncoming Silver Tsunami, to decrease the gap between their life expectancy and Healthy Adjusted Life Expectancy, and to transform the problem and deficit-model of aging into the opportunity and asset-model of Longevity, they need to embrace the development of such analytical frameworks, and utilize them to proactively prioritize Healthy Longevity as a major component of their national agendas.

The overall size, complexity and market capitalization of Longevity is set to dwarf all other industries, from real-estate to energy and many, many others. As a consequence, the challenges and opportunities it poses to its participants and stakeholders will also grow.

Conclusions:

- The Longevity Industry's ongoing growth will eventually reach an inflection point where many of the holders of the world's wealth will recognize the opportunity in front of them, and understand that they have the chance to participate in something uniquely profitable that can deliver a greater benefit to humanity than any other endeavour in history. Momentum will multiply and the industry will experience a self-perpetuating growth.
- This will attract manpower at an exponential rate. For various types of professionals, a working life outside this expansive industry will be inconceivable.
- Longevity already attracts the best and brightest scientists and medical professionals working today, as it is already the forefront of biotechnology and biomedicine.
- The borders of Longevity expand to incorporate more of the above-mentioned sectors and related sectors; we will see the most skilled entrepreneurs migrating to the Longevity sector.
- In order to be productive, entrepreneurs entering Longevity will need to be highly skilled, intelligent, and adhere to a rigorous ethical code, as the repercussions of both fraud and honest mistakes in this industry are greater than in others. There will come a day when it will be almost unthinkable for any smart business

professional or investor to not be actively involved in Longevity, considering its scope and benefits.

- Longevity Industry 1.0 explores the current state and prospects of this highly complex, multidimensional, nascent but rapidly expanding industry which will help to address the challenges and obstacles we will need to overcome as the world's global population continue to age.
- It explains how and why the Longevity Industry will be the biggest and most complex in history, as well as the most ethical, with the greatest potential to benefit humanity.
- Chapter by chapter, we will explore the innovations that must take place in science, medicine, technology, finance and governance.

Chapter 2: Formulating the Longevity Industry Framework

Key Points:

- While many Longevity Industry participants and analysts consider its scope to be limited to the core "geroscience" (advanced forms of biomedicine that target the root causes or "hallmarks" of aging), the Deep Knowledge Group has a much broader and more realistic understanding of the full scope of the global Longevity Industry, which encompasses not just biomedicine but also technology, finance and governance.
- We have cultivated that understanding through years of study and data aggregation on behalf of our Longevity-focused analytical subsidiary Aging Analytics Agency, which was created in 2013 with the explicit purpose of obtaining a comprehensive yet deep understanding of the entire Longevity Industry in all its aspects.
- Aging Analytics Agency was the first entity to formulate a comprehensive and inclusive Longevity Industry Framework that encompassed the full range of its sectors, domains and technologies, some of which have only recently been recognized by the wider scientific, business, finance and investment communities as legitimate aspects of the industry.
- Utilizing this framework, Aging Analytics Agency was also the first entity to predict in 2014 the substantial rise in Longevity Industry investments that occurred during 2017-2018, three years in advance.
- The creation of this framework, and the accompanying 1300+ page analytical reports series on the global Longevity Industry in which it was introduced, laid the foundation and provided the understanding of the full scope of the Longevity Industry activity that has enabled Aging Analytics Agency to conduct its more targeted, precise and actionable analytics on the full scope of the global Longevity Industry since that time.

"A mere three years ago the current rise of the Longevity Industry would have been unthinkable. Now, a few years later, it has become unthinkable that biomedicine should not have healthy Longevity among its objectives. The time has come to establish a framework for the rising Longevity Industry."

Dmitry Kaminskiy, in *Longevity Industry Landscape Overview Volume II: The Business of Longevity* (Aging Analytics Agency, 2018)

During the period of 2016-2017, Aging Analytics Agency undertook the challenge and opportunity of profiling the entire scope of the global Longevity Industry for the very first time, which was documented in its 1300+ page series of analytical reports, *Longevity Industry Landscape Overview Volume I: The Science of Longevity* and *Volume II: The Business of Longevity*.

Landscaping the entire international Longevity sphere proved to be a significant but worthwhile challenge, and it laid the foundation for all of the more targeted analytical reports produced by Aging Analytics Agency in the several years since then. These first two volumes introduced the Longevity Industry Framework, which serves as the basis for sector classification and categorization, and provided the initial volume of data necessary to gain a deeper understanding of the industry's current state, near-future trajectory of development, and main players, trends and bottlenecks.

"It is now our mission to share this multi-level understanding of the full scope of the industry with the public through this book."

Dmitry Kaminskiy and Margaretta Colangelo

Most people naturally equate the idea of "Longevity" with progress in the science of advanced biomedicine in the study of aging, with the ultimate aim of delaying its diverse diseases. However, in reality, it consists of many more distinct yet intersecting fields. Progress in Longevity is no longer simply a question of progress in geroscience (the science of aging) or advanced biomedicine; it is now driven more by the synergetic convergence of multiple distinct technological sectors and sub-sectors.

Throughout the production of its many industry analytical reports and special case studies on the Longevity Industry, Aging Analytics Agency has formulated a broad industry classification framework that categorizes the Longevity Industry into four distinct segments:

- Geroscience R&D;
- P4 Medicine;
- AgeTech;
- Novel Financial System.

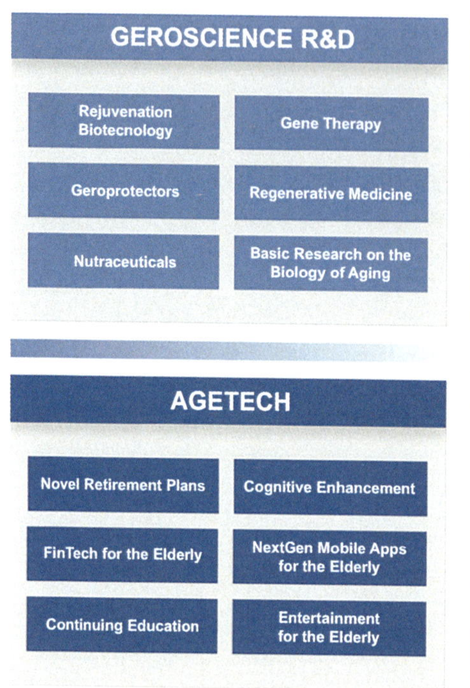

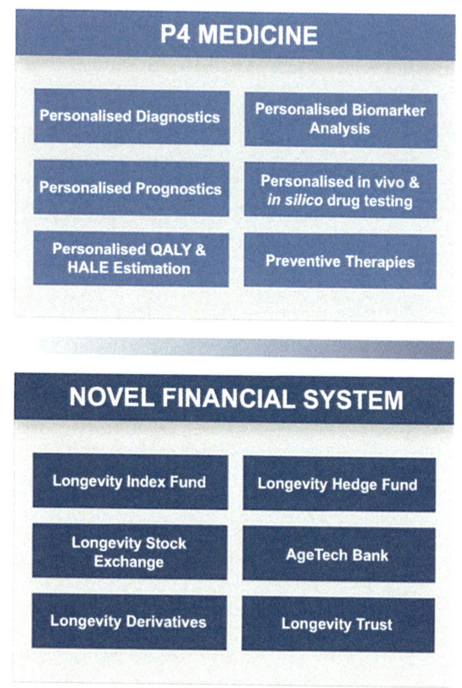

If Longevity only consisted of biomedicine and there were not so many intersections with other industries, then analysis and forecasting might be a comparatively simple task, similar to the analysis of the current BioTech Industry.

However, in reality, ***Longevity inevitably involves a synergy between advanced biomedicine, AI, digital health, financial industry, pension and national healthcare systems, governmental initiatives and even political issues partially related to stagnating economies due to the Silver Tsunami***, which together create a very diverse and dynamic ecosystem whose already-rapid pace of progress and diversification only continues to accelerate, creating challenges for a concrete understanding and a practical forecasting.

Global Longevity Industry Landscape

In 2014, Dmitry Kaminskiy predicted the 2017-2018 boom in Longevity Industry investments and activity, three years in advance, noting the inevitability of its growth considering the impact it would have on global healthcare systems and the business models of modern medicine, its extreme prospects for profitability and the fact that it is the most ethical form of business, with the potential of simultaneously delivering substantial ROIs while providing more benefits to humanity than any other industry in history.

The initial aim will be to identify novel Longevity and healthy aging biomarkers to accelerate diagnosis of age-related health decline.

The Longevity Industry has gone from an underrepresented field of R&D to the rapidly expanding and diversifying frontier of advanced biomedicine.

Then researchers will develop solutions for personalised physical, mental and financial health to better implement and promote healthy lifestyles for longevity, such as modifying patterns in sleep, nutrition, physical activity, environmental exposure and financial planning.

Today, ***the Longevity Industry's advanced dynamic of progress and its strong trajectory of growth and diversification is quite obvious***, with thousands of Longevity companies active around the globe, dozens of Longevity-focused investment firms, and the fact that in more recent years, it has begun to be embraced by even the most conservative of entities, including top-tier business and finance media brands like The Economist, Financial Times, Bloomberg and others, by large financial institutions and investment banks (who now regularly host conferences and release analytical reports on the topic of Longevity for their institutional and HNWI clients), and even politicians and parliamentarians (the recent launch of the **All-Party Parliamentary Group** being perhaps the best example of the recent emergence of Longevity Politics).

Longevity Industry in the UK: Landscape Overview Q4 2018

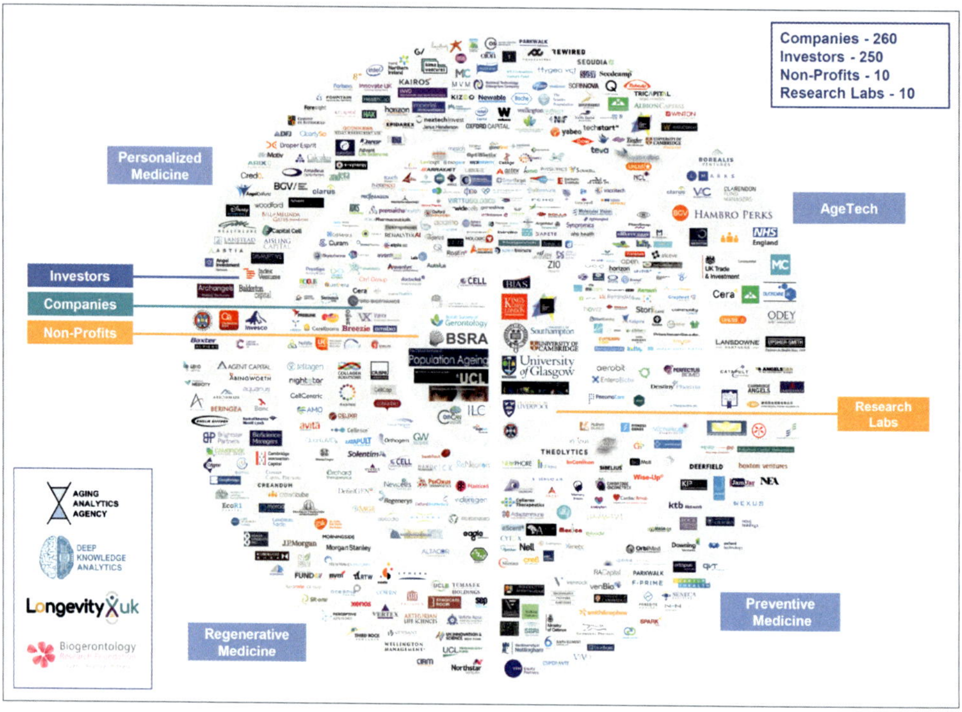

Companies - 260
Investors - 250
Non-Profits - 10
Research Labs - 10

Personalized Medicine

AgeTech

Investors

Companies

Non-Profits

Research Labs

Preventive Medicine

Regenerative Medicine

AGING ANALYTICS AGENCY

DEEP KNOWLEDGE ANALYTICS

Longevity uk

Biogerontology

Longevity Industry in Singapore: Landscape Overview 2019

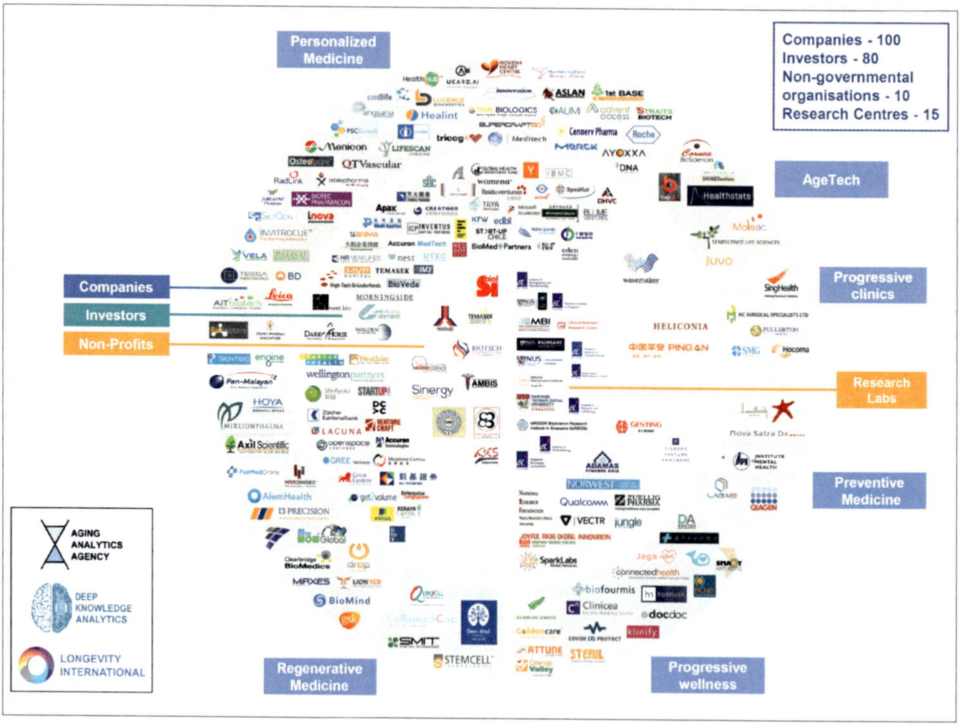

Companies - 100
Investors - 80
Non-governmental organisations - 10
Research Centres - 15

Personalized Medicine

AgeTech

Companies

Investors

Non-Profits

Progressive clinics

Research Labs

Preventive Medicine

Regenerative Medicine

Progressive wellness

AGING ANALYTICS AGENCY

DEEP KNOWLEDGE ANALYTICS

LONGEVITY INTERNATIONAL

Longevity Industry in California Landscape Overview 2019

Longevity Industry in Switzerland Landscape Overview 2019

Geroscience R&D — The Science of Aging and Longevity

The first segment of the Longevity Industry is Geroscience R&D — the segment of biomedical science and research that aims to treat the root causes of aging.

Some of the most early-stage forms of geroscience attempt to treat aging as an engineering issue to be solved using advanced biomedical engineering.

These areas are at the very forefront of BioTech and biomedicine, and so, even these alone require highly specialized approaches to assessment and forecasting, beyond the ones that have proven adequate for the BioTech Industry generally.

Longevity Industry Landscape Overview Volume I:
The Science of Longevity

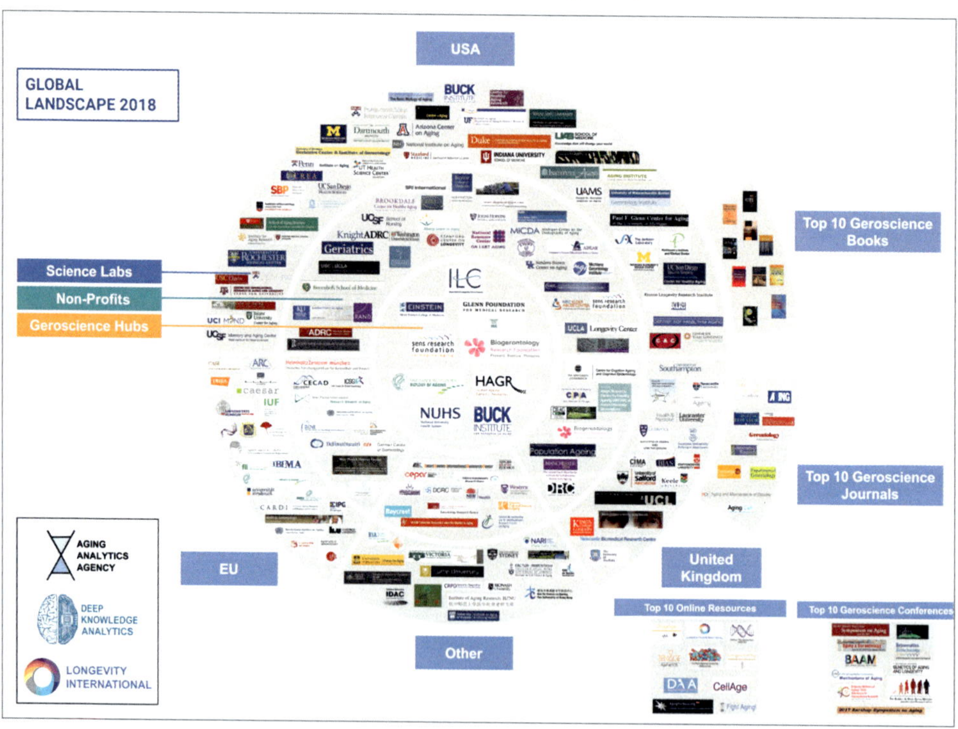

P4 (Preventive, Precision, Personalised and Participatory) Medicine

P4 Medicine: leading edge technologies that have already achieved a state of market-readiness and clinical implementation.

This segment has a clear history of paradigm shifts toward greater precision, personalisation, prevention and patient participation, driven forward and enabled by advances in biomedicine, Data Science and Artificial Intelligence.

Drug development companies will transition from the current form of "blockbuster drugs" (standard drug formulations applicable to many millions of patients) to P4 Medicine, tailoring drugs to specific patient cases based on age, gender, ethnicity, state of health and genetics.

The **first and second "P"** in P4 Medicine are "personalised" and "precision", which refers to the drugs and treatments that will be designed and applied using precise, individually-tailored methods of dosing, cocktail compositions of micro-dosages, and efficient methods of delivery.

AI for R&D in drug discovery will become more sophisticated and drugs will become more customized to specific diseases and even to specific patients.

Such advances also represent a move towards greater prevention (the **third "P"** in P4 Medicine), and a shift away from reactionary treatment towards optimized disease prevention applying micro-dosages of drugs, long before the underlying pathology develops into an actual chronic disease.

Healthy Longevity means prevention rather than treatment, through the maintenance of optimal states of health via continuous monitoring of disease-associated biomarkers, and micro-adjustments in therapeutic, lifestyle and behavioural regimes to normalize those biomarkers.

The **fourth "P"** in P4 Medicine is "participatory", which refers to the increasingly active role that patients are taking in managing their own health, culminating in a situation where citizens are empowered with the tools, approaches and services capable of enabling continual micro-adjustments to their regimes in response to continuous AI-empowered monitoring of micro-changes in biomarkers that measure state of health and predict risk of diseases long before their actual onset and progression.

> *This paradigm is described very precisely in the book* The Patient as CEO: How Technology Empowers the Healthcare Consumer *by Robin Farmanfarmaian, a contributor of Longevity Industry 1.0.*

These changes are already being embraced by the medical communities and healthcare systems of progressive countries. In coming years, as P4 becomes the new norm, the new definition of failure will be when patients are forced to get doctors involved.

In a world in which P4 Medicine triumphs, citizens will have no need to engage with doctors until the very end of life.

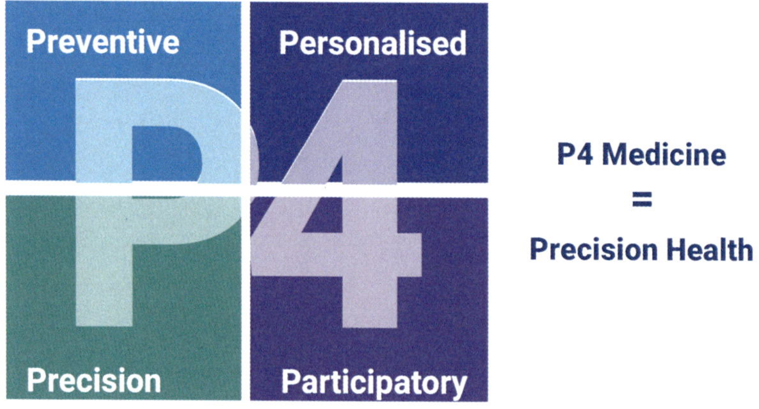

The term **"Precision Health"** is becoming increasingly common, and refers to the notion that the ideal and most comprehensive case of P4 Medicine will naturally and inevitably lead to a state of Precision Health, in which diseases and other sub-optimal forms of health are delayed for as long as possible, until near the very end of life.

The role of AI in P4 medicine is already remarkably apparent, especially in places such as the UK, USA, Switzerland and Singapore.

For example, we have seen very proactive efforts by the UK government, both through their AI Industrial Grand Challenge and their aging Industrial Grand Challenge, for the rapid application of AI to Preventive Medicine, advanced biomedicine and digital health, and the recent establishment of the **All-Party Parliamentary Group for Longevity**, where Aging Analytics Agency was proactively involved.

Furthermore, its high degree of complexity necessitates innovative frameworks not only for general benchmarking and forecasting, but also for the general assessment of its technologies and therapies basic safety and efficacy. *Take, for example, the common use of model organisms to assess the safety and efficacy of therapeutics.*

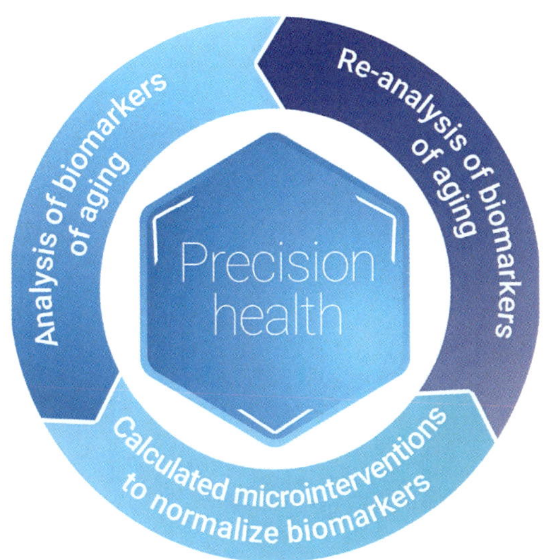

Biomarkers of Aging

Key Points:

- The development of precise and actionable biomarkers of aging is one of the most prevalent and important areas of Longevity research today, as well as an area in which practical implementation is lagging behind the science.
- This is one of the most important diagnostic services that could be offered, and yet ***it does not receive the attention it deserves compared to the amount of tangible benefits it can deliver***.

How do we know when a biomarker is a biomarker of aging?

It depends on how it is sourced. The current approach to biomarkers is to take them from people at various stages of a disease's known progress, which in practice means sourcing them from hospital patients. Isolating biomarkers of aging, however, means collecting data which mark the difference between healthy people only, e.g. between the young and the even younger, with no traces of any officially recognised diseases.

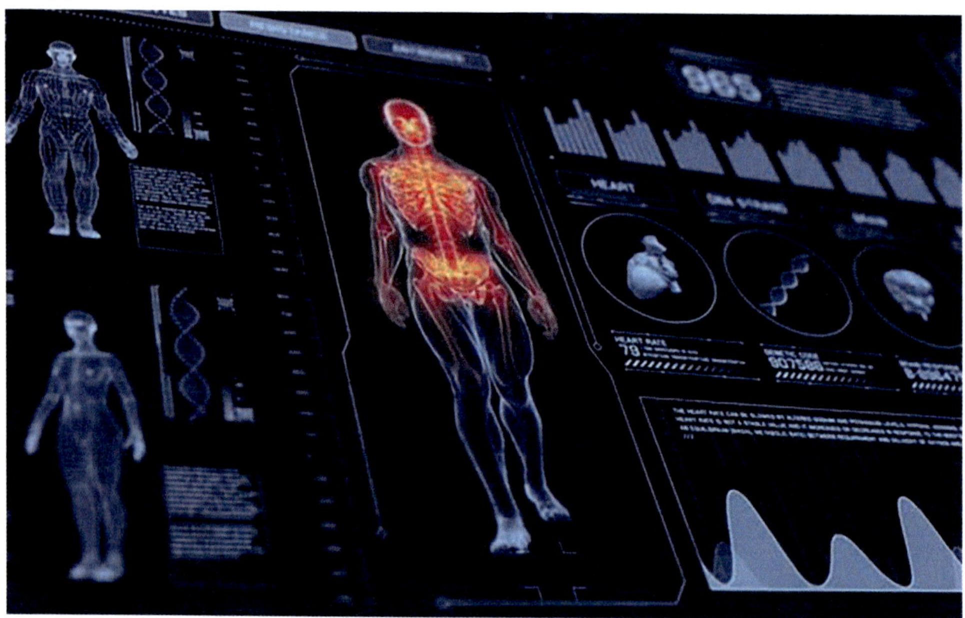

This presents a challenge because whereas hospital patients remain in dedicated areas, and are available for analysis at the doctor's convenience, collecting biomarkers of aging means collecting vast amounts of data from the daily lives of people who have no reason to be in hospital. There are however options available for aggregating such data.

Also important is the degree of emphasis on achieving a panel of biomarkers which are not only comprehensive but also actionable.

A panel of less precise but easily implementable biomarkers of aging would be much better than an extremely precise and comprehensive panel of biomarkers of aging that is too hard or expensive to translate easily into widespread practical use across nations.

For example, a panel of aging biomarkers was developed recently based on Deep Learning analysis of standard blood biomarkers, which is less precise than the most precise available biomarkers of aging (DNA methylation clocks), but is nonetheless precise enough, and can be implemented by any researcher, doctor and clinician that has access to routine blood tests.

As a further example of actionability, consider the biomarkers of aging that have been constructed using Deep Learning-based analysis of photographs of mice, which could quite easily be extended to humans. Their accuracy alone is not enough to make them a research priority, but the increasing video capabilities of smart-phones mean that this rapid development of photographic biomarkers of aging (e.g. of the face or the eye) could now be a very actionable area of research whose practical level of precision and accuracy will develop quite rapidly in coming years.

However, the use of AI in R&D in geroscience is lagging behind its application in other areas.

While there is a small handful of companies that are working at this frontier, the overall proportion in comparison to the total size of the Longevity Industry is still quite small.

Deep Knowledge Ventures has been identifying and supporting companies working on the frontlines of AI for Longevity since 2014, when it provided the seed funding for Insilico Medicine, now a leader in the application of AI for Longevity research, drug discovery and biomarker development.

AI for Longevity

As the complexities of the Longevity science and technology increase, and as the volume of data continues to amass, the role of AI in both analyzing and understanding becomes completely necessary for continued progress and industry development.

While AI for Longevity is still an emerging and underrepresented sector within the **global Longevity Industry**, its extreme disruptive potential makes the eventual emergence of this sector as a core and integral area of growth and development inevitable. AI for Longevity will become one of the most impactful sectors within the industry in the next several years, and will demonstrate its potential to accelerate the continued development of the industry in almost every sector, from Longevity R&D to therapeutic development, P4 Medicine, biomarker discovery, and even non-biomedical sectors such as the Longevity Financial Industry.

Precision Medicine, with its DNA sequencing, high-tech diagnostic tests and individually targeted therapies, might be significantly less costly than conventional approaches.

Awareness of the importance of utilising Artificial Intelligence within aging and Longevity research is rapidly increasing in academia and industry. Modern deep learning techniques used to develop age predictors offer new possibilities for diverse data types, enabling a holistic view to identify novel geroprotectors, biomarkers, drug discovery and biotechnology in the healthcare and pharmaceutical industry.

- ***The main concept of Precision Medicine is providing an individually tailored healthcare based on a person's genes, lifestyle and environment. This, together with the advances in genetics, artificial intelligence and the growing availability of health data, presents an opportunity to make precise personalised patient care a clinical reality.***
- ***A second important application of AI for Longevity is on the so-called "Lifetime Wellness" — non-medical factors that impact quality of life and functionality for seniors, ranging from financial wellness, continuing education, happiness, psychological well-being, neuroplasticity and active social involvement.***

Considering the vast amount of life data and information about citizens being collected in the most developed nations by financial institutions, telecom companies, etc., there is a large number of options and avenues for how AI, Big Data analysis and predictive analytical techniques could utilize that data to create personalised recommendations for how citizens 60 years and older can optimize their lifestyles and behaviours to achieve a high degree of wellness, stability, happiness, social involvement and life activity.

The number of companies, researchers, projects and technologies active in this space (AgeTech, FinTech for the Elderly, Continuing Education, Brain Training, etc.) is significant, and rapidly growing. Therefore, the demand for practical and sophisticated AI-driven approaches for improving and optimizing the products and services in this space is also very high.

Accelerating the Development of Precision Health through AI

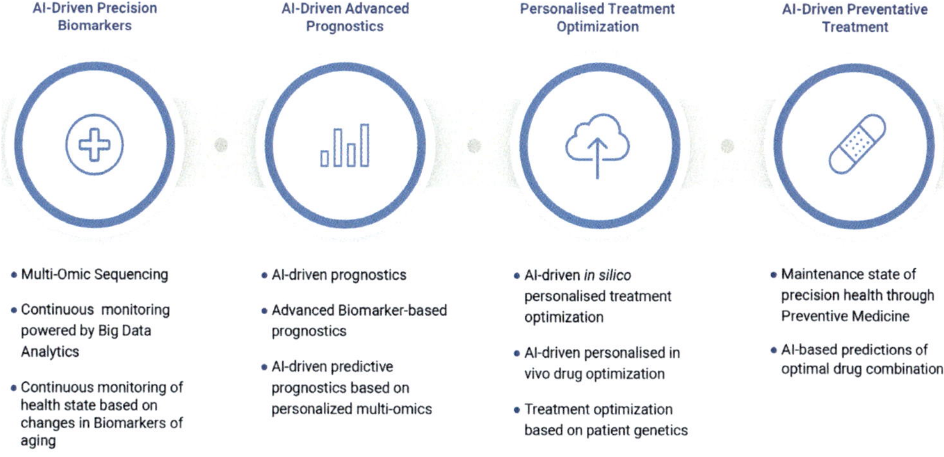

- Multi-Omic Sequencing
- Continuous monitoring powered by Big Data Analytics
- Continuous monitoring of health state based on changes in Biomarkers of aging

- AI-driven prognostics
- Advanced Biomarker-based prognostics
- AI-driven predictive prognostics based on personalized multi-omics

- AI-driven *in silico* personalised treatment optimization
- AI-driven personalised in vivo drug optimization
- Treatment optimization based on patient genetics

- Maintenance state of precision health through Preventive Medicine
- AI-based predictions of optimal drug combination

The intensive application of AI to all stages of Longevity and Preventive Medicine R&D has the potential to rapidly accelerate the clinical translation of both validated and experimental diagnostics, prognostics and therapeutics, to empower patients to become the CEOs of their own health through continuous AI-driven monitoring of minor fluctuations in biomarkers, and to speedily develop the ***global Longevity Industry to scale****.*

Longevity and the AgeTech Market

The third segment of the Longevity Industry is **AgeTech**, which broadly refers to all IT and digital technologies that help to maintain a greater functionality into older age, and improve the quality of life using non-medical means. **This segment of the market is a rapidly growing one, with the number of people in retirement globally growing past 1 billion.** It also includes such things as advanced and progressive forms of social care, as well as products and services that help to preserve neuroplasticity into older ages.

While AgeTech can provide little benefit to the actual slowing of biological aging, it can provide innumerable benefits for retaining functionality and improving quality of life into older ages, enhancing psychological well-being, mental functioning and neuroplasticity, and increasing levels of independence and social activity. As such, it is one of the sectors of the Longevity Industry poised to grow the most in the shorter-term horizon.

AgeTech - Digitally Enabling the Longevity Economy

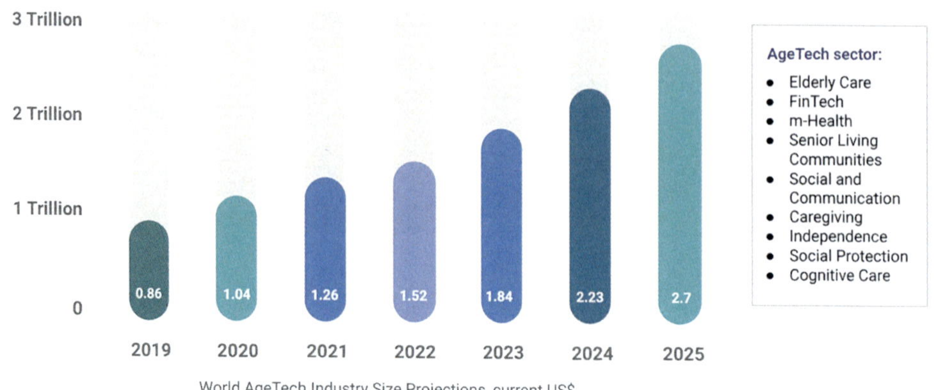

World AgeTech Industry Size Projections, current US$

While the global Longevity Economy is projected to reach US$27 trillion in 2025, the AgeTech potential within it will reach US$2.7 trillion by 2025.

This would imply a 21% annual growth in the global AgeTech market. This growth is driven by the general development of the elderly care sector enhanced by advancing IT, FinTech and other digital technologies.

The Longevity Financial Industry

The final and most recent segment of the Longevity Industry is the Longevity Financial sector, **which has emerged naturally out of the clear economic and socioeconomic consequences of an aging population and a Healthy Longevity for national economies, pension funds, insurance companies and other financial institutions**.

The above factors have come together to produce an inevitable coming paradigm shift in the standard operating procedures, products, services and core business models of global finance within the next 2-5 years. The global finance industry is currently worth several tens of trillions of dollars, and for the last 50 years it has been marked by a distinct lack of innovation, a resistance to embrace technological change and to re-tune business models in a manner that is relevant for the dynamic of scientific and technological progress. However, we can already see fundamental changes taking place specifically due to innovations in Longevity.

Evolution of the Longevity Financial Industry

Deep Knowledge Ventures and **Aging Analytics Agency** consider this topic particularly important, and are working on it in various ways. We are, for example, launching a Longevity-focused hybrid investment fund Longevity.Capital, which will utilize data-driven analytical assessment and forecasting frameworks combined with innovations in InvestTech specifically adapted for Longevity, with longer-term plans to develop the concept of a specialized Longevity Stock Exchange, Index and marketplace for tradable financial instruments and derivatives tied to the Longevity sector.

Chapter 3: From BioTech Stagnation to Longevity Prosperity: Forecasting on the Future of Longevity Biomedicine

"The demand for AI technologies and AI talent is growing in the pharma and healthcare industries and driving the formation of a new interdisciplinary field — data-driven drug discovery/healthcare. Acquiring the best AI start-ups will dominate the biopharma industry."

Margaretta Colangelo in *AI for drug discovery will be driven by biopharma and the rise of Asian tigers* (Outsourcing Pharma, April 2019)

Key Points:

- In practice, the Longevity Industry's extreme levels of complexity and multidimensionality lead to accelerated rates of industry development, and the transition from scientific R&D into practical technological implementation.
- BioTech and BioPharma are currently in the midst of a paradigm shift, away from treatment (one-size-fits-all blockbuster drugs) towards Personalised, Preventive Medicine and Precision Health.
- This shift is being accelerated by the application of AI to drug discovery and development, which exemplifies the way that frontier technologies and DeepTech domains at the very forefront of advanced science accelerate the rate of industry innovation and new technology adoption and disruption.
- The near-future paradigm of AI-enabled precision health will pave the way towards the implementation of true Longevity therapeutics within the next 5-7 years, enabling patients to become the CEOs of their own health, and creating an ecosystem for the widespread adoption of AI-enabled Longevity technologies to scale.
- Within the next 10 years, AI will replace doctors, sick care will be replaced by preventive, precision, continual maintenance of an optimal state of Healthy Longevity until the final stages of life,

and every major BioPharma and healthcare corporation will have Longevity as a central component of its R&D.

Longevity Mega-Complexity Fuels Paradigm Shifts and Accelerates the Rate of Practical Technological Implementation

The complexity of the Longevity Industry, and its extreme pace of change and innovation, is increasing specifically due to the intersection of multiple scientific and technological domains.

The fact that an industry possesses an extreme degree of complexity, and is driven by progress at the crest of the wave of the most advanced spheres of science and technology, necessarily means that the pace of overall industry growth and diversification is proportionally more rapid when compared to other industries, and that the fruits of its progress will be translated into practical implementation at a faster rate than slower-moving sectors.

Whereas five years ago it was possible for DeepTech and frontier technology industry innovations to be driven by advancements in a single domain or sector, today it is simply impossible, with the vast majority of such changes occurring at the intersection of two, three or more scientific and technological domains.

And this is just the beginning of a rapidly expanding trend, because the degree of complexity behind these fields, and the number of points at which they are converging and intersecting, are increasing at an exponential pace.

Currently, these convergent paradigm shifts are occurring in industries that are already dominated by deep science and emerging technologies. However, within the next 3-5 years, due to the pressures imposed by ongoing innovations and the arrival of advanced technologies, especially in the fields of AI and Advanced Biomedicine, we will begin to see other, much more conservative and slow-moving industries being shocked as well and transformed by innovations at the intersection of these technologies, literally forcing them to evolve in the face of significant technological change, despite their complete natural conservatism.

Consider, for example, the management of entire countries, or the governance of entities such as pension funds.

However, under the pressures of emerging technologies and AI in particular, it is inevitable that at least some entities in ultraconservative domains and sectors such as the ones mentioned will also soon come to be driven by similar paces of disruption and innovation absorption, marshalling towards new frontiers of science and technology.

The Shift from Treatment to Prevention, From Prevention to Precision Health, and from Precision Health to Healthy Longevity

We are currently witnessing a paradigm shift in the BioTech and BioPharma industries in real time: the disruption of drug discovery and the development of Data Science and AI, and the transition from one-size-fits-all blockbuster drugs towards targeted, individualized treatments.

As the Longevity, Preventive Medicine and Precision Health industries grow and develop to scale, we will see an increasing emphasis on the creation and validation of a wide diversity of biomarkers of aging, which will enable the extension of healthspan and the main-

tenance of optimal health for the majority of citizens' lifespans via continuous, AI-empowered monitoring of fluctuations in personalised biomarkers of aging.

The goal of applying AI for Drug Discovery is finding more efficient and targeted ways to discover new drugs. The AI for Drug Discovery sector is currently focused on designing new blockbuster drugs. Blockbuster drugs typically are considered drugs that can generate at least US$1 billion annually for one given Pharma corporation.

These AI for Drug Discovery companies are focused on the needs of Pharma corporations, which develop these blockbuster drugs aimed at a single disease and optimized for effectiveness in all patients equally. The Pharma business model, which was established over 30-40 years ago, has not evolved significantly since that time, and has some very obvious apparent limitations.

As AI for Drug Discovery becomes more sophisticated, it will focus on Personalised Precision Medicine. When we reach this milestone in the evolution of drug discovery, drug development companies will switch from "blockbuster drugs" towards personalised Precision Medicine: drugs will be designed and applied using precise, individually-tailored methods of dosing, drug cocktail composition, and accurate efficient delivery.

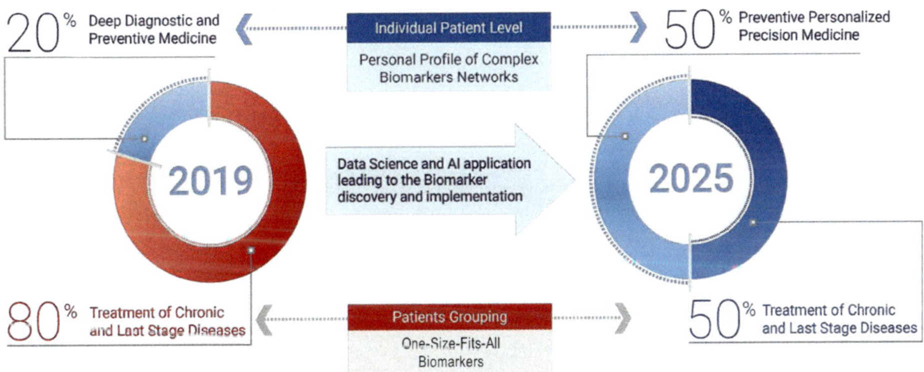

Jamie Metzl for Longevity.Technology: "First, we're increasingly understanding the biomarkers of aging, and that is giving us a language of measurement. We can assess with more precision whether certain interventions are working or not working. With the new tools of AI and machine learning we're really seeing a super convergence of different technologies that are all pushing forward, including the science of human Longevity."

Medicine will be optimized for each individual person and varied according to their genetics, current state of health, age, and many other parameters.

The current state of medicine and healthcare is being disrupted by the application of P4 medicine, causing a shift away from "one-treatment-fits-all" blockbuster drugs and towards personalised, precision, preventive and participatory diagnostics, prognostics and therapeutics.

Thus, the next major innovation in drug discovery will be moving away from single drugs optimized for entire patient populations, and towards increased personalization. In the most advanced stage, AI for Drug Discovery will focus on Precision Health and Healthy Longevity rather than Precision Medicine. The Longevity sector is the most complex area of AI for Drug Discovery because Longevity focuses on prevention rather than treatment.

Longevity requires the complete optimization of health at the deepest level targeting biological systems that control diseases. This stage will mark the shift from Precision Medicine towards precision health, developing drugs not just for single diseases, but entire states of patient health. The Precision Health stage is the most complex and will require the most advanced next-generation technologies.

Forecasting on the Future of Longevity Biomedicine: Patient as CEO and the Inevitable On-Boarding of Longevity into BioPharma and Healthcare

The most sophisticated tools will be required to assess companies working in the field of Precision Health and Longevity.

Compared to the current business models and technical approaches to the discovery, design and delivery of drugs, the shift towards Personalised Precision Medicine will be 10 times more complex and multidimensional, and correspondingly the further shift from Precision Medicine to Precision Health will be 100 times more multidimensional and complex.

As a result, the methods and approaches for industry analysis, investment target identification, and due diligence applied to companies will be proportionately more advanced, multidimensional and sophisticated than they are today.

However, those methods in common use today are even below the bar of the current complexity of the AI for Drug Discovery landscape, and therefore they will prove to be increasingly ineffective tools for strategic decision-making as the level of complexity in the BioPharma increases more and more during the shift from blockbuster drugs to Personalised Precision Medicine and finally towards Precision Health.

Biomarkers for Paradigm Shift from P4 Medicine to Precision Health

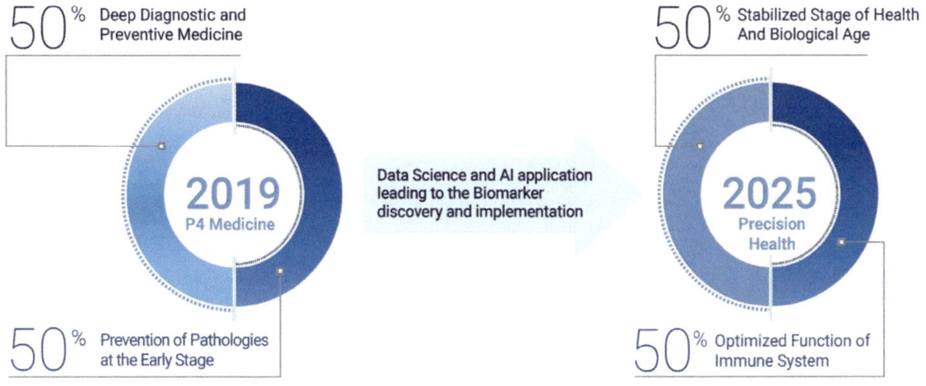

Since 2013, Deep Learning systems have surpassed human performance in multiple applications, such as face and image recognition. Predictors of chronological age, and biological age — or functional age — are rapidly gaining popularity and with this a deep outburst of research and development is awakened, both in the scientific and industrial spheres. A new market is brewing. AI has shown that it is possible to overcome the best human ophthalmologists or radiologists and the best conventional predictors of complex pathologies such as Parkinson's and Alzheimer's have been surpassed. And in this framework, AI-driven biomedical research and development efforts are now already facing aging.

Advances in P4 Medicine will converge and culminate in the emergence of a new paradigm of "Precision Health", which denotes the continuous stabilization of health and the maximum-obtainable maintenance of a young biological age via the routine application of P4 medicine in response to ongoing fluctuations in biomarkers of aging and health.

The assumption that these coming shifts will not occur until the far future is incorrect, and our current methods of industry analysis and tangible, quantifiable forecasting have informed us that it is quite reasonable to expect that the approaches and business models underlying Precision Health will be the norm in developed countries by the year 2027-2030, and that in some countries and regions, significant elements of this approaches may be in place as early as 2023-2024.

Furthermore, we can expect to see intermediate progress towards the full realization of this shift, like the widespread use of AI for blockbuster drug discovery, and even the shift from single-drug-fits-all business model towards personalised Precision Medicine as early as 2022-2023. During the time major shifts will occur in healthcare. Healthcare decisions will be transferred from doctors to IT-systems. Progressive healthcare clinics will be managed by technical engineers and IT-companies executives.

While many analysts consider these events to be decades away, our forecasting and industry analysis shows that this will be standard by 2030. In many countries, significant elements will be achieved much sooner and become reality by 2027.

Intermediate steps, like personalised advanced biomedicine, capable of delivering some elements of precision health, will be achievable by 2024.

Precision Diagnostics

- Multi-Omics Sequencing
- Non-invasive continuous monitoring of biomarkers
- Multi-modal total-body imaging
- Qualitative functional tests
- Whole-body and organ specific biological age calculation based on biomarkers
- 3D integration of cross-sectional tissue and organ imaging

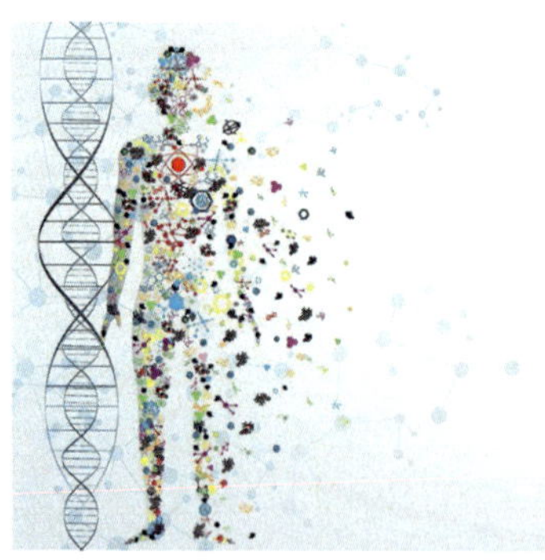

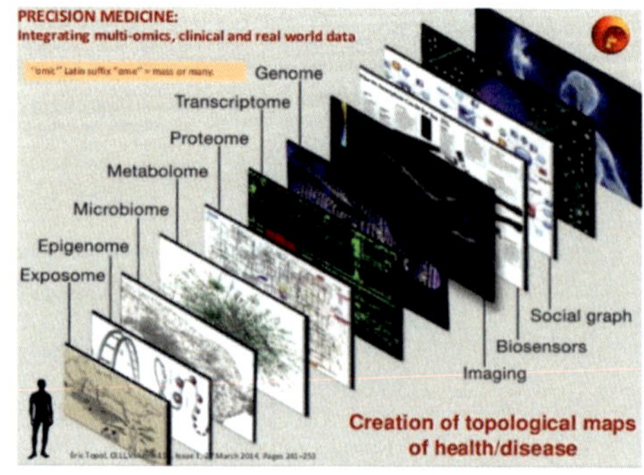

Not only new methods of standard industry benchmarking and forecasting need to be developed to combat the issues of overcomplexity and multidimensionality in the Longevity Industry, but new methods of testing the basic safety and efficacy of Longevity and Precision Health **diagnostic, prognostic and prevention** need to be adapted as well, moving away from the use of model organisms, towards a more human-centric approach.

The importance of AI and the shift from treatment towards prevention and maintenance of patient health will cause a transfer from doctors to IT-systems, and clinics will be engineered and managed by people who think as aerospace engineers and managers of IT-corporations do now, whereas doctors will be like those people who are now mechanical engineers in the aerospace sector — the practitioners, but not the designers and strategic decision makers.

In many cases, the patients, being empowered by sophisticated Data and AI systems, will be capable of becoming CEOs of their own health.

Conclusions:

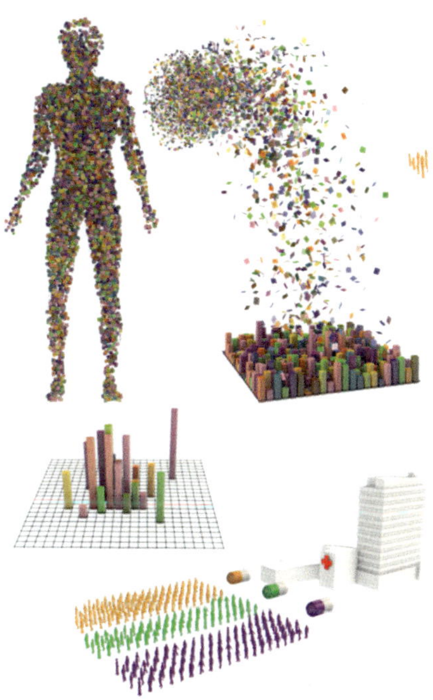

- The healthcare industry is currently dominated by BioPharma corporations.
- In 7-10 years, it will be dominated by healthcare corporations, who will take the form of either IT-giants, or tech corporations who have merged with or acquired the most progressive Pharma corporations, and will eventually sell to their clients subscriptions to Precision Health, in the same way that today they are selling subscriptions to Netflix and Amazon Prime.
- **Deep Knowledge Analytics and Aging Analytics Agency** have been working over multidimensional approaches to industry analytics, to serve as the leading tools and solutions for strategic decision-making, with the aim of developing such frameworks to the levels required by the rapidly complexifying nature of the global healthcare system.

Chapter 4: Longevity Investing 1.0: Disproportions in the Current Longevity Industry Investment Landscape

"Because investment in the biotechnology and life science sectors requires a greater deal of technical expertise in order to successfully assess the viability and achievability of new ventures than in other sectors, there is a greater potential for big fails and an ensuing bubble. In a similar vein, there is a greater potential for over-promising or over-hyped ventures to receive large investments in place of ventures that are more realistic and don't over-promise and over-hype in a similar fashion, which also contributes to an economic climate that is more susceptible to growth rates beyond achievability and financial success, in turn further exacerbating the potential for a bubble to form and burst."

Dmitry Kaminskiy in *Global Trends - The Rising Longevity Industry* (Biogerontology Research Foundation, November 2016)

Key Points:

- The current perception regarding the leading investment funds in Longevity is mostly related to funds that, from the point of view of LPs, are making very risky bets on the forefront of core geroscience and biomedical Longevity research, with a very high risk of failure of translation into humans.
- There remains a significant unmet need for funds using a sophisticated investment strategy with robust diversification and pragmatic de-risking approaches.
- The right strategy shall both include diversification over a significant scope of Longevity Industry domains, including such topics as Artificial Intelligence, Precision Medicine, AgeTech and even Longevity FinTech and WealthTech, and avoid focusing too narrowly on geroscience and rejuvenation niches.
- There should also be diversification over regions, not placing all bets on the Silicon Valley, and diversification over the level of port-

folio company maturity. Lastly, it should employ a reasonable exit strategy, taking into account that, in case of projects related to clinical trials, it might take at least 7-10 years to get intermediate positive results in humans.

The Current State of Investing in Longevity

There are several hundred investment funds that could be considered investors in the Longevity space. Among them, approximately 20-30 could be considered the leading and really proactive funds.

Longevity Investment Funds

	Longevity Investment Fund	Website	Founded	Investor Type	Investment Stage
1	Advent Life Sciences	adventls.com	2010	Venture Capital	Early Stage Venture, Seed, Venture
2	Apollo Ventures	apollo.vc	2016	Venture Capital	Early Stage Venture, Seed
3	ARCH Ventures	archventure.com	1986	Venture Capital	Early Stage Venture, Seed, Venture
4	Deep Science Ventures	deepscienceventures.com	2016	Accelerator	Seed
5	F-Prime Capital	fprimecapital.com	1946	Venture Capital	Early Stage Venture, Late Stage Venture, Seed
6	Ferghana Partners	ferghanapartners.com	1991	Investment Bank	Late Stage Venture
7	Forbion Capital Partners	forbion.com	2007	Venture Capital	Early Stage Venture, Late Stage Venture
8	Forever Healthy	forever-healthy.org	2016	Accelerator	Early Stage Venture
9	Front Seat Capital	frontseatcapital.com/	N/A	Angel Investor	Late Stage Venture
10	Generator Ventures	generatorvc.com	2017	Venture Capital	Convertible Note, Early Stage Venture, Late Stage Venture, Seed
11	IDO Investments	ido.om/	2016	Venture Capital	Late Stage Venture
12	Juvenescence	juvenescence.ltd	2016	Venture Capital	Early Stage Venture, Late Stage Venture
13	KIZOO	kizoo.com	2000	Venture Capital	Early Stage Venture, Seed
14	Life Biosciences	lifebiosciences.com	2017	Venture Capital	Seed, Incubator, Ecosystem
15	LifeSci Venture Partners	lifesciventure.com	2017	Venture Capital	Early Stage Venture
16	Longevity Vision Fund	lvf.vc	2018	Venture Capital	Early Stage Venture, Late Stage Venture
17	Longitude Capital	longitudecapital.com	2006	Venture Capital	Debt, Early Stage Venture, Late Stage Venture, Private Equity
18	Methuselah Fund	methuselahfund.com	N/A	N/A	Early Stage Venture
19	Nest.Bio Ventures	nest.bio	2016	Venture Capital	Early Stage Venture, Late Stage Venture, Private Equity, Seed
20	Orbimed	orbimed.com	1989	Angel Investor	Debt, Early Stage Venture, Late Stage Venture, Private Equity

	Longevity Investment Fund	Website	Founded	Investor Type	Investment Stage
21	OS Fund	osfund.co	2014	Venture Capital	Early Stage Venture, Seed
22	Qure Ventures	qureventures.com	2012	Venture Capital	Early Stage Venture
23	RA Capital Management	racap.com	2001	Venture Capital	Early Stage Venture, Late Stage Venture, Post-Ipo, Private Equity
24	ScienceVest	sciencevest.com	N/A	Venture Capital	Early Stage Venture, Late Stage Venture
25	Sofinnova Investments	sofinnova.com	1974	Venture Capital	Early Stage Venture, Late Stage Venture
26	Tectonic Capital	tectonic.vc	2013	Venture Capital	Early Stage Venture, Seed
27	The Longevity Fund	longevity.vc	2011	Venture Capital	Early Stage Venture, Seed
28	Thiel Capital	thielcapital.com	2011	Venture Capital	Venture
29	Vickers Venture Partners	vickersventure.com	2005	Venture Capital	Early Stage Venture
30	Y Combinator	ycombinator.com	2005	Accelerator	Debt, Early Stage Venture, Seed

However, there is a significant issue with language and classification frameworks surrounding the field, and specifically with classifying and identifying what exactly is or is not related to the Longevity Industry, and what exact domains of scientific research are within the scope of the Longevity space.

Historically, what happened is that within the scope of scientific research, some hubs and figures became much more well-known within the Longevity Industry, and spinoffs from the individuals and research hubs became more famous and promoted across the industry.

Some of these projects, being based in the Silicon Valley, had the advantage of being more visible just due to their location (specially from a media perspective), while others, due to the famous scientists and executive management they have at their helm.

Many of these projects are related to what could be named "rejuvenation biotechnology" or radical life extension, with a focus on scientific research domains such as senolytics, mitochondrial gene therapies and telomere extension.

However, this is very particular and typical for the Silicon Valley, and it might be considered oversaturated to many reasonable investors, while many other domains do not receive sufficient investment, and, from a commercial point of view, have much less visible attention, without any reasonable logic, given their potential.

Longevity Investment Funds Investment Strategies

	Longevity Investment Fund	Investment Focus	Research Focus	Funding Round Focus	Geographical Distribution of Assets	Investment Strategy
1	[illegible]	Diversified Portfolio	Human Life Extension	Diversified Portfolio	Diversified	Balanced
2	[illegible]	Diversified Portfolio	Human Life Extension	Diversified Portfolio	Concentrated	Balanced
3	[illegible]	Diversified Portfolio	Human Life Extension	Diversified Portfolio	Diversified	Balanced
4	[illegible]	Digital Health	Human Life Extension	Early Stage Venture	Concentrated	Middle Risk Level
5	[illegible]	Digital Health	Human Life Extension	Early Stage Venture	Diversified	Middle Risk Level
6	[illegible]	Drug Discovery	Human Life Extension	Diversified Portfolio	Diversified	Middle Risk Level
7	[illegible]	Drug Discovery	Human Life Extension	Diversified Portfolio	Diversified	Middle Risk Level
8	[illegible]	Diversified Portfolio	Preclinical Trials (Mice)	Early Stage Venture	Diversified	Middle Risk Level
9	[illegible]	Drug Discovery	Human Life Extension	Diversified Portfolio	Diversified	Middle Risk Level
10	[illegible]	Drug Discovery	Preclinical Trials (Mice)	Diversified Portfolio	Diversified	Middle Risk Level
11	[illegible]	Diversified Portfolio	Diversified	Early Stage Venture	Diversified	Middle Risk Level
12	[illegible]	Digital Health	Human Life Extension	Early Stage Venture	Concentrated	Middle Risk Level
13	[illegible]	Diversified Portfolio	Human Life Extension	Early Stage Venture	Diversified	Middle Risk Level
14	[illegible]	Diversified Portfolio	Human Life Extension	Late Stage Venture	Concentrated	Middle Risk Level
15	[illegible]	Digital Health	Human Life Extension	Early Stage Venture	Concentrated	Middle Risk Level
16	[illegible]	Diversified Portfolio	Preclinical Trials (Mice)	Diversified Portfolio	Diversified	Middle Risk Level
17	[illegible]	Drug Discovery	Preclinical Trials (Mice)	Early Stage Venture	Diversified	High Risk Level
18	[illegible]	Drug Discovery	Preclinical Trials (Mice)	Diversified Portfolio	Diversified	High Risk Level
19	[illegible]	Drug Discovery	Preclinical Trials (Mice)	Late Stage Venture	Diversified	High Risk Level
20	[illegible]	Drug Discovery	Human Life Extension	Early Stage Venture	Concentrated	High Risk Level
21	[illegible]	Drug Discovery	Preclinical Trials (Mice)	Early Stage Venture	Concentrated	High Risk Level
22	[illegible]	Diversified Portfolio	Preclinical Trials (Mice)	Early Stage Venture	Diversified	High Risk Level
23	[illegible]	Drug Discovery	Preclinical Trials (Mice)	Early Stage Venture	Concentrated	High Risk Level
24	[illegible]	Drug Discovery	Preclinical Trials (Mice)	Early Stage Venture	Concentrated	High Risk Level
25	[illegible]	Drug Discovery	Preclinical Trials (Mice)	Diversified Portfolio	Concentrated	High Risk Level
26	[illegible]	Drug Discovery	Preclinical Trials (Mice)	Diversified Portfolio	Diversified	High Risk Level
27	[illegible]	Drug Discovery	Preclinical Trials (Mice)	Early Stage Venture	Concentrated	High Risk Level
28	[illegible]	Drug Discovery	Human Life Extension	Early Stage Venture	Concentrated	High Risk Level
29	[illegible]	Drug Discovery	Preclinical Trials (Mice)	Diversified Portfolio	Diversified	High Risk Level
30	[illegible]	Diversified Portfolio	Preclinical Trials (Mice)	Early Stage Venture	Diversified	High Risk Level
31	[illegible]	Drug Discovery	Human Life Extension	Early Stage Venture	Concentrated	High Risk Level
32	[illegible]	Drug Discovery	Preclinical Trials (Mice)	Diversified Portfolio	Concentrated	High Risk Level
33	[illegible]	Drug Discovery	Preclinical Trials (Mice)	Diversified Portfolio	Diversified	High Risk Level
34	[illegible]	Drug Discovery	Preclinical Trials (Mice)	Early Stage Venture	Concentrated	High Risk Level
35	[illegible]	Drug Discovery	Preclinical Trials (Mice)	Diversified Portfolio	Concentrated	High Risk Level

Many of these technologies and hypotheses are already now working and showing some intermediary positive results in model organisms, including mice. This gives such projects substantial leverage and opportunity to be over-promoted. However, there are very strong and rational reasons to doubt that such technologies and projects will be efficiently translatable to humans in the foreseeable future as it was common in the traditional BioTech industry aiming to design drugs for specific disease targets rather than for complex biological aging. The clinical trials framework which worked well for the BioTech Industry is unlikely to be applicable for clinical trials in the Longevity Industry.

Therefore, all venture funds which are making bets on projects dependent on showing results in model organisms and don't have yet intermediate positive results in humans might be considered quite risky, especially if those funds do not have substantial portfolio diversification in many areas of aging research science and, moreover, in areas that do not require clinical trials at all to offset this risk (such as Longevity FinTech, AgeTech, and other domains that are already market ready).

More in-depth details on the specific innovations in investment strategy tailored to be maximally relevant for the Longevity Industry which are being developed and deployed by Deep Knowledge Group, Deep Knowledge Ventures and its specialized Longevity-focused hybrid investment fund Longevity.Capital, beyond those described in the present book, will be presented in its sequel, *Longevity Industry 2.0*.

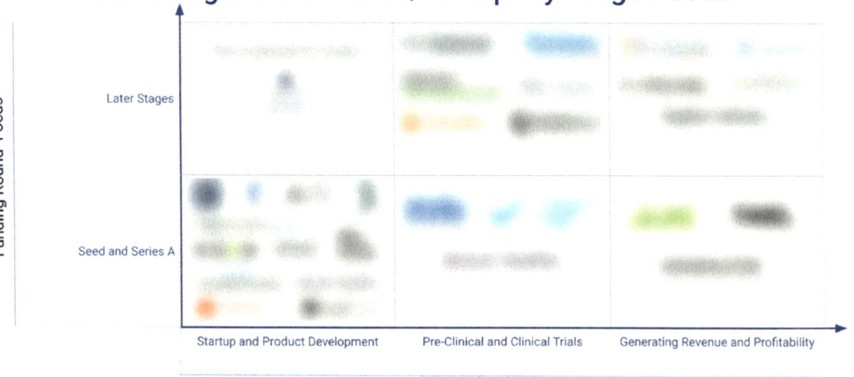

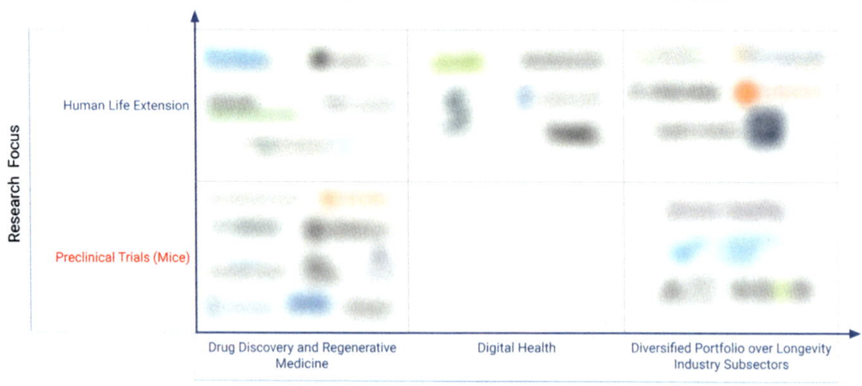

Comparison of Longevity Investment Funds
Number of Investments / Geographical Distribution of Assets

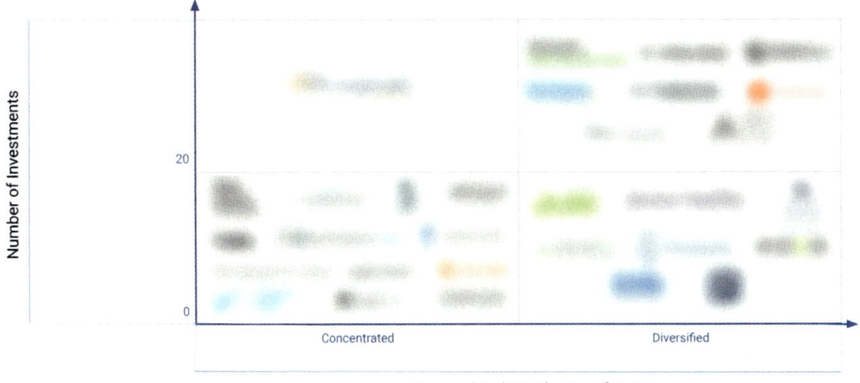

Comparison of Longevity Investment Funds
Investment Specialization / Investment Approach

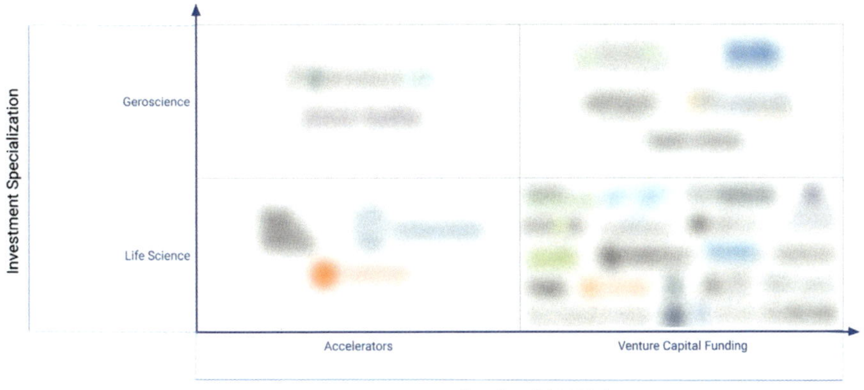

Major Trends, Challenges and Opportunities in "Investing in Longevity"

- **The majority of Longevity investment funds invest in drug discovery and depend on the success of clinical trials.** Such investors are highly exposed to clinical trial risks because most of the drug discovery companies in the portfolio only have results in model organisms, and model organisms (in the case of Longevity) have very limited concordance with human pathology, due to general differences in biology, and specific differences in the nature of aging.
- To minimize the risk of failed clinical trials and increase the probability of successful commercialization of treatment, researchers

should determine the effects of the drug on the human body using similar methods (e.g. via the use of *in silico* models of human biology, via human cells and tissues in vitro, and via in vivo micro-dosing and measuring of effects).

- **Lack of portfolio diversification over Longevity Industry subsectors:** Proprietary analytics performed by Aging Analytics Agency indicate that a very select few investment funds with interests in the Longevity sector show sufficiently-diversified investment portfolio both regarding Longevity subsectors and the level of companies maturity, investing into AgeTech, Drug Discovery, and P4 Medicine projects at different funding.
- **Lack of effective de-risking investment strategies in terms of "time diversification" and company stage:** The Longevity Industry will inevitably grow, but correcting current disproportions in investment strategy will accelerate progress.

Chapter 5: Longevity Investing 2.0: Why Traditional BioTech Analytics Fail Against the Longevity Industry's Extreme Complexity

"The Longevity Industry will dwarf all other industries in both size and market capitalization and will require unprecedented sophistication in its approach for assessment and forecasting from the start to neutralize challenges and manifest opportunities. The Longevity sector has both unprecedented levels of multidimensionality and intersectionality and unprecedented prospects for growth and profitability. Although challenges to realistic assessment and forecasting are great, they are not insurmountable. Established practices for forecasting and assessment already exist in other complex high-tech industries, and progress in Big Data analysis and AI for modeling can be adapted for use in Longevity. It is precisely this mission — the formulation of relevant, quantitative, analytical frameworks for Longevity Industry assessment, benchmarking, forecasting and optimization — that has been a central component of the mission of Deep Knowledge Group and its Longevity-focused analytical subsidiary, Aging Analytics Agency, for the past several years."

Dmitry Kaminskiy in *Introducing Longevity Industry 1.0*

Key Points:

- The Longevity Industry's unprecedented complexity is a result of the fact that it is a sector located directly at the intersection of the most advanced domains of science, technology, medicine, finance and governance in human history.
- As these many sectors merge and interact to create the multidimensional integrated assembly that is the Longevity Industry, they combine not via simple addition, but my multiplication, making the whole not just the sum of its parts' complexity and sophistication, but the exponential doubling and quadrupling of them.

- This creates significant challenges to relevant, realistic and tangible industry benchmarking and forecasting. The approaches that proved successful in the traditional BioTech and biomedicine sectors will fail when faced with the extreme complexity and sophistication of the Longevity Industry, substantially complicating any efforts to manifest the sector's opportunities and neutralize its risks.
- Aging Analytics Agency has spent the past five years developing sophisticated multidimensional analytical frameworks of equal complexity to the Longevity Industry itself, in order to build the necessary tools for relevant industry forecasting, benchmarking and analytics, which can be leveraged to enable relevant and actionable strategic decision-making within the sector.
- Today, these frameworks encompass the full scope of the global Longevity Industry, from science to business, including the Longevity financial industry, the Longevity policy and governance sphere, and more.

Longevity Industry Mega-Complexity: Challenges, Issues, Opportunities

> It is precisely the mission of formulating relevant, quantitative analytical frameworks for Longevity Industry assessment, benchmarking, forecasting and optimization that has been a central component in the mission of Deep Knowledge Group and its Longevity-focused analytical subsidiary, Aging Analytics Agency, for the past several years.

One of the foremost issues presenting challenges to Longevity Industry assessment is how extremely broad the sector is, which means that an analysis of many hundreds of sectors, industries and domains of science and technology must be performed in order to obtain a concrete and comprehensive understanding of the dynamics, trends and directions of the industry. This is a situation entirely unique to the Longevity Industry.

Despite its unprecedented levels of multidimensionality and intersectionality, the Longevity Industry also has equally unprecedented prospects for growth and profitability.

Due to this extreme level of complexity, realistic assessment and forecasting are extremely challenging, and the methods currently being applied for assessment of the BioTech and biomedical industries have proven completely inadequate.

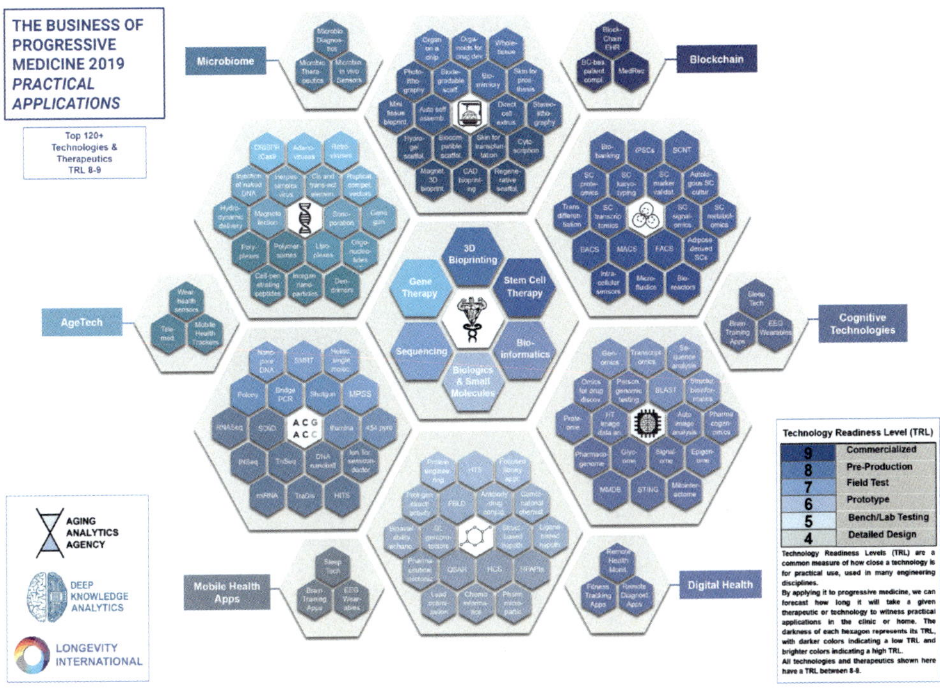

In the coming years, the frontline of other types of professionals, including entrepreneurs and investors, will also gravitate to the Longevity Industry, after realizing its extreme potential for growth and profitability, combined with the fact that it is the most ethical form of conducting business, and the industry with the greatest beneficial impact for humanity.

The quantitative and tangible assessment of technologies, methods, therapies and companies within the Longevity space necessitates the use of novel approaches to technological, scientific and industry benchmarking, utilizing methodologies like Technology Readiness Levels (TRLs), which use the expertise of science and technology professionals to assess the market-readiness of products and services, and forecast when their clinical translation will become a reality.

These levels of complexity also present substantial risks, given that they significantly complicate the ability of companies, investors and even national governments to anticipate challenges (such as risk of fraud) and recognize opportunities.

These challenges will need to be addressed in national Longevity development strategies that various nations are currently devising in response to the pressures of the looming Silver Tsunami.

Though the challenges of realistic assessment and forecasting are great, they are not unsolvable. There already exist established practices for forecasting and assessment in other complex high-tech industries, especially taking into account progress in Big Data analysis and AI for forecasting, scenario building and modeling, which can be adapted for use in Longevity.

The Need for a New Generation of Industry Analytics to De-Risk and Optimize Industry Growth and Stability

The previous chapter outlined the remarkable growth of the Longevity Industry in recent years, driven by the multiplicative intersection of many frontier domains of science and technology, the rise of Longevity as a clear MegaTrend embraced across many sectors and domains, and the increasingly rapid diversification that the industry is currently undergoing.

As all these changes progress, the number of points at which these sectors intersect increases. This progress obviously will not be driven by advances in a single technological domain or sector. Each of the necessary breakthroughs will occur at an intersection of two, three or more technologies.

Due to its complexity, the Longevity Industry requires extremely sophisticated analytical frameworks for assessment and forecasting. This becomes increasingly important as it progresses and grows, because the scope for costly mistakes increases proportionately.

Many such mistakes will be made with good intentions as a simple result of the sheer complexity of the Longevity landscape and the difficulties of forecasting, but there will also be room for actual cases of fraud, as exemplified by the Theranos scandal.

And due to the fact that it will be an industry dwarfing all others in the history of mankind regarding its size, the cost and overall repercussions of such mistakes will also be of an unprecedented size and scale. In order to prevent such outcomes, and neutralize the likelihood of a Longevity boom and bust, participants in Longevity need to utilize approaches of assessment, forecasting and strategic decision-making precise enough to match its level of complexity.

Longevity Industry Analytics 2.0 for Modern Benchmarking and Forecasting

While the industry does indeed require new forms of analysis and forecasting to match its runaway complexity, this does not mean that such solutions cannot be created over the next several years, or that they are not already being created today. This is made easier by the fact that there are already existing methods of technological and scientific assessment practiced in other high-tech industries, such as the use of Technology Readiness Levels in the Aerospace Industry for assessing how close to market-readiness certain technologies are, or scenario analysis in politics and warfare.

There are also similar assessment practices in the fields of AI, machine learning, deep learning and Big Data analysis, such as the use of synthetic data and metadata (i.e. "synthetic" data extrapolated from existing data when such data cannot be directly measured) to benchmark, assess and extrapolate existing trends into the future.

While the level of complexity is rising, the pace of progress in technologies, tools and techniques for assessing and forecasting is also increasing, and if proactive measures are applied, the levels of precision and efficiency of such methods can be made to keep pace with this increasing complexity.

In order to neutralize these challenges and unleash the industry's potential, **Aging Analytics Agency** and **Deep Knowledge Analytics** have been working over the course of the past five years on designing and validating increasingly sophisticated and multidimensional approaches to industry analytics, to serve as the leading tools and solutions for strategic decision-making, with the aim of developing such frameworks to the levels necessitated by the rapidly complexifying nature of the global healthcare system.

They have been applying systematic methodologies to create different types of analytical frameworks that define and classify distinct scientific domains, technologies and applications very clearly, in a way that allows them to be quantitatively compared, continually refining them to maintain their relevance against the changing dynamics of the industry sectors.

Above it is shown an example of the Aging Analytics Agency's 3-D Longevity Industry Analytical Framework, whose production was necessary because of the complexities of the sector, and required to obtain a tangible and pragmatic understanding of the industry in order to structure investment strategies in a relevant way.

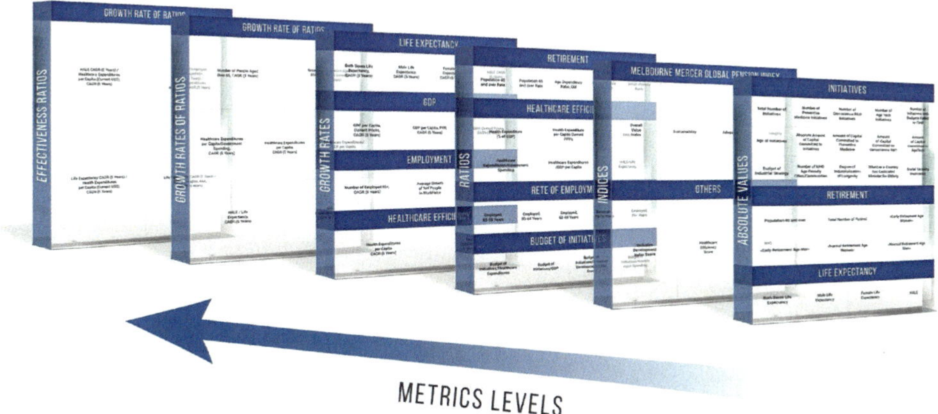

This is the 6-Layer Analytical Framework used for benchmarking of countries according to their levels of Longevity Progressiveness, used in Aging Analytics Agency's National Longevity Development Plans: Global Landscape Overview 2019 report. Metrics are categorized into 6 distinct layers, and include both indicators of potential (or lack thereof) and indicators of actual success (or lack thereof). Thus, the ranking system reflects both strengths and opportunities of different countries regarding the development of National Longevity Development Strategies.

The metrics developed for and used in Aging Analytics Agency's *National Longevity Development Plans: Global Overview 2019* report are broken down into 6 distinct layers, with:

- Specific ratios being derived from 1st layer metrics.
- Specific metric ratios and growth rates of ratios being derived from 3rd layer metrics.
- Effectiveness measurements being derived from 4th layer metrics.
- Effectiveness measurements of growth rates being derived from 5th layer metrics.

Aging Analytics Agency has begun to direct significant resources to the production of sophisticated open-access and proprietary analytics on the topics of Longevity governance and governmental development plans, the intersection of Longevity and the advancing financial industry of pension funds and insurance companies, and the global market of financial instruments and derivatives related to so-called "Longevity Risk".

Longevity Industry Analytical Framework: Company Harmonization Analysis

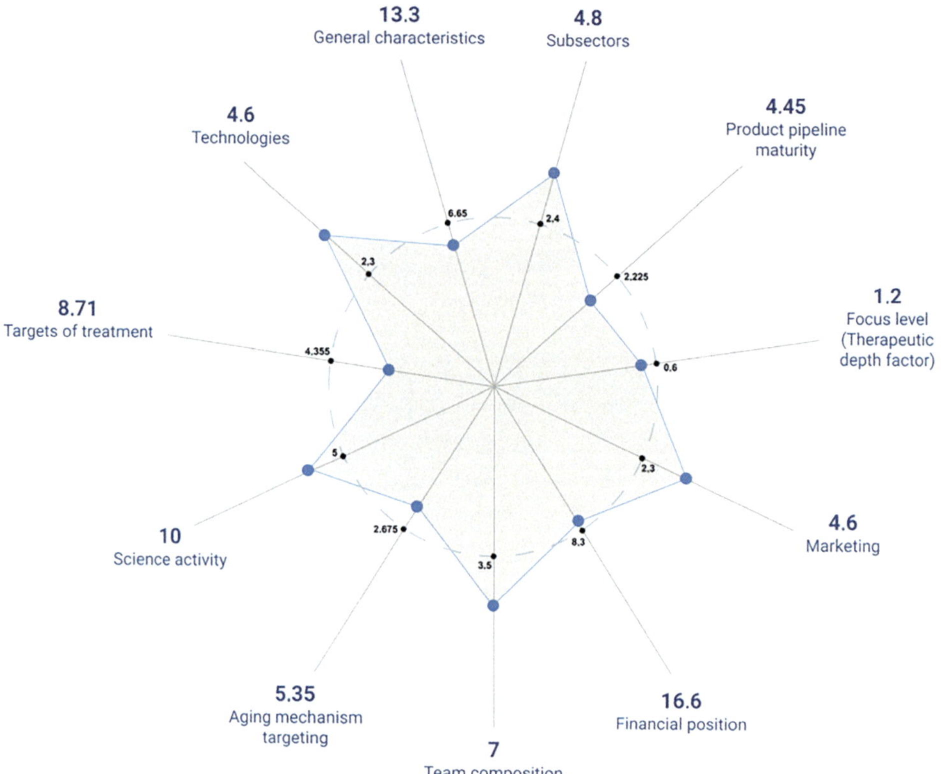

The proprietary reports of Aging Analytics Agency utilize a variety of insightful comparative analyses, including company harmonization analyses showing how companies compare in terms of the ratio of their strengths in key areas including scientific validation, business development, marketing, financial position, executive management composition, technology pipelines and other relevant domains.

These analytical reports include comparison charts showing the ratio of therapeutic breadth to therapeutic depth of companies' product and service pipelines.

Aging Analytics Agency has continued to refine these comparative analysis systems over the past several years, refining the specific metrics used to conduct its market studies, as well as the mathematical formulas used to combine them, and the advanced visualization techniques used to make its forecasts, rankings and determinations as clear as possible.

Precision Medicine Clinic Product and Service Pipeline Therapeutic Depth vs. Breadth Analysis

Conclusions:

- Deep Knowledge Group and Aging Analytics Agency will continue to increase and enhance the breadth, depth and overall re-tunability of these analytical frameworks, and to extend them to additional relevant domains, including benchmarking of projects and initiatives in the realms of the Longevity Financial Industry and Longevity politics, governance and national development plans.
- It was necessary to begin the process of developing these analytical frameworks early, and to continue to evolve the approaches used for assessment, benchmarking and forecasting continuously, in step with the rapidly shifting dynamics of Longevity.
- We are now standing at the dawn of a golden age of Data Science and AI that will deliver significant progress in the development of comprehensive yet actional panels of biomarkers of aging, and rapidly-intensifying dynamics of progress on the forefront of Preventive Medicine, Precision Health and advanced biomedicine.
- These will form the central metrics of a vast, multi-faceted industry which will swallow up surrounding industries including biotechnology and finance. Its end product is, after all, humanity's

most valuable asset upon which all other assets depend: additional years of healthy functional active life.

Meanwhile, **Deep Knowledge Group** will continue its mission to strategically assist, support and optimize the trajectory of development of the global Longevity Industry by supporting the ongoing work of its Longevity-focused analytical subsidiary Aging Analytics Agency, and by utilizing it as the brain behind the body of its Longevity-focused subsidiary hybrid investment fund, Longevity.Capital, to transform deep market intelligence into practice via a relevant and modern investment strategy fully equipped to face the mega-complexity posed by the rising Longevity Industry.

Chapter 6: Longevity Analytics 2.0 - Modern Analytical and IT Solutions to Manage Longevity Complexity

"The convergence of AI, advanced data science, and Longevity research will accelerate important medical, technological and financial breakthroughs that will benefit all of humanity. I know that advanced technologies can save lives. I know this because advanced technologies saved my life. I'm actually an early adopter of life extension technology. This is why myself and Dmitry were compelled to write this book — to present our understanding to the public, and arm Longevity Industry participants, investors and even government representatives to transform the notion of aging and Longevity from a challenge into an opportunity and source of massive socioeconomic growth, stability and prosperity."

Margaretta Colangelo in *A Preview of Our New Book Longevity Industry 1.0*

In 2020, Deep Knowledge Group set out on a mission to systematize and unite the wide array of Longevity Industry analytics across the domains of science, technology, finance, policy and governance that its Longevity focused analytical subsidiary, Aging Analytics Agency, had developed over the past 5 years into a single integrated ecosystem, backed by the Big Data analytics and sophisticated data visualization capabilities of Deep Knowledge Group, in the form of a single coherent Global Longevity Big Data Analytics IT-System.

The ultimate aim of this system is to deliver strategic decision makers across the private sector, global investment community, financial industry and governance and policy ecosystem access for the first time to Big Data analytics and visualization, market intelligence, competitive analysis, technology and company benchmarking, SWOT analysis, practical recommendations and other strategic toolsets capable of handling the unprecedented complexity and multidimensionality of the full-scope Global Longevity public and private sector ecosystem.

Longevity Industry Big Data Analytical System Architecture

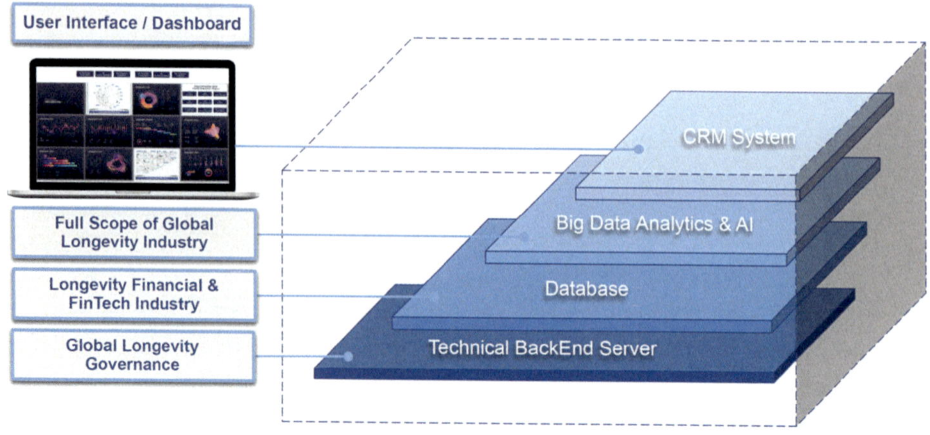

Longevity Industry IT-Platform and BigData Analytics System

LONGEVITY ECOSYSTEM
Longevity Ecosystem Dashboard

LONGEVITY MARKETPLACE
Fitness
Life Style
Nutrition
Health
Vitamins
Beauty
B2C Dashboard

BUSINESS ECOSYSTEM
B2B Dashboard

INVESTMENT ANALYTICS
Investment Analytics Dashboard

FINANCIAL INDUSTRY
Longevity Finance Dashboard

NATIONAL HEALTHCARE
Longevity Governance Dashboard

The Longevity Dashboard and IT-Platform is a single project with 6 individual component dashboards. The majority of Front End and Back End systems and features will be applicable to all 6 individual component dashboards, with some adjustments and additional dashboard-specific features integrated required on a case-by-case basis for each individual dashboard.

General Features will include:

1. Interactive real-time data visualization in form of mindmaps, charts,

lists, region maps, bar graphs, etc.;

2. Access to merged databases of entities, products, services and technologies related to Longevity and HeathCare Industries;
3. Incorporated AI-driven vendor-client smart-matching based on client's geography and existing unmet needs and preferences;
4. Sophisticated Big Data analysis of Longevity Market and Industries Trends, future strategies and national plans;
5. Tailored recommendation packs;
6. Entities quantitative ranking and benchmarking (both positive and negative);
7. Filters implementing, so to sort entities via names, categories, locations, overall activity, investments and financing, etc.

Longevity IT-Platform Super Dashboard FrontEnd

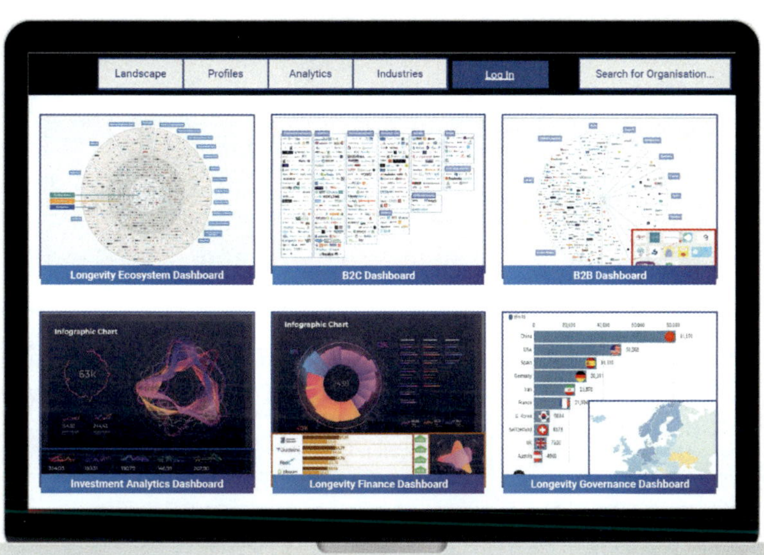

Longevity Dashboard Architecture

Global Longevity Ecosystem

- Centralized and integrated Global Longevity Industry Ecosystem IT-Platform
- Created by integrating all previous region and domain-specific Longevity IT Platforms

- Will also integrate 2 new/upcoming Longevity reports and IT-Platforms: Longevity Industry in Alpine Europe, and mHealth in Alpine Europe
- Will be used as basis for building stage-2 platform, only containing entities relevant for Longevity Bank's marketplace and candidate partners and ambassadors

B2C Dashboard

- Web dashboard aggregating relevant vendors of products and services across full scope of Longevity and Healthy Living
- Includes: physical and psychological health, fitness, cosmetics, financial wellness ("wealthspan"), clinics, sport and exercise, diet and supplements, precision health clinics, diagnostic and prognostics etc.), for exclusive use by Longevity Card holders
- Incorporates AI-driven vendor-client smart-matching based on client's geography and existing unmet needs

B2B Dashboard

- Second-level Marketplace Dashboard available only for Longevity Bank Institutional and Corporate Clients, and B2C marketplace vendors, allowing clients to list market and distribute their products and services to other businesses (clients and/or B2C marketplace vendors)
- Uses AI-driven smart-matching to enable B2B transactions between Longevity Bank Corporate Clients on the one hand, and approved B2C Marketplace Vendors
- Clients get rewards based on volume of B2B transactions

Investment Analytics Dashboard

- Provides advanced, sophisticated and quantitative Big Data analysis on Longevity companies and Longevity investment strategy.
- Will contain more in-depth data and analytics on the companies featured in the B2C and B2B Dashboards
- SWOT analysis tailored to clients' geographical, development stage and sector-specific focus
- The results of the analysis will be used to provide tailored recommendation packs to hedge risks and maximize diversification

Longevity Finance Dashboard

- Market intelligence on the Longevity-related activities of hundreds of major financial institutions (investment banks, pension funds, insurance companies, retail banks)
- SWOT analysis and competitive landscaping
- Quantitative ranking and benchmarking (both positive and negative) of financial corporations
- B2B marketplace of relevant Longevity financial products and services
- Big Data, Machine Learning and AI Analytics capabilities
- Combines the sophisticated technological and data visualization resources of Deep Knowledge Group's IT department with the quantitative multidimensional industry analytics of Aging Analytics Agency
- Provides progressive financial institutions interested in capturing the massive rising tide of Longevity Finance with the necessary set of tools required to structure, optimize and execute their business models, products, services and strategic decision making in a way that is relevant for the extreme complexity and multidimensionality of Longevity

Longevity Governance Dashboard

- Applies Big Data analysis to identify social policy, healthcare, medical, financial and socioeconomic factors having the greatest effect on the gap between life expectancy at birth and Health-Adjusted Life Expectancy (HALE) for 100 regions
- Identifies factors and practices behind certain regions' success in maintaining a high degree of National Healthy Longevity and a low gap between HALE and Life Expectancy
- Provides tangible and practical recommendations tuned to the specifics of individual countries, providing the necessary set of tools to allow countries currently leading the international Healthy Longevity race to maintain and improve their current standing
- Features region-specific recommendation packs to enable governments currently lagging behind others to reduce their HALE gap and improve their comparative global standing, transforming the deficit and challenge of the silver tsunami into the asset and opportunity of Healthy Longevity for the mutual benefit of their citizens and their economy

Dashboard N1 - Global Longevity Industry Ecosystem: Main Features

The Global Longevity Ecosystem dashboard will be in the form of an interactive mindmap with 50,000+ entities, containing individual profiles of Longevity-focused companies, investors and R&D Hubs. This dashboard will serve as the foundation for Dashboards N2-N6.

- Mindmaps are sophisticated tools for visualizing market segmentation and connections between Longevity Industry entities and stakeholders, particularly companies, investors, personalities, government organizations, non-profits and R&D Hubs.
- The mindmaps are divided into layers, or sectors, and sectors are segregated into groups. Each group relates to a particular category, sector or practical application, for example AgeTech, P4 Medicine, etc., and logos of companies that are connected to this very group are putted in specially designated place for this.
- Aging Analytics Agency's interactive mindmaps and IT-Platforms are a unique and major hallmark of their brand, and one of the main factors that has established them as the leader of sophisticated, quantitative and multidimensional Longevity Industry analytics.

Dashboard N1: Overview

20,000 + entities (category-specific scope and estimated quantity):

Companies (~6000): Longevity and Wellness related companies developing therapeutic, diagnostic, medical and consumer devices, products and services to address and maintain the full scope of Healthy Longevity, from biological, psychological and social health to financial wellness.

Investors, Funding Agencies (~4000): Main organizations which invest in key players in the Longevity and Aging sphere, support bodies and lenders helping to aid the efforts of relevant companies, labs, centres, etc.

R&D Centres, Hubs, Clinics (~5000): Labs, R&D centres, hubs, universities and institutes, clinics and hospitals etc. functioning in the Longevity Industry, dedicated to scientific research in related fields and emerging approach for multiple diseases (as well as aging-associated conditions) treatment and prevention.

Personalities (~5000): Public and private-sector professionals working to grow the Longevity landscape through their efforts in business, science, policy, philanthropy and thought-leadership, with a focus on entrepreneur-scientists, technologists, and professionals working on practical applications in humans and translational research, rather than on animal models and so-called "basic scientific research" that is far away from real-world implementation.

Financial institutions (~500): Investment banks, insurance companies, pension funds and FinTech companies with tangible interests or activities within the Longevity financial sphere, seeking to leverage the rising tide of Longevity, the convergence of increasing healthspans and wealthspans, and the 1 trillion opportunity of 1 billion people in retirement.

Regions and Territories (~200): National governments trying to increase their National Healthy Longevity, reduce the gap between Health-Adjusted Life Expectancy and unadjusted Life Expectancy, and facilitate Longevity industrialization.

Dashboard N2 - B2C Longevity Marketplace: Main Features

The B2C Longevity Marketplace Dashboard will serve as a virtual online store where clients will use their Longevity Card to purchase products and services across the full scope of Longevity; for example, a list of companies that provide medical check-up services.

These products will be both searchable based on keywords, filters and market segments, as well as automatically suggested in the form of recommendations, and clients will have, via machine-learning enabled automated data, analysis of their current needs, goals, age, gender and geography.

For example, a user specifies a **goal** or **unmet need** (e.g. losing weight), and receives notifications recommending local providers of supplements that increase breakdown of fat, healthy restaurants near his location, well-reviewed personal trainers, and progressive gyms that provide intensive fitness courses.

Dashboard N2: Major Use Cases

Longevity Cardholders and Longevity Bank Clients:

- Access to a highly diverse marketplace of products and services across the entire scope of Longevity, Wellness and Healthy Living (all the way from healthspan to wealthspan)
- Discounts on Marketplace purchases obtainable through Longevity

Reward Points that are generated every time they use their Longevity Card

- Targeted real-time recommendations on local and global products and services best-suited to help to achieve and surpass their current Longevity goals

Longevity Vendors:

- Suppliers of Longevity, health and wellness-focused products and services will be able to obtain access to a much larger, and extremely relevant (i.e., highly focused) client base by joining the platform
- Capacity to significantly expand their market and target demographic in exchange for giving up a small portion of their profits (access fee for being a vendor on the platform), AKA the "GroupOn" business model
- Heightened marketing and public visibility, and access to Longevity Bank's sophisticated Marketing Engine
- Potential visibility to investors via the Investment Analytics Dashboard

Major Corporate Vendors

- Some large corporate vendors, such as major pension funds and insurance companies interested in Longevity, can benefit from gaining access to a highly targeted and qualified set of individuals looking to maintain very healthy lifestyles, with a large unmet desire for progressive financial institutions willing to financially underwrite their efforts to maximize their Healthy Longevity

Dashboard N3 - B2B Longevity Marketplace: Main Features

B2B is the Second-level Marketplace Dashboard available only for Longevity Bank Institutional and Corporate Clients, and B2C marketplace vendors. Corporate clients and vendors will benefit by using the Longevity marketplace to distribute their services, and to obtain services from other relevant clients and vendors at discounted, premium prices.

What such companies will sacrifice in terms of % of profits from marketplace sales going to Longevity Bank and exclusive client discounts, they will make up for by gaining an expanded user base for their products and services.

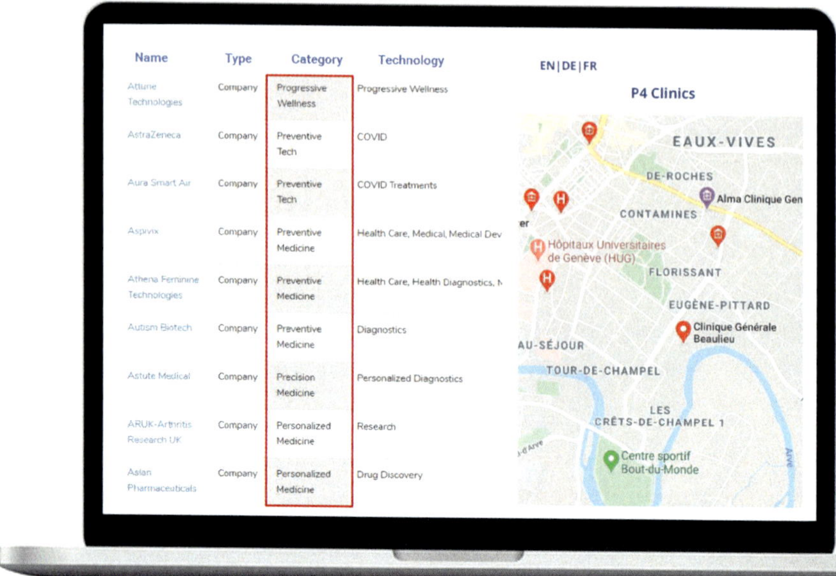

The B2B dashboard will incorporate smart matching by geography and product category, in order to connect relevant clients with relevant vendors. For example, it makes sense to match a local Geneva-based fitness club only to Geneva-based citizens or Longevity Bank clients that are currently visiting the region.

Thus, smart-matching should occur by grouping different vendors and clients based on geography, geographic scope of their product and service, and their specific product/service needs.

Dashboard N3: Major Use Cases

Corporate Longevity Cardholders and Clients:

- Access to a highly diverse marketplace of potential produce and service providers, enabling supply chain optimization
- Discounts on B2B marketplace purchases obtainable through Longevity Reward Points that are generated every time they use their Longevity Card

- Targeted real-time recommendations on local and global products and service providers
- Free-of-charge analytics on how supply chains can be optimized

Longevity Vendors:

- Suppliers of Longevity, health and wellness-focused products and services will be able to obtain access to a much larger, and extremely relevant (i.e. highly focused) client base by joining the platform
- Capacity to significantly expand their market and target demographic beyond retail users and towards corporate and institutional buyers
- Heightened marketing and public visibility
- Potential visibility to investors via the Investment Analytics Dashboard

Dashboard N4 - Investment Analytics: Main Features

The Investment Analytics Dashboard is targeted toward investment funds with an interest or focus on Longevity, providing clients access to quantitative, sophisticated and multidimensional analytics on many potential future portfolio companies and investment prospects.

1. **The platform will provide real-time analytics** and data feeds on potential investment candidates, providing insight into their development prospects over time and their future growth potential.
2. **Provides advanced, sophisticated and quantitative** Big Data analysis on Longevity companies and Longevity investment strategy.
3. **Will contain more in-depth data and analytics** on the companies featured in the B2C and B2B Dashboards.
4. **SWOT analysis tailored** to clients' geographical, development stage and sector-specific focus.
5. **Results of the analysis** will be used to provide tailored recommendation packs to hedge risk and maximize diversification.

Dashboard N4: Major Use Cases

Longevity Investors:

- Access to quantitative, sophisticated and multidimensional analytics on many potential future portfolio companies and investment prospects
- Real-time analytics on potential investment candidates, providing insight into their development prospects over time, their future and ongoing growth potential, visibility on which companies are growing the fastest, which are consistently making or losing money, etc.
- Targeted and intelligent smart-matching between investors and portfolio candidates based on specified sectors and qualifying criteria (e.g. highly-targeted ratios of rankings in specific areas)

Longevity Vendors:

- Heightened visibility to a professional community of Longevity-focused investors and investment funds
- Objective and quantifiable analytics and rankings, enabling companies to gain investor interest based on real, fact-based analysis of current prospects and future potential, rather than on MarkTech and superficial optics
- Targeted smart-matching based on specified criteria (e.g. the type of investors different companies are specifically looking for, such

as funds of a certain size, ones providing both monetary and in-kind [e.g. mentorship] opportunities, etc.)

Dashboard N4: Main Concepts/Interface

The fourth Investment Analytics Dashboard will be for internal use only, and will be leased by Longevity Bank to its strategic partner Longevity.Capital.

Investment Analytics Dashboard

Will contain more in-depth data and analytics on the companies featured in the B2C and B2B Dashboards, suitable for investment analytics, due diligence and forecasting.

Will be utilized to inform and instruct future investment strategy and decision making of Longevity.Capital, and allow it to structure investment decision making.

Multidimensional and Quantitative Longevity Industry Analytical Frameworks

Technically, the back end of this dashboard should automatically (in real time) collect additional forms of company data, including: **description, products, board members and employees, patents, grants, publications, clinical trials, brand scalability, financing and revenue.**

The dashboard's analytics will be driven by the sophisticated Longevity Industry intelligence of Aging Analytics Agency, which developed their 3-D Longevity Industry Analytical Frameworks in order to meet the demands presented by the overwhelming and unprecedented complexities of the sector, in order to obtain a tangible and pragmatic understanding of the industry in order to structure investment strategy in a relevant way.

Dashboard N4: Main Types of Users

The main types of users for the Investment Analytics Dashboard component of the platform and marketplace will consist of investors that are seeking to:

- gaining exposure to the global Longevity Industry, both generally and in specific relation to one of its different subsectors,
- obtaining quantitative investment analytics on a number of prospective investment targets within the Longevity Industry, and
- obtaining access to the dashboard's smart-matching platform, allowing them to connect and curate dealflow directly with relevant companies (similar to Pitchbook).

Institutional VC	Family Offices	Investment Banks
Corporate Investment Divisions	HNWI Angel Investors	Angel Groups
Accelerators	Incubators	Sovereign Wealth Funds
Industrial Strategy Funds	Government Investment Funds	Financial Corporations

Dashboard N5 - Longevity Finance: Main Features

The Longevity Finance Dashboard will be released as a sophisticated, technological data visualization that will be in the form of dynamic infographics and 3D mindmaps. Aging Analytics Agency (that provides a database for the Dashboard) will produce a comprehensive analytical overview of the emerging Longevity Financial Industry.

The platform will feature a number of specific components that together encompass the entire scope of the Longevity finance sector, providing: market intelligence on the Longevity-related activities of hundreds of major financial institutions, SWOT analysis and competitive landscaping, quantitative ranking and benchmarking (both positive and negative) of financial corporations, forecasting, B2B marketplace of relevant Longevity products and services, and Big Data, Machine Learning and AI Analytics capabilities.

Dashboard N5: Major Use Cases

Financial Institutions (retail banks, investment banks, insurance and FinTech)

- The dashboard consists of a licensed white-label solution offered to a variety of external financial corporations (major retail banks, investment banks, insurance companies, FinTech companies, etc.) looking to transform their business model toward Longevity-focused banking and Health as New Wealth, in order to capture the massive untapped multi-trillion market of 1 billion people in retirement globally.

- The dashboard provides out-licensed access to Longevity Bank's B2C and B2B dashboards, where external financial institutions first sign a non-competition agreement obliging them to focus on markets and regions that are not within the scope of Longevity Bank's target market, and pay a premium in exchange for access to Longevity Bank's ecosystem and marketplace of Longevity products and services.
- The dashboard enables financial institutions interested in Longevity to select and filter Longevity products and services available within their region, in order to aggregate a set of vendors capable of providing their own clients with relevant products and services designed to maximize Healthy Longevity across the full scope of the global Longevity ecosystem (from healthspans to wealthspans).
- Clients will also gain access to advanced analytics showing relevant benchmarking parameters for available vendors within each specific product and service category, enabling them to conduct cost-benefit analyses and determine which vendors are best suited to meet the needs of their clients within their specific target demographic and regional market.
- The dashboard will also provide continuous monitoring and market intelligence of the specific Longevity-focused activities, products and services developed and deployed by 500 financial corporations globally, to continually track, analyze and rank best practices within the Global Longevity Financial Industry.

Dashboard N5: White Label Solution for Longevity Financial Industry Analytics

End-to-end solution of proprietary analytics and practical recommendations on the Longevity Financial Industry

Large financial institutions lack the deep industry expertise required to transform their business models in a relevant Longevity-focused manner and to develop new Longevity financial products and services in a relevant manner

Aging Analytics Agency (major provider of analytics for Longevity Bank) has been producing advanced Longevity Industry analytics for 5+ years, and produced the first ever analytical report on the Longevity Financial Industry

The agency is in an unparalleled position to offer the SWOT analysis, customized practical recommendations, benchmarking, forecasting and guidance needed to transform financial institutions for the Longevity future

Major topics include: Integrated AgeTech & WealthTech Solutions for Clients 80-100+, Longevity FinTech 2.0, AI for Financial Wellness, Longevity De-Risking, How to Develop Novel Longevity-Focused Financial Products

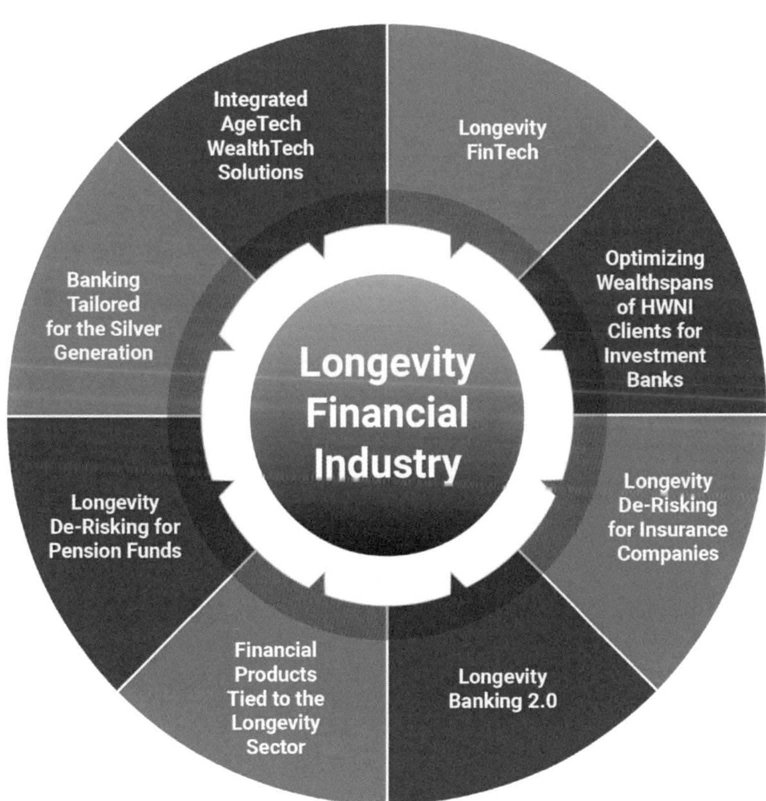

Dashboard N5: Major Features & Components

Deep Knowledge Group's Longevity Finance Dashboard combines the sophisticated technological, data visualization and software solution resources of Deep Knowledge Group's IT department with the quantitative multidimensional industry analytics of Aging Analytics Agency (the first entity to produce a comprehensive analytical overview of the emerging Longevity Financial Industry) in order to provide progressive financial institutions interested in capturing the massive rising tide of Longevity Finance with the necessary set of tools required to structure, optimize and execute their business models, products, services and strategic decision making in a way that is relevant for the extreme complexity and multidimensionality of Longevity. The dashboard features a number of specific components that together encompass the entire scope of the Longevity Finance sector, providing: **market intelligence** on the Longevity-related activities of hundreds of major financial institutions (investment banks, pension funds, insurance companies, retail banks), **SWOT analysis** and **competitive landscaping**, quantitative **ranking** and **benchmarking** (both positive and negative) of financial corporations, **forecasting, B2B marketplace** of relevant Longevity products and services, and **Big Data, Machine Learning and AI Analytics** capabilities.

Dashboard N6 - Longevity Governance: Main Features

The Longevity Governance Dashboard applies Big Data analysis to identify social policy, healthcare, medical, financial and socioeconomic factors having the greatest effect on the gap between life expectancy at birth and Health-Adjusted Life Expectancy (HALE) for 100 regions.

The dashboard focuses on identifying the factors and practices behind certain regions' success in maintaining high National Health Longevity, and a low gap between Health-Adjusted Life Expectancy (HALE) and unadjusted Life Expectancy. It utilizes the results of its region-specific analysis to offer tangible and practical recommendations tuned to the specifics of individual territories, providing the necessary set of tools to enable national governments, individual economy, healthcare and industrial development industries, international policy organizations and other responsible stakeholders to formulate and implement policies and development strategies capable of transforming the challenge of aging into the opportunity of Healthy Longevity for the mutual benefit of their citizens and their economy.

Dashboard N6: Major Use Cases

Government Agencies, Healthcare, Economy & Industrial Development Ministries, & International Policy Organizations

- The Longevity Governance Dashboard delivers access to continuous monitoring of the specific governmental policy activities directly impacting both National Healthy Longevity and Longevity Industrialization, and to consistently track and analyze data points related to government-led Longevity Development initiatives.
- Applies **Big Data analysis** to identify social policy, healthcare, medical, financial and socioeconomic **factors** with the greatest effect on the **Gap** between life expectancy and **Health-Adjusted Life Expectancy (HALE)** for 100 regions.
- Identifies factors and practices behind certain regions' success in maintaining a high degree of **National Healthy Longevity** and a low gap between HALE and Life Expectancy.
- Provides **tangible** and **practical recommendations** tuned to the specifics of individual countries, providing the necessary set of tools to allow countries currently leading the international Healthy Longevity race to **maintain** and **improve** their current standing.
- Features region-specific recommendation packs to enable governments currently lagging behind others to reduce their HALE gap and improve their comparative global standing, transforming the deficit and challenge of the silver tsunami into the **asset** and **opportunity** of Healthy Longevity for the mutual benefit of their citizens and their economy.

Longevity Governance	
Recommendation Packs	Industrial Strategies
Precision Health	Advanced IT-Solutions
Analytics & Benchmarking	Modernization

Dashboard N6: Practical Recommendation Packs

The Longevity Governance Dashboard applies Big Data analysis to identify social policy, healthcare, medical, financial and socioeconomic factors having the greatest effect on the gap between life expectancy at birth and Health-Adjusted Life Expectancy (HALE) for 100 regions.

Many governments are putting policies on Longevity at the centre of their growth strategies and budget planning, while others lag behind. Identifying the factors and practices behind certain regions' success is critical to enabling national governments and interactional policy organizations to formulate and implement policies and development strategies capable of transforming the challenge of aging population into the opportunity of Longevity.

The dashboard utilizes the results of its analysis to offer **tangible and practical recommendations** tuned to the **specifics** of individual countries and territories, providing the necessary set of tools to allow regions currently leading the international Healthy Longevity race to maintain and improve their current standing, and to allow countries currently lagging behind others to improve their comparative global standing, enabling inflection points within the opposed megatrends of Aging Population and Advanced Biomedicine to be leveraged to enable economic growth and increases in quality of life.

Key Topics for Analysis and Practical Recommendations

- What specific features of healthcare systems, socio-economic conditions, environmental factors affect public health the most?
- How does the impact of such factors differ across regions?
- What constellation of factors contributes the most to Healthy Longevity?
- Which factors are the main drivers of health-adjusted life expectancy and disability-adjusted life years?
- What regions are leaders in Longevity governance?
- Why do disproportionate healthcare expenditures in the United States contribute to poor healthcare system performance and a decline in overall life expectancy in recent years?

- Why is the healthcare system in Singapore considered as one of the most efficient in the world?
- What can be done to improve National Healthy Longevity in each territory globally?

Dashboard N6: Big Data Analytics Framework

Data Collection

- 100 regions
- 200 parameters per region
- 20,000 parameters in total

Data Cleaning

Aggregation of data by 5 dimensions

- Economic conditions
- Demography
- Health care and Longevity
- Environment
- Social factors

Model Creation

- Factor analysis of LE-HALE gap determinants (multiple regression)
- Analysis of variance of major Longevity parameters across groups of countries (ANOVA)
- Defining leading countries in Longevity governance (ranking)
- Estimation of relationships between metrics (intraclass correlation)
- Assessment of effectiveness of health care systems

Model Validation

- Hypothesis testing
- Sensitivity analysis

Development of Recommendations

- Incorporation of research results in practical region-specific and department-specific recommendations

Chapter 7: Longevity.Capital: Specialized Hybrid Investment Fund for Longevity Industry De-Risking and Diversification

"Longevity-oriented start-ups, if successful, could bolster continuing increases in funding in the Longevity Industry and facilitate its ongoing growth. However, early failures due to over-funding and over-valuation of over-hyped technologies and therapeutic approaches could turn the Longevity Industry into little more than a Longevity bubble. As the dawn of the Longevity Industry is confidently visible on the horizon, it is these challenges and risks that should be analyzed and mitigated while the real opportunities are fostered and nurtured, so as to create a landscape of realistic opportunity rather than one of unrealistic promise and potential."

Dmitry Kaminskiy in *Global Trends - The Rising Longevity Industry* (November 2016)

Key Points:

- The complexities of the Longevity Industry not only require the development of a new generation of analytics for relevant and realistic industry benchmarking and forecasting, but also a new approach to intelligent, stable and de-risked Longevity Industry investing.
- Deep Knowledge Group has spent 5+ years nourishing and developing what can be considered an advanced Longevity Industry Brain via the activities of its Longevity-focused subsidiary Aging Analytics Agency, in order to develop sophisticated analytical frameworks capable of delivering a deeper understanding of Longevity Industry dynamics and enabling relevant, tangible and actionable strategic decision-making.
- Longevity.Capital utilizes novel InvestTech solutions to provide liquidity similar to hedge funds with Venture Capital-style objectives, bridging the gap between the Longevity start-up communi-

ty on one hand and the conservative investment community on the other hand.

- In 2019, the Deep Knowledge Group launched its Longevity-focused hybrid investment subsidiary fund, Longevity.Capital, to serve as the body, muscle and actuator to put the intelligence of that "Longevity Cortex" (a very broad and deep Longevity informational ecosystem) into practice, executing a modern and relevant investment strategy that gives investors enhanced access to the full scope of the Longevity Industry, while providing growing Longevity companies with the levels of funding they need in order to prosper and translate their products and services into practice.
- Leveraging the extreme cross-sector multidimensionality, intersectionality and complexity of the Longevity Industry for its advantage rather than its detriment, Longevity.Capital provides portfolio diversification across the full scope of this industry, encompassing 10 sectors spread across the domains of BioTech, Technology and Finance, transforming the enormous cross-sector scope of the Longevity Industry into a source of diversification and de-risking.

Similar to how a revolution was needed in the area of Longevity Industry analytics in order to create relevant and realistic methods of benchmarking and forecasting in the face of the sector's unprecedented levels of complexity at the intersection of the most advanced fields of frontier science and technology, a revolution is also needed regarding how those analytics are applied in practice to the challenge of formulating a modern, intelligent and capable framework for investment strategy, investment target identification, and portfolio de-risking and diversification.

Deep Knowledge Group has spent years of hard work and effort in order to understand the global Longevity Industry, with the ultimate aim of delivering industry analytics capable of equipping industry players and participants with the tools, solutions and knowledge necessary to make intelligent decisions within the scope of its dynamic trajectory of development.

Just as the Longevity Industry presents outstanding and unprecedented opportunities for ethical profit and the enrichment of society, both at the level of the citizen and the economy, it also presents equally extreme challenges and areas for risk and failure.

In order to ensure an optimal future trajectory of growth for the Longevity Industry, the main drivers of progress (Longevity entrepreneurs and investors) need to act with care, foresight, and deep intelligence, to ensure that the practical benefits of Longevity (an increase in societal health and wealth) are delivered as quickly as possible, in a manner as distributed as possible, and in a way that does not jeopardize the future credibility and stability of the industry.

Thus, in 2019, Deep Knowledge Group decided to take the Longevity Cortex that it had been developing over the past five years (Aging Analytics Agency), and to connect it to an equally sophisticated and data-driven body, muscle and actuator: Longevity.Capital, a Longevity-focused hybrid investment fund backed by the deep market intelligence of Aging Analytics Agency, employing novel InvestTech solutions to de-risk, diversify, stabilize and optimize Longevity Industry investment.

Portfolio De-Risking and Diversification by Betting on the Entire Longevity Industry

Longevity Capital Fund is a Novel InvestTech Solution:
Specialised Investment Fund focused on the Longevity Industry

While interest in the Longevity sector from conservative investors continues to mount, a large, unbridged gap exists between the financial needs of Longevity companies and the unwillingness of investors to lock their money into sectors that, while extremely promising, lack liquidity and are still the sole vanguard of VC funds.

> ***Many conservative investors and UHNWIs are personally interested in Longevity, both as a prospective market with the capacity for unprecedented growth, and also due to their interest in their own personal life extension.***

The past few years have seen an unprecedented rise in interest on the part of large financial corporations (including investment banks, pension funds and insurance companies) in the topic of Longevity, demonstrating the obvious interest from even the most conservative sectors of the global financial industry.

Such parties now very clearly understand that the Longevity sector is one of the most prospective and relevant sectors to invest in, with full confidence that such investments will lead to relatively low-risk and stable profitability in the long term. Therefore, financial innovations that can provide liquidity to Longevity companies and technologies, and form a bridge between the Longevity Industry and conservative financial markets, are the tools required to neutralize this big gap.

Problems with Traditional Funds: Low Liquidity and High Entry Fees

The exponential progress in the Longevity sector is readily apparent. What was considered fringe science by analysts and investors a mere five years ago is now an exponentially growing sector with hundreds of active companies financed by an even larger number of investment firms.

Interest in the topic from both the public and investors continues to mount at an incredible pace; yet, the barrier for entering, facing potential investors, remains high, thus preventing the access for most traditional investors. The vast majority of Longevity companies are start-ups, and venture capital (VC) firms remain the sole vanguard of start-up financing. This makes it impossible for investors not willing to lock up large amounts of capital for a long term to participate in this growing industry.

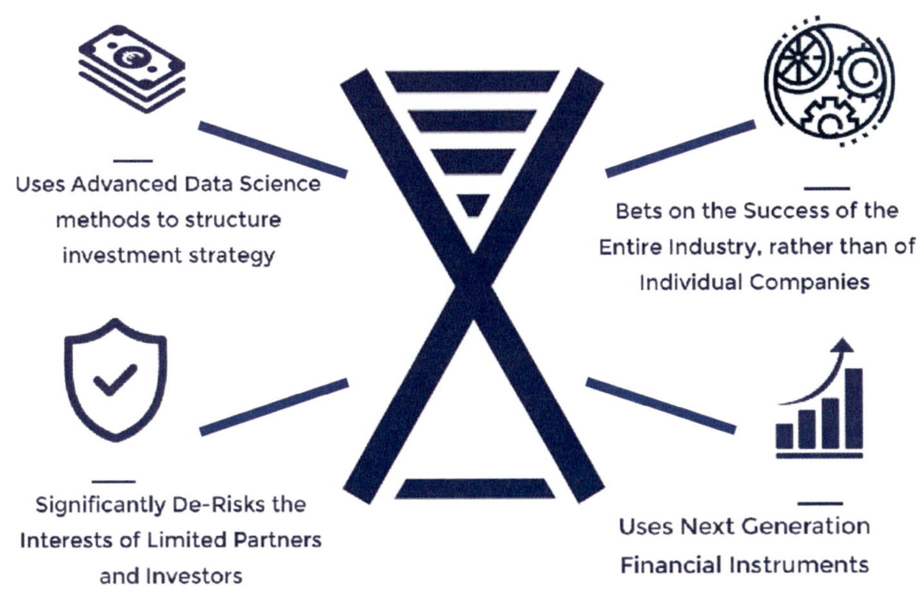

Modern Relevant Investment Strategy for the Mega-Complex Longevity Industry

- Longevity.Capital is a hybrid investment fund specifically focused on the Longevity Industry, backed by seasoned professionals who have been active in both the investment banking and the Longevity industries for 25+ years, long before the sector was recognized as a serious prospect by the overwhelming majority of investors. The fund structures its portfolio based on sophisticated industry intelligence and comparative analytics provided by the world-leading Longevity analytics entity Aging Analytics Agency, which uses hundreds of quantitative and fact-based parameters to identify prospective investment targets for the fund, utilizing multidimensional analytical frameworks as complex as the industry itself.

- Longevity.Capital delivers capital appreciation through investment in a carefully selected portfolio of companies in the Longevity sector, using the best Longevity Industry analytics available. Its management team includes Dmitry Kaminskiy, one of the authors of this book and a well known DeepTech investor who made his first investments in the Longevity Industry in 2014.

The life sciences and biotechnology industries carry certain inherent risks due to the complexity of the field, the high standards required for scientific validation, low clinical trial success rate and the necessarily long duration of development required to bring any drug through regulatory testing and ultimately to market. These complexities are multiplied by the even greater degree of scientific, technological and regulatory complexity surrounding the Longevity and Preventive Medicine industries.

In order to face and neutralize these challenges, **Longevity.Capital will employ several novel and sophisticated tools, techniques and approaches** to portfolio diversification and de-risking of investments in order to combat the extremely high levels of complexity of the Longevity Industry, and to significantly decrease the scope and levels of risk associated with investments in the industry, based on the unique, quantitative analytical frameworks developed by Aging Analytics Agency for Longevity and Preventive Medicine industry assessment, benchmarking and forecasting.

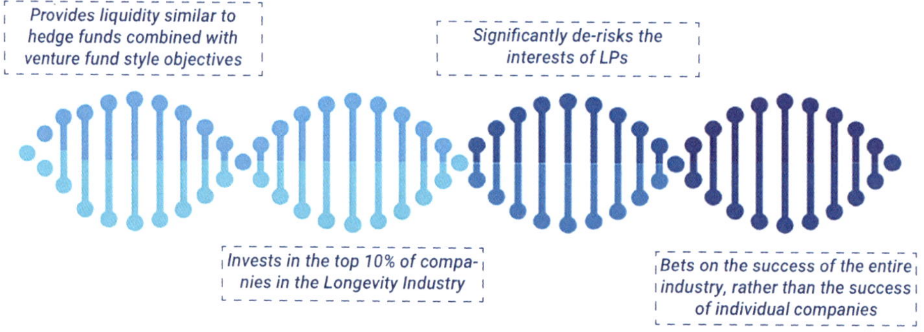

Leveraging the Deep Market Intelligence of Aging Analytics Agency

Aging Analytics Agency serves as the main source of expertise behind Longevity.Capital, providing sophisticated Longevity Industry analytics in order to develop and de-risk the fund's sophisticated investment strategy. Established in 2013, Aging Analytics Agency has the longest track record of any Longevity Industry analytics globally; it was the first to produce Global Longevity Industry Landscape Overviews (over 1000 pages in length), and successfully predicted the sharp rise in Longevity Industry investments in 2017-2018 three years in advance.

Aging Analytics Agency currently serves as a major source of expertise and analytics for the UK All-Party Parliamentary Group on Longevity, and is serving as one of the contributors to the development of the upcoming blueprint of a UK National Development Strategy for Healthy Longevity.

> The agency was the first company to apply rigorous and tangible methodologies for assessing the market-readiness of products in the life sciences and BioTech space (such as Technology-Readiness Levels, or TRLs), and to establish a validated approach for assessing timelines for clinical translation of Longevity and Preventive Medicine therapies, comparing prospective investment targets using multiple parameters to differentiate levels of maturity and scientific and technical advantages in an objective manner.

For early-stage start-ups, it applies assessment based on several dozen parameters, whereas for the more advanced leading companies more than 100 factors are considered.

The higher degree of complexity of the Longevity Industry requires novel, more sophisticated approaches to be aligned with the increased complexity of the industry landscape, in order to be capable of deploying relevant industry intelligence and analytics to develop and guide modern and applicable investment strategies for the Longevity sector. Aging Analytics Agency is uniquely positioned to provide unparalleled Longevity Industry market intelligence aggregated and refined through its 5+ years history as the only analytical firm exclusively dedicated to Longevity Industry analytics, benchmarking and forecasting.

At the request of Longevity.Capital, Aging Analytics Agency has developed a sophisticated multidimensional analytical framework to benchmark the full scope of companies within the global Longevity Industry via advanced comparative and competitive analyses in order to identify the top-40 most promising Longevity companies distributed across 10 distinct market sectors, revealing the untapped bottom of the Longevity Industry iceberg.

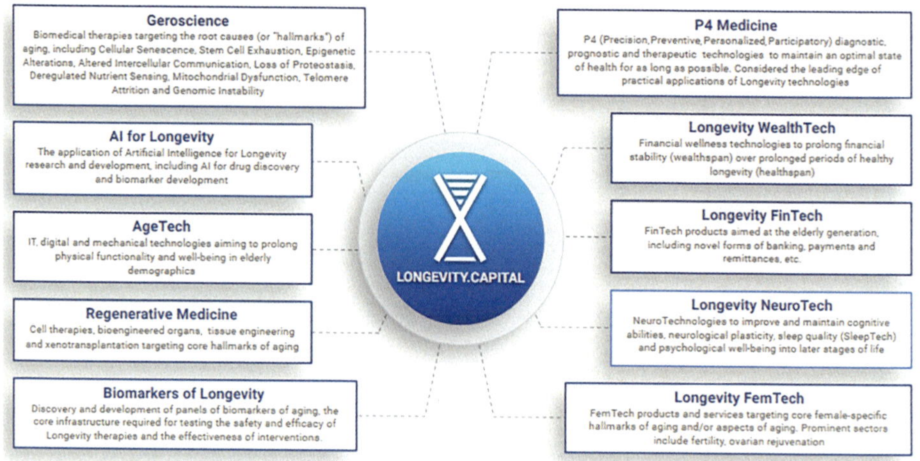

Portfolio De-Risking and Diversification by Betting on the Entire Longevity Industry

This benchmarking is first applied to the full scope of Longevity companies globally, comparing hundreds of active players in the space side by side, which are then segregated into progressive levels of advancement and potential.

The only way to identify the most promising players in an industry distinguished by extreme levels of complexity and multidimensionality is to use advanced comparative analytical frameworks of equal complexity.

This analytical methodology is the data-driven foundation upon which Longevity.Capital's 2020 target portfolio is structured, and also forms the basis for the structuring of the fund's general investment strategy, company valuation procedures, and due diligence processes.

Aging Analytics Agency has been continually developing sophisticated and quantitative analytical frameworks for Longevity Industry analysis, benchmarking, competitive landscaping and forecasting for over 5 years, enabling Longevity companies to be evaluated and analyzed in a validated and tangible manner for the first time.

> In contrast to traditional BioTech, the Longevity Industry is an extremely advanced domain of science and technology, and can be considered as the very cutting edge of advanced biomedicine.

This poses unique challenges to standard approaches for forecasting, investment target identification and due diligence. In an industry marked by extreme levels of complexity and multidimensionality, the old approaches which proved successful in BioTech break down and become ineffective. Being situated at the intersection of many frontier technologies and domains of science, Longevity Industry benchmarking and analysis need to be as complex and multidimensional as the sectors they are applied to in order to be relevant.

Conclusions:

- Since first developing quantitative analytical frameworks for Longevity Industry analysis in 2013, Aging Analytics Agency has continued to refine these comparative analysis systems, both in terms of the specific metrics used to conduct its market studies as well as the mathematical formulas used to combine them, and the advanced visualization techniques used to make its forecasts, rankings and determinations maximally concrete and understandable.
- Today, these analytical methodologies have evolved to incorporate 3-D frameworks where metrics and sub-metrics can be visualized simultaneously, as well as the development of advanced "timeline machines" to study the changing state of a company's strength in specific areas ranging from scientific validation to business development and R&D over time and projected into the future, based on the statistical properties of its past behaviour.
- The quantitative frameworks developed by Aging Analytics Agency form the basis for Longevity.Capital's investment target identification, portfolio structuring and optimization, and due diligence processes.
- Aging Analytics Agency was the first entity to take validated approaches for market-readiness forecasting developed in other ad-

vanced industries like aerospace and apply it in the life sciences and the Longevity Industry.

- Technology Readiness Levels (TRLs) use a ranking of 1 to 9, with 9 being the most mature technology. Specific levels are assigned to specific technologies by a group of relevant scientific experts.
- The use of TRLs provides a uniform metric, enabling consistent discussions of maturity across different types of technologies. In the coming years, TRLs can underpin efforts to shed light on the most important technologies and reveal those currently furthest away from practical applications.
- Therefore, TRLs enable the right timing and focus to ensure each emerging technology accomplishes its specific endpoints, and highlights the interactions that are possible between technologies.
- These new financial tools designed specifically for the Longevity Industry will enable the most reliable and fastest transition to a competent and powerful new ecosystem.
- This will be adequately placed to deliver the promises of AI, P4 Medicine, AgeTech, rejuvenation biotechnology and others, to the highest benefit of the largest number of patients.

PART II

Longevity Policy and Governance

Longevity Technocracies & MegaHubs

- **The Rise of Progressive Longevity MegaHubs and Technocracies**
- **Longevity as a Major National Priority Item of Progressive Governments' Strategic Agendas**
- **Longevity Progressive and Regressive Nations**
- **National Longevity Development Plans**
- **International Longevity Cooperation Initiatives**
- **The Current State of National Healthy Longevity (Health-Adjusted Life Expectancy)**
- **Longevity Policy and Governance as the Next Great Frontier of Longevity**
- **The Emergence of Longevity-Focused Parliamentary Groups and Government Bodies**
- **National Longevity Industrial Strategies and Healthy Longevity Development Plans**
- **How Longevity Will Determine the Outcome of National Elections by the Year 2025**

Chapter 8: The Rise of Longevity Technocracies and MegaHubs: Governance and Policy as the Next Great Longevity Frontier (Contributor: Eric Kihlstrom)

Multiple times in the course of modern history humanity has seen fit to create international networks, unions, leagues, blocs and alliances: the UN, the European Union, G8, G20, and so on. Most of the existing ones were created in the 20th century, the age of oil, wars, and geopolitical instability. In the 21st century, structures such as these are being used less for resolving and averting conflict and more for facilitating peaceful cooperation.

This repurposing of international institutions has been accompanied by a repurposing of technology. Nuclear technology is a clear example of this: what began as fuel for weapons and a source of global tension, is now a fuel for neighbourhoods and a potential source of clean energy.

Likewise, 21st century innovations which currently risk becoming objects of international tensions and rivalry – **such as advanced AI and advanced genetics for example** – could also be peacefully and productively deployed, provided that society finds a cause worthy enough to unite people of most creeds and nations behind its peaceful and productive deployment. ***That cause, I believe, is Healthy Longevity***.

After years in this line of work, it became obvious that the next stages would consist of the ever more rapid assembly of ever more sophisticated frameworks to proactively guide and inform the activities of industry and governmental participants.

Then, in early 2019, I joined the ranks of Aging Analytics Agency as its Strategic Director, and later as Partner of Deep Knowledge Group and, more recently, its Longevity-focused specialized hybrid investment fund, Longevity.Capital, and I quickly understood that there were dedicated teams actively working not just to foresee such frameworks, but to build and execute them in order to accelerate progress in delivering the asset of Healthy Longevity to the masses.

This is what the Longevity Industry and the world's nations need — proactive professionals with engineering mindsets dedicated to creating the necessary frameworks to understand how to transform the deficit of aging into the asset of Healthy Longevity.

What we did agree on was this: that a great many countries are currently wasting a great deal of money in trying to find solutions to their own demographic problems, while a small handful, usually but not always small technocratic countries with large aging populations, had become what we came to call **"Longevity-progressive"**, meaning they possessed the will, means and foresight to ***facilitate cooperation between diverse technological sectors in order to meet the challenges of aging at every stage in their emergence, from the genetics right through to the geriatrics***.

Those are the nations which, in our view, ought to be forming the international unions and leagues of the future, such as a Longevity League of Nations, a set of national strategies working together, each contributing in its own way — each pooling its scientific and financial resources with the rest, each developing its Preventive Medicine frameworks, AI and Data Science — in order to convert global Longevity into an asset, and in turn profit and benefit from it.

We are only a few steps away from this future, and the purpose of this section of the book is to describe those steps.

Governments have two roles in moving the Longevity Industry forward:

1. **National Initiatives** such as social care, financial reforms, and infrastructure for Precision Medicine ecosystems;
2. **Intergovernmental Initiatives** for marshaling key technologies, resources, and experts from nations around the world.

Longevity development strategies are necessary on a national scale in order to enact these reforms, and on an international scale to utilize the long term strengths of each individual state. Any government wishing to seize the Longevity Dividend must develop a national Longevity development strategy.

National Longevity Initiatives

Governments are responsible for driving forward the development of many facets of the Longevity Industry ranging from social care to financial reforms, and also for developing and supporting the missing technological synergies, such as the integration of Big Data and healthcare, that currently serve as roadblocks for further industry growth.

Given the central immediate role of P4 in advancing the industry, what is now needed is Big Data analytics to develop optimal panels of biomarkers of aging, and to determine which Preventive Medicine technologies are effective. In this regard, progress hereafter is less a biotechnology problem (which requires us to wait on breakthroughs), and more a data mining, analysis and management problem. This, in turn, makes it a government problem.

International Longevity Initiatives

It is necessary for leading Longevity-progressive nations to establish intergovernmental initiatives that would leverage key strengths of different nations in order to launch programs that yield synergistic, multiplicative effects, enabling the sharing of key technologies, resources and experts. The United Kingdom, the world's soft-superpower, may play a key role here.

The Future of Longevity Governance Lies in National Longevity Development Plans

Recently, we have witnessed an explosion of disconnected government initiatives around the world, each addressing the impending demographic crisis in its own way. However, all of them currently fall short of the necessary requirements of a national Longevity development plan. In other words, none are doing all they can to achieve the industrialization of Longevity.

Some government initiatives are more integrated than others, more synergistic, more long term, and more focused on bringing Healthy Longevity to the people on an industrial scale.

For practical purposes, these fall into three main categories:

- **Independent or municipal programs** — one plan per project or per city, e.g. urban planning solutions for accommodating the elderly.
- **National or metropolitan master plans**, such as plans which bring together multiple government departments and take place at levels of government.
- **Industrial strategies**, by which the entire industrial economy of a nation is reconfigured with a preconceived set of objectives in mind.

A national Longevity development plan would be a form of national industrial strategy which recognizes the aging demographic as a challenge and specifically seeks to reconfigure the industrial economy so as to facilitate cooperation between the four main sectors discussed in this book (advanced biomedicine, AgeTech, AI and the Longevity Financial Industry) with the goal of reversing the global aging demographic trend and transforming the challenge of aging into the opportunity of Healthy Longevity.

A Brief Survey of Government-Led Longevity Initiatives Around the World

Aging Analytics Agency's recent **Longevity Policy and Governance reports** coincide with an explosion of disconnected government initiatives around the world, each attempting to grapple with the demographic challenge in its own unique way.

In recent years we have been seeing increasingly frequent references to the "aging society" in official government strategic documents around the world. At every layer of government planning, ranging from *ad hoc* projects such as municipal plans to grand industrial strategies, the aging society is cited as a challenge to be overcome.

Lifestyle and Fitness Programs such as:

- Japan's plans for an Ageless Society
- Singapore's smart-homes, residential master plans
- The Seoul Metropolitan Government's 2020 Master Plan for the Aged Society
- Preventive medicine initiatives such as the UK's genomic medicine service
- The Swiss Personalised Health Network initiative

Intervening in the biology of aging itself such as:

- The Netherlands' Deltaplan for Dementia
- Switzerland's Masterplan for the Promotion of Biomedical Research
- BIRAX Aging, the joint UK-Israeli Geroscience research initiative

We have even seen financial innovations such as the **Swiss city of St. Gallen's elderly bank**. However, while these efforts are all steps in the right direction, no true national level Longevity development strategy currently exists anywhere in the world. We do, however, see the beginnings of one in the UK's existing initiatives, which lay a good foundation for the development of such a plan.

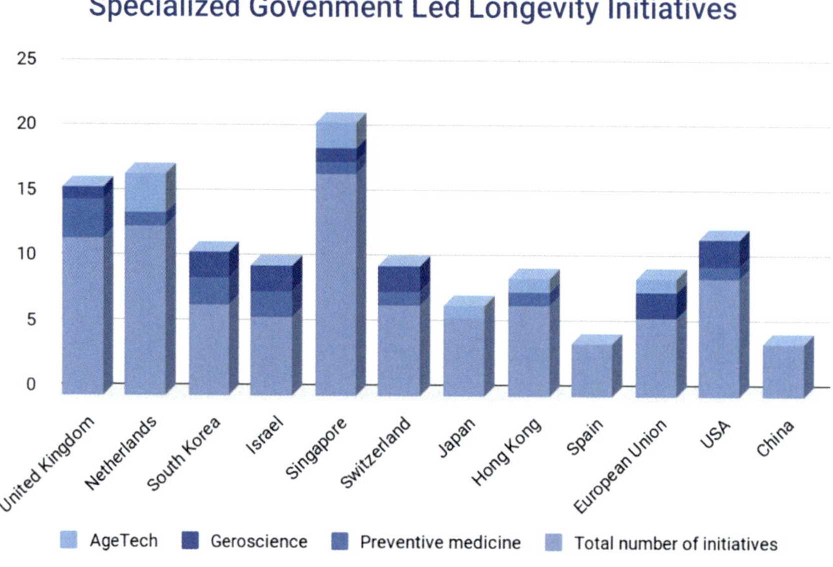

Represented here are the total number of relevant initiatives in the UK, the Netherlands, South Korea, Israel, Singapore, Switzerland, Japan, Hong Kong, Spain, the European Union, the USA and China.

Different governments have been offering a myriad of *ad hoc* solutions for adapting to the demographic crisis: Lifestyle and Fitness Programs such as **Japan's plans for an Ageless Society**, whereby people aged 65 or older will not be automatically regarded as seniors but will be encouraged to stay healthy and work, remaining economically active.

AgeTech programs, such as the **Singapore Government's initiatives** focused on smart-homes to improve the quality of life and well-being of the elderly, and increase their digital literacy. Residential master plans, such as the Seoul metropolitan government's **2020 Master Plan for the Aged Society** embracing the vision of Seoul as "a city whose citizens enjoy healthy and active lives of up to 100 years" under the banner of an "age-friendly city".

Age-Friendly Cities and Communities

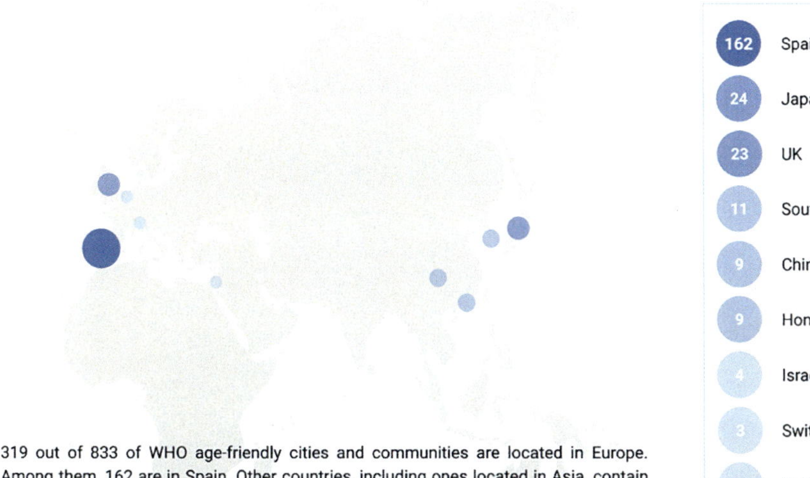

319 out of 833 of WHO age-friendly cities and communities are located in Europe. Among them, 162 are in Spain. Other countries, including ones located in Asia, contain significantly less number of WHO age-friendly cities/communities.

A number of these cities, such as Seoul in South Korea or Akita in Japan, are the products of detailed government master plans. Such master plans are recorded as instances of government initiatives in this document.

Source: WHO Global Network

Above it is shown an infographic from Aging Analytics Agency's National Longevity Development Plans report, with the global distribution of cities currently signed up to the WHO "age-friendly cities" guidelines. Although WHO sets an ambitious standard, at present many of these neighbourhoods amount to little more than especially effective retirement communities. Aging Analytics Agency offers its own advice on the development of truly smart age-friendly cities, integrating all facets of the Longevity Industry documented in its reports.

We have seen initiatives for Preventive Medicine approaches to aging, such as the **UK's genomic medicine service** and the **Swiss Personalised Health Network**.

We also have seen initiatives for intervening even further upstream, in the biology of aging itself, with Geroscience initiatives such as the **Netherlands' Deltaplan for Dementia,** the **Switzerland's Masterplan for the Promotion of Biomedical Research**, and **BIRAX Aging,** the **joint UK-Israeli Geroscience research initiative**.

Besides that, we have even seen financial innovations such as the **Swiss City of St. Gallen's elderly bank**, where retired volunteers "deposit" hours worked looking after elderly people (and in return can use any time saved up for their own care provision later in life).

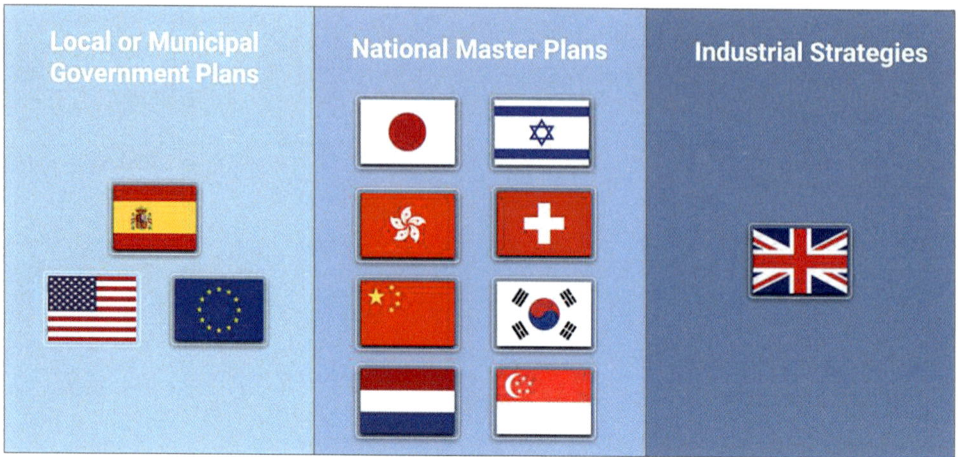

Above it is shown an overview of relevant Longevity projects and initiatives in 12 different regions globally, classified into National Master Plans, Industrial Strategies, and Municipal Government Programs.

Initiatives such as these, however, remain uncoordinated across the globe, and without solid national and international development strategies in place, they will remain as such, with low potentials for practical results in increasing the national Healthy Longevity or decreasing the gap between life expectancy and HALE. The Agency is engaged in dialogue with a number of government associated organizations around the world on the benefits of national and international development plans for Longevity.

When Healthy Longevity itself becomes a short-term issue with near-term consequences, it will become an electoral talking point.

Governments that promise it could appeal to their citizenries' desire for healthier and happier lives, and before long this will be in the interests of other governments who wish to be reelected to use the current progress in Longevity as rapidly as possible for the benefit of all.

Country Ranking by Size of Gap Between Healthy Longevity and Life Expectancy

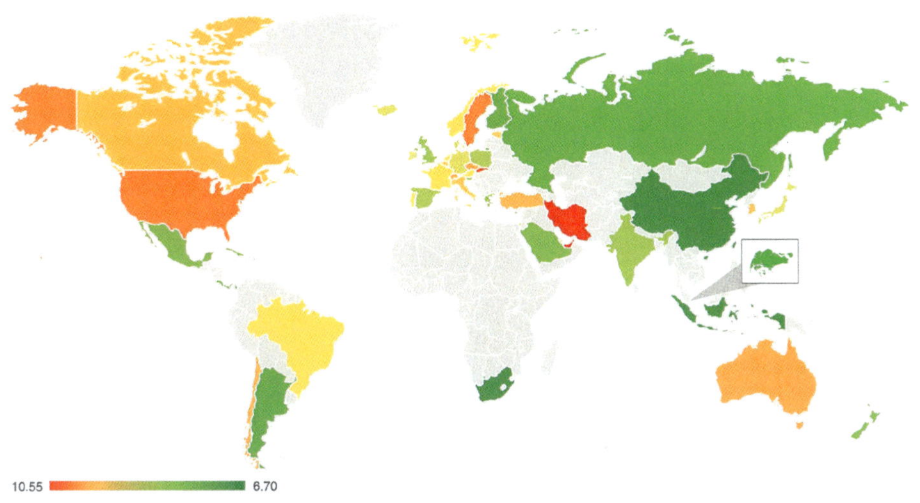

Health-Adjusted Life Expectancy (HALE), used here as a measure of Healthy Longevity, is the average number of years an individual can expect to live free of chronic age-related disease.

Life expectancy (LE) at birth reflects the overall mortality level of a population. It summarizes the mortality pattern that prevails across all age groups in a given year – children and adolescents, adults and the elderly.

HALE (Health-Adjusted Life Expectancy) is a measure of population health that takes into account mortality and morbidity. It adjusts overall life expectancy by the amount of time lived in less than perfect health, and is already viewed by policy makers as a key metric internationally.

In addition to the aforementioned technological and political facets of the industry, the financial industry will also need monitoring, development and optimization.

> With the use of a business model reform (and the development of novel financial instruments tied to Longevity) based on **Aging Analytics Agency's** quantitative analytics, financial institutions such as investment banks, pension funds and insurance companies can either sink or swim when hit by the oncoming Silver Tsunami.

A range of novel specialized financial institutions could ride this rising tide: **AgeTech Banks, Longevity index fund and hedge funds, and even a Longevity stock exchange for Longevity start-ups, that will issue specialized derivatives.**

It is by such means that increased ***global Longevity will be transformed from a threat into an opportunity***, and conservative investors of the future will be able to provide unlimited liquidity to the Longevity Industry, thereby establishing a self-perpetuating cycle capable of transforming aging as a source of economic loss and stagnation into Healthy Longevity as a source of economic growth and stability.

These and other aspects of the rising Longevity Financial Industry will be explained in greater detail in Part III of this book.

Longevity Policy and Governance as a New Analytical Priority of Aging Analytics Agency

In 2019, following the appointment of myself as its Strategic Director, Aging Analytics Agency prioritized the development of open-access and proprietary analytics on the topic of Longevity Policy and Governance in general, and on government-led National Longevity Development Plans in particular.

> These reports place a specific emphasis on identifying the specific social policy, healthcare, financial reforms, and socioeconomic factors that are most likely to enable governments to develop integrated Longevity Industries and ecosystems to scale, and to help them reduce their national gap between life expectancy and Health-Adjusted Life Expectancy (HALE).

Our first dedicated Longevity Governance report, National Longevity Development Plans: Global Overview 2019, was presented at the inaugural APPG (All-Party Parliamentary Group) for Longevity Advisory Board Meeting, and distributed at the APPG's official launch event.

Aging Analytics Agency's prioritization of Longevity policy and politics analytics coincides with an explosion of disconnected government initiatives around the world, each attempting to address the demographic challenges of the aging population in its own unique way, each of which is documented in the report.

The Agency's strategy is to harness the rise of Longevity-focused political initiatives to maximum synergetic effect.

The initiatives documented in the report are currently uncoordinated across the globe. The Agency recommends the coordinated creation of national and international Longevity development plans to those nations ranking highest in terms of the strength, relevance and proactivity of their current Longevity initiatives.

Governments that make Healthy Longevity a core electoral talking point with near-term results will have an advantage over those that don't.

Healthy Longevity Heat Map

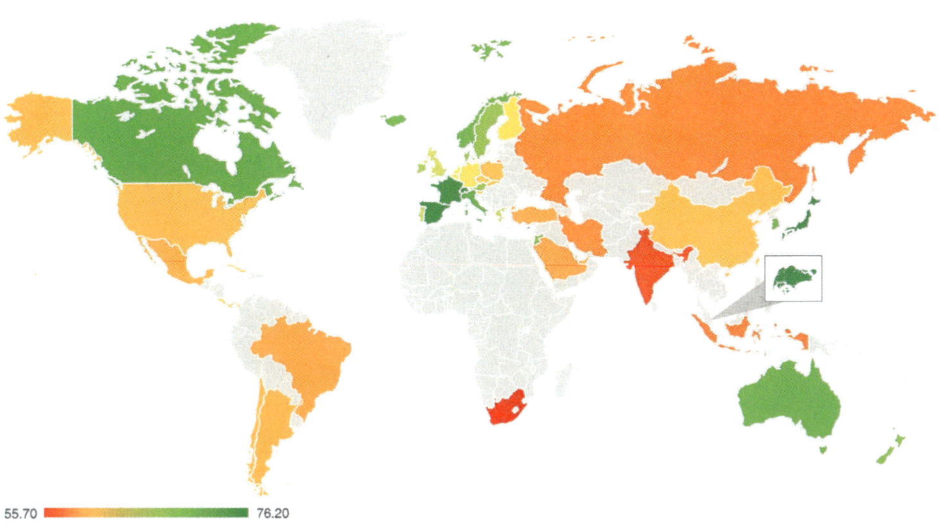

The Rise of Longevity-Progressive Governments

Nations most likely to initiate Longevity reforms will be countries characterized as ***Longevity-progressive*** with strong scientific bases in biotechnology and likely to integrate AI into their economic, financial, and healthcare systems. Much of the responsibility for these initiatives lies with governments.

We consider the UK central to the emergence of the global Longevity Industry over the next decade owing to the UK government's 2017 industrial strategy prioritizing the Aging Society as a Grand Challenge, and their recently published green paper for a Preventive Medicine National Strategy, making the UK the first country to officially implement P4 Medicine into its national healthcare system.

Progress in Longevity is no longer simply a question of progress in Geroscience or advanced biomedicine. Progress is driven by the synergetic convergence of intersection of multiple distinct technological sectors and sub-sectors. The political conditions surrounding the Longevity sector are some of the most important factors on which its future depends. Concerted efforts to synergize government-led Longevity development plans and related efforts are very important and may very well determine the shape, rate and trajectory of the industry's development in the years to come.

All-Party Parliamentary Group for Longevity

Preventive Medicine
Innovations in Healthcare
Problem of Ageing Population
Financial Reform for Pension System

"Longevity UK" is the secretariat for APPG for Longevity

www.longevityinternational.org

On April 30th 2019, Dmitry Kaminskiy and Eric Kihlstrom convened with parliamentarians, policy directors and researchers at the UK Parliament, to participate in the inaugural meeting of the APPG for Longevity and to discuss key goals for the group's strategic agenda for the coming year.

The APPG for Longevity signals the United Kingdom's commitment **to prioritize Healthy Longevity as a key component of the country's national agenda.**

The APPG for Longevity:

 It is the first dedicated parliamentary group to make the maintenance and extension of Healthy Longevity, innovations in Preventive Medicine and healthcare, and financial reform for pension systems its mission.

 Its current objective echoes the UK government stated commitment to adding 5 extra years on the UK's national HALE by 2035.

The biomedical technologies and therapies necessary to meet this goal are already in place, and what is now needed is Big Data analytics to develop optimal panels of biomarkers of aging and to determine what Preventive Medicine technologies are effective. Progress hereafter is less of a biotechnology problem (which requires us to wait on BioTech breakthroughs), and more of a data mining, analysis and management problem. This, in turn, makes it a government problem to some extent, as only government-led initiatives would be capable of providing the necessary infrastructure for such a project on a national level.

The rate of progress in Precision Medicine, which plays a pivotal role in the future of HALE, relies on government coordination. It would therefore be counterproductive for the government to limit its ambitions for decreasing the gap between life expectancy and HALE. The UK Government has already published a green paper for a National Strategy for the integration of P4 Medicine into its healthcare system.

Aging Analytics Agency sees no excuse for UK strategists to base their goals for increasing National Healthy Longevity and Health-Adjusted Life Expectancy (HALE) on historical rates of progress in advanced biomedicine and BioTech, because in the shorter term the greatest gains in this arena will come from analyzing and applying existing Preventive Medicine tools and technologies to scale, making it not a BioTech problem but a data aggregation and analysis challenge.

Key Highlights and Conclusions of Aging Analytics Agency's "National Longevity Development Plans: Global Overview 2019"

An effective international Longevity development strategy requires playing to the long term strengths of each individual state. Aging Analytics Agency's activities involving analytics and recommendations pertaining to the national policy of Longevity are not limited to the UK.

The agency puts significant emphasis on analyzing how each individual state around the world can maximize its strengths and assemble its existing resources for optimal effect.

All of this requires realistic, comprehensive analysis of each of them, both at the outset and as the industry develops. The Agency has adjusted its analytical focus accordingly. As an adjunct to its efforts in the realm of Longevity governance, policy and politics, the agency has begun to direct significant resources to the production of sophisticated open-access and proprietary analytics on the topics of Longevity governance, policy and politics, and on government-led Longevity development plans.

Aging Analytics Agency's *National Longevity Development Plans: Global Overview 2019* was presented in the UK Parliament on April 30th, 2019 as part of the APPG for Longevity's Strategic Advisory Board Meeting, and distributed to the APPG's officers, members and advisors at its official Launch Event on May 7th. The report provides a detailed international overview of the projects, initiatives and efforts that different countries across the globe are making in order **to combat** the issues associated with the global demographic challenge of an aging population, **to promote** the extension and maintenance of their citizens' Healthy Longevity.

Pictured above is Health Secretary Matt Hancock who has recently had his position renewed by the incoming Prime Minister Boris Johnson standing alongside the cover of the analytical report. The cover of the report details how close various countries are to achieving **National Longevity Development Plans**. The flags represent the countries whose government initiatives have been assessed and documented in the report. Dmitry Kaminskiy presented the *National Longevity Development Plans: Global Overview 2019* to parliamentarians, policy directors and researchers at Room M, Portcullis House, Houses of Parliament at the Strategic Advisor Board meeting of the APPG for Longevity.

The report documents and assesses government initiatives in the hope of offering governments some idea of the building blocks available for the construction of what could become the world's first Longevity National Development Plan. It gives special mention to the UK and illustrates how far the UK is already ahead of the game in this regard, *and why it is, therefore, the potential cradle of the fourth industrial revolution.*

The special analytical case study identified the broad categories of a government initiatives to be considered:

- the different orders of magnitude, ranging from small municipal programs to national industrial strategies;
- the different areas of intervention, from the financial to the biomedical.

The report also analyzes and visualizes:

- a number of data relevant to each country's current challenges and opportunities relating to Healthy Longevity and Aging Population, ranging from healthcare expenditure and efficiency to gaps between their Health-Adjusted Life Expectancy (HALE) and standard life expectancy, projected dates of insolvency for state-funded pension systems and social security systems, etc.

The chapter titled Report Methodology describes in detail the methods for evaluating various initiatives and ultimately ranking countries according to how close they come to executing actionable developments with a practical impact on the aging population.

As such, our analysis also includes the final ranking of twelve countries according to the strength and relevance of their Government-led aging and Longevity-related projects and initiatives, as well as their likelihood of achieving tangible deliverables such as increases in Healthy Longevity, and decreases in the economic burdens posed by aging populations.

Ranking Countries on the Strength, Scope and Relevance of their Government Longevity-Related Projects and Initiatives

POSITION	COUNTRY	COUNTRY SCORE
1	United Kingdom	5.29
2	Netherlands	4.36
3	Singapore	4.15
4	South Korea	4.00
5	Israel	3.94
6	Switzerland	3.93
7	Hong Kong	3.41
8	Japan	3.10
9	USA	3.07
10	Spain	1.94
11	European Union	1.88
12	China	1.85

The subsequent chapters serve as an overview of government initiatives from various countries which are contending with the Silver Tsunami in their own way, ranging from:

- ***Young parliamentary democracies*** with limited histories of government programs such as Spain, which produce government initiatives for the elderly in abundance but show little concerted effort for bringing about comprehensive solutions for dealing with the demographic crisis, and instead produce a succession of short-term plans and *ad hoc* regulations in order to ameliorate the experience of their aging societies.

Technocratic tiger economies such as Singapore, Hong Kong and South Korea. These countries tend to resemble what this report series has defined as Longevity-progressive countries: small technocratic countries with aging populations, who are therefore galvanized to produce coordinated solutions. We can observe in these countries a large overall quantity of aging and Longevity-related initiatives. However, the budgets of these initiatives are much smaller than those allocated by larger countries with greater GDP. Also, these countries have begun implementing their initiatives comparatively recently — from 12 years in Singapore to 20 years in Hong Kong.

Strong and established parliamentary democracies such as the UK and Japan. These are the states that have been facing the challenge of Longevity for some time and are already making an effort to manifest the dividend in Longevity and to overcome the demographic challenges posed by an aging population. Moreover, they have already demonstrated the political will for developing bold industrial strategies. This combination of factors puts them a cut above the tiger economies. Currently, the main challenge for these countries is continuing to assure consistent policy in this area, as well as continuing to innovate.

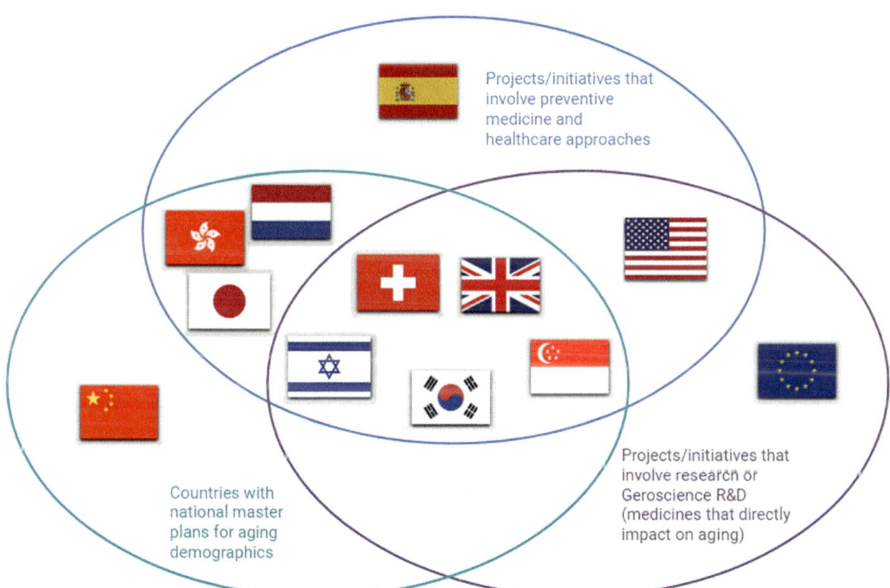

Above it is shown an infographic from *National Longevity Development Plans: Global Overview 2019*. The countries at the centre have come the closest to developing fully integrated industrial strategies for Longevity, whereas the ones near the periphery are those who have put forth more *ad hoc* and less comprehensive strategies.

Above it is shown a multi-faceted look at Longevity-relevant government initiatives globally: overall, there are 6 levels of proprietary metrics which differ based on the nature of the parameters of which they consist. Indicators, their growth rates and their ratios are calculated separately and then integrated in the final metrics system.

The whole of the metrics can also be subdivided into 2 categories based on the logic of the parameters, namely:

- **indicators of potential (or lack thereof);**
- **indicators of actual success (or lack thereof).**

Thus, the ranking system reflects both strengths and opportunities of different countries regarding the development of national Longevity strategies. It can be applied for the evaluation of the current state of a country, as well as of its prospects.

A complex, multi-dimensional analytical framework applies specifically-tuned weightings to a number of tangible, quantitative metrics and parameters, including quantitative metrics relating to Longevity, aging population and its effects on the national economy with regard to variables such as **life expectancy, HALE, GDP, healthcare efficiency, number of retirees, projected insolvency dates of relevant programs** such as social security and pension schemes, and many others, as well as **specific novel metrics** unique to Aging Analytics Agency's comparative analytics framework for the mentioned report, which applies specific importance factors to unique quantitative and qualitative parameters in order to classify and prioritize specific types of initiatives, and to measure the strength of Longevity-related initiatives and their likelihood of translating into tangible deliverables like increased Healthy Longevity and economic growth.

Using this proprietary framework, the report compares the overall strength, efficiency, and focus of each government regarding the sum of its projects and initiatives focused on Healthy Longevity and aging population.

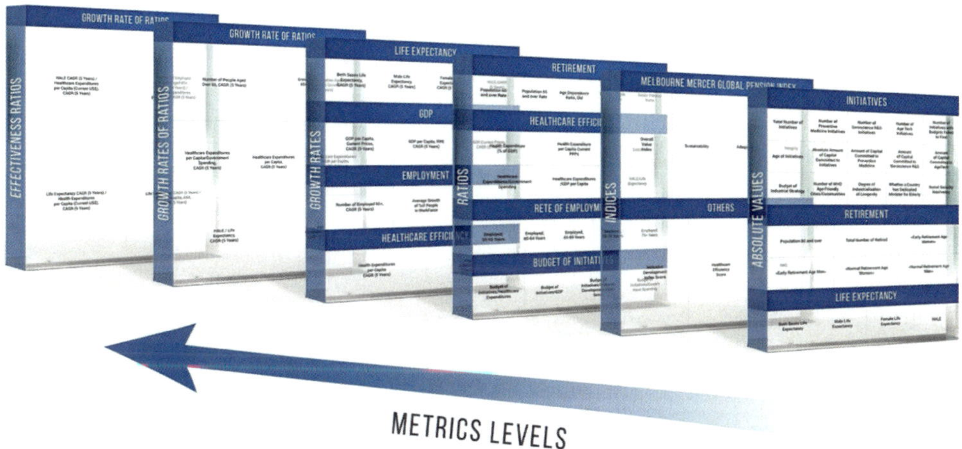

As already mentioned in Part I of this book, the metrics developed for and used in Aging Analytics Agency's ***National Longevity Development Plans: Global Overview 2019*** report are broken down into 6 distinct layers, with specific ratios being derived from 1st layer metrics, specific metric ratios and growth rates of ratios being derived from 3rd-layer metrics, effectiveness measures being derived from 4th layer metrics, and effectiveness measure growth rates being derived from 5th layer metrics.

Insolvency Predictions for Government-Funded Schemes

Figure showing predicted insolvency dates for various countries' retirement programs. The U.S. Medicare and Social Security programs are headed toward insolvency by 2026 and 2035 respectively. Spain's Social Security Reserve Fund had run out of money by 2018 which only added to concerns over Spain's financial situation. South Korea's National Pension Service is expected to run dry by 2056. The China Academy of Social Sciences reported that China's pension funds could become insolvent by 2035. The second pillar of Switzerland's pension system is under severe pressure, and pension schemes are projected to go down by 2025, with the rejection of a main reform proposal in a public referendum.

The Current State of Healthy Longevity Around the World

In late 2019, Aging Analytics Agency released *Global Longevity Governance Landscape: 50 Countries Big Data Comparative Analysis of Longevity Progressiveness*, a 540-page open access special analytical case study that utilized sophisticated multidimensional Big Data analytics to provide intelligible and fact-driven benchmarking of 50 nations in relation to levels of Healthy Longevity, as measured by Health-Adjusted Life Expectancy (HALE), their current gaps between HALE and unadjusted life expectancy, their current levels of success in growing and maintaining National Healthy Longevity and dealing with the issue of aging, and tangible policy recommendations on how to either maintain or improve their standing and optimize their National Healthy Longevity.

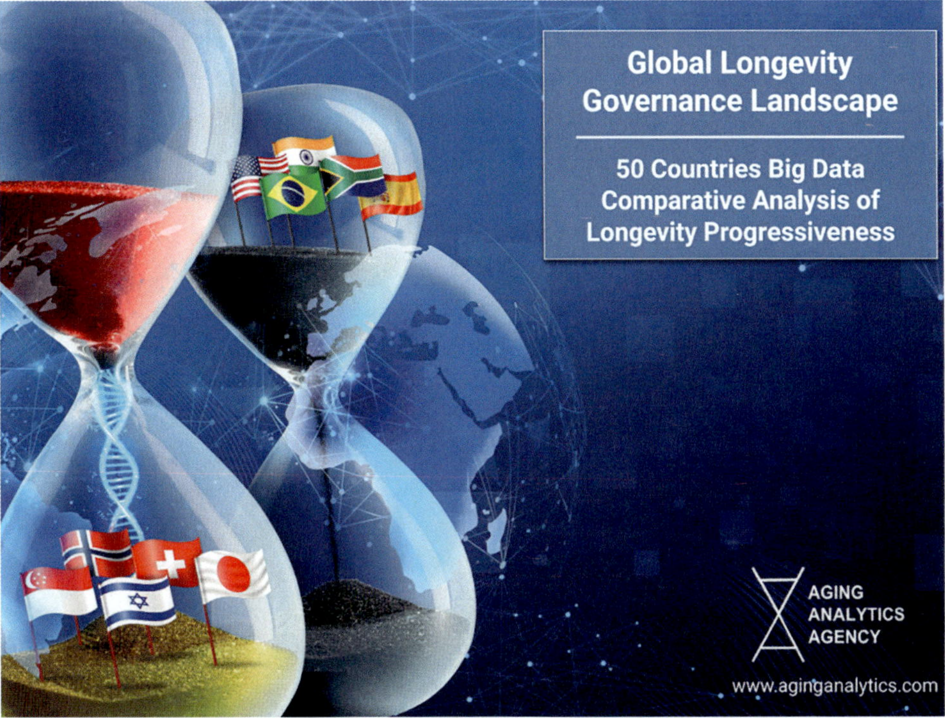

The report aims to answer a number of key questions, including:

- What specific features of healthcare systems, socio-economic conditions and environmental factors affect public health the most?
- How does the impact of such factors differ across countries?
- What constellation of factors contributes the most to Healthy Longevity?
- Which factors are the main drivers of health-adjusted life expectancy and disability-adjusted life years?
- What countries are leaders in Longevity governance?
- Why do disproportionate healthcare expenditures in the United States contribute to poor healthcare system performance and a decline in overall life expectancy in recent years?
- Why is the healthcare system in Singapore considered as one of the most efficient in the world?
- What can be done to improve National Healthy Longevity in each country globally?

It is a follow-up to Aging Analytics Agency's previous *National Longevity Development Plans: Global Landscape Overview 2019 (First Edition)* report, which utilized comprehensive analytical frameworks to rank the strength, relevance and proactiveness of government-led Longevity projects and initiatives in 12 different regions around the world.

50 countries were compared using **200 parameters** each, encompassing **10,000 data points** in total, integrated and assembled via sophisticated analytical frameworks that were used to identify the specific factors that should be either adjusted, neutralized or maintained to enable an increase in National Healthy Longevity as efficiently as possible, with a specific emphasis on governmental industry, medical and financial policy recommendations to transform the deficit and liability of an aging population into the opportunity and asset of National Healthy Longevity.

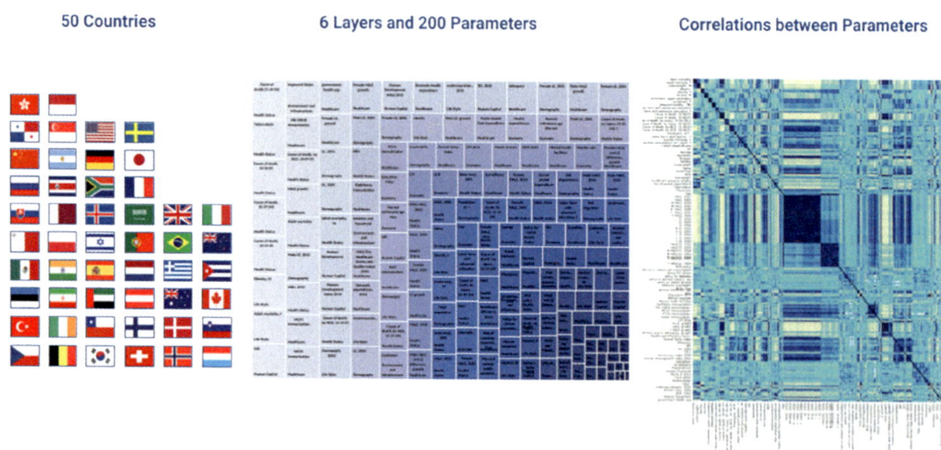

Today's increased global Longevity is a **"problem of success"**, in which the rise in global life expectancy seen in the last several decades has not been accompanied by a commensurate extension in health.

As a result, increased global Longevity is producing a global aging demographic, an impending crisis frequently referred to as the "Silver Tsunami".

In order to float rather than sink, Longevity must become an asset.

And this means altering the nature of aging entirely by compressing the period of financial and social inactivity in the final years of life, utilizing technology to ensure that these longer lives are also healthy, productive and financially active, creating a system of government frameworks and financial incentives to sustain this state of affairs.

By analyzing the specific circumstances of Longevity outliers — nations with an unusually large or small gap between healthy-adjusted life expectancy and unadjusted life expectancy — the study of these special cases is able to derive insights into the factors likely to either increase or decrease this gap.

The healthcare system in Singapore, for example, appears more geared toward raising up all its citizens than on achieving excellence in a few high-profile areas.

By contrast, the United States (which is the subject of another policy-focused analytical report, *Metabesity and Longevity: USA Special Case Study*) spends a disproportionate amount on healthcare, and yet has the lowest level of healthy life expectancy among high-income developed countries.

This illustrates the extreme disparities and variation in healthcare efficiency across the globe, exemplified by the enormous gap between HALE and life expectancy in different countries (e.g. Singapore's gap of 6.7 years vs. a gap of 10.0 years in the USA).

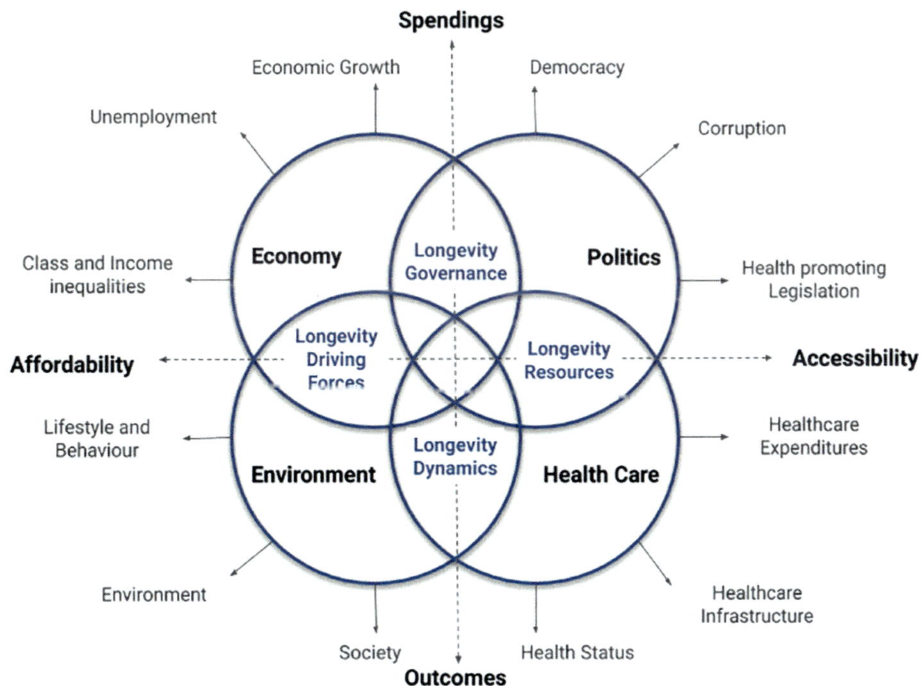

By identifying the factors with the greatest likelihood of enabling governments to develop integrated Longevity strategies and ecosystems to scale, and to reduce as much as possible their national gap between life expectancy and Healthy Longevity, the special analytical case study is able to offer tangible and practical recommendations tuned to the specifics of individual countries, providing the necessary set of tools to allow:

- countries currently leading the international Healthy Longevity race to maintain and improve their current standing,
- countries currently lagging behind others to reduce their Healthy Life Expectancy gap and improve their comparative global standing to the mutual benefit of their citizens and their economies.

Health-Adjusted Life Expectancy (HALE) and Life Expectancy

HALE and Life Expectancy (LE)	Countries	Gap
High HALE and LE	Australia, Austria, Canada, France, Italy, Luxembourg, Norway, Switzerland, Sweden, Republic of Korea	Big Gap between HALE and Life Expectancy
Medium HALE and LE	Belgium, Chile, Czech Republic, Denmark, Finland, Germany, Ireland, Slovenia	
Low HALE and LE	Estonia, Iran, Turkey, United Arab Emirates, United States of America	
High HALE and LE	Iceland, Israel, Japan, New Zealand, Spain	Medium Gap between HALE and Life Expectancy
Medium HALE and LE	Cuba, Greece, Malta, Netherlands, Portugal, Qatar, United Kingdom of Great Britain and Northern Ireland	
Low HALE and LE	Brazil, India, Mexico, Poland, Slovakia, Saudi Arabia	
High HALE and LE	Hong Kong, Singapore	Small Gap between HALE and Life Expectancy
Medium HALE and LE	China, Costa Rica, Panama	
Low HALE and LE	Argentina, Indonesia, Russia, South Africa	

Focus on healthcare status and lifestyle

High levels of life expectancy and health-adjusted life expectancy are strongly impacted by the burden of diseases and the harmful impact of behavioural factors.

The public-private balance

It is important for Longevity governance to find an effective combination of universal health coverage system, support from citizens, and the private sector. Evolving stages of socioeconomic development should reflect changing priorities in public health — from environmental measures to personal lifestyles and healthcare consumption.

Large focus on delivery of care

Today, Longevity is about social inclusiveness, high quality of life, technical innovations in care delivery and medical treatment, and modified business and governmental models.

Financial protection and fairness of financing

Healthcare affordability is becoming more important because rising premiums and out-of-pocket payments place an increasingly large financial burden on households with lower and middle incomes.

Low socioeconomic inequality and reduced disparity in health outcomes

Many health outcomes — everything from life expectancy to infant mortality and obesity — can be linked to the level of economic inequality within a given population. Greater economic inequality appears to lead to worse health outcomes.

Corruption in healthcare

Corruption significantly weakens overall healthcare system performance, and has been found by multiple studies to have a significant negative impact on important health outcomes.

Level of economic development

Healthcare performance is strongly dependent on the economy, but also on national healthcare systems themselves. Investment in health is not only a desirable, but also an essential priority for most societies.

Developed and wealthy nations tend to have more favourable and optimal health outcomes.

Global Trends in Health-Adjusted Life Expectancy (HALE)

Healthy life expectancy is affected by many factors such as:

- Socioeconomic status, demography, income, well-being, healthcare quality, efficiency, progressiveness and access,
- Health and lifestyle behavioural factors such as tobacco and excessive alcohol consumption, poor nutrition and lack of exercise, social factors, genetic factors,
- Environmental factors including overcrowded housing, lack of clean drinking water and inadequate sanitation.

In countries with low HALE, we see an accompanying lack of access to modern healthcare and a generally underdeveloped medical infrastructure.

Hence, it must be noted that the countries that have the highest life expectancy and HALE indicators are generally the most developed countries and tend to have the happiest citizens.

Utilising Artificial Intelligence in Preventive Medicine

As the paradigm shift from treatment to prevention continues forward, governments should heavily prioritize funding and development of AI for Preventive Medicine, which represents the most efficient mean of accelerating progress in Preventive Medicine to scale.

Conclusions:

A wide range of independent Longevity-related government initiatives have recently been appearing around the world.

- This includes social and educational programs, urban planning solutions, biotechnological investment programs, and national health data infrastructures.
- The United Kingdom has already turned its attention to cross-sector collaboration, particularly between artificial intelligence and healthcare. There has also been a general recognition of the central role of technology, and financial technology in particular, in improving the lives of the elderly.
- The official formation of the UK All-Party Parliamentary Group for Longevity in March 2019, and their commitment to assist the UK government in meeting its goal of adding 5 years of Healthy Life Expectancy to its population by the year 2035, has served to further strengthen the nation's prospects for attaining a prominent international position as a Longevity-Progressive country and a leader of Healthy Human Longevity.
- While many countries are taking steps towards prioritizing Longevity as a major national concern, more work needs to be done in the explicit formation and execution of government-led National Longevity Development Plans, and in concerted development of the full scope of the Longevity Industry (biomedical, technological, financial) in a way that leverages cross-sector synergy across government, industry and academia.
- Citizens of progressive technocracy driven countries can expect healthier, happier and longer lives. As smart governments utilize progress in all sectors of the Longevity Industry to maximize the health, wealth, and wellness of their citizens, Longevity will become a major electoral talking-point and policy priority that will determine the success of parties and politicians.

Chapter 9: Longevity Progressive and Regressive Nations: Israel, Singapore and the USA

Israel

"Longevity governance and progressive government-led Longevity development initiatives will reshape the political and socioeconomic landscape of nations around the world."

Margaretta Colangelo in *Longevity Initiatives Will Reshape the Political & Socioeconomic Landscape of Nations Around the World* (Official LinkedIn Longevity Newsletter, November 2019).

- ***National master plan on aging***
- ***Strong Political Support for the elderly***
- ***Joint geroscience research initiative with the UK***

Israel's proactive stance on Longevity parallels its progressive general outlook. The country's healthcare system is highly advanced compared to other nations of similar economic status. This is because the Israeli healthcare system greatly emphasizes disease prevention, promotion of healthy nutrition, early medical screening and Preventive Medicine.

Public health in Israel has seen an astonishing improvement over the last decade – notably, a 50% reduction in the incidence of heart attacks. Much of the nation's technological strengths and the maturity of its innovation ecosystem stems from the government taking a highly interdisciplinary approach to the problems it seeks to solve and the products it aims to develop.

Israel has also made substantial efforts to foster its digital health industry. According to Israeli tech innovation non-profit group, Startup Nation Central, the number of Israeli digital health start-ups increased from 65 in 2005 to almost 400 in 2016.

This explosion of the digital health sector shows no signs of stopping, with a 27% increase in investments in 2016 alone. Both Israel's private and public sectors have worked jointly to create this growth in the sector.

The program aims to facilitate a distributed, continuing education program to help medical professionals stay abreast of the newest and best techniques available.

The nation's proactive stance on Longevity has only intensified in the past year. **In July 2018, the Knesset Committee on Science and Technology held a landmark session titled "Strengthening the research and development for improving the quality of life and Longevity and prevention of aging-related diseases", which was dedicated to bolstering R&D for healthy Longevity.** The session featured leading Israeli scientists and representatives of various Israel ministries.

A recent article in National Geographic attributes this to lifestyle interventions including their Mediterranean-style diet and low alcohol consumption; strong social, family and cultural values, which help to combat the loneliness and detachment often present in the elderly population of developed nations; and a strong healthcare system that greatly emphasizes personalised treatment and Preventive Medicine.

> ***Israel currently ranks 5th in the world for healthy Longevity according to the United Nation's 2018 World Happiness Report.***

Bloomberg's annual Healthcare Efficiency Index ranks Israel 6th in the world, up one place from the previous year. The index arrives at its ranking by:

- A weighted average of life expectancy (60%).
- National per capita healthcare spending as a proportion of overall GDP (30%).
- Per capita spending on health in dollars (10%).

Experts are concerned, however, that declining public spending on healthcare may not allow Israel to keep its current rank. Israel spends 7.3% of the GDP on public health, which is below the OECD average of 9%. The UK, for instance, spends 16.8% of the GDP on public health but ranks quite low, at 35th globally, due to its low life expectancy of 79 years. This does suggest that Israel is using the funds it allocated to public health in a highly efficient and proactive manner, but may simply be indicative of the relative difference in size of populations between the two nations. Nonetheless, spending on public health in Israel is declining (currently at 63%), while private spending is increasing (currently at 36%).

The Israeli government needs to refocus efforts on public health, as it has done in the past, to keep its country's overall health from slipping. By renewing concentration on personalised and preventive healthcare tactics and placing greater emphasis on the maintenance and extension of healthy Longevity, it has the power to maintain its current ranking and even surpass it. The possibility is there, and it is merely the will and commitment of the government that needs to be in place to make that goal a reality.

More generally, Israel is home to a very strong BioTech industry, boasting over 1,450 companies in the life science sphere with headquarters in the country. The majority of these were founded in just the last 10 years, with an average of 130 companies launching each year.

Much of this progress is due to proactive and progressive policies put forward by the Israeli government. In 2018, two units of the country's Ministry of Economy partnered to establish a new grant program that aims to cover as much as 20-30% of the costs associated with BioTech companies making the transition from R&D to full-scale manufacturing.

These two departments are the Israel Innovation Authority, the government's technology investment arm, and the Israel Investment Center, a government body that oversees the country's peripheral regions and job creation.

Whereas the transition from R&D to scaled manufacturing traditionally takes up to 15 years, the government hopes that this new program can accelerate the shift. Companies located in the country's central district will receive grants covering 20% of the cost of this transition, while that number rises to 30% for those at more peripheral regions.

Authorities hope that this will create a more favourable landscape for investors interested in providing financing for Israeli life science and BioTech companies, and lower the number of companies unable to survive the transition due to financial stress. The grant program thus creates a very strong life sciences foundation upon which a more specialized Longevity Industry can grow and prosper.

Furthermore, if the government can combine their progressive support of BioTech with support for Longevity companies, they may significantly accelerate the overall development of a national Longevity Industry agenda.

Over the past several years, Israel has intensified its focus on the preventive and personalised treatment of aging, and BIRAX Ageing

(Britain Israel Research and Academic Exchange Partnership) is the culmination of these activities.

Currently, although 130 new life science companies are founded each year in Israel, roughly 65 of those are forced to shut down due to financial pressures.

Through BIRAX Ageing, in the last year the Israeli government has taken a large first step towards recognizing aging as a condition amenable to biomedical intervention.

They have also taken progressive stances on a number of related and convergent areas, including Preventive Medicine and digital health.

The program's budget for 2015 provided up to NIS 15 million (about US$4.2 million) in grants for Israeli researchers working toward practical solutions for the elderly, and encouraged interdisciplinary research projects in technology, life sciences/medical sciences and social/behavioural sciences.

The program particularly emphasizes:

- personalised diagnosis and treatment
- advanced techniques
- information and communication technologies
- nanomedicine-based diagnostics and treatments
- medical robotics and bioengineering

The program was developed as a result of discussions during Israel's largest aging and Longevity-focused conference, held at Bar-Ilan University during Israel Science Day and hosted by the Israel Ministry of Science.

Israel has established a strong record over the past decade for high healthcare efficiency, a strong focus on Preventive and Personalised Medicine, and within the last five years an increasingly prominent focus on aging research and healthspan extension.

The nation has all the necessary resources to grow its academic geroscience landscape and their burgeoning Longevity Industry into a full-fledged Longevity-focused national agenda. The only missing element is a coordinated effort to unite these trends and resources into a coherent, synergistic national development plan.

Due to its emerging Longevity Industry and remarkably mature geroscience landscape, Israel has excellent potential to become a notable force on the international Longevity scene. Although the past five years have witnessed excellent progress, additional steps are required to realize Israel's full potential. Specifically, the country needs to further maintain and cultivate its existing strengths, including:

- Government Support of Longevity Research & Development. The Israeli government has made an excellent first step toward cementing Longevity as a core priority, but it needs to further strengthen its Longevity agenda and position the healthspan extension as the centre of a major national development plan, akin to the UK's successful decision to list the problem of an Aging Population as the 2nd grand challenge in its industrial strategy. It needs to commit more government funding for basic aging research and the development of therapies to extend healthspan.
- Highly Mature Academic Geroscience Landscape. For a number of years, Israel has outputted high-volume, high-quality research into the fundamental biology of aging and potential healthspan extension interventions. Most compellingly, 100% of Israeli universities have now established dedicated facilities for aging research, including several labs and interdisciplinary centres.
- Attractive Technology and Innovation Hub. The amount of funding raised by high-tech start-ups in Israel continues to grow, reaching US$6.47 bln in 2018 through 623 deals. Israeli start-ups are also acquired much faster than their foreign counterparts. On average, Israeli start-ups are acquired four years after founding, compared to an average of six years in Europe. This accelerated return on investment makes the tech industry in Israel very attractive for international investors. We are also seeing large IT and tech giants opening locations in Israel.
- For example, in 2016, Google established an R&D centre in Israel, where many of the company's most important products (including Google Suggest, Google Trends, and Google Live Results) were developed.
- Google was not the first US company to invest in Israel's potentials; Intel, for instance, set up its first international R&D lab in Israel in 1974 after recognizing the country's strengths in technology innovation.

Singapore

Tiger Economy

Diverse Government Programs with strong focus on continuing education for the elderly and developing AgeTech

In a 2017 article for the Straits Times, Dr. Brian Kennedy, former CEO of the Buck Institute for Research on Aging and the new Director of the Center for Healthy Aging at the National University Health System (NUHS), noted that although Singaporean life expectancy is rising, its healthspan expectancy is lagging behind.

However, the stress of Singapore's aging population, combined with the government's progressive aim as a global leader in healthcare efficiency, may spur Singapore to lead human aging research on a global scale.

The newly established Center for Healthy Aging puts this commitment into action.

The centre promotes research into behavioural and lifestyle interventions, such as exercise and fasting, and Longevity-extending drugs to delay aging.

Dr. Kennedy cited a 2012 global study which concluded that from 1990 to 2010, lifespan in Singapore grew by 5.4 years for women and 6 years for men. In contrast, healthspan only increased 3.4 and 4.1 years, respectively, during the same period.

The studies will determine whether healthspan-extending interventions similarly affects different population demographics and ethnicities. Furthermore, the centre will collaborate with the Institute for Aging Research at the Albert Einstein College of Medicine in the US to determine whether the common diabetes drug metformin can extend human healthspan.

According to the Natixis Investment Managers' Global Retirement Index, this year Singapore ranked 28th globally and 3rd in Asia (behind Japan and South Korea) for the strength of their retirement security.

The index ranks countries according to 18 different performance indicators that cover key aspects of retirement security, including the material means to live comfortably; access to quality financial services to help preserve savings value and maximize income; access to quality health services; and a clean and safe environment.

Singapore has enthusiastically embraced the rising AgeTech sector to improve the quality of life and levels of social engagement of its elderly population. AgeTech, which encompasses any digital technologies that aid the elderly, is being rapidly adopted by medical institutions and nursing homes across the nation.

One illustrative device is the Bond Stick, which is a three-in-one walking stick, alarm sensor and MP3 player.

The stick reduces dementia through sensory stimulation, and its auto-fall sensor alerts caregivers to potentially devastating falls. At the 9th annual Aging Asia Innovation Forum, a recent conference showcasing AgeTech devices, Singapore's Senior Minister of State for Health, Dr. Amy Khor, noted that "rethinking aged care and supporting our aged population is not a task that can be accomplished overnight. To succeed in these efforts, the public, private and people sectors will have to work in partnership to re-imagine new possibilities and solutions."

The market for products and services targeted for Singaporeans aged 50 and over is projected to triple from SGD 33 billion (US$ 24 billion) in 2015 to SGD 91 billion (US$ 66 billion) in 2025.

Interestingly, pioneering companies at the forefront of Singapore's AgeTech market are almost entirely technology start-ups, with very limited private sector interest from larger corporations other than Singapore's multinational healthcare technology companies.

Wong Poh Kam, Director of the National University of Singapore's Entrepreneurship Center, commented:

"The awareness of big corporations towards aging population might be lower than you expected [in Singapore], compared with other advanced economies like Japan."

The Agency for Science, Technology and Research (A*STAR) is a statutory board under the Ministry of Trade and Industry of Singapore. The agency supports R&D that is aligned to areas of competitive advantage and national needs for Singapore. These span the following four technology domains set out under the nation's five-year R&D plan (RIE2020):

- Advanced Manufacturing and Engineering (AME)
- Health and Biomedical Sciences (HBMS)

— Urban Solutions and Sustainability (USS)
— Services and Digital Economy (SDE)

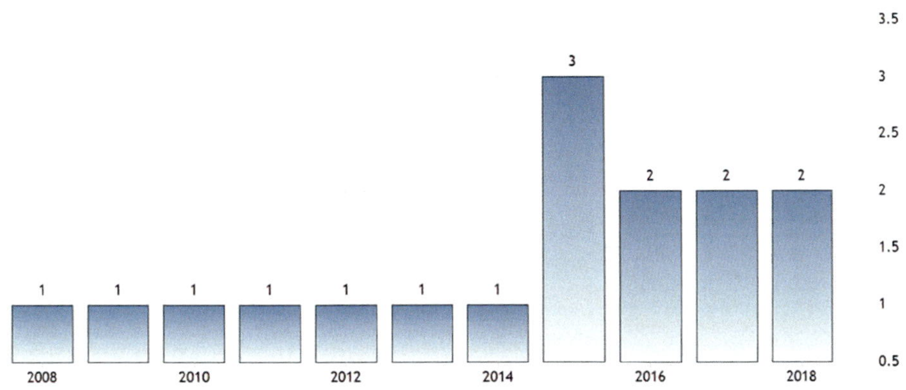

A*STAR was established in 1991 with the primary mission of advancing the economy and improving lives by growing the knowledge-intensive biomedical, research, scientific and engineering fields.

The Biomedical Research Council (BMRC) oversees research entities that serve to support key industry clusters in Biomedical Sciences, such as pharmaceuticals, medical technology, biotechnology and healthcare services.

Speaking to Straits Times, Dr. Finian Tan, the chairman of Vickers Venture Partners, stated that Vickers invested in Samumed, a San Diego-based regenerative medicine firm, due to its highly optimal risk-reward profile, "because the discovery here is not the drug, but the biological pathway that regulates stem cell differentiation and how it can be manipulated to spur the regeneration of hair for a bald person, or retina for a blind person, or cartilage for someone with osteoarthritis. Is this a platform play? Signalling is the cause of all cellular growth and death. You can't patent the pathway, but you can patent the drugs that work on the pathway, and there's no one entering the clinic that's doing what we do".

The number of Singaporean venture funds that invest globally in Longevity companies is relatively few. Vickers Venture Partners, through astute investment choices, has found itself in a leadership position. Its investment in Samumed came at a time when most investors and business analysts were still skeptical of the Longevity Industry's viability and long-term profitability.

It remains to be seen if this success will be a catalyst for other Singaporean VCs to make similar high reward investments, but success is often imitated and eventually improved upon. This could help spur the growth of the industry in Singapore and well beyond.

United States of America

This country is an economic giant with a strong scientific base, with a federal government that demands integrated aging strategies from all its member states.

The USA holds the greatest share of the multitrillion dollar global Longevity economy and the majority share of global Longevity Industry companies and players. Despite this fact, the USA currently has a gap between Health-Adjusted Life Expectancy (HALE) and un-adjusted life expectancy of 10 years, compared to just 6.7 years in Singapore. Meanwhile, its HALE is 7.7 years less than Singapore, 6.3 years behind Japan and 5 years behind Switzerland.

Its life expectancy at birth lags behind 25 countries, and yet its healthcare expenditures are the highest among all developed countries in the world (18% of the GDP).

Other countries are maintaining a much higher state of Healthy Longevity with much lower rates of spending. This is not due to inherent genetic differences – the USA is simply not implementing the right policies to spend their healthcare dollars in effective ways.

The United States needs a new approach that shifts away from "sick care" to a model of empowering overall health and wellness, providing patients with access to proactive care that identifies risk and manages chronic disease early to prevent escalation and deterioration.

It is a nation equipped with all the resources necessary to become a global leader in Longevity, Preventive Medicine and Precision Health, and National Healthy Longevity, but lacks national prioritization by its federal government, and a strategy to unite the activities of its Longevity, Artificial Intelligence and Preventive Medicine industry ecosystems to work in synergy, rather than in discoordination.

Singapore	United States
HALE: 76.2	HALE: 68.5
HALE GAP: 6.7	HALE GAP: 10.0
Life Expectancy: 82.9	Life Expectancy: 78.5
Healthcare Efficiency Rank: #2	Healthcare Efficiency Rank: #25
% GDP Healthcare Spending: 4.5%	% GDP Healthcare Spending: 18%

The USA holds the greatest share of the multitrillion dollar global Longevity economy and the majority share of global Longevity Industry companies and players.

An increase in Healthy Longevity would be of universal benefit for both the American economy and society. It would decrease the burden of the old on the young, create a reinvigorated workforce and consumer market, and have innumerable benefits to the USA economy as a whole, besides putting the country in a position to become a global Longevity leader, leveraging scientific progress for the betterment of all society.

As mentioned, the USA has all the resources necessary to become a global leader in Longevity, Preventive Medicine and Precision Health, and National Healthy Longevity, so the country's low HALE and high gap between HALE and LE is not a scientific problem, but a policy problem.

Too Much Emphasis on Aging, Not Enough on Longevity

The United States is home to the world's top universities, laboratories and scientific talent, and some of the world's biggest technological and financial hubs and greatest technological feats. But unlike some of its constituent states, one of which we shall examine in the next section, the US Federal Government has a relatively scant record of government initiative relating to Longevity, and of all the countries listed in this chapter, the USA falls the furthest short of anything even resembling a comprehensive industrial strategy, let alone a national Longevity development plan.

The Federal Government's most integrated strategy on aging is the 1965 Older Americans Act, which has created a large number of State Units on Aging. These in turn have been largely responsible for each US state's individual initiatives.

The Older Americans Act was signed into law on July 14th 1965. The Act authorizes a wide array of service programs through a nationwide network of 57 state agencies on aging and 665 area agencies on aging, supports the sole federal job creation program benefiting low-income older workers, and is a major source of federal funding for an extensive grant program for training, research, and demonstration activities in the field of aging. The Act has been amended 13 times since the original legislation was enacted.

It established the Administration on Aging within the Department of Health, Education and Welfare, and called for the creation of State Units on Aging (SUAs).

In 2018, The Building Our Largest Dementia (BOLD) Infrastructure for Alzheimer's Act was introduced by senators and developed in close partnership between the sponsors, the Alzheimer's Association and AIM. The bill quickly developed enormous bipartisan support. More than half of the 115th Congress — 58 Senators and 256 Representatives — cosponsored the bill. The bill unanimously passed in the Senate on December 12th and passed in the House 361-3 on December 19th.

Its purpose was to create an Alzheimer's public health infrastructure across the country to implement effective interventions focused on public health issues such as increasing early detection and diagnosis, reducing risk and preventing avoidable hospitalizations.

Its key measures were:

- Supporting early detection and diagnosis
- Reducing risk of avoidable hospitalizations
- Reducing risk of cognitive decline
- Enhancing support to meet needs of caregivers
- Reducing health disparities
- Supporting care planning and management

The US is no stranger to geroscience (i.e. the science of Longevity) initiatives either. The National Institute of Health (NIH) has a geroscience initiative, supporting the conducting of genetic, biological, clinical, behavioural, social and economic research related to the aging process. It is published in a document titled *Aging Well in the 21st Century*.

Leveraging The USA's Unique Strengths to Boost its International Longevity Standing

The Gap Between the USA Health and Wealth: High Healthcare Expenditure, Low Health-Adjusted Life Expectancy (HALE)

Despite having one of the highest rates of healthcare spending, the United States is a complete outlier in terms of life expectancy at birth, Health-Adjusted Life Expectancy (HALE), and healthcare efficiency.

> It's important to reemphasize that other developed countries are maintaining a much higher state of Healthy Longevity with much lower rates of healthcare spending. This is not due to inherent genetic differences — the USA is simply not implementing adequate policies and practices to utilize their healthcare dollars in effective ways.

The Needed Shift from Sick Care to Preventive Medicine, Followed by Precision Health and Then Economic Prosperity

As the population ages, sick care will become increasingly expensive and ineffective. The USA needs to rapidly implement a broad-based shift from treatment to population-wide prevention.

An array of tools is available ranging from simple digital-supported education to Precision Health approaches, using deep diagnostics and prognostics in combination with biomarkers of aging. These tools can both reveal and confirm effective interventions and guide their optimal selection for the individual. The aim is to thereby delay the onset of disease with as minimal intervention as possible, as early as possible.

Synergies of Longevity research, P4 Medicine and Artificial Intelligence have the potential to enable rapid and widespread policy and infrastructural transformation of healthcare in America to quickly boost National Healthy Longevity (healthspan). However, this can only be possible with sufficient public and private commitment at every level and step.

Policy Implications: National Government Strategy to Narrow the Gap Between Life Expectancy and HALE

The United States holds the greatest share of the multitrillion dollar global Longevity economy and the majority share of the global Longevity Industry companies and players. It also has one of the highest rates of healthcare expenditures.

While the US has all the resources necessary to become a global leader in Longevity, Preventive Medicine and Precision Health, and of

National Healthy Longevity, it lacks such prioritization among government and private healthcare stakeholders.

A cohesive strategy is lacking for enabling the Longevity Industry, AI, and Preventive Medicine to work in synergy, rather than in discoordination. The USA's low HALE and large gap between HALE and life expectancy is not because of a lack in scientific knowhow. What is needed are policies to apply the science.

Chapter 10: The Swiss Longevity Valley: How Switzerland May Become A Global Longevity Financial Industry MegaHub by 2025 (Contributor: Stefan Hascoet)

Key Points:

- Switzerland possesses completely unique strengths and synergies in the spheres of BioTech, Preventive Precision Medicine, International Policy, Financial Industry and Advanced AI-Empowered InvestTech Solutions.
- This unique intersection of frontier technologies and domains can be leveraged to transform the nation into a world-leading Longevity Valley in the coming years.
- Its specific strengths in international finance and FinTech in particular make it poised to become the world-leading Longevity Financial Industry Hub, if its unique advantages and potentials are leveraged in the right way.
- **Deep Knowledge Group** has been increasing its activities in the Swiss Longevity ecosystem for some time, with the recent launch of Deep Knowledge Swiss and the **Longevity Swiss Foundation**, and the planned launch of AI Centres for Longevity and Financial Wellness in Switzerland, as components of the global **Longevity AI Consortium**, which was recently launched and inaugurated at King's College London.

As a Switzerland-based Financial Industry professional, the nation's unique strengths in the financial sector and international policy sector have been clear to me for a long time. But it was not until I met Dmitry Kaminskiy, General Partner of Deep Knowledge Group, that Switzerland's equally-unique strengths and prospects in the Longevity Industry — and its potentials to reap extremely promising synergies between these two domains — became apparent to me.

I am excited to promote this agenda and to help steer the direction of the ongoing Swiss-based Longevity activities towards a future that can enable the nation to become a world-class Longevity MegaHub.

The Longevity Industry in Switzerland

Switzerland is thought to be second only to Japan in terms of the number of people who have reached 100 (Switzerland has the highest life expectancy in Europe at 83.7 years, according to Eurostat). According to a study conducted by the Institute for Social and Preventive Medicine, about 40 out of every 10,000 people born in 1900 in Switzerland made it to their 100th birthday. Life expectancy has increased by 98% for men and 96% for women in the past century and a half. A slight dip was due to an influenza epidemic in 1918.

Switzerland is one of the most efficiently regulated and supervised financial centres in the world today. The country is an international centre of finance where investment banks are acutely aware of the demographic challenge and the incentives to do something about it. Switzerland's financial sector is of significant importance to the national economy, employing about 5% of the total workforce and accounting for 9% of the economic output. The financial sector ensures that the Swiss economy is never short of the necessary capital or financial services. Switzerland has been leading transformative developments emerging from the digitalization of its banking and financial sector. Even the Swiss Board of Advisors names now digitization as the most important topic.

Switzerland has made large strides towards accommodating innovation — both domestic and foreign — in the fields of FinTech, blockchain, and cryptocurrencies in the last few years. For example, there were 220 FinTech companies in Switzerland by the end of 2017, with 32 new companies being incorporated throughout the year.

It is leading the digitization of financial markets and establishing itself as a catalyst for financial innovation on a global level. Switzerland sits at one end of the BioValley, one of the leading life science clusters in Europe. The cluster is unique because it spans across three countries: Switzerland, Germany and France. This includes the global life science hub of Basel, Switzerland.

10% of all global European FinTech enterprises are located in Switzerland, with 46% of them located in Zurich.

BioValley brings together important ingredients for a successful BioTech cluster: a concentration of companies, rich availability of skills and experience within Life Sciences, and a research base that is world-class.

Switzerland spends the highest percentage of its GDP on healthcare (around 11.4%) compared to all EU countries. Basic health insurance is compulsory in Switzerland, although you are free to choose your own Swiss health insurance company. In the EU's latest statistics, Switzerland was the only country, compared to the EU, to total more than EUR 4,500 per inhabitant on healthcare expenditure. Healthcare is largely organised by Switzerland's individual communes.

The health ministers from all cantons form the Swiss Conference of the Cantonal Ministers of Public Health (GDK), which aims to promote cooperation and implement common policies between cantons.

Moreover, Switzerland is known to be one of the most Longevity-progressive countries, which means it is not simply a country with high investment in biotechnology, but one of the most capable to integrate AI into its economic, financial and healthcare systems.

What Makes Switzerland a Longevity-Progressive Country?

Longevity-progressive countries normally have large aging populations. The Swiss population is one of the oldest on the planet. This is a consequence of low fertility, increased life expectancy (in 2018 Swiss life expectancy ranked 5th in the world, with an annual life expectancy of 83.5 years) and a societal appreciation for preventative health and healthy aging.

An aging population has two Longevity-progressive benefits:

Voting power	Spending power
It galvanises government action. The challenges of an aging society make themselves felt at all levels, and this forces governments to confront the global "Silver Tsunami" head on.	Wealth is concentrated in the hands of the elderly, and is more likely to be directed toward solutions which improve the lives of the elderly.

This voting power factor is especially strong in Switzerland because of its tradition of direct democracy and popular initiatives. As a consequence, the Swiss political establishment is acutely aware of the democratic consequences of its demographics, and has therefore taken extensive initiatives to address Switzerland's demographic challenge.

The digitization of finance, and novel financial systems which treat Longevity as a dividend, will play an integral role in the future Longevity Industry and economy. Switzerland is an international centre of finance where investment banks are acutely aware of the demographic challenge and of the incentives to do something about it.

Switzerland's financial sector is of significant importance to the national economy, employing about 5% of the total workforce and accounting for 9% of the economic output.

As the financial sector ensures that the Swiss economy is never short of the necessary capital or financial services, and **the country is one of the most efficiently regulated and supervised financial centres in the world today as well,** it has all the elements necessary to become a leading Longevity financial hub, also due to other factors such as a lean political system that facilitates rapid implementation of integrated government programs, a strong research environment for geroscience, a strong research and business environment for digital health, and most importantly, international financial prowess.

Switzerland Age/Employment Range

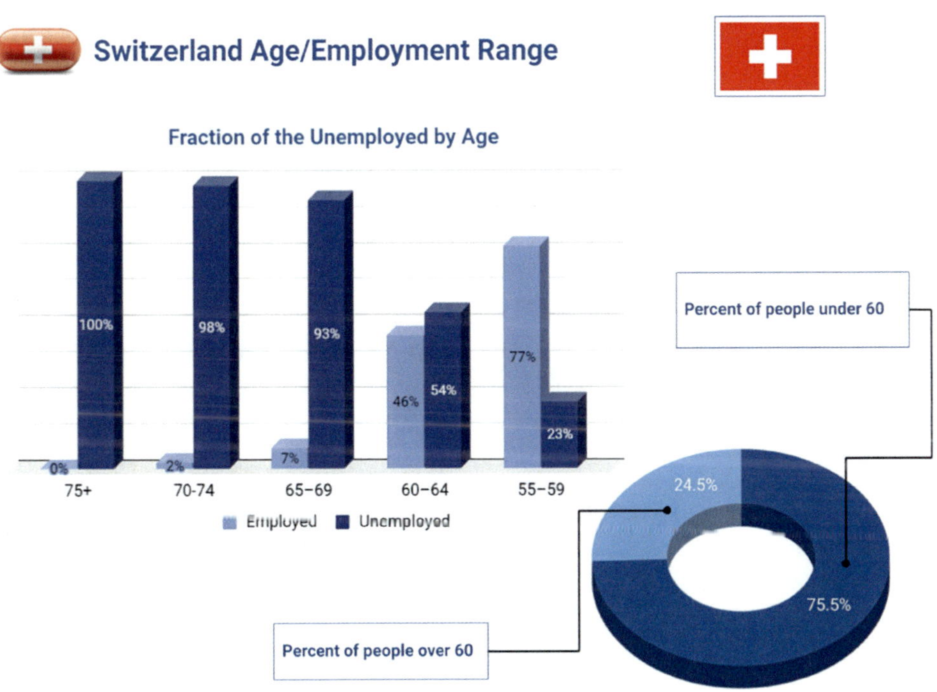

That accounts for both population aging (which threatens to destabilize the current business models of insurance companies and pension funds) and the potential for widespread healthspan extension, and the development of a national strategy for intensively developing its geroscience and FinTech to a state so advanced that it propels Switzerland into a central role in the internationally competitive Longevity business ecosystem, where it can rise to become a global leader in the specific field of Longevity Finance.

Switzerland sits at a crossroads of European geroscience, and has a strong and productive geroscience community. The Swiss Institute for Bioinformatics, for example, has recently identified large numbers of genetic markers directly linked to human life expectancy.

Switzerland is also home to the prestigious Vontobel Prize for Aging Research.

The top universities in Switzerland for clinical medicine, based on their reputation and research in the field, are Zurich, Bern, Basel, Geneva, Lausanne and the Swiss Federal Institute of Technology.

While the word "Longevity" is often associated with the likes of "Silicon Valley" and the life extension community of supporters, according to the Aging Analytics Agency, this may soon change.

The Longevity Swiss Foundation, a Geneva-based non-profit and think tank, is aiming to turn the nation into a world-leading Longevity hub, calling it a new "Longevity Valley".

While tech had Silicon Valley as its incubator, Longevity will require something more powerful. It is not just about vast amounts of money for investment, nor the innovation that draws talent. It covers complex phenomena that include political drive, synergy between finance and new BioTechs, and demographics that allow the new therapies to have a huge impact on the economy and on people's well-being.

Dmitry was correct when he said, in a press release on the publication of Aging Analytics Agency's **Longevity Industry in Switzerland** report published in 2019, that:

> **"Switzerland has a long-standing reputation as a hub for both international policy and the financial industry. The nation has extremely strong potentials to leverage these existing assets in order to become the leading European hotspot for the rising Longevity Financial Industry."**

In examining Switzerland's Longevity-progressive characteristics, we find that the country possesses the following unique strengths and weaknesses:

Strengths

1. A lean political system that facilitates rapid implementation of integrated government programs.

2. A strong research environment for geroscience.

3. A strong research and business environment for digital health.

4. An abundance of political will to address the demographic challenge and international financial prowess.

Weaknesses

1. The absence of any specific Longevity business community. For example, it is a site of digital health summits, not Longevity summits.

2. The absence of any industrial strategy for Longevity, like the UK's recognition of "aging in society" as an industrial challenge.

3. The heterogeneity of health data infrastructures has slowed the development of a nationwide personalised health ecosystem as compared to countries with more homogeneous national health systems.

Given Switzerland's small geographical size, and its reliance on international cooperation, its inevitable function will be as a small but important node. The most productive way forward for Switzerland, given its strengths, might be as follows:

- Developing a Longevity progressive pension system and insurance company ecosystem that accounts for both population aging (which threatens to destabilize the current business models of insurance companies and pension funds) and the potential for widespread healthspan extension.
- Creating a national strategy for intensively developing Longevity, Precision Medicine and FinTech to a state so advanced that it propels Switzerland into a central role in the internationally competitive Longevity business ecosystem, where it can rise to become a global leader in the specific field of Longevity Finance.

The Current State of Longevity Progressiveness in Switzerland

In a recent open-access analytical report, ***Global Longevity Governance: 50 Countries Big Data Comparative Analysis of Longevity Progressiveness***, Aging Analytics Agency performed fact-driven benchmarking of 50 nations using 200 parameters per country and 10,000 data points in total to rank their respective levels of Healthy Longevity and their current gaps between health-adjusted life expectancy and unadjusted life expectancy, and to provide tangible policy recommendations on how to optimize their National Healthy Longevity. **Regarding the analysis of Healthcare System in Switzerland:**

- The Swiss health system is highly valued by patients and allows them to see a specialist directly (free choice of doctor).
- Switzerland and the EU have signalled a mutual interest in intensified and institutionalised cooperation in the area of public health. The priorities are the fight against communicable diseases, general health concerns, food safety, and production security in general.

- The health system performs very well with regard to a broad range of indicators. Life expectancy in Switzerland is one of the highest in Europe, and healthy life expectancy is several years above the EU average.
- Developed network of P4 clinics to make medicine more Precise, Preventive, Personalised and Participatory.

- Health insurance premiums are increasing quicker than Swiss incomes.
- Switzerland's level of health spending is high compared to most EU countries (most of which have single-payer systems).
- The system remains highly fragmented as regards both organization and planning as well as healthcare provision.
- Non-communicable diseases account for more than 85% of the burden of disease in Switzerland.

By identifying the factors with the greatest likelihood of enabling governments to develop integrated Longevity strategies and ecosystems to scale, and to reduce as much as possible their national gap between life expectancy and Healthy Longevity, the special analytical case study is able **to offer tangible and practical recommendations** tuned to the specifics of individual countries, providing the necessary set of tools to allow countries currently leading the international Healthy Longevity race **to maintain and improve their current standing**, and to allow countries currently lagging behind others **to reduce their Healthy Life Expectancy gap and improve their comparative global standing** to the mutual benefit of their citizens and their economies.

Perhaps not surprisingly, Switzerland was ranked well among the 50 countries analyzed, but was still surpassed by other nations, such as Singapore and Cyprus, indicating that Switzerland does indeed have a reputable international standing in terms of its levels of Healthy Longevity and Longevity-progressiveness, but that there is still room for improvement.

Some practical recommendations given by the special analytical case study on ways that Switzerland can work to maximize its National Healthy Longevity and minimize the gap between its Health-Adjusted Life Expectancy and unadjusted life expectancy include:

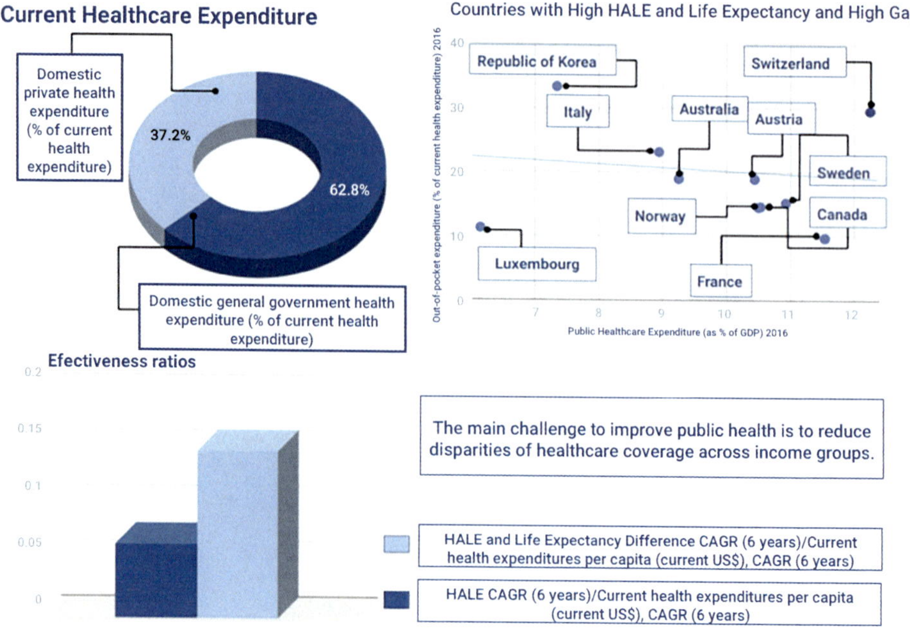

- **The greater use of medical guidelines, investments in patient safety, and the reduction of waste** by improving coordination within and between different levels of care, further improving efficiency.
- **Following trend towards greater transparency in healthcare,** extending the amount of healthcare data and rising consumer expectations of patients and the public.
- **Improving financial protection and fairness of financing.** This is becoming more important because rising premiums and OOP payments place an increasingly large financial burden on households with lower and middle incomes.
- **Enabling patient-centred care with information technology systems.** Embracement of technology in healthcare will lead to personalization and improvement of the quality of medical care through close coordination between patients, caregivers and professionals.
- **Strengthening disease prevention and health promotion with a focus on non-communicable diseases,** which remains an issue. Favourable living conditions in Switzerland, such as good housing conditions, a high-quality education system and low rates of unemployment contribute to healthy living conditions.

- **Utilising Artificial Intelligence in Preventive Medicine.** AI has great potential in terms of tackling the problem of bureaucracy and inefficient administration, relieving doctors from time-consuming administrative tasks and giving them more time to spend with their patients. By automating and improving processes, AI can benefit both patients and medical staff. By optimising patient processing planning it can reduce the waiting time and length of stay for patients, and it can also help medical staff in their day-to-day work.
- **Promoting healthy lifestyle and health education,** which could potentially have a large impact on further improving the very good health status of the population.

The Launch of the Longevity AI Consortium at King's College London, and its Expansion into Switzerland

In late 2019, Europe's first Longevity AI Consortium (LAIC) was launched at King's College London with strategic and financial support from Deep Knowledge Group and the Biogerontology Research Foundation. **AI for Longevity is an underrepresented sector in the Longevity Industry despite having more potential to increase Healthy Longevity in the short term than any other sector.**

The initial aim will be to identify novel Longevity and healthy aging biomarkers to accelerate diagnosis of age-related health decline. Then researchers will develop personalised physical, mental and financial health to better implement and promote healthy lifestyles for longevity, such as modifying patterns in sleep, nutrition, physical activity, environmental exposure and financial planning.

The Consortium will serve as the leading R&D hub and industry-academic hotspot for advanced AI-driven personalised preventive diagnostics, prognostics and therapeutics. This represents a paradigm shift from treatment to prevention and a new frontier — **from Precision Medicine to Precision Health, enabling the UK to**

The Longevity AI Consortium will work to facilitate the shift from treatment to prevention and from Preventive Medicine to real-world Precision Health.

become the first global hub for the application of AI to Longevity and Precision Health.

As part of its continuing development efforts over the next several years, the Consortium will expand to include centres in Switzerland, Israel, Singapore, United States and Japan. **The first country where the Consortium is expanding to is Switzerland.** The LAIC is developing collaborative research projects with Dynamics of Healthy Aging and the Digital Society Initiative at the University of Zurich initially funded by Deep Knowledge Ventures. The collaboration will utilize AI technologies to predict future cognitive ability of individuals using multimodal neuroimaging and risk factor data.

By mid-2020 we expect LAIC to have established several collaborative projects with several universities in Switzerland, including some funded through the KCL Longevity AI Accelerator.

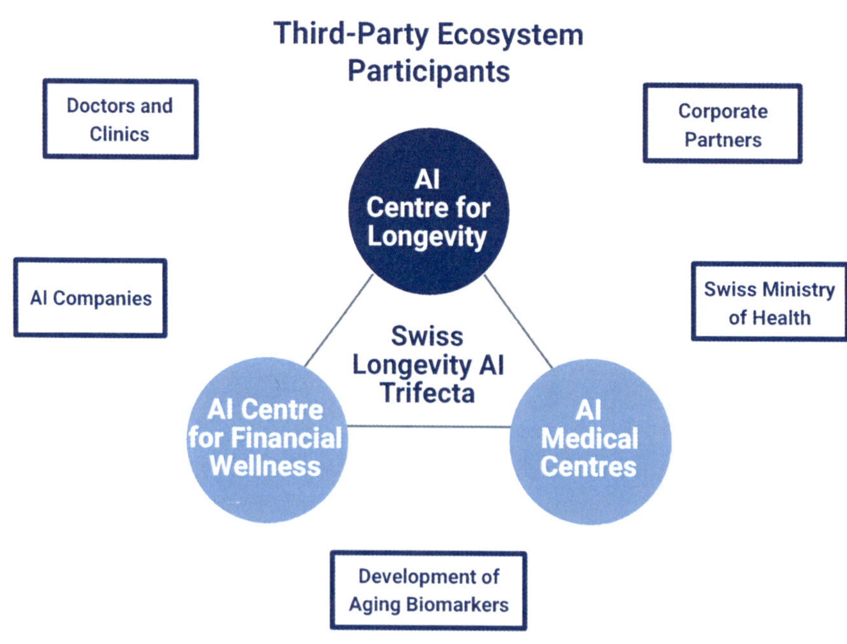

The joint R&D between Aging Research at King's and the University of Zurich forms the first phase of the global Longevity AI Consortium that will be extended to Israel, Singapore, Japan and the US.

1 Billion People in Retirement Globally - a New Multitrillion Opportunity

"The one billion retired people globally are a multi-trillion dollar opportunity for business"

Dmitry Kaminskiy interview in the Financial Times

Rising Financial Hubs for the New Financial Industry

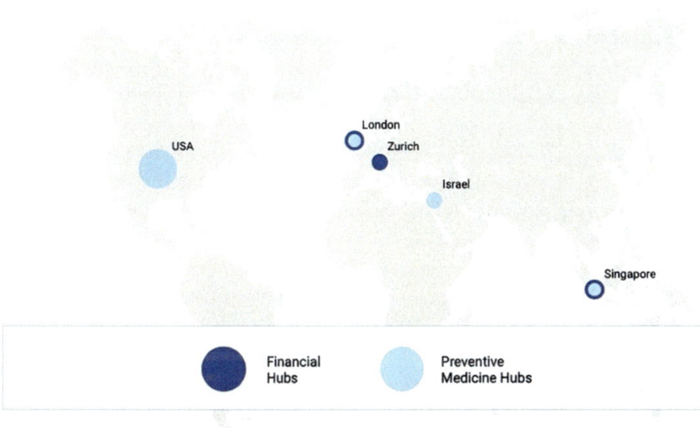

This map identifies four major global preventive medicine hubs (London, Singapore, Israel, and USA}, which for various reasons constitute hotspots of R&D and industry development in the precision and preventive medicine industry, as well as three major financial hubs, which for various other reasons represent epicentres of innovation and technological development in the finance industry.

It is notable that London and Singapore are distinguished as being hubs for both the financial industry and the preventive medicine industry, and as such have extremely strong potential to become global leaders at the emerging intersection of longevity and the advancing financial industry.

A major component of the Switzerland-based AI for Longevity Center, besides cutting-edge Longevity R&D, biomarkers of Longevity research and clinical translation, will be the concept of developing AI-enabled technologies for extended wealthspan: financial wellness over prolonged healthspans.

The planned development of AI Centers for Financial Wellness will enable financial stability over extended periods of healthy Longevity for Swiss citizens, applying advances in **WealthTech** and **AgeTech**.

Given both its status as an international BioTech epicentre and its reputation for being one of the most progressive countries in terms of financial industry and the FinTech sector, the prospects for Switzerland to lead the world in the development of its Longevity Financial Industry are extremely strong.

As a core component of its mission to develop Switzerland into a leading international Longevity Financial Industry hub, Longevity Swiss Foundation also plans on roadmapping the development of AI Centres for Financial Wellness.

Whereas the proposed AI Centres for Longevity would focus on optimizing health, this centre would focus on the **application of AI to the creation of methods and technologies to promote wellness in the elderly in all aspects of life besides health**, including:

- **Financial wellness**
- **Continuing education**
- **Happiness**
- **Psychological well-being**
- **Neuroplasticity and active social involvement**

Development of AgeTech and WealthTech in Switzerland

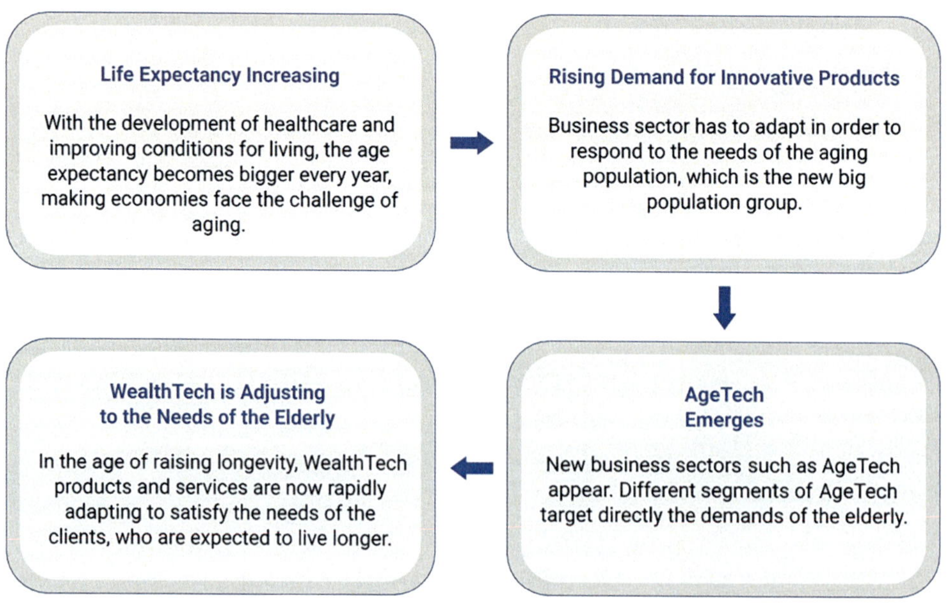

The Recent Launch of Longevity Swiss Foundation: Making Switzerland a Leader of International Longevity Policy

Another development related to Deep Knowledge Group's increasing interest in the Swiss Longevity sphere is the recent launch of the Longevity Swiss Foundation, a leading Geneva-based Longevity policy non-profit and think tank working to leverage the national strengths and potentials of Switzerland in order to turn the nation into a world-leading Longevity Hub through the **coordinated development of Longevity Politics and Governance, the Longevity BioTech Industry, Preventive Medicine, Precision Health and the emerging Longevity Financial Industry.**

Leveraging Switzerland's existing reputation as a hub for independent international policy organizations like **the World Economic Forum**, **the United Nations**, **UNESCO**, **the World Health Organization** and others, Swiss Longevity Foundation aims to turn Switzerland into the leading international hub for cross-sector and cross-nation Longevity Development projects and initiatives, including:

1. Interfacing with Swiss government agencies and representatives to build a national Swiss Longevity development strategy.
2. Supporting the nation-wide launch of Swiss AI centres for Precision Health and AI centres for Financial Wellness.
3. Dedication to turning Switzerland into an international Longevity, Preventive Medicine and Precision Health hub.

Longevity Swiss Foundation will work with the participation of proactive corporate and institutional partners to interface with relevant Swiss governmental ministries, departments, agencies and members of the Swiss Parliament to establish a **National Swiss Longevity Development Framework**, as well as a parliamentary body equivalent to the United Kingdom's All-Party Parliamentary Group on Longevity, to transform the economic burden of an aging population into a source of economic growth and increased national Healthy Longevity.

The foundation is also interested in cooperation, collaboration and initiating dialogue with a number of relevant organizations actively involved in **Swiss governance**, ranging from government ministries, agencies and departments, to relevant policy-focused NGOs and think tanks, and members of Swiss Parliament in order to establish a framework for the coordinated development of the nation's Longevity politics and governance sphere.

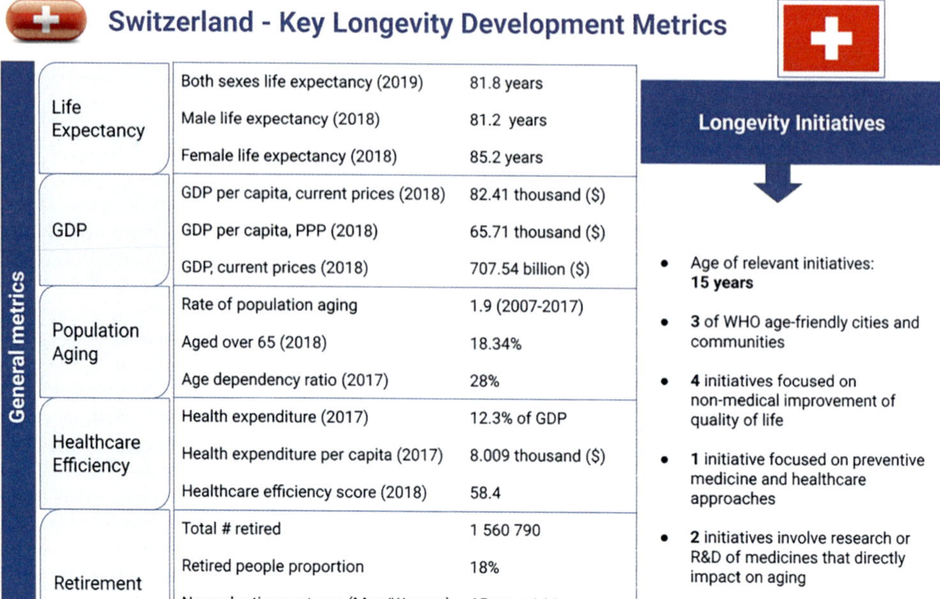

Switzerland - Key Longevity Development Metrics

General metrics

Life Expectancy	Both sexes life expectancy (2019)	81.8 years
	Male life expectancy (2018)	81.2 years
	Female life expectancy (2018)	85.2 years
GDP	GDP per capita, current prices (2018)	82.41 thousand ($)
	GDP per capita, PPP (2018)	65.71 thousand ($)
	GDP, current prices (2018)	707.54 billion ($)
Population Aging	Rate of population aging	1.9 (2007-2017)
	Aged over 65 (2018)	18.34%
	Age dependency ratio (2017)	28%
Healthcare Efficiency	Health expenditure (2017)	12.3% of GDP
	Health expenditure per capita (2017)	8.009 thousand ($)
	Healthcare efficiency score (2018)	58.4
Retirement	Total # retired	1 560 790
	Retired people proportion	18%
	Normal retirement age (Man/Woman)	65 years/ 64 years
	Early retirement age (Man/Woman)	63 years/ 61 years

Longevity Initiatives

- Age of relevant initiatives: **15 years**
- **3** of WHO age-friendly cities and communities
- **4** initiatives focused on non-medical improvement of quality of life
- **1** initiative focused on preventive medicine and healthcare approaches
- **2** initiatives involve research or R&D of medicines that directly impact on aging

In order to bootstrap its activities in the realms of Longevity policy, politics, governance and synergetic industry development, the Longevity Swiss Foundation is seeking donations from key institutional and individual sponsors that are keen to see the nation manifest its latent strengths and prospects, and become the leading Longevity nation that it has the potential to be.

Longevity Swiss Foundation plans to work with a number of key Swiss Longevity Industry participants and stakeholders to develop a framework and blueprint for a Government-led National Longevity Development Plan to increase the national Health-Adjusted Life Expectancy of all Swiss citizens.

The scope of this plan also includes financial reform to **boost Swiss GDP and reduce the economic burden of an aging population**. In order to support this sphere of activity, Swiss Longevity Foundation is keen to work alongside large Swiss financial institutions including pension funds, insurance companies, private wealth banks and asset management firms to roadmap initiatives and policy proposals capable of turning the problem of an aging population into the economic opportunity of Healthy Longevity by means of Longevity policy, politics, and scientific R&D.

Conclusions:

- Switzerland's existing strengths in BioTech and BioPharma, industry-academic collaboration, international policy, FinTech and the financial industry make it the perfectly-poised hotspot to rapidly develop the full scope of the Longevity Industry ecosystem, encompassing biomedicine, tech and finance.
- Its specific strengths in FinTech and progressive financial products, services and solutions give it stronger prospects than any other country in the world to become the global leader specifically in the area of the Longevity Financial Industry, encompassing novel financial products and services for the elderly, fully integrated AgeTech/WealthTech solutions, and sophisticated AI and data-driven platforms for maintaining wealthspan over extended periods of healthspan.
- **Deep Knowledge Group** is utilizing its many resources to help advance this agenda, and secure Switzerland's place as the Longevity Valley of the near future, by supporting the full scope of Longevity Industry developments in the nation, including the Longevity Biomedicine and Financial Industries via the activities of its Switzerland-based subsidiary, Deep Knowledge Swiss, AI for Longevity via the activities of the upcoming Swiss branch of the Longevity AI Consortium, and the domain of International Longevity Policy via the activities of the Swiss Longevity Foundation.

Chapter 11: The Longevity Leadership Role of the UK: The Emergence of Longevity-Focused Parliamentary Groups and Government Bodies (Contributor: Eric Kihlstrom)

"The UK has most of the required compounds in place to make the best possible assembly of resources to shift the nation's focus from the problem of aging to the opportunity of Healthy Longevity, and ignite the co-ordinated development of a world-leading intersectional Longevity, Advanced Biomedicine, Artificial Intelligence and Financial Industry Hub."

Eric Kihlstrom in Aging Analytics Agency release *Global Overview of Government-Led Longevity Development Initiatives: UK Well Positioned to Execute World-Leading National Longevity Development Strategy*

"Given that the Longevity Industry is one of the only sectors where there can be no competitors, but only collaborators, with each counter-parties' efforts serving to further the global good of healthier, more productive lives, our new analytical report gives specific focus on promoting a greater degree of cross-sector collaboration both within nations' own borders and between countries whose unique strengths and resources can be allied for mutually-beneficial Longevity-focused international initiatives, learning from some countries' previous mistakes, and working to implement the proven best practices of other countries to strengthen the collective Longevity-progressive efforts of all nations together."

Dmitry Kaminskiy in Aging Analytics Agency release *Global Overview of Government-Led Longevity Development Initiatives: UK Well Positioned to Execute World-Leading National Longevity Development Strategy*

"We have in the UK the biggest tech sector — FinTech, BioTech, MedTech, NanoTech, GreenTech, every kind of tech — in London, which is the biggest tech sector anywhere in Europe, with perhaps half a million people working in tech alone."

UK Prime Minister Boris Johnson, September 24th 2019, United Nations General Assembly

Aging Analytics Agency, for which I serve as Strategic Director, has examined the United Kingdom in great detail — its scientific base, its detailed industrial strategy, its economy, its financial leadership, its popular and political will to tackle its demographic challenges head on — and concluded that the country is in a unique position to spearhead the global Longevity Industry.

This requires intelligent coordination, the prospects for which will be described in the following pages.

However, the British Government must extend its existing efforts and create a framework for changing the deficit model of the "Aging Society" to an asset model around "Longevity", and develop a fully integrated National Longevity Development Plan for harnessing the "Longevity Dividend" to benefit all people in society.

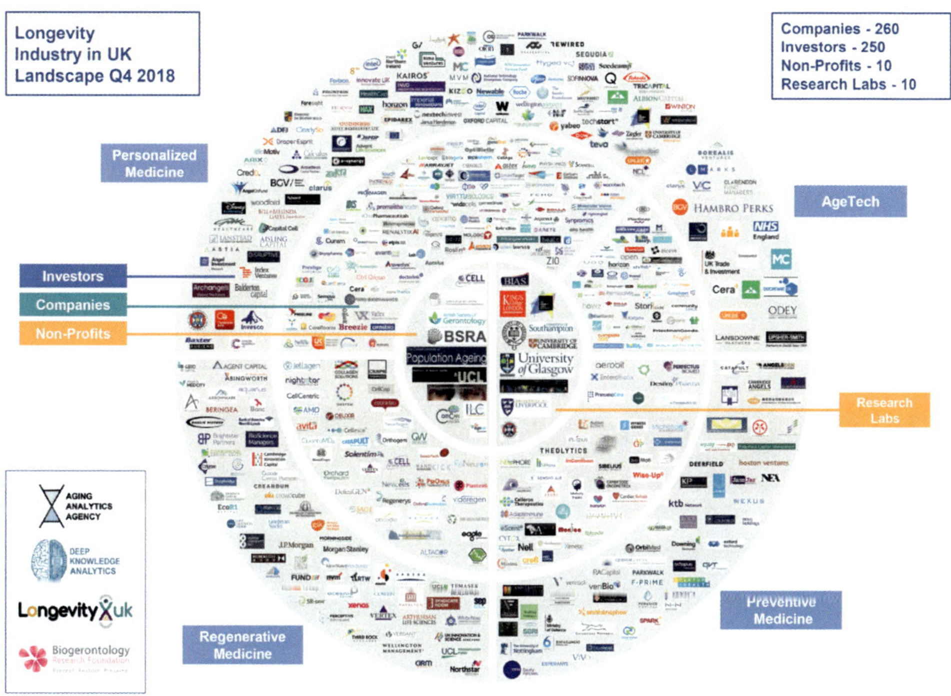

As we can see from the above graphic, the United Kingdom is an ideal ecosystem for integrating finance with biomedical technology and preparing for the challenge of an aging society.

These companies and institutions represent an amazing hub of:

- 250 UK-based Longevity investors
- 50 Longevity scientific articles authored by UK-based scientists
- 50 UK-based Longevity non-profit organizations
- 25 UK-based Longevity-focused scientific journals
- 50 Longevity books authored by UK-based authors or published by UK-based publishers
- 55 UK-based Longevity influencers
- 25 UK-based Longevity research labs and university-based R&D hubs

The United Kingdom is the first country with the global power, influence and strategic initiative necessary to spearhead this industry.

Its strengths are:

Artificial Intelligence (AI): AI is essential for ensuring that the choices made are data-driven and factual, and the UK is the world leader in AI.

- **Health Data:** For the purposes of AgeTech and Longevity, the centralized healthcare system of the NHS (National Health Service) along with the data-rich electronic healthcare records put the United Kingdom in an even stronger position.
- **International Scientific Leadership:** The UK also plays a leadership role in BioTech research and development, as well as having an excellent tradition of not only collaboration between industry and academia, but also a strong cooperation between the divergent elements in their cross-regional science and technology development hub.
- **Scientific Leadership:** This is especially apparent on the academic side with the London-Oxford-Cambridge BioTech triangle. The most relevant minds, institutions, publications, idea pools and conferences on Longevity-based BioTech happen there. It is an international and pan-global nexus for intellectual talent and thought leaders. In short, "Move over, Silicon Valley!"

We can get a better idea of the rate of progress by looking at a summary of recent developments.

Feb 2018: AgeTech & Longevity Hub Established

London's Innovation Warehouse, originally founded in 2010 as a community for digital start-ups, established an AgeTech & Longevity Hub, providing mentoring and corporate finance services to early-stage FinTech enterprises, with the stated aim of "extending healthier lifespans and maintaining quality of life for our growing, aging population".

12th March 2018: Industrial Strategy Challenge Fund Allocated

Innovate UK, the UK's technology strategy board (which reports directly to BEIS), allocated £300 million from their Industrial Strategy Challenge Fund to develop methods to help the global aging population, with opportunities for businesses and researchers to work together.

1st April 2018: United Kingdom Research and Innovation (UKRI) Created

United Kingdom Research and Innovation (UKRI) is created by the Government to direct research funding. It takes control of Innovate UK, which ceases to report to BEIS, and brings it together with the seven existing research councils of the UK under the same coordination.

16th April 2018: *AI in the UK: ready, willing and able?* - Lords Report Published with Implications For Personalised Preventive Medicine and Diagnostics

pact of Longevity on society) and Just Group (UK financial services group focusing on attractive segments of the UK retirement income market) announce shortlisted entries for the Innovating for Ageing competition from 77 submissions.

They are:

- **Behavioural Insights (social purpose company that aims to connect the elderly through a low-cost and accessible buddying platform to combat social isolation).**
- **The Chatty Cafe Scheme (a signage scheme for cafés to set aside a table so that customers can meet others and encourage strangers to talk to each other).**
- **Digital Care Planning (uses artificial intelligence-enabled voice technology to help individuals and families take an active role in planning and managing their care).**
- **Echo, Ferret Information Systems, Fuss Free Phones, MorganAsh, MyCareMatters (an online tool that collects and shares a person's non-medical needs and preferences so they can receive dignified and tailored care when they are no longer able to engage in these conversations), and others.**

5th November 2018: Longevity Forum Held in London

Longevity Forum held in London, hosted by Jim Mellon, brings together scientists, insurance and medical industry functionaries, biotechnology investors, and political figures.

Consensus is that large financial institutions are not currently well positioned for any sort of upward leap in life expectancy in old age.

19th November 2018: Government AI Strategy Debated in Parliament

The government's response to *Ready, Willing and Able?* report, which contained key suggestions for applying AI to Personalised and Preventive Medicine therapies and diagnostics, is debated in parliament and a motion is agreed to implement these.

Lord St John of Bletso, present at the NHS healthcare data parliamentary debate, also played a prominent role here.

4th February 2019: Longevity Leaders Conference

Thought leaders, KOLs, CEOs, innovators and disruptors from the world of life sciences, technology, financial services, government and the investment community convene in Aldersgate, London, to discuss how the grand challenges of Longevity can be tackled, how the significant opportunities can be seized, and how to forge partnerships and relationships to succeed in this new age.

March 2019: Launch of the All-Party Parliamentary Group (APPG) for Longevity

Launch of the All-Party Parliamentary Group for Longevity, the first APPG dedicated to aging and Longevity.

The group was created in order to address the scientific, technological and socio-economic issues relating to the aging demographic and promote living younger, healthier and longer lives.

The APPG is aiming to produce, with partners and experts, a draft National Strategy by the end of 2019 setting out what the United Kingdom needs to do to meet the goal set by the Government of five more years of healthy life expectancy by 2035 (HLE + 5) and at the same time to close the large social gap in healthy life expectancy.

Through an ambitious action plan in 2020, the APPG aims to turn the "problem" of aging into one of the most promising opportunities of the 21st century — and to secure Britain's place as a global leader in Longevity by providing access to the "Longevity Dividend" to everyone equitably in society.

November 2019: London Longevity Week

November has now been established as the month when London becomes a networking hub for the entire industry, where many of the same scientific, financial, medical and political figures attend the Master Investor Conference, where multi-millionaire and billionaire investors specialised in multiple sectors liaise strategy, and:

- Jim Mellon and Andrew Scott's Longevity Forum.
- International Longevity Policy and Governance Summit, hosted by Longevity International UK (APPG for Longevity Secretariat), held for its first year at King's College London, and where both myself and Dmitry Kaminskiy spoke alongside key policy makers and government representatives around the world.

The Current State of Longevity Policy and Governance in the United Kingdom

Reviewing these initiatives, we can see that the UK has already turned its attention to cross-sector collaboration, particularly between Artificial Intelligence and healthcare. There has also been a general recognition of the central role of technology, and financial technology in particular, in improving the lives of the elderly.

What is still missing is any explicit intention of directing these agendas toward improving Healthy Longevity as a metric in itself. If the UK government wants to optimise its existing initiatives for solving the aging population problem, it must create a veritable industry of healthy Longevity itself, which in turn requires:

- A greater focus on promoting biomedical innovations focused on extending Healthy Longevity.
- A greater focus on financial reform to neutralize economic risks posed by an aging society.
- A greater focus on combining these technologies in order to meet strategic goals. For example, it is not clear how much the UK government knows about the impact of its own biomedical initiatives on the "aging society" grand challenge.

In other words, the United Kingdom needs a fully integrated Longevity National Development Plan. This in turn requires the establishment of a governing body equivalent to the UK's recently-created Office for AI.

This is an objective of the recently established All-Party Parliamentary Group (APPG) for Longevity, and its secretariat company, Longevity International UK, for which I serve as Head of Industry Collaboration, leveraging my experience as the former Interim Director of the UK government-led £98 million Healthy Ageing Industrial Strategy Challenge Fund, in order to assist Longevity International UK and the APPG for Longevity to transform the challenge and deficit-model of aging into the opportunity and asset-model of healthy human longevity.

It should be noted that regardless of who is in residence at 10 Downing Street, the UK government, broadly speaking, is a progressive one, which would allow for the implementation of the societal will across sectors to mobilize and realize a vision of the magnitude described in this book.

> **Government action has become the final missing element in further Longevity development: the political will need to take action, marshal global resources and provide the necessary momentum to succeed in the future.**

Luckily, there are some politicians, such as West Suffolk MP Matt Hancock, who have begun to take action. In November 2018, Matt Hancock, serving as the UK Health Secretary, laid out a new path for public policy when he released a paper on behalf of the ministry called *Prevention is better than cure: Our vision to help you live well for longer*.

This was a follow-up to a speech he gave in September of that year at the NHS Innovations Expo in Manchester, in which he addressed the issue and its disruptive nature, stating that "I'm not looking for people to blame. I'm looking for people to step up and lead."

> This has led to the creation of the **All-Party Parliamentary Group (APPG) for Longevity**, under the guidance of Conservative MP from Ashford, **Damian Green**, as chair.

This committee has been formed with the express intent of identifying the opportunities in an aging population.

Due to our long history of leadership in the Longevity field and our willingness to explore novel methodologies and disruptive tech investment and research, Dmitry and I were named, along with Collider

Health CEO Tina Woods, as part of the strategic advisory board for Longevity International, the public arm of the APPG.

Tina sits as the CEO of the organization with me as head of industry collaboration, and Dmitry responsible for guiding international development. **Dmitry's views on the strategically central role of the UK mirror my own:**

"The UK is very well positioned to become an international leader of Healthy Longevity, and was ranked number 1 in this report's proprietary analysis for several reasons including its reputation as a BioTech R&D and Financial Hub, a strong history of industry-academia partnerships focusing on scientific and technological synergies, and its commitment of £300 million to its Ageing Population Industrial Grand Challenge. The nation has all the necessary compounds in place to leverage and channel its existing strengths into an efficient, Government-led campaign to make both the promotion of Healthy Longevity and the financial reform to neutralize the economic burden of an aging population a key priority of its national strategic agenda."

Eric Kihlstrom in Aging Analytics Agency release *Global Overview of Government-Led Longevity Development Initiatives: UK Well Positioned to Execute World-Leading National Longevity Development Strategy.*

The express purpose of the APPG is bringing together start-ups, industry, academic and governmental stakeholders under one umbrella to provide a unified voice, and being a coordinating vehicle for positive discourse and change to ensure the "Longevity Dividend" is accessible to everyone.

Dmitry had already spoken on this topic to the APPG for AI, the predecessor to the APPG for Longevity. He spoke on the importance of AI and how the UK was moving forward to a leadership role. In his opinion, a convergence of advances in AI and machine learning with Preventive Medicine and Longevity science could create what he coined as a "fourth industrial revolution".

The All-Party Parliamentary Group (APPG) for Longevity, established in March 2019, is the first dedicated parliamentary group to make the maintenance and extension of Healthy Longevity, innovations in Pre-

ventive Medicine and healthcare, and financial reform for pension systems its mission.

Aging Analytics Agency has participated in a number of the APPG for Longevity's advisory board meetings, and despite the fact that such meetings brought together the most progressive and forward thinking experts, specialists and thought-leaders dedicated to the mission of Healthy Longevity, because the field is so overwhelmingly complex, diverse and multidimensional, a number of potential issues and points of debate among parties arose regarding the optimal formulation of the APPG's planned Blueprint and Framework for a UK National Healthy Longevity Industrial Strategy. In light of the points raised during those meetings, some of the major key points included:

- Prioritized emphasis on international cooperation with other Longevity-progressive countries in the development of the Blueprint for a National Healthy Longevity Industrial Strategy.
- Seeking maximum synergy between the UK's Longevity strategy on the one hand and its AI Industrial Strategy on the other, given the substantial accelerative effect that AI brings to advanced biomedicine and practical applications (P4 Medicine).
- Incorporating the use of maximally-relevant metrics for measuring Healthy Longevity, and specifically for measuring the effectiveness of its initiatives by examining their cost versus the practical effect they can achieve in terms of increasing national Healthy Longevity. In response to these concerns, Aging Analytics Agency has compiled a comprehensive list of metrics and parameters with specific weight factors.
- Such metrics can serve as an excellent foundation upon which relevant governmental bodies and authorities can structure the list of metrics they will be using to judge both where they stand in terms of National Healthy Longevity currently, and to measure the real-world effectiveness of Industrial Strategies for Healthy Longevity as they move forward and develop.
- The formation and development of multiple AI Centres for Longevity in key R&D, academic, industrial and metropolitan centres throughout the UK, such as Birmingham, Liverpool and Edinburgh, modelled on the recent precedent of the multiple Centres for AI and Healthcare across the UK.

In an August 2019 report, Longevity International CEO Tina Woods lays out some of the more specific and most ambitious plans yet of APPG.

The main goal set for the year 2035 is to produce five more years of healthy life expectancy. This is to be achieved by employing **the four-tired approach:**

- **The first** is the prediction and prevention of diseases, a task that will become increasingly applicable with ongoing advances in genetic sciences, genomic technologies and other methods of diagnosis.
- **The second** is developing a more precise and specific understanding of each individual's biochemistry and genetic makeup to allow in turn for more precise diagnosis and to avoid divergent conditions with very similar symptoms.

- **The third** element, an extension of the previous two, is the advancement of pharmacogenomics and the recognition of the differences between individual patients in how they metabolise and react to medicines, based on their unique genetics.
- **The fourth and final factor** is, through the use of wearable technology and other advances, to increase real time and personalised information on patients and to give them a much greater participator role in their own diagnosis and ongoing care.

Left to right: Dmitry Kaminskiy, Andrew Scott, Geoffrey Filkin, Eric Kihlstrom, Tina Woods, Health Minister Matt Hancock, and Damien Green convene in the UK Parliament at the inaugural Advisory Board Meeting of the UK APPG for Longevity on 30th April 2019.

The idea of international cooperation and the UK's role were further expanded upon by Dmitry in a July 2019 speech to the APPG, in which he called for the establishment of embassies staffed by UK ambassadors in Longevity progressive regions.

This would allow them to liaise with and provide leadership and guidance to all stakeholders, whether they be government, researches, R&D hubs or Longevity oriented start-ups.

The United Kingdom, if it continues on the path of technological and public policy leadership, has extremely strong prospects to leverage its unique strengths, and continue to build its already-established leadership position in the specific realms of Longevity Policy and Governance, and the development of Longevity Industrial Strategies, to transform the challenge and deficit of an aging population into a massive financial, medical and socioeconomic opportunity of Healthy Longevity.

The Future of Longevity Policy and Governance in the United Kingdom

While the past decade has witnessed the emergence of a wide variety of strategies and plans focused on aging and Longevity, no truly nation-level Longevity development strategy exists anywhere in the world. Nonetheless, we can see the rudiments of one in the UK's existing initiatives, which lay a good foundation for the development of such a plan, having taken several crucial early steps.

Indeed, just a few months ago the UK Government published the green paper of its Preventive Medicine National Strategy, entitled *Advancing our health: prevention in the 2020s – consultation document.*

In practice, this indicates that the UK will be the first country to officially implement P4 (Personalised, Preventive, Precision and Participatory) Medicine into its national healthcare system. This is the newest development in a series of large steps that the UK government has made in recent years towards the development of a proactive, progressive and technology-driven national Healthy Longevity development strategy, beginning with the formation of the Ageing Industrial Grand Challenge (prioritizing the problem of aging population as one of four key national industrial development challenges for the nation) in 2017, followed by the launch of the £98 million Government-led Healthy Aging Industrial Strategy Challenge Fund in 2018, and the launch of the All-Party Parliamentary Group for Longevity in 2019.

These are some of the major factors that led to the UK being ranked as number 1 in Aging Analytics Agency's *National Longevity Development Plans: Global Overview (First Edition)* analytical report, which used quantitative metrics to rank the strength, proactivity and relevance of various nations' Longevity development projects and initiatives. This new green paper strengthens and reaffirms the conclusion made in that analytical report, on the UK's leading position as a country that prioritizes the issue of aging population and the opportunity of Healthy Longevity as key national priority items of the nation's government.

There are a number of countries (including Singapore, Switzerland, South Korea, Israel, the Netherlands, Spain and Japan) that are currently ahead of the UK in terms of the gap between life expectancy and Health-Adjusted Life Expectancy (HALE), which can be considered one of the most robust measures of Healthy Longevity. However, this fact may be due to the comparatively smaller size of these countries' populations, among other factors, which makes the implementation of national policy and preventive healthcare initiatives easier.

However, one of the foremost reasons that the UK was ranked as number 1 in Aging Analytics Agency's *National Longevity Development Plans* analytical report, despite the country's comparative large gap between life expectancy and Healthy Longevity, is that the nation is taking boldly progressive, science and technology-driven steps to launch initiatives that can rapidly decrease this gap, and not just putting forth optimistic rhetoric — actually following through on its promises with concrete and tangible actions.

Given the UK's large GDP, the proactive efforts of its government to make Healthy Longevity a major priority of its national agenda, and the many steps they have taken to prove their seriousness on this topic, it is quite likely that the UK can become the clear leader in terms of government-led National Longevity Development Plans, and can achieve very practical and tangible results in increasing their National Healthy Longevity within the next 5 years.

The UK's potential leadership position in international Longevity development planning is also the reason why Aging Analytics Agency dedicated two regional case studies in the Longevity sphere in the UK (the first edition released in 2018 with 875 pages, and the second edition published in 2019 with 1000+ pages, due to the unprecedented degree of development that occurred between the start of 2018 and the middle of 2019).

Early steps taken by the UK government include:

- The UK has recognized an "aging society" as one of its 4 core industrial grand challenges, and allocated £300 million to overcome this challenge, out of which £98 million goes towards its Healthy Aging Industrial Strategy Challenge Fund.
- This £98 million will drive the development of new products and services which will help people to live in their homes for longer, tackle loneliness, and increase independence and well-being.
- The UK has allocated £210 million towards its Data to Early Diagnosis and Precision Medicine program.
- The Centers of Excellence in Genomic Science (CEGS) program, which aims to develop novel and innovative genomic research projects using the data sets and technologies developed by the Human Genome Project.
- Innovate UK's Digitalization of Medicines Manufacturing Challenge Fund.
- In June 2018, Theresa May, the prime minister at the time, announced a commitment to harness AI to provide five more years of healthy independent lives by 2035.

Reviewing these initiatives, we can see that the UK has already turned its attention to cross-sector collaboration, particularly between Artificial Intelligence and healthcare.

There has also been a general recognition of the central role of technology, and financial technology in particular, in improving the lives of the elderly.

However, there is no explicit intention of directing these agendas toward improving Healthy Longevity as a metric in itself yet. If the UK Government wants to optimize its existing initiatives for solving the aging population problem, it must create a veritable Industry of Healthy Longevity itself, which in turn requires:

- A greater focus on promoting biomedical innovations focused on extending Healthy Longevity, and on financial reform to neutralize economic risks posed by an aging society.
- A greater focus on combining these technologies in order to meet strategic goals. For example, as already mentioned, it is not clear how much the UK government knows about the impact of its own biomedical initiatives on the aging society grand challenge.

Existing efforts must be extended to create a framework for changing the deficit model of the "Aging Society" to an asset model around "Longevity", and to be bold with a national strategy to harness the "Longevity Dividend" to benefit all people in the society. In other words, a fully integrated Longevity National Development Plan is needed. This requires intelligent coordination.

Chapter 12: California - Longevity Hype in Silicon Valley: Will Traditional Approach to BioTech Investment Lead to a Longevity Boom, Bubble or Bust? (Contributor: Kate Batz)

Key Points:

- California in general and Silicon Valley in particular are considered the **birthplace of Longevity BioTech**, home to the largest proportion of Longevity-focused companies globally, and many prominent Longevity research foundations and influencers.
- However, California's stronghold on this rapidly developing industry is gradually slipping as other nations begin to catch up in the race, with major government policy and industry-led developments and initiatives now in place from other nations like the United Kingdom, Switzerland, Singapore, Israel and others.
- Furthermore, much of what originally helped California establish its global predominance in Longevity entrepreneurship and investment has now become a source of risk: namely, Longevity Hype, and a specific focus on some particular biomedical niches that leave other sectors neglected as well as predominant reliance on the results of preclinical trials using model organisms like mice, which due to the complexity of the biology of aging, are likely to have higher failure rates than BioTech in general.
- This combination of factors, if not addressed and neutralized, has the potential of leading to a Longevity boom and bust cycle, with the overfunding of overvalued companies leading to a failure to deliver on their promises via positive clinical translation in humans, casting a shadow of doubt over the entire scope of the Longevity Industry.
- Fortunately, emerging solutions at the intersection of AI, Preventive Medicine and Precision Health offer a new paradigm to therapeutic validation that is more human-centric and more likely to lead to

clinical translation. California has the potential to neutralize these risks if it acts now, and to maintain a leading position within the Global Longevity Industry as other Longevity-progressive countries begin to scale up their efforts aimed at the industrialization of Longevity.

"Aging Analytics Agency ***has been producing landscape overviews of both the Global Longevity Industry and related regional case studies for a number of years, long before mainstream recognition of this sphere. These analytical reports were necessary to grasp the entire scope of the Longevity Industry and to gain a concrete understanding of its key players, laying the foundation for the agency's proprietary analytics and industry benchmarking.***

The choice of California for our regional case study was obvious, and it is clear that the state is one of the leading catalysts of the Global Longevity Industry and a literal nuclear reactor for advancing Longevity science, driven by progress in AI, precision and preventive biomedicine and geroscience. California will undoubtedly continue to play a prominent role in this trajectory, helping the industry grow into the multitrillion dollar giant it is destined to become."

Kate Batz in *California: a Key Player in the Global Longevity Scene*

"I have always been extremely pissed off about the idea of death. Your whole life you work, you try to improve yourself, save money, invest wisely, and then all of a sudden — poof. It's over."

Former California Governor Arnold Schwarzenegger

As a long-time California resident, ever since I joined the ranks of **Deep Knowledge Group**, **Aging Analytics Agency** and more recently **Longevity.Capital** after meeting Dmitry Kaminskiy, I have been witness to both the specific strengths, as well as the specific weaknesses of the Longevity Industry in California generally, and in Silicon Valley in particular.

Compared to the rest of the United States, Californians take a progressive stance on Longevity — the state ranked second for life expectancy at birth and third for healthy life expectancy.

This is in stark contrast to the United States as a whole, which has one of the largest gaps between life expectancy and Health-Adjusted Life Expectancy (HALE), on the order of 10 years, compared to just 6.7 years in Singapore.

However, on a global scale, California is lagging behind other leading world regions with respect to these parameters, especially considering the amount of corresponding health expenditures.

While the government of California has been among the pioneers for addressing the societal implications of aging for decades, the state is far from being immune from the associated challenges.

The Golden State is following the global aging trend and is becoming the Graying State – its vast Baby Boomer cohort started entering retirement and by 2030, older Californians are projected to outnumber children for the first time in history.

This so-called Silver Tsunami brings about a number of significant challenges such as higher overall healthcare costs, retirement and long-term care crises as well as poverty among seniors. However, increased Longevity also introduces a multitude of possibilities – **people in the 50+ age group have the largest spending power, many are willing to work past the traditional retirement age and most can infuse societies with transformative social benefits as caregivers and volunteers while themselves benefitting from such purposeful activities.**

California is home to a plethora of top-ranked universities and research institutions which lead the nation in biomedical research grants from NIH (at 15.1% or US$3.9 billion), further driving innovation. Academic excellence drives the state's vibrant life sciences ecosystem, which boasts four mega-clusters in San Francisco Bay Area, Los Angeles, Orange and San Diego counties.

It is the world's fifth-largest economy and, at almost 40 million people, is the most populous U.S. state.

For decades, California has been implementing a thoughtful public policy aimed at supporting the life sciences industry through tax incentives, encouraging more investment, as well as via state-sponsored initiatives promoting the use of advanced computing and technology to better understand and treat diseases.

Due to the state's healthy business climate as well as a strong success record of its life sciences companies, California has long been a magnet for BioTech investment – it consistently leads the nation in attracting venture capital funding.

California boasts 10 institutions in the Shanghai's Index of the world's 100 top universities. In 2016, the state graduated more than 4,900 science and engineering PhDs, by far the most in the United States.

Academic excellence drives the California's vibrant life sciences ecosystem, which offers many advantages, such as:

- The mentioned four life sciences mega-clusters: the Bay Area, Los Angeles, Orange and San Diego counties.
- State's research institutions receiving the most NIH funds in the nation (15.1%), further driving innovation.
- California's world-class research generates new companies, health technologies and improved care.

California's thoughtful public policy plays a critical role, supporting a healthy business climate as well as improved access to diagnostic and therapeutic technologies.

The life sciences industry is also an economic engine — **in 2017, the sector's revenue exceeded US$178 billion,** generated US$18.8 billion in federal and local taxes and is second only to computer technologies in employment among high-tech industries.

As California companies have a strong record of translating science into products that help patients, the state has long been a magnet for investment:

US$7.6 billion were attracted by local life sciences companies in venture capital funding in 2018, leading the nation once again.

At **US$3.9 billion** California also attracted the most VC funding in US in the digital health sector.

California plays an important role on the global Longevity scene:

- Its sheer economic power;
- World-renowned academic and research institutions producing top talent and fostering innovation;
- Thoughtful public policy supporting the state's vibrant life sciences ecosystem as well as dynamic venture capital scene help secure such position.

The state views healthy Longevity as a priority, as evidenced by a multitude of government-sponsored initiatives aimed at understanding disease and improving the health of its residents as well as by a network of agencies tasked with addressing the needs of the elderly.

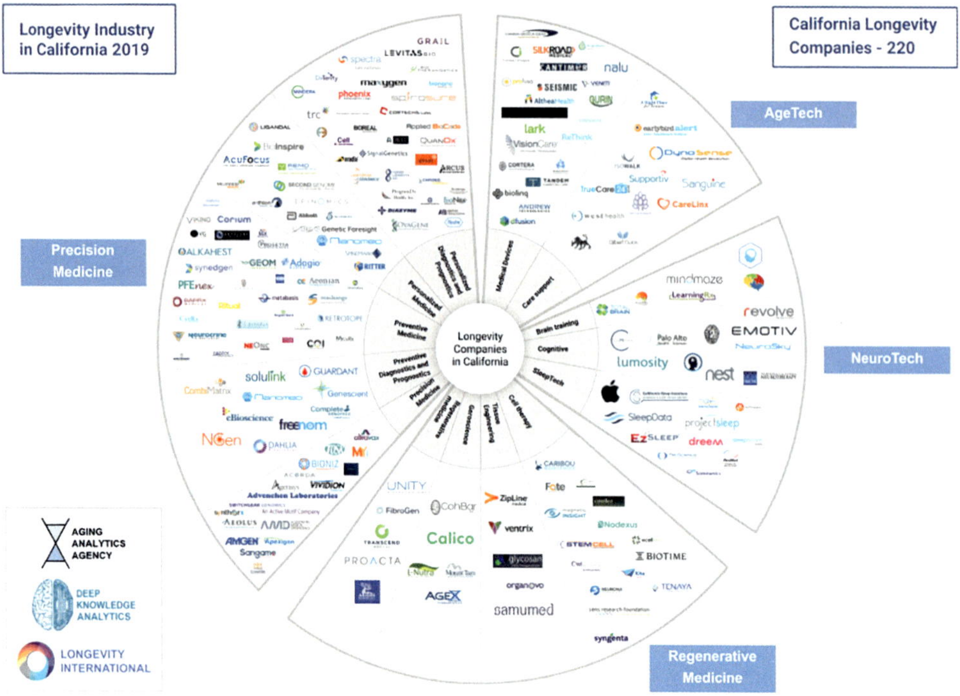

Longevity Industry in California 2019

California Longevity Companies - 220

AgeTech

Precision Medicine

NeuroTech

Regenerative Medicine

Longevity Companies in California

Medical Devices

Care support

Brain training

Cognitive

SleepTech

Cell therapy

Tissue Engineering

Gerosciences

Regenerative Medicine

Precision Medicine

Preventive Diagnostics and Prognostics

Preventive Medicine

Personalized Medicine

Personalized Diagnostics and Prognostics

AGING ANALYTICS AGENCY

DEEP KNOWLEDGE ANALYTICS

LONGEVITY INTERNATIONAL

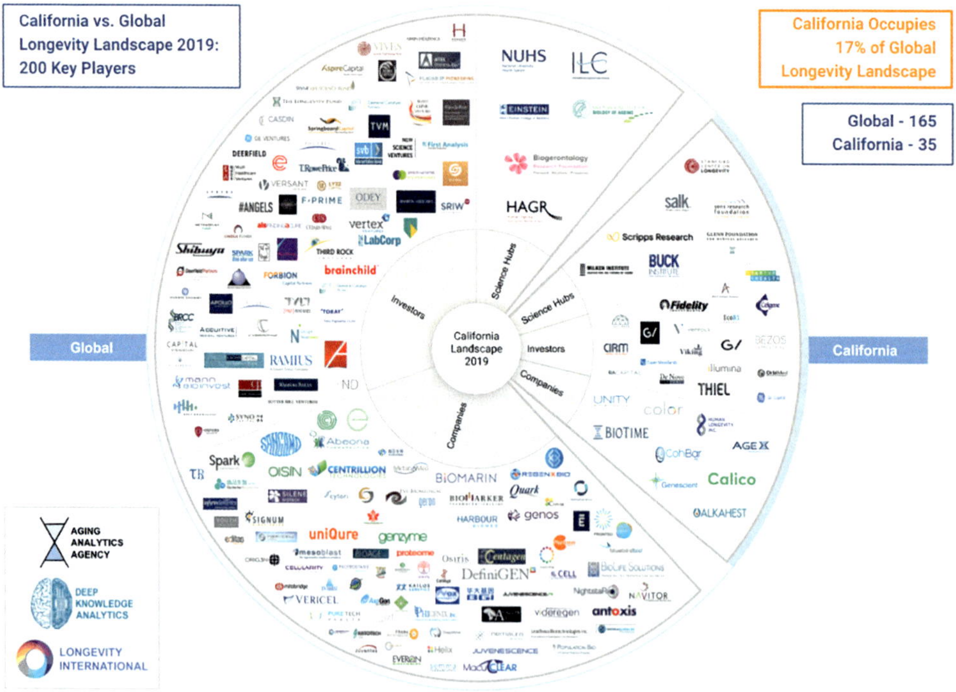

California vs. Global Longevity Landscape 2019: 200 Key Players

California Occupies 17% of Global Longevity Landscape

Global - 165
California - 35

Global

California

California Landscape 2019

Science Hubs

Investors

Companies

AGING ANALYTICS AGENCY

DEEP KNOWLEDGE ANALYTICS

LONGEVITY INTERNATIONAL

California's State Unit on Aging (SUA) is the California Department of Aging, which submits a State Plan to the federal Administration on Aging at least every 4 years. The current plan is perhaps strategically advanced in the USA, and has a number of key goals and strategies for seniors and their caregivers. In February 2019, the State introduced legislation to develop a Master Plan on Aging. Senate Bill 228 sets out the following preliminary goals:

- **Expand access to coordinated, integrated systems of care**
- **Strengthen access to long-term services and supports**
- **Prepare families to plan and pay for long-term services and supports**
- **Support California's family caregivers**
- **Increase access to oral healthcare**
- **Develop affordable housing options**
- **Enhance access to transportation**
- **Develop a culturally-competent paraprofessional and professional workforce**
- **Prevent exploitation and abuse (financial or physical) of older adults**
- **Streamline state administrative structures to improve service delivery**

This shift from a routine state plan on aging to a "master plan" suggests a glimmer of government recognition of the need for ever more integrated solutions. Moreover, California is home to the transhumanist movement, the Longevity community's biggest group of supporters.

We hope therefore that the California government will be amenable to popular pressure to develop further solutions that take account of its scientific and technological strengths in its master planning.

The Current State of the Longevity Industry in California

In 2019, **Deep Knowledge Group**'s Longevity-focused analytical subsidiary Aging Analytics Agency released a 1130-page analytical report titled ***Longevity Industry in California: Landscape Overview 2019*** which delivered a comprehensive overview of the history, present state and near-future trajectory of the Longevity Industry in California, profiling:

The choice of California as the subject of Aging Analytics Agency's regional Longevity Industry report series is justified for a number of reasons.

California plays one of the key roles on the global Longevity scene — its sheer economic power, population demographics, world-famous academic and research institutions producing top talent and fostering innovation, thoughtful public policy supporting the state's vibrant life sciences ecosystem as well as dynamic venture capital scene help secure such a position.

As stated before, compared to the rest of the United States, Californians take a progressive stance on Longevity — the state ranked second for life expectancy at birth and third for healthy life expectancy. However, on a global scale, California is lagging behind other leading world regions with respect to these parameters, especially considering the amount of corresponding health expenditures.

While the government of California has been among the pioneers for addressing the societal implications of aging for decades, the state is far from being immune from the associated challenges.

Increased Longevity also introduces a multitude of possibilities

- people in the 50 plus age group have the largest spending power;
- many are willing to work past the traditional retirement age;
- most can infuse societies with transformative social benefits as caregivers and volunteers while themselves benefitting from such purposeful activities

Silicon Valley, Longevity Hype and the Future of Longevity Investments

While most people consider the Longevity Industry to be of a much more limited scope, consisting of core geroscience therapies at the forefront of advanced biomedicine, Deep Knowledge Ventures Group has been working for the past 5+ years to landscape and understand the global multifaceted Longevity Industry, through the work of its analytical subsidiary Aging Analytics Agency, which has gained such an understanding through tens of thousands of pages worth of public and proprietary Longevity Industry analytical reports, including its 2019 **Longevity Industry in California Landscape Overview 2019**.

The perception of the Longevity Industry, in both its scope and its main trends, in the USA in general and in Silicon Valley in particular, is different than in other places, including the UK and Switzerland.

Here in California, it is most often conflated with biomedical moonshots — very advanced biomedicine not yet on the stage of human clinical trials — and this is an angle that severely underestimates technologies which we consider to be within the scope of the Longevity Industry, which are very actionable and closer to market readiness.

Conclusions:

- While California in general and Silicon Valley in particular are in many ways the birthplace of Longevity industrialization, and still to this day home to a larger proportion of core geroscience-focused companies than any other region, it is beginning to lose its overwhelming regional dominance due to the rapid advance of Longevity Industry developments, diversification and growth in other Longevity-progressive regions including the UK, Switzerland, Israel, Singapore and others.
- Silicon Valley's focus on some specific, narrow niches within the biomedical sector of the Longevity Industry, while generally positive, leaves other sectors (such as AgeTech, Longevity WealthTech and FinTech, and others) vastly underrepresented, and puts the region at risk by not exhibiting enough sector-based diversification.
- Moreover, the majority of leading Longevity investors are still operating under the paradigm and model of therapeutic validation

(and, by extension, company valuation) that worked in the broader BioTech and BioPharma industries, leading to enormous company valuations following successful preclinical trials in model organisms such as mice.

- However, due to the complexities of the biology of aging and the high degree of science, technology and sector-intersectionality in the Longevity Industry, failures are likely to happen: much higher clinical trial failure rates, and ultimately a failure for many companies to provide real ROIs proportional to their valuations.
- If this trend continues, it could lead to general pessimism about the Longevity Industry among investors, and harm the prospects of the entire Longevity Industry globally, including non-biomedical sectors, by association.
- There is, however, still time to neutralize these risks by embracing new, more sophisticated approaches to investment analytics, due diligence, and company valuation, equal to the complexity, intersectionality and multidimensionality as the Longevity Industry itself.
- This is one of the foremost objectives of our new Longevity-focused hybrid investment fund, **Longevity.Capital** — a relevant, modern strategy for Longevity investment de-risking and diversification by investing across the entire scope of the Longevity Industry (biomedicine, tech, finance) using sophisticated, multidimensional analytical frameworks and market intelligence of Aging Analytics Agency.
- In a similar vein, there is also still time to embrace more sophisticated and more human-centric approaches to therapeutic validation, less likely to lead to enormous clinical trial failure rates, which is a subject that will be explored in further detail in the fourth part of this book.

Chapter 13: The Future of Longevity Governance: How Longevity Will Become a Major Priority Item for the National Agendas of Progressive Countries by 2025

In the next few years, several technologically advanced small smart states will emerge as global competitors in the development of integrated Longevity Industry ecosystems. Some will focus on specific sectors.

Others will seek to create fully integrated hubs encompassing the entire scope of the industry. The potential of governments to bring this about is not to be underestimated. A parallel can be drawn with what the Swiss have done in embracing the crypto economy.

The previously underdeveloped Zug canton in Switzerland has, after a set of legislative initiatives and some government coordination, quickly become known worldwide as the **"Crypto Valley"**. All that was required was for the cantonal authorities to foster a legislative environment (combined with some international promotional efforts) that would incentivize relevant expertise to relocate there and set up business.

In other words, the government created conditions which attract a self-selecting population of crypto entrepreneurs. Some countries are now mimicking this procedure, selling their citizenship to foreigners who are present and working in those countries for a certain period, thereby utilizing the same technique of selectively attracting human expertise that was used by Singapore in the creation of its technological megahub.

We expect, five years from now, to see a "new normal" of small technocratic nations selling their citizenship selectively to people committed to advancing Longevity-related technologies, in exchange for access to some of the most sophisticated and advanced **healthcare, life insurance, MedTech, AgeTech and WealthTech ecosystems** available.

These same countries will undertake projects such as smart towns and cities that integrate all subsectors of the multifaceted Longevity Industry to create an optimized ecosystem for the maintenance of health and wealth.

The development of these **Longevity megahubs** would incentivize the elderly to relocate in exchange for access to the best forms of AgeTech, WealthTech and other technologies, products, services and social policies capable of enabling the highest possible quality of life, social activity, mental wellness and overall functionality. Meanwhile, the middle-aged would be incentivized to relocate in exchange for access to the highest-quality MedTech, HealthTech and P4 medicine services, and the most sophisticated life and health insurance systems that reward their clients for the maintenance of an optimal state of health.

Among this assortment of initiatives, there will be:

age-friendly cities ***age-friendly towns***

This term refers to a formal commitment by city authorities to attaining a particular existing World Health Organization urban planning commitment for towns supportive of aging populations. Towns and cities whose municipal authorities have made this commitment currently amount to little more than high-end retirement communities. But a truly age-friendly city, and more importantly, a truly "Longevity-friendly city", would combine all the facets of the Longevity Industry discussed previously, from AgeTech to P4 medicine, WealthTech, advanced InsurTech as well as societal infrastructures for maintaining an optimal state of wealth and health in the age of Healthy Longevity, empowering the elderly and the middle-aged physically, mentally and financially.

It is with this vision in mind — **a globally coordinated Longevity Industry led by Longevity-progressive countries, small versatile nations each intensively developing its own infrastructure for Longevity BioTech hubs, Longevity finance hubs, Precision Medicine ecosystems, AgeTech towns and age-friendly cities** — that Longevity.Capital and Aging Analytics Agency are advising the following:

To government bodies and authorities, we are saying that when Healthy Longevity itself becomes a short-term issue with near-term consequences, it will become an electoral talking point. Governments that promise it could appeal to their citizenries' desire for healthier and happier lives, and before long it will be in the interests of other governments who wish to be reelected to utilise current progress in Longevity as rapidly as possible for the benefit of all.

To industry players, scientists, companies, investors and stakeholders we say they should consider already being present in those countries poised to become Longevity MegaHubs, in advance, in order to be ahead of the curve.

PART III

The Longevity Financial Industry

Novel Financial Instruments and Health as New Wealth

- **The Increasing Role of Longevity in Global Finance**
- **Formulating the Framework for the Longevity Financial Industry and Novel Financial System**
- **Longevity FinTech**
- **Longevity Embraced by the World's Biggest Financial Corporations: Investment Banks, Insurance Companies, Asset Management Firms**
- **New Financial Instruments and Derivatives: New Business Models and Novel Financial Instruments Tied to the Rising Longevity Industry**
- **Integrated AgeTech, WealthTech, FinTech Solutions**
- **AI, Data Science and Mathematical Technologies Driving the Evolution of the Longevity Financial Industry**
- **FinTech 2.0 and the Rise of Longevity Banks**
- **Projected Evolution of the the Longevity Financial Industry**
- **Longevity Stock Exchanges, Financial Marketplaces and AgeTech-Longevity Banks**

Chapter 14: The Longevity Financial Industry and Novel Financial System

"There have been many well-documented efforts to predict the future of biomedical progress, but is there any good reason why the same logic can't be applied for the financial sphere? Many thought leaders have made reasoned predictions on how some fragments of the collapsing financial system will evolve, adapt and adjust to the increasing life expectancy. We should work to assemble the framework of scenarios regarding the evolution of the financial system in the next 10 years, and create the pathways that will be able to neutralize collapses and accelerate the dynamic of progress of the Longevity Industry, with a focus on extension of the healthy period of life for the betterment of all of humanity."

Dmitry Kaminskiy, in *Longevity Industry Landscape Overview Volume II: The Business of Longevity* (Aging Analytics Agency, 2018)

"Today, banks have a small number of clients who are over 100 and they are outliers. In the next decade that demographic will increase dramatically. In the next few years, age-friendly FinTech companies and Longevity Banks will develop new financial products designed for clients who are planning to live extra-long lives and want to remain high functioning and financially stable throughout."

Margaretta Colangelo in *AI Will Give Rise to FinTech 2.0 and Longevity Banks* (Forbes, January 2020)

In Part I we explained why the Longevity Industry will be the biggest and most complex industry in human history, that it is much more than just geroscience, and that it concists of multiple sectors — Aging Biomedicine, P4 Medicine, AgeTech, and Novel Financial System.

The increasing interconnection and synergy between these domains will eventually make Longevity itself (currently a liability) into an asset — **a new asset class itself**, in fact. Aging should be considered not only one of the most acute problems of our time but also one of the most promising opportunities. Financial institutions such as investment banks, pension funds, insurance companies can either sink or swim when hit by the oncoming Silver Tsunami.

Whether they succeed at riding the wave or drown under it will depend not only on their willingness to deploy new business models adapted to the aging population and the emerging industries of AgeTech, WealthTech and Longevity Finance but also on the quality of Longevity analytics that they use to formulate such business models.

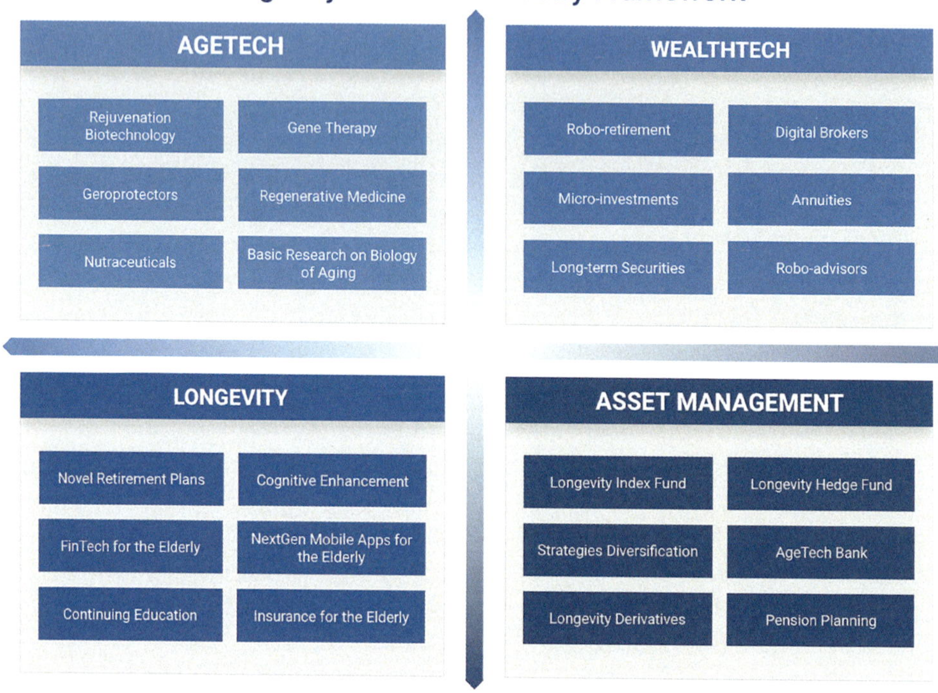

The Increasing Role of Longevity in Global Finance

As people are being rescued from death, and to some extent from disease, but not from general infirmity, their period of being economically unproductive is increasing.

The relevance of this to finance has already been well recognised among the international financial community. Each year an increasing number of forums and conferences are held on the topic of Longevity in finance, and renowned and respected brands such as The Economist and the Financial Times now regularly host conferences and panel discussions on the subject of aging and the business of Longevity.

Also, the biggest investment and private wealth banks are issuing analytical reports for their clients on this topic.

Credit Suisse featured Health and Aging as one of the four main themes in their 2018 Global MegaTrends Conference

Julius Baer held a major forum on the topic of "Investing in Longevity" featuring a keynote presentation by Aging Analytics Agency Co-Founder Dmitry Kaminskiy

UBS featured "Living to 150" as one of the six major topics in their 2018 Healthcare Summit, featuring a keynote presentation by prominent Longevity entrepreneur Alex Zhavoronkov of Insilico Medicine.

UBS also issued a report on the "largest survey of wealth investors in the world to date", concluding: "Don't let skepticism about living to 100 keep you from planning for it. Life expectancies are rising, and it's a real possibility. In fact globally, 9 in 10 investors are already adjusting how they are planning for their life and their legacy."

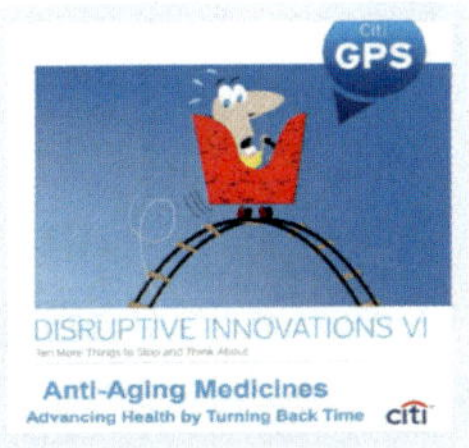

CitiBank released a landmark report detailing the rise of the Longevity Industry, highlighting rapidly rising sectors being driven by disruptive scientific innovation.

Frost and Sullivan also released two prominent reports on the emerging Longevity Industry, and in 2018 created the "Award for Innovation in Artificial Intelligence for Aging Research and Drug Development".

The global spending power of those aged 60 and over will reach $15 trillion annually by 2020.

The one billion retired people globally are a multi-trillion dollar opportunity for business.

Dmitry Kaminskiy interview in the Financial Times

Comparison of Health-Adjusted Life Expectancy with Life Expectancy of developed countries in 2016

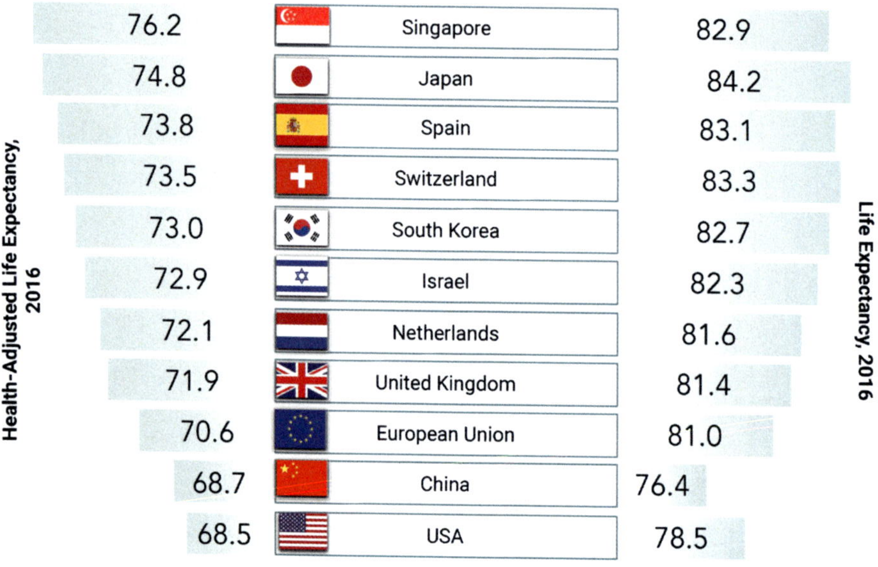

Sources: *Government Longevity National Development Plans Global Overview 2019, GHO Life expectancy and HALE*

The Gap between life expectancy and Health-Adjusted Life Expectancy (HALE) varies widely among developed countries, and to some extent a Gap could be seen between the nations which have and those who have not made efforts to embrace the paradigm shift from treatment to Precision Health in response to the Silver Tsunami.

Some countries, upon reaching this inflection point, have taken financial initiatives, while some others have stagnated. Japan, for example, experienced an economic boom 50 years ago that nearly allowed it to exceed the USA in GDP while its life expectancy nearly overtook the USA, although without an equal increase in its citizens' healthspan. This gap had an initial negative impact on Japan's national economy, which has been stagnating for the past 20 years as a result. Now, however, Japan's government is making great efforts in financial engineering to account for this gap.

It should be noted however that they have only succeeded in delaying the collapse of their economy, not fixing the fundamental cause behind it. Japan and its major financial institutions are motivated more than any other nation today in adopting a combination of advancements in biomedicine and advancements in the financial sphere to synergistically avoid stagnation and collapse in the face of this big gap.

However, there are alternative positive scenarios available, which are more likely to be explored by the most progressive, technocracy-driven nations and financial institutions. There are two main scenarios, described in the graph below, of how the **collision of two megatrends — Advancing Biomedicine and the Silver Tsunami** — is going to develop:

Country Benchmarking Based on Levels of National Healthy Longevity

A range of **novel financial institutions** that could ride this rising tide and bring about a positive scenario are expected to appear and develop: Longevity-focused venture funds, Longevity-AgeTech banks, Longevity index funds and hedge funds, and even a specialized stock exchange for Longevity-focused companies and financial products.

Above it is shown the Longevity financial institutions of the future, presented in chronological order of their likely emergence. Furthermore, the mentioned trends will influence the development of the AgeTech and WealthTech industries.

Healthspan Meets Wealthspan: The Integration of AgeTech with WealthTech

Increases in life expectancy and the encroachment of the Silver Tsunami have resulted in the emergence of AgeTech and WealthTech, technologies targeting people expecting to live 100 years or more. These three industries are expanding in a synergistic manner. Increased life expectancy creates demand for and investment in AgeTech, AgeTech creates healthy functioning centenarians, and healthy functioning centenarians enable WealthTech, which supports greater healthy Longevity. This makes their ongoing emergence and growth almost inevitable.

Development of AgeTech and WealthTech

Life Expectancy Increases

With the development of healthcare and improving conditions for living, the age expectancy becomes bigger every year, making economies face the challenge of aging.

Rising Demand for Innovative Products

The business sector has to adapt in order to respond to the needs of the aging population, which is the new big population group.

AgeTech Emerges

New business sectors, such as AgeTech, will appear. Different segments of AgeTech will target directly the demands of the elderly.

WealthTech Adjusts to the Needs of the Elderly

In the age of rising Longevity, WealthTech products and services will now rapidly adapt to satisfy the needs of the clients, who are expected to live longer.

Source: *Advancing Financial Industry: Longevity / AgeTech / WealthTech Volume II*

AgeTech, previously introduced, among many other things, covers an emerging new trend of smart homes for elderly. This is connected to the fact that some fraction of the elderly prefer staying at home for most of the time and require special care, which can be provided using AI products and services.

Meanwhile, the **WealthTech** industry comprises any product or service (again, almost invariably IT-based) that either simplifies or enhances the creation and maintenance of Wealth – from savings to investment – for all ages of society.

The term covers the new generation of financial technology companies that create digital solutions to transform the investment and asset management industry. New companies are arriving on the scene offering advice based on Artificial Intelligence and Big Data.

These include:

Robo-advisors: automated services that use machine-learning algorithms to provide users with advice based on the most profitable investment options, yield targets, user's risk aversion profile and other variables.

- *Robo-retirement: another version of robo-advisors that is especially popular in the United States. Companies in this category specialize in managing retirement savings.*
- *Digital brokers: online platforms and software tools that put stock market information and the possibility of investing within anyone's reach.*
- *Financial products designed for investors expecting to live 100 years and beyond.*

The WealthTech industry is currently anticipating the emergence of new wealth management technologies. With the use of such technologies, and by adapting existing products and services, financial service innovators have an opportunity to greatly enhance the financial lives of the people who are over 60.

The depth and diversity of this group create an incredible opportunity to implement innovations on their behalf and address their financial health challenges head on. As AgeTech and WealthTech converge, the financial industry is likely to see the emergence of AgeTech-Longevity banks.

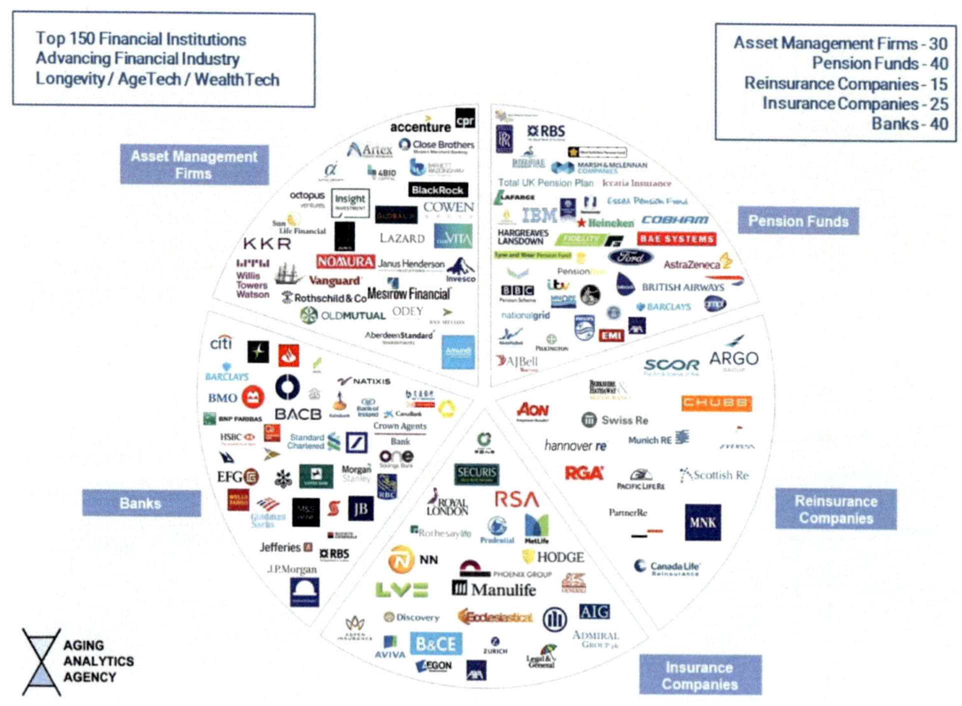

The sectors and subsectors of Longevity Financial Industry — what to expect from AgeTech and WealthTech in the next few years:

- Rising life expectancy will create major opportunities for the financial sector, because the elderly as a special social group have common characteristics and common needs to satisfy.
- All in all we can expect to see the WealthTech industry becoming more old-age-oriented, offering an increasing number of products and services to those aged over 60.
- Over the next few years, it is likely that AgeTech and WealthTech will come to be regarded as complementary functions within a single product or service.
- The AgeTech segment's potential is forecasted to reach US$2.7 trillion by 2025, showing a 21% annual market growth.
- This explosive growth will be accompanied by a proliferation of products that concentrate on satisfying the demand for different individual types of savings, specialized retirement plans and financial advising of the elderly.

Novel Longevity Financial Instrument and Specialized Stock Exchange

Specialized stock exchanges are nothing new. One example is LME (London Metal Stock Exchange), which was founded in 1877 and is the futures exchange with the world's largest market in options and futures contracts on base and other metals. NASDAQ fits that profile as well; it was created as a stock exchange for IT and Tech companies and is currently the home of tech-oriented stocks.

The most relevant example is the recently launched Silicon Valley Stock Exchange backed by Marc Andreessen, and other tech heavyweights, that will give high-growth technology companies more options to list their shares outside of the traditional New York exchanges.

Specialized stock exchanges typically form when an industry grows by a sufficient amount, and with the Longevity Industry in its present state of maturation, a Longevity stock exchange now appears to be inevitable.

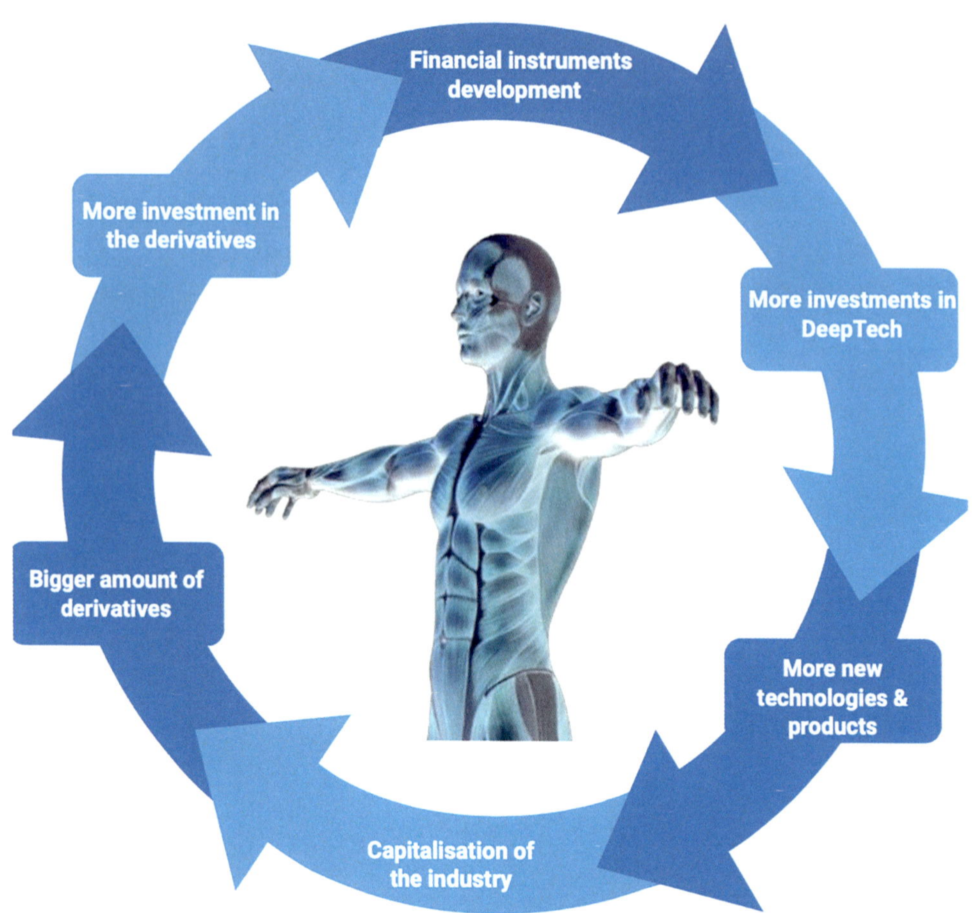

A Longevity Stock Exchange provides increased liquidity, which in turn would enables greater flexibility and a greater leverage for the further growth of the companies listed on the exchange, and as such, greater opportunities for the advancement of the Longevity Industry as a whole globally.

Setting up a Longevity Stock Exchange would require the public listing of at least 100 Longevity-focused companies to create good enough diversity and potential volume for trading.

Thereafter, the more advances there are in Longevity, the more even the most conservative investors will want to invest. By that point they will have been well advised that Longevity is an industry like no other. It is by such means that increased global Longevity will be transformed from a threat into an opportunity.

Longevity Offers Opportunities Only to Those Who Can Adapt

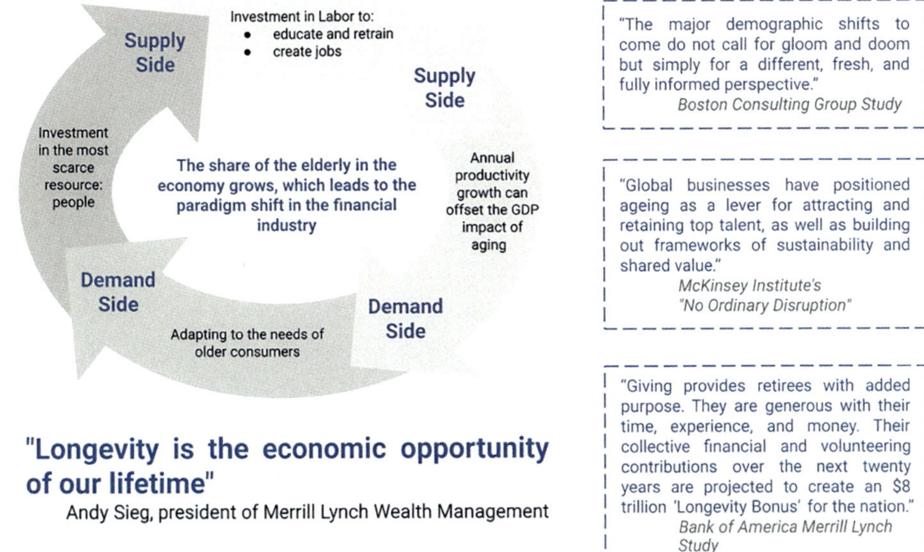

Sources | Global Ageing Report | World Economic Forum | Finances in Retirement

Self-perpetuating cycle of Longevity Finance

As the share of the elderly in the economy grows, this leads to a self-sustaining cycle of growth in the financial industry whereby the effect of aging on GDP is repeatedly offset and the resulting wealth is repeatedly reinvested into technologically reinvigorated human capital.

The greater the progress in achieving Healthy Longevity, the more the owners of wealth will want to invest in the labour force, and as it is endowed with greater healthspans, it will bring further growth and even greater healthspans, and so on.

During the past several years, a quite clear disproportion has emerged between various DeepTech sectors, in particular between the Longevity start-ups on the one hand, and the entire business model of venture capital funds on the other. There have also been big gaps and disruptions in the global financial system.

There is a highly irrelevant big gap between progress in science and technology, and the outdated bureaucracy, in which most financial institutions remain mired, as though both exist in parallel universes.

This is happening for multiple reasons:

- At one end, DeepTech start-ups (including Longevity start-ups) have been suffering from a lack of access to relevant levels of seed investment.
- Although venture funds are by definition supposed to prioritize investments into the most disruptive technologies and start-ups, in reality, most of them prefer to specifically avoid DeepTech sectors, or to enter investment rounds at much later stages.
- As a consequence, the start-ups are forced to deal with angel investors. This creates a growth gap phenomenon known as the "Death Valley": 99% of DeepTech start-ups do not survive the stage of growth between seed financing and the beginning of revenue generation or even "A" rounds.

Meanwhile, at the other end, there is an extreme abundance of significant assets being held and preserved in bank accounts or in comparatively stable derivatives on a scale of tens of trillions. For instance, there is a tremendous volume of money on the scale of at least €1 trillion currently being stored in Swiss bank accounts with negative interest rates, which is an illogical phenomenon of a modern financial world itself.

Yet the owners of these financial assets would nonetheless prefer to avoid investing them into venture funds, who are equally reluctant to invest into Longevity start-ups.

Thus, the major source of these disproportions comes down to the issue of illiquidity.

There are many thousands of HealthTech start-ups and hundreds of Longevity start-ups in the UK, EU, USA and Asia-Pacific region and 99% of them are not publicly traded, which means that they are limited to seeking funding from angel investors and venture investors, which represents a very small fraction of the available global wealth.

This situation creates an extreme funding deficit and a major illiquidity problem.

This is a problem facing almost all DeepTech sectors, but the negative repercussions are particularly bad for the Longevity Industry, as it leads on the individual level to reduced quality of life and unnecessary deaths, and threatens to inflict crippling economic effects on national healthcare systems, pension and social security systems, and economies.

Therefore, an extreme abundance of financial assets ends up preserved rather than invested.

> In many cases, angel and venture investors are operating as sharks, exploiting this gross illiquidity for their own financial advantage, to the detriment of Longevity and other DeepTech start-ups.

There are enormous amounts of financial assets being conserved within the umbrella of family offices (and we can estimate that there are around 5,000 of these) and hundreds of very conservative financial institutions, which hoard this capital simply due to a lack of safe, stably growing and predictable financial derivatives into which to invest. There is no relevant methodology to assess the amount of such assets, as they tend to keep this a secret. But this is at least several tens of trillions of dollars.

At the same time, many owners of these vast sums of wealth are nonetheless personally interested in Longevity, both as a prospective market with the capacity for unprecedented growth, and as a mean to their own personal life extension.

Even the most conservative investors, and the owners of the largest financial assets, now very clearly understand that the industries of AI and Longevity, separately, are two of the most prospective and relevant sectors to invest in, with full confidence that such investments will lead to relatively low-risk and stable profitability in the long term. **However, due to the lack of liquid tradable instruments related to the AI and Longevity industries, owners and managers of these assets still prefer to avoid any significant investments into these sectors.** Nevertheless by the time of publishing this book, the things in the AI industry have started to change significantly and many AI companies during 2019-2020 became publically traded, with AI in industry itself being considered by conservative financial institutions as investable and bankable.

Therefore, financial innovations that can provide liquidity to Longevity companies and technologies, and form a bridge between the Longevity Industry and conservative financial markets, would inevitably enable the injection of something around 1% out of those tens of trillions of dollars currently lying inert as "preserved money" within the global Longevity Industry. In practice, this means that once such liquidity bridge is established, it will have an immediate ability to attract around 300-500 billions dollars, pessimistically, just within the first few years and at least several trillions within a 5-7 years horizon.

Currently, the typical approach of these family offices and large financial institutions is to allocate 10% into alternative investments. Our most pessimistic estimate is that 10% of that wealth (and 1% of the multitrillion total) could be reasonably invested into the Longevity Industry, but only under one very specific condition: that mechanisms exist to provide investors with enough liquidity to be able to withdraw at least some of their investment within more reasonable timeframes than the typical lock-in periods of venture capital firms.

We could expect that 90% of that conservative wealth would be invested into tradable financial synthetic instruments and derivatives built on top of the Longevity Industry's companies, products, services, science and technology, and 10% as actual equity investment into the companies directly.

Considering the current natural pace of innovation in the Longevity and Financial industries, even without any specific innovations in the InvestTech field, the current problem of illiquidity will likely be resolved naturally in 7 to 10 years, but with these new bridges in place, within 3 to 5 years.

It is important that these solutions take into account the interests of both groups — start-ups wishing to acquire additional funding, and conservative investors wishing to keep their funds in secure tradable financial instruments.

In the meantime, one method of dealing with illiquidity is the creation of more modern hybrid investment funds, which would serve as the above-mentioned bridge between conservative investors and Longevity start-ups, and can provide more liquidity for investors (LP's) in comparison with the usual venture funds. Elements of such solutions are already present in other industries and can be returned and further improved using the modern tools of financial engineering and InvestTech.

A second, more innovative method of neutralizing these disproportions and inefficiencies would be the establishment of a specialized stock exchange for Longevity start-ups. Such an entity would be the first of its kind in the world, and if it is supported by key government officials, and integrated with the Longevity start-ups ecosystem, it could easily secure the position as a leading, progressive Longevity financial hub.

AIM (Alternative Investment Market — which is a subsidiary exchange of the London Stock Exchange) is one of the relevant examples, which is helping to develop London as a progressive hub of Europe providing simplified ways for mid-level companies to become public.

It would also benefit the regional financial markets, enabling a multiplicative leap in the development of the host nation's healthcare, Preventive Medicine, Precision Health, Longevity and financial industries.

This specialized stock exchange focused on Longevity companies should aim to make IPOs for at least 100 Longevity start-ups within several years of its launch, and to launch specialized financial derivatives with ties to the nation's industry, and subsequently launch several specialized Longevity ETFs (exchange traded funds).

The nation and stock exchange that does this would be capable of attracting up to $1 trillion of investment into the Longevity index within the next 5-7 years, guaranteeing nearly unlimited opportunities for the growth of its Longevity, Preventive Medicine and Precision Health industries beyond any current expectations, the only potential obstacles being global black swans such as unprecedented, global financial recessions or events similar to Covid-19 pandemics.

The ultimate goal of this project would be the deployment of a Longevity Industry index (similar to the NASDAQ-Composite, which serves as an indicator of expectations on the growth of the USA tech industry).

The first nation to establish a specialized Longevity Stock exchange will have effectively created something resembling a perpetual motion machine for the further growth of its national Longevity Industry, having built an engine for providing its companies with sufficient investment and accelerating the market-readiness of their technologies, products and services.

The nation that establishes marketplaces for both shares in publicly-traded Longevity companies and financial instruments and derivatives built as a second layer upon its Longevity Industry would be capable of attracting several trillions of potential wealth that is currently inaccessible and locked away.

To take this concept even further, if that nation were to then build a Longevity Index as a third layer on top of this Longevity Stock Exchange, to create the analogue of a NASDAQ Composite Index for its HealthTech, Preventive Medicine, Precision Health and Longevity industries, this could become one of the most predictable, stably growing and rapidly-growing investment opportunities, capable of attracting trillions dollars from conservative investors.

Furthermore, because Longevity is very much a science and technology-driven industry, it is much, much more simply predictable than, for example, the larger tech market or real estate market.

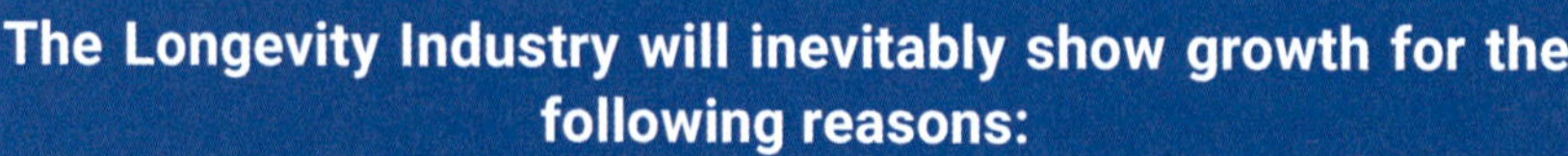

- it has a significant market size due to the increase in global life expectancies and other external factors;
- it is beneficial for investors, as it accelerates their access to biomedical technology and life extension;
- it is of great benefit to humanity, creating the products and services that will transport us all to a new era of long, comfortable and productive lives;
- it is the most ethical way of conducting business, and it is the way to generate enormous profits, bringing investors closer to the most advanced Longevity technologies, and delivering more health to humanity.

The threats and opportunities of global Longevity are of increasing interest to global finance, and are an increasingly frequent topic of discussion at international conferences, where there is an ever-greater consideration among attendees regarding the future shape of global finance.

The increased liquidity that these would provide would set in motion a self-perpetuating cycle of Longevity Finance: with greater rogress in achieving healthy Longevity, more the owners of wealth will want to invest in the repeatedly reinvigorated labour force endowed with a greater healthspan, leading to further growth and greater Healthy Longevity.

- The nation that initiates these reforms would be capable of attracting several trillions in potential wealth that is currently inaccessible and locked away.
- Such nation is more likely to be among the nations which Aging Analytics Agency has in the past characterized as "Longevity-progressive", the definition of which could extend from small technocratic nations to large financial centres with detailed industrial strategies such as the UK.
- Many countries, including the US, China and Switzerland, are heading towards insolvency as the number of retirees skyrockets.
- The Longevity-progressive countries that first develop a fully functional and integrative Longevity Financial Ecosystem will succeed to spawn a whole new industry, the capitalization of which could exceed anything ever considered by financial markets.
- This will also produce a large quantity and diversity of derivatives, which in turn will support a second and third layers of derivatives, which in turn will give rise to the biggest possible market for derivatives imaginable.

Chapter 15: Major Longevity Financial Industry Trends, Predictions and Insights

Over the past 100 years, the financial industry has largely excluded people in retirement, despite the fact that the most valuable client demographic in terms of purchasing power are the citizens of the 7th Continent which is made up of 1 billion people over 60 years of age. Financial services innovators have an opportunity to enhance the financial lives of a billion people by designing new solutions and adapting existing products, effectively de-risking the problem of the aging population, and converting it into a source of growth and untapped market potentials.

The global spending power of this demographic is expected to be $15 trillion in 2020. Longevity Banks and FinTech 2.0 services will attract people 60+ who expect to live to 100 years and beyond, who recognize Health as New Wealth, and who have unprecedented demand for technologies able to optimize their wealthspan in step with increasing healthspans. In the next few years, age-friendly FinTech companies and Longevity Banks will develop new financial products designed for clients who are planning to live extra long lives and want to remain highly functioning and financially stable throughout.

The impending maturation of Longevity-focused investment products in the next 5 years has a promising outlook. Novel products that can enable liquidity, tradability, and exposure to private equity markets, are emerging. For the first time, such risk-averse exposure to the Longevity market will be available to accredited investors and the conservative investment community.

Financial institutions are going to be introduced to the opportunity to mitigate and convert their Longevity-based risks to financial products and services which will help to synchronize clients wealthspans (period of extended financial stability) and Healthspans (period of Healthy Longevity) through AI integration. There is a level playing field with regard to the size of opportunity for well established institutions compared to newer entrants in this space.

On one hand, new entrants have few systemic bottlenecks in terms of reformulating existing business models, and on the other hand, large corporations have a large client base and reservoirs of wealth, making them ideally suited to on-board Longevity products, services and strategies at scale very quickly.

Projects may arise out of JV's between large financial institutions and new innovative companies. We have seen many examples of such JV's in the FinTech sphere, and recently several at the intersection of InsurTech and HealthTech.

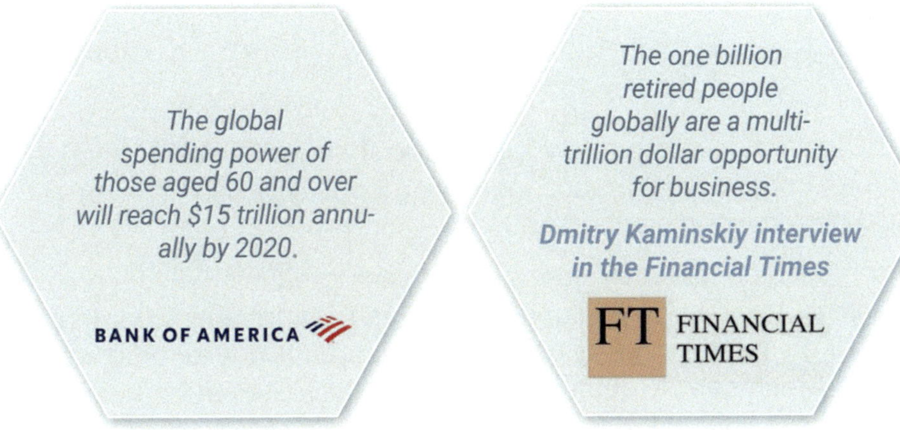

Exchange Traded Funds Landscape

There will be a significant number of Longevity-themed exchange traded funds (ETF) emerging rapidly in the next 3-5 years. One example is the Long Term Care ETF (OLD) which holds a portfolio of companies focused on senior housing, nursing services, Bio-Pharma companies and Real Estate Investment Trusts (REITS) that specialize in senior living. The weakness of such ETFs is their lack of focus on the full scope of the Longevity Industry.

This void will be filled by funds which seek to encompass all relevant Longevity sectors across medicine, technology and finance in a data-driven manner with well-balanced profitability/risk strategies. Such ETFs will be paramount to allow larger institutions to park their money in stable and risk averse environments — which is a major need for many institutional investors.

Financial Advisory Sector

Longevity is a new focus for financial advisors whose client base is entering retirement. Whereas banks need to adapt their products and services to an increasingly healthy older generation, financial advisors need to adapt their guidance to the rising Silver Generation. It would be prudent to keep an eye on Longevity-themed investment basket portfolio holdings of large institutions (especially pension funds). Although there are clearly many considerations to keep in mind, Longevity is definitely an asset class that is coming into its own.

Insurance Sector

In the insurance sector, we expect several Longevity-based products such as Longevity insurance, qualifying Longevity annuity contracts, and deferred income annuities.

With a pending influx in older people, such products will become increasingly relevant and valuable (in terms of premiums). Companies with the greatest Longevity risk are pension funds and insurance companies, which can be seen in the ongoing increase in the number of Longevity swaps.

However, there still remains a major unmet need, and growing trend, for insurance companies to "gamify" Longevity by offering financial incentives (such as discounted rates on life and health insurance) in exchange for clients maintaining a healthy lifestyle and meeting certain health-related goals.

Longevity insurance companies are not simply tools to hedge Longevity risk for institutions such as pension funds and insurance companies. There are most definitely synthetic micro-investment opportunities for individual investors through deferred annuities and other strategies. Nothing stops individual investors from taking advantage of the "silver wave" by investing in Longevity-themed indices which are a risk averse setting for lifetime savings, and through modern and innovative approaches they will, for the first time, be able to gain liquid exposure to DeepTech and Frontier Technology industries.

"Longevity is a blessing. And as an investor, it provides you opportunities to benefit from compounding and to have a longer investment horizon. But if you don't prepare for it, you are left with two options: work longer in life, perhaps much longer than you'd like, or hope you've been good to your children and that they'll be willing to care for you in your old age. And, second, I hope you'll speak out. Longevity is an issue of social justice that will have a more profound impact on your generation than on any generation before. If we don't start to address it – not just in this country but globally – we're going to see fewer job prospects for yourger people, higher unemployment, lower growth and many older people – maybe your parents – left without the means to support themselves."

Larry Fink, Chairman of Blackrock Capital

"I'm actually pretty optimistic about the U.S. economy. But Europe's got real challenges. A lot of that is due to the demographics in Europe. China has been the engine of growth for the world for the last 20 years, or the last 10 years in particular, but that's not sustainable. So you're looking at a world where growth is going to be more challenged than it's been, unless you see some really big jumps in productivity."

Bill McNabb, Chair of Vanguard

"The new technology wave is changing who we are. There is research going on in biology, regeneration of body parts, enzymes and so on. If we make progress in what we are doing in trating cancer, it will prolong life expectancy by a number of years. Now, in Switzerland, every new baby is expected to have a life of more than 100 years."

Klaus Schwab, Founder and Executive Chairman of the World Economic Forum

FinTech Sector Landscape

We can estimate that the next several years will be the time where FinTech will actually merge into FinTech 2.0, when advances in AI, InsurTech, MarkTech (marketing technology), LegalTech and RegTech will collide into a single integrated and advanced technology.

This technological convergence will deliver the more sophisticated results that were expected to be delivered in recent years by the FinTech industry, but which ultimately failed to occur.

What challenger banks were proposed to deliver (the integrated collision of FinTech with other advanced AI, IT and data-driven technologies) did not happen, but it is reasonable to expect that by 2022-2024 this will happen in practice.

And yet the entire FinTech and financial industries are missing a very simple yet strong point: that the biggest and most valuable and capable client demographic in terms of purchasing power are those aged 50+, the citizens of the so-called 7th continent.

Clients 50+ (and even younger who are expecting to live 100 years and beyond) are also diverse in their interests and desires, and can be segregated into different layers (e.g. the interests and desires of clients 50-60 years old are a little bit different from those aged 60-70, and the interests of clients 70-80 are different than their comparatively younger peers, etc.).

Integrated AgeTech-WealthTech Solutions

Taking into account AgeTech in particular (advanced IT solutions for elderly people), if you are a banker and considering yourself as a progressive FinTech executive, you should not be surprised to consider FinTech products designed specifically for clients around 95 and even 100 years.

If the first decade of 2000 was inspired by expats looking for tax havens (e.g. from NY to Caribbean islands), the second decade of 2020 had many expats looking for political stability from different emerging countries without stable political and social ecosystems.

We can expect that the third decade of the 2000s (2020-2030) will be remembered as the period when wealthy (but first of all smart) people seek to relocate to places where they will have maximum probability to live a longer and healthiest life, AKA, where they can maximize their HALY (Health-Adjusted Life Years), and QALY (Quality-Adjusted Life Years), or their healthy and high-functioning period of life.

If the fourth industrial revolution is estimated to deliver significant breakthroughs in biotechnology, the fifth industrial revolution will deliver exact, tangible, significant results in terms of this maximum life expectancy combined with efficient extension of healthy and high-functioning period of life, maximum HALY and QALY, and health for the vast majority of their maximum life expectancy.

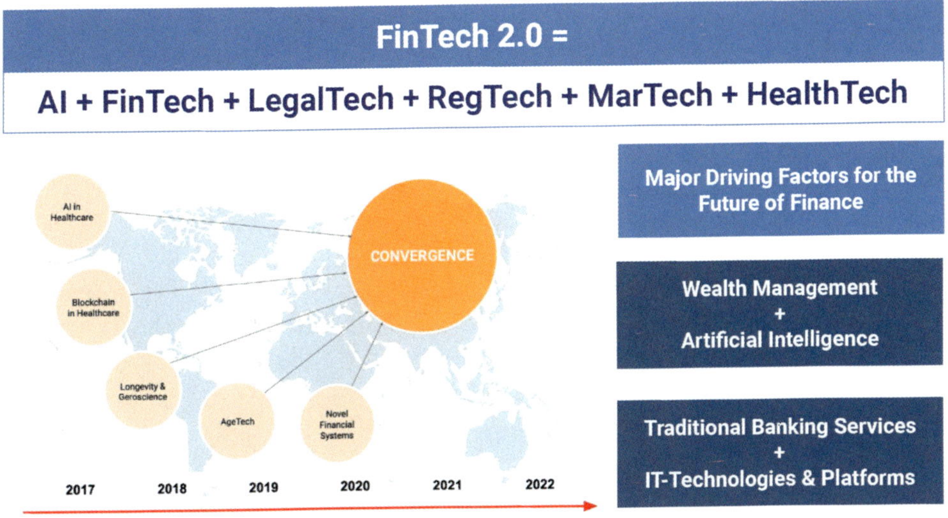

Banking Sector Landscape

Here is a significant unmet need to make financial institutions friends of their customers, their health and wellness coaches. This is why technologies such as HealthTech and AgeTech, implemented in the Longevity Card, are crucial for the future of banking. Traditional Banking is already in the past for almost 10 years and the current approach of modern challenger banks is lacking behind the technological progress for almost 5 years, and it can be assumed that in the nearest future investors will start to take money out from their current FinTech portfolio companies and reinvest into health-focused ventures.

Banks need to start tapping into the market potential of the Senior Generation, a generation which on the one hand provides the world's wealthiest clientele for financial institutions, and on the other hand happens to be the most in need of financial and technological inclusion and disruption. Today we can see the rise of Challenger Banks, which redefine the banking industry by connecting with a New Generation of mobile-first consumers. Yet none of them offers financial products to meet the needs of the rapidly-expanding 60+ Generation. Instead, Challenger Banks are developing financial products for a limited age range only, chasing the Middle-Aged and Younger generations, while missing out on a 1 billion consumer — or 15 trillion dollar — market opportunity locked up in the older demographic.

Where Wealthspan Meets Healthspan

Yet this older demographic provides the world's wealthiest clientele, which happens to be the clientele most in need of high-tech financial services.

It is here that AgeTech may play a role. AgeTech refers to a diverse range of digital technologies designed to support the elderly, increase functionality and social activity, and reduce the negative consequences of aging in everyday life. AgeTech innovations such as elderly fraud protection, large text options, higher accessibility, adaptive user interfaces and voice commands will allow banks to adapt to the older demographic and capture the whole opportunity of the Longevity Industry in the coming years.

One of the only companies we are aware of that is taking this massive unmet need to heart, and actively tapping into the multitrillion market of 1 billion people in retirement globally, is Deep Knowledge Group's portfolio company Longevity Bank, via its flagship product, Longevity Card. There will be several layers of implementation of the Longevity Bank project: 2020 launch of the Longevity Marketplace for retail clients with Longevity Card as a flagship product (USA launch in Q2 2021); Q3 2021 launch of the B2B Marketplace and technological ecosystem (optimization of business processes and supply chain for SME in the HealthTech sphere); 2022 launch of the Longevity Investment Bank.

The Rise of Longevity Derivatives and Financial Instruments Tied to Longevity

Longevity-based derivatives are going to be a preferred option for investors such as survivor bonds which pay a coupon based on the "survivorship" of a stated population group along with Longevity notes which reference a pool of pre-defined lives. Due to the rise in such Longevity-themed financial instruments and investment options, the gov-

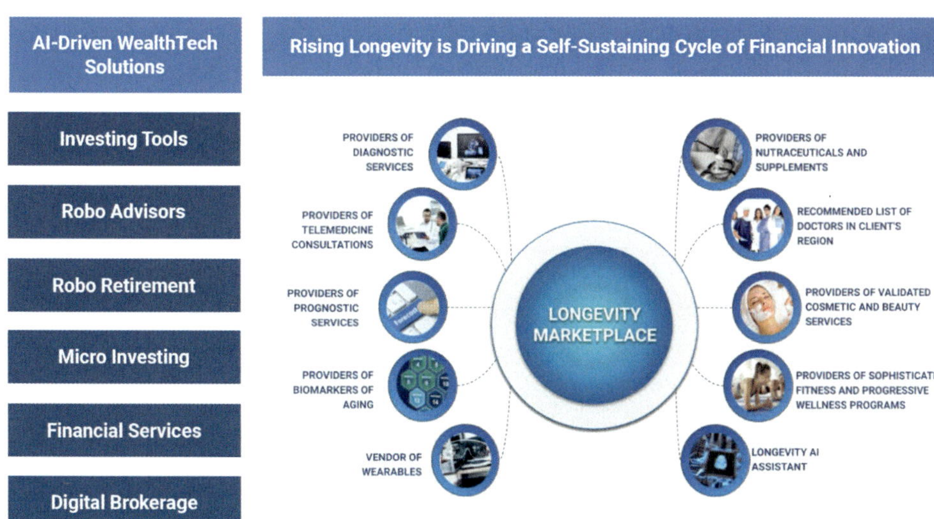

ernment mortality indices will be closely watched in the coming years. There will also be a significant increase in investment to adapt existing technologies and infrastructure to the aging population.

Today, the majority of Longevity indices and derivatives are packaged as risk management solutions. The current synthetic Longevity products are emerging Longevity indices, Longevity notes, Longevity swaps and other Longevity derivatives such as survivor bonds. The attraction of Longevity-based financial products that take on Longevity risk is that they are standardized and tradable which allows massive liquidity to larger institutions that buy them such as pension funds and asset management companies. Since the Longevity risk on insurance and annuity contracts are swappable, the secondary insurance market might see minimal increases in liquidity, although life insurance products and annuities might not necessarily be extremely liquid in the future. These kinds of practices are the simplest and least modern form of this general trend.

Investors Have Appetite for Longevity, But No Optimal Frameworks for Exposure

There are enormous near term opportunities for liquid Longevity indices and derivatives focused at individual investors (and HNWIs in particular), that enable exposure to the rising tide of the global Longevity Industry. This is a key mechanism for matching wealthspans to rising healthspans. Such products are evolving to create liquidity in derivatives that have historically been illiquid or have had no liquidity. Existing InvestTech solutions have the potential to give investors exposure to relevant Longevity companies in a highly liquid and tradable manner, but are not being utilized sufficiently.

Several major investment banks have introduced Longevity-themed baskets and portfolios tied to various sectors of the Longevity industry. The objective is to give the massive global investment community exposure to the rapidly growing Longevity Industry. Some specific examples include AXA's WF Framlington Longevity Economy Fund, and Julius Baer's Longevity Basket Tracker Certificate. The only drawbacks of such companies and funds is that they are limited to publicly-traded companies when the vast majority of true Longevity companies are privately held, and they are only very weakly and superficially tied to the actual Longevity industry partly as a result of being limited to public companies. Thankfully, there are existing InvestTech solutions and liquidity-generating approaches that can neutralize what we refer to as the Big Longevity Liquidity Gap.

Bridging the Longevity Liquidity Gap to De-Risk Longevity Exposure

During the past several years, a quite clear disproportion has emerged between various DeepTech sectors, in particular between the Longevity start-ups on the one hand, and the entire business model of venture capital funds on the other. There have also been big gaps and disruptions in the global financial system. There is a highly relevant big gap between progress in science and technology, and the outdated bureaucracy, in which most financial institutions remain mired, as though both exist in parallel universes.

This is happening for multiple reasons: At one end, DeepTech start-ups (including Longevity start-ups) have been suffering from a lack of access to relevant levels of seed investment. Although venture funds are by definition supposed to prioritize investments into the most disruptive technologies and start-ups, in reality, most of them prefer to specifically avoid DeepTech sectors, or to enter investment rounds at much later stages. As a consequence, the start-ups are forced to deal with angel investors. This creates a growth gap phenomenon known as the "Death Valley": 99% of DeepTech start-ups do not survive the stage of growth between seed financing and the beginning of revenue generation or even "A" rounds.

Meanwhile, at the other end, there is an extreme abundance of significant assets being held and preserved in bank accounts or in comparatively stable derivatives on a scale of tens of trillions. For instance, there is a tremendous volume of money on the scale of at least €1 trillion currently being stored in Swiss bank accounts with negative interest rates, which is an illogical phenomenon of a modern financial world itself. Yet the owners of these financial assets would nonetheless prefer to avoid investing them into venture funds, who are equally reluctant to invest into Longevity start-ups. Thus, the major source of these disproportions comes down to the issue of illiquidity.

There are many thousands of HealthTech start-ups and hundreds of Longevity start-ups in the UK, EU, USA and Asia-Pacific region and 99% of them are not publicly traded, which means that they are limited to seeking funding from angel investors and venture investors, which represent a very small fraction of the available global wealth. This situation creates an extreme funding deficit and illiquidity problem.

Making Longevity Investments Attractive to the Global Financial Community

This is a problem facing almost all DeepTech sectors, but the negative repercussions are particularly bad for the Longevity Industry, as it leads on the individual level to reduced quality of life and unnecessary deaths, and threatens to inflict crippling economic effects on national healthcare systems, pension and social security systems and economies.

Therefore, an extreme abundance of financial assets ends up preserved rather than invested. There are enormous amounts of financial assets being conserved within the umbrella of family offices (and we can estimate that there are around 5,000 of these) and hundreds of very conservative financial institutions, which hoard this capital simply due to a lack of safe, stably growing and predictable financial derivatives into which to invest. There is no relevant methodology to assess the amount of such assets, as they tend to keep this a secret. But this is at least several tens of trillions of dollars.

At the same time, many owners of these vast sums of wealth are nonetheless personally interested in Longevity, both as a prospective market with the capacity for unprecedented growth, and as a mean to their own personal life extension. Even the most conservative investors, and the owners of the largest financial assets, now very clearly understand that the industries of AI and Longevity, separately, are two of the most prospective and relevant sectors to invest in, with full confidence that such investments will lead to relatively low-risk and stable profitability in the long term.

However, due to the lack of liquid tradable instruments related to the AI and Longevity industries, owners and managers of these assets still prefer to avoid any significant investments into these sectors. And in many cases, angel and venture investors are operating as sharks, exploiting this gross illiquidity for their own financial advantage, to the detriment of Longevity and other DeepTech start-ups. Therefore, financial innovations that can provide liquidity to Longevity companies and technologies, and form a bridge between the Longevity Industry and conservative financial markets, would inevitably enable the injection of something around 1% of the tens of trillions of dollars currently lying inert as "lazy money" within the global Longevity Industry.

Longevity InvestTech to Make Liquidity

In practice, this means that once such a liquidity bridge is established, it will have an immediate ability to attract around 300-500 billions dollars, pessimistically, just within the first few years and at least several trillions within a 5-7 years horizon. Currently, the typical approach of these family offices and large financial institutions is to allocate 10% into alternative investments. Our most pessimistic estimate is that 10% of that wealth could be reasonably invested into the Longevity Industry, but only under one very specific condition: that mechanisms exist to provide investors with enough liquidity to be able to withdraw at least some of their investment within more reasonable timeframes than the typical lock-in periods of venture capital firms.

Considering the current natural pace of innovation in the Longevity and Financial industries, even without any specific innovations in the InvestTech field, the current problem of illiquidity will likely be resolved naturally in 7 to 10 years, but with these new bridges in place, within 3 to 5 years. It is important that these solutions take into account the interests of both groups — start-ups wishing to acquire additional funding, and conservative investors wishing to keep their funds in secure tradable financial instruments. In the meantime, one method of dealing with illiquidity is the creation of more modern hybrid investment funds, which would serve as the above-mentioned bridge between conservative investors and Longevity start-ups, and can provide more liquidity for investors (LP's) in comparison with the usual venture funds. Elements of such solutions are already present in other industries and can be returned and further improved using the modern tools of financial engineering and InvestTech.

Instruments Tied to Healthy Longevity

We can also envision the emergence of financial instruments and analytical tied to biomarkers of aging (which serve as proxies for measuring the current state of individuals and populations' biological aging), and to the technological and scientific validation currently possessed by Longevity-focused start-ups. More specifically, we envision the development of 3 types of analytical products.

All of these products will be derived from sets of biomarkers of aging and Longevity, and panels of biomarkers which are off the shelf analytical dashboards.

An analytical panel will be launched for hedge funds and investment banks to predict success or failure of particular molecules in the later stages of clinical trials and provide investors with the signals to form long or shorting positions.

Technological due-diligence for venture investors to evaluate the claims of emerging companies whether their technologies can deliver actual results on humans will be made available in detailed formats.

An analytical panel could also be launched for InsurTech-HealthTech companies focused on the retails clients. Currently we are aware of at least 6 companies working on similar types of solutions, and we can envision the emergence of another 10-20 such companies in the next 2-3 years.

Depending on the management, scientific team, and business executive team, we will see a variety of specific structuring of biomarker panels and actual analytical/financial products based on them.

Traditional VC	Longevity Investing 2.0
High Minimum Entry Fees	Competitive Minimum Entry Fees
Long Fund Lock-in Periods	Higher Liquidity
Low Liquidity	Offers Different Ratios of Liquidity to Profitability
Risky (bets on single companies rather than industries)	De-risking Investments by Betting on Entire Longevity Subsector
Ineffective due-diligence processes for sectors as complex as Longevity	Capable of Beating Market Index via Active Portfolio Management

New Longevity Markets: Longevity Stock Exchange

A second, more innovative method of neutralizing the disproportions and inefficiencies behind the Big Longevity Liquidity Gap is the establishment of a specialized stock exchange for Longevity start-ups. Such an entity would be the first of its kind in the world, and if it is supported by key government officials, and integrated with the Longevity start-ups ecosystem, it could easily secure the position as a leading, progressive Longevity financial hub. *The ultimate goal of this project would be the deployment of a Longevity Industry index (similar to the NASDAQ-Composite, which serves as an indicator of expectations on the growth of the USA tech industry).*

Alternative Stock Exchanges are usually associated with uprising wealth within regional boundaries. They facilitate brokers to do their business in the selling of shares to companies and vice versa with heightened efficiency. It enhances companies' access to capital and the chance to also increase their views and their public image. All savvy businesses can increase the power of stock sharing to expand and enhance their companies. While advantages to financial and regulatory costs are connected with being listed on the alternative stock exchange, the benefits far outdo the disadvantage. A Longevity based stock exchange would provide further access to capital, profile enhancement, control maintenance, reduction of the cost of capital and increases the ability to attract more investment.

The first nation to establish a specialized Longevity Stock exchange will have effectively created something resembling a perpetual motion machine for the further growth of its national Longevity Industry, having built an engine for providing its companies with sufficient investment and accelerating the market-readiness of their technologies, products and services. The nation that establishes marketplaces for both shares in publicly-traded Longevity companies and financial instruments and derivatives built as a second layer upon its Longevity Industry would be capable of attracting several trillions of potential wealth that is currently inaccessible and locked away.

Longevity Composite Exchanges and Longevity Indexes

To take this concept even further, if that nation were to then build a Longevity Index as a second layer on top of this Longevity Stock Exchange, to create the analogue of a NASDAQ composite for its HealthTech, Preventive Medicine, Precision Health and Longevity industries, this could become one of the most predictable, stably growing and rapidly-growing investment opportunities, capable of attracting trillions of pounds worth of lazy money from conservative investors.

Furthermore, because Longevity is very much a science and technology-driven industry, it is much, much more simply predictable than, for example, the larger tech market or real estate market.

The threats and opportunities of global Longevity are of increasing interest to global finance, and are an increasingly frequent topic of discussion at international conferences, where there is an ever-greater consideration among attendees regarding the future shape of global finance. The increased liquidity that these would provide would set in motion a self-perpetuating cycle of Longevity Finance: with greater progress in achieving healthy Longevity, more the owners of wealth will want to invest in the repeatedly reinvigorated labour force endowed with a greater healthspan, leading to further growth and greater Healthy Longevity.

As mentioned before, the nation that initiates these reforms would be capable of attracting several trillions in potential wealth that is currently inaccessible and locked away. Such a nation is more likely to be characterised by a technocratic government structure with large financial centres and detailed industrial strategies. Many countries, including the US, China and Switzerland, are heading towards insolvency as the number of retirees skyrockets. The Longevity-progressive countries that first develop a fully functional and integrative Longevity Financial Ecosystem will succeed to spawn a whole new industry, the capitalization of which could exceed anything ever considered by financial markets.

Major Benefits of Longevity Derivatives and Instruments Over Traditional Longevity VC		
Hedge Fund-style Liquidity with VC Objectives	Bets on the Success of the Entire Longevity Industry	Significantly De-Risks Exposure to Longevity

Longevity Stock Exchange

Current financial products' levels of sophistication are limited by status quo financial and legal frameworks, but new technologies platforms and frameworks have the potential to allow for the creation of truly innovative financial products and systems. In our view, the ideal solution for designing novel financial instruments and products is to establish a new specialized financial marketplace in the form of a specialized stock exchange with a formal license, to serve as the base and launching pad for a wider variety of financial instruments and systems tied to the Longevity Industry.

Eventually, this could take the form of a Longevity Industry financial index, similar to the NASDAQ composite, which would represent the current state of the Longevity Industry in one particular region. We suspect that these types of frameworks will most likely emerge in regions that have recognition within the broader international financial community, stability, and a prospective domestic Longevity Industry, yet which are large enough to encompass the behaviour of the Longevity Industry globally. At the present time, we see London and the US as the most prospective regions in this regard, although Switzerland, Singapore and Hong Kong have fairly strong prospects as well. A Longevity Stock Exchange provides increased liquidity, which in turn would enables greater flexibility and a greater leverage for the further growth of the companies listed on the exchange, and as such, greater opportunities for the advancement of the full-scope Longevity Industry as a whole globally.

Specialized stock exchanges are nothing new. Currently, for example, investors can dig into about 50 major commodity markets worldwide. Those include markets for soft commodities such as wheat, coffee, cocoa and other agricultural products, and markets for commodities that are mined, such as gold and oil. NASDAQ fits that profile as well; it was created as a stock exchange for IT-companies and is currently the home of tech-oriented stocks. The most relevant example is the recently launched Silicon Valley Stock Exchange backed by Marc Andreessen, and other tech heavyweights, that will give high-growth technology companies more options to list their shares outside of the traditional New York exchanges. Specialized stock exchanges typically form when an industry grows by a sufficient amount, and with the Longevity Industry in its present state of maturation, a Longevity stock exchange now appears to be inevitable.

De-Risked & Optimized Longevity Exposure

Setting up a Longevity Stock Exchange would require the public listing of at least 100 Longevity-focused companies to create good enough diversity and potential volume for trading.

Thereafter, the more advances there are in Longevity, the more even the most conservative investors will want to invest. By that point they will have been well advised that Longevity is an industry like no other. It is by such means that increased global Longevity will be transformed from a threat into an opportunity.

Several examples of the successful implementation of innovative approaches to legal and regulatory frameworks, administration and management exist, which lay good groundwork for structuring the right approach to establishing a Longevity Stock Exchange, including the Alternative Investment Market (AIM), a subsidiary of the London Stock Exchange, which gives medium-sized companies opportunities to be publicly listed in an intermediate way, providing them with a framework for raising tens of millions of pounds (rather than just several millions at best) by opening up access to the broader conservative investment community, which prefer to deal only with tradable, highly liquid assets.

If a similar approach were to be taken for the Longevity Industry start-ups, this can provide a very effective method for leapfrogging roadblocks in the growth and effective funding of the sector (in a way that bridges the gap between supply and demand). Additionally, this approach may also provide a promising tool for attracting foreign investors, including those from the EU and the Gulf Region. The Long-Term Stock Exchange, a Silicon Valley-based Stock Exchange for tech companies established by Andreseen Horowitz, which creates an interesting and more innovative alternative to the NASDAQ, tuned to the specifics of DeepTech start-ups in Silicon Valley.

More broadly, Singapore as a smart city-state currently has the smallest gap between Health-Adjusted Life Expectancy (HALE) and life expectancy, and is very well known for rapidly implementing frameworks for the balanced strategic support of innovative start-ups and technologies, and for quickly attracting foreign talents for highly focused industry development, which may serve as an efficient basis and ecosystem not only for accelerated technology innovation, but for financial innovations as well.

Financial Instruments & Futures Markets Tied to National Longevity Economies

Another prospective type of Longevity-focused financial product and market that we can expect to emerge in the next several years are National Longevity Economy financial instruments and Futures Indexes, which are tied to either the current or predicted future state and performance of entire National Economies with respect to Healthy Longevity and Aging Population.

More specifically, such instruments would be tied to the extent with which national governments, individual economy, healthcare and industrial development industries, international policy organizations and other responsible stakeholders formulate and implement policies and development strategies capable of transforming the challenge of aging into the opportunity of Healthy Longevity for the mutual benefit of their citizens and their economy.

The ability to invest in individual countries' longevity based economic conditions (e.g. social security, etc.) is a large opportunity for institutional investors to try and reach untapped markets and produce significant alpha whilst taking on minimal risk. The emergence of governmental Longevity based indices would add another avenue for investors to safely park large amounts of money with large investments on long and short bias' on systematic longevity based risks taken on by governments around the world.

These types of instruments can also be broken down in a more granular fashion, tied to specific global regions, and to specific individual components of entire national economies, such as the current state of Longevity success and progressiveness of different region's social security systems, national healthcare systems, government-funded pension funds, level of Healthy Adjusted Life Expectancy (HALE), gap between HALE and unadjusted life expectancy, and others.

Futures Markets Tied to National Pension, Healthcare & Social Security Systems

Such instruments and markets could be either structured and traded individually, or in the form of segregated baskets (multi-future instruments) and markets. This futures market would create a framework for forecasting positive and negative scenarios surrounding the intersection of what we refer to as the Opposed Longevity MegaTrends of Aging Population and Advanced Biomedicine.

Meanwhile, in addition to creating a new type of Longevity-focused investing (taking long positions or shorting based how well specific regions are facing the challenge and opportunity of National Longevity and Aging Population), this type of system would also provide tangible inputs of investors and financial corporations on the most prospective regions to actually invest in from a Longevity Industry standpoint.

Additionally, this type of marketplace would be ideally suited for sovereign wealth funds in particular, which typically make their investments with the specific economic prospects of their own region in mind.

In reality, Longevity serves as a highly optimal target sector for investment by sovereign wealth funds, in that it has the potential to deliver straightforward, direct value to citizens by:

- Promoting the extension of Healthy Longevity,
- Generating lucrative and stable returns by being at the intersection of the most promising an sophisticated technologies and companies, and
- Promoting growth and stability of their entire economy due to ancillary benefits relating to increasing their region's National Healthy

Longevity (including reducing the economic burden of their aging population and increasing the productivity of their workforce, and overall economic participation of their Silver Generation).

Possible Forms of Futures Markets Based on National Longevity Economies		
Instruments Tied to Current State of Health-Adjusted Life Expectancy (HALE)	Futures Betting on Future HALE and Gap Between HALE and Life Expectancy	Instruments & Futures Tied to National Healthcare Economies
Instruments & Futures Tied to National Pension Systems	Instruments & Futures Tied to National Social Security Systems	Instruments & Futures Tied to National Longevity Financial Systems

The Unmet Need For Sophisticated Financial Industry Related Longevity Analytics

One of the major hallmarks of the global Longevity Industry in general is its unprecedented complexity, which creates significant challenges for getting an understanding of the scope and scale of the market landscape, as well as major trends and forecasts, required to properly formulate business models and structure long and short-term strategy. The same is true, if not more so, for the Longevity Financial Industry.

Although increased Longevity represents a major threat for the pension funds, it may still be beneficial for some of them. Only those pension funds and insurance companies that are better adapted, with business models that account for the Longevity factor, will survive. Thus, these companies should focus on managing Longevity risk properly.

Insurance and reinsurance companies provide risk transfer mechanisms for institutions (pension funds predominantly). There is a $750bn+ opportunity globally in pension closeouts for insurers. In addition, Longevity risk is a natural hedge for insurers vs. mortality risk, and it is an efficient way to use insurance subsidiary capital. Insurers, AMCs, private and retail banks are poised to benefit from Longevity, as long as they can adapt to the changes in time.

Venture funds have already changed their investment targets and are about to shift from seed and series A, B, C funding methods to implementing TRLs (Technology Readiness Levels) and other tangible metrics as benchmarks for a company's assessment. Hedge funds are going to follow venture funds by shorting the stock of outdated biopharma companies. They are also developing so-called "negative ratios" to assess the degree of outdatedness, i.e. if a pharma company is not using AI in its core R&D, this would add to its negative ratio.

In view of the looming fall of inefficient BioTech industry, the rising of BioTech Industry 2.0 (Longevity Industry) is anticipated, and hedge funds will have an outstanding opportunity to thrive on this transition, shorting the stagnating part of the industry. However, in order to succeed in practice in doing any of this, financial institutions need to develop sources of industry and sector analytics as multidimensional, complex and sophisticated as the domains that they are applied to.

White Label Solutions For Financial Institutions Market Intelligence & Swot Analysis

Deep Knowledge Group is currently working on the development of a dashboard that combines proprietary Big Data analytics, real-time monitoring, market intelligence and advanced, interactive data visualization on active players within the Longevity Financial Industry. The platform is targeted towards analysts, executives and decision makers working at large financial institutions (insurance companies, pension funds, investment banks and asset management firms), with the aim of structuring and developing their short and long-term strategies, obtain precise analysis of their competitors' activities, derive best-case examples from the market and optimize their Longevity Financial Industry strategy.

The Longevity Finance Dashboard will be a licensed a white label solution offered to a variety of external financial corporations (major retail banks, investment banks, insurance companies, FinTech companies, etc.) looking to transform their business model toward Longevity-focused banking and Health as New Wealth, in order to capture the massive untapped multi trillion market of 1 billion people in retirement globally. A major focus is placed upon parameters that quantify an institution's Longevity-related products, services, instruments, funds, activities and strategies. Also, ancillary factors that make them optimally tuned to switch to capturing Longevity as major short and long-term strategies (such as their alignment with Longevity trends and designing solutions for aging populations, team composition and their data processing metrics), which allow the dashboard to keep track of institutions' capacity to adapt to advancing Longevity trends.

The ultimate objective of the dashboard is to serve as a sophisticated source of Big Data analytics and market intelligence on the Longevity-related activities of 500 financial institutions globally. The platform will feature a number of specific components that together encompass the entire scope of the Longevity finance sector, providing: market intelligence on the Longevity-related activities of hundreds of major financial institutions, SWOT analysis and competitive landscaping, quantitative ranking and benchmarking (both positive and negative) of financial corporations, forecasting, B2B marketplace of relevant Longevity products and services, and Big Data, Machine Learning and AI Analytics capabilities.

B2B & B2C Longevity Finance Marketplaces for Product/Service Pipeline Optimization

The dashboard consists of a licensed white label solution offered to a variety of external financial corporations (major retail banks, investment banks, insurance companies, FinTech companies, etc.) looking to transform their business model toward Longevity-focused banking and Health as New Wealth. It provides out-licensed access to Longevity Bank's B2C and B2B dashboards, where external financial institutions first sign a non-competition agreement obliging them to focus on markets and regions that are not within the scope of Longevity Bank's target market, and pay a premium in exchange for access to Longevity Bank's ecosystem and marketplace of Longevity products and services. The dashboard enables financial institutions interested in Longevity to select and filter Longevity products and services available within their region, in order to aggregate a set of vendors capable of providing their own clients with relevant products and services designed to maximize Healthy Longevity across the full scope of the global Longevity ecosystem.

Smart-Matching & Advanced, Quantitative Longevity Financial Industry Analytics

Clients will also gain access to advanced analytics showing relevant benchmarking parameters for available vendors within each specific product and service category, enabling them to conduct cost-benefit analyses and determine which vendors are best suited to meet the needs of their clients within their specific target demographic and regional market. It will also provide continuous monitoring and market intelligence of the specific Longevity-focused activities, products and services developed and deployed by 500 financial corporations globally, to continually track, analyze and rank best practices within the Global Longevity Financial Industry. The dashboard is powered by Deep Knowledge Group and developed by Aging Analytics Agency, the the world's first entity to conduct a dedicated analysis of the Longevity Financial Industry (and even coined and defined the term) in it's 2019 open-access analytical report ***Advancing Financial Industry: Longevity / AgeTech / WealthTech***.

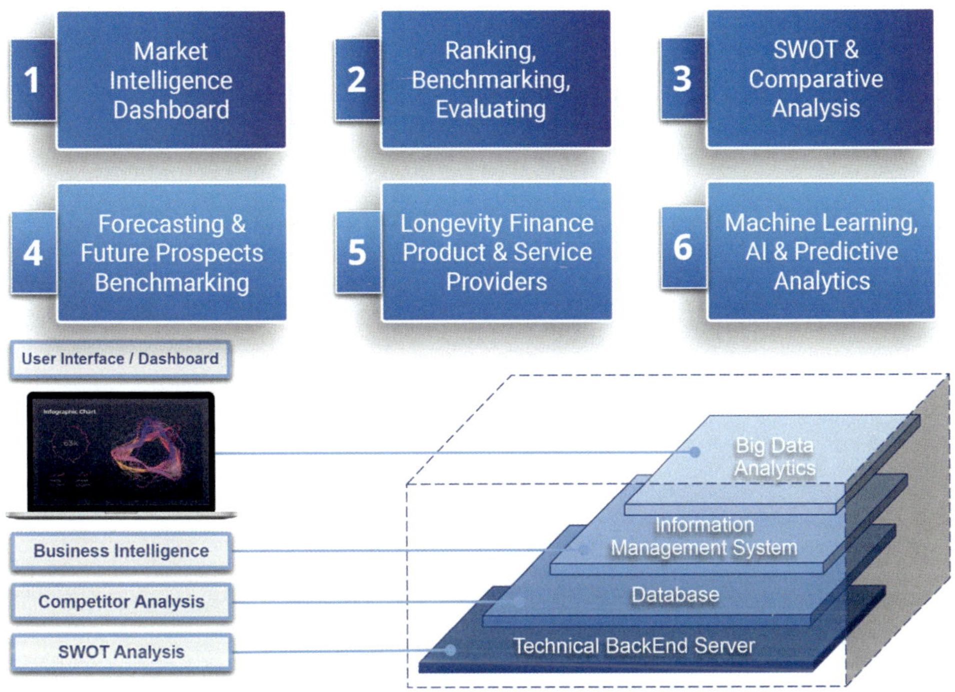

Novel Longevity-Focused Strategies

Equity strategies regarding pharmaceutical companies on a global scale provide funds with a large scope of possibilities. Since pension funds are highly exposed to Longevity-based risks due to increased clientele lifespans, shorting pension investment funds on global stock exchanges is a strong avenue for large financial institutions to consider.

Pension funds with low TRL's and high defined benefit plan clientele are increasingly risky and are bound to have higher volatility and eventually decrease in value. Contract default swaps are a nuclear option for dynamic aggressive equity strategies although spotting challenger banks through multiple data sets that are susceptible to Longevity-based risks and have exorbitant evaluations is a strategy that can and should be implemented. Investing in pension investment funds with Longevity progressive systems, high TRL's and low amount of defined benefit plan clientele is another promising investment strategy that could take advantage of the growing Longevity Industry and longer average lifespans. Investing in Longevity focused exchange traded funds that are passive in nature is a credible avenue to invest in the Longevity Industry in a relatively higher liquid manner. Acquiring distressed companies and assets to incorporate Longevity-based risk mitigation systems and reselling them is another investment opportunity for larger investment outfits.

Global Financial Ramifications & Outlook

The global financial economy will undergo a fundamental structural change driven by the globalization of business on one hand and by the revolution in artificial intelligence and biotechnology on the other. The Longevity Industry is posed to revamp the economic growth of countries through the governmental backing of Longevity-based policies. The influx of capital in Longevity-related industries due to increasing liquidity in financial derivatives is on track to serve as a novel avenue for capital generation. However, there is a severe lack of forecasting technological capabilities of governments and relevant large financial institutions. Due to this, they are on track to lose out on benefiting from the progressing biomedical revolution. The few governments and countries that are able to capture the entirety of the opportunity presented will benefit immensely, while governments and institutions that cannot grasp this shifting dynamic of megatrends will suffer sizable losses because of their exposure to Longevity-related risks.

Government Challenges & Opportunities

Governments in particular bear a significant amount of Longevity risk. Their Longevity exposure comes through public pension plans and social security schemes. An unexpected increase in Longevity would increase spending in public schemes, which typically provide benefits for life. The economic and fiscal effects of an aging society are generally recognized by policymakers, but the financial consequences associated with the risk that people live longer than expected — Longevity risk — has received less attention. Unanticipated increases in the average human lifespan can result from misjudging the continuing upward trend in life expectancy, introducing small forecasting errors that compound over time to become potentially significant. A three-pronged approach should be taken to address Longevity risk, with measures implemented as soon as feasible to avoid a need for much larger adjustments later.

Measures to be taken include: (1) acknowledging government exposure to Longevity risk and implementing measures to ensure that it does not threaten medium- and long-term fiscal sustainability; (2) risk sharing between governments, private pension providers, and individuals, partly through increased individual financial buffers for retirement, pension system reform, and sustainable old-age safety nets; and (3) transferring Longevity risk in capital markets to those that can better bear it. An important part of reform will be to link retirement ages to advances in Longevity. If undertaken now, such measures can be implemented sustainably.

Public policy is paramount to allowing the people who are part of the growing aging demographic to adapt to the "silver wave" and have affordable retirement plan solutions tailored for the elder demographic. The 2019 US Secure Act did an effective job in making small business owners who plan on retiring to set up "Safe Harbour" retirement plans that are cheaper and easier to use. In another way, the Japanese government stepped in and disallowed shorting of the Government Pension Investment Fund (GPIF) in 2019 preventing short sellers from benefiting from the grave dangers that pension funds are dealing with (growing deficits, underfunding, etc.) due to Longevity risks. Monetary and fiscal policy has to take into account the growing elderly population along with significant integration with the private sector to allow the public to ease into this transition of a larger older population.

Chapter 16: Longevity FinTech (Contributor: Sergey Balasanyan)

"As increasing numbers of high-net-worth individuals (HNWI) and regular middle-class individuals age, financial institutions enhance and extend their clients' health spans and wealth spans in equal measure. Modern challenger banks are chasing income from the middle-aged and younger generations, missing a US$15 trillion market opportunity, whilst banks like HSBC, UBS and Barclays are making their first steps in the AgeTech industry. It's an outdated approach to challenge traditional banks, and the future is in synergetic cooperation.

Challenger banks should challenge themselves rather than challenging traditional banks. New technologies in finance have unlimited opportunities, and yet many of these opportunities have not surfaced despite the huge, and illogically disproportionate, amount of investment in the sector. This is the failure of challenger banks, and this unmet need is what the Longevity Bank and Longevity FinTech company aim to correct. Currently we can't disclose the exact concept of the product, but this product will make online and mobile banking experience easy and safe for the senior generation, raising trust to modern banking technology among 60+ aged people. It will initially set itself up as a bank attracting net-new customers, but the goal is to also become a third-party provider to major banks."

Sergey Balasanyan in *Challenger Longevity Bank positions itself for the silver generation* (FinTech Futures, 2020)

"Today, FinTech for social good is a rising trend that is attracting significant attention from both governments, NGOs, companies and investors alike. It represents more than just financial inclusion; it represents a clear path toward humanitarian good, and towards accelerating the socioeconomic development of underdeveloped countries so as to give them greater opportunities for acquiring basic human amenities."

Dmitry Kaminskiy, in *FinTech for Social Good* (Deep Knowledge Analytics, 2018)

If you have read this book to the current stage, you will have an idea of what FinTech is, both in general and for an aging user base.

Now I would like to delve a little deeper into the money and economics but perhaps more so into how this affects our lives both individually and as a society.

One of the greatest drawbacks of the pre-Longevity Industry mindset is that in both subtle and overt ways it is death obsessed and views aging and the elderly as a problem and a burden — yesterday's men and women robbed of both their vitality and relevance.

> **So you see, FinTech most certainly already exists, and is already growing, so what is this fuss over making it aging friendly? Why not just have a "large-sized font" option which is already readily available on most smartphones and be done with it?**

Well, that comes down to a question of two things, money and who we are as a collective human population and our value systems. In the world right now there are three massive markets. The first two are the United States and China, which should do little to surprise you, but the third might. Amazingly, it is people over the age of 50. Is it not amazing that this massive market exists and yet it is ignored as FinTech companies and FinTech-enabled banks spend massive amounts of time and treasure chasing the under-30 market? This is a group that does certainly spend, often on a whim, but that is also going to be at the start of their careers and not nearing the end, and are much less likely to do things such as buying a new car or spending money on vacations as their older neighbours.

Of course I am not saying that the under-30 market should be kicked to the curb, *but rather that it makes no sense, financially or morally, to ignore the aged market*. Both can be served, and certainly any benefits that the aged may have accrued through this stronger focus on them can also benefit younger clients or at worst have a neutral impact.

On a societal level of economic endeavour, with huge image, marketing and advertising sectors, the defining aspects are who is it all about, who is the audience they are talking to and most importantly catering to. Regrettably, aged people have not been the biggest focus, but thankfully this is something that can and will be corrected as FinTech companies become educated about it and integrated into the Longevity Industry.

This is a move that I would say is both morally correct as it is one that will result in massive economic reward. It creates a stronger trust and relationship, not only with their older customers, but also with their younger ones who not only realize that one day they will be the older customer, but who also see their older friends and family members catered to and allowed to act in the world in a dignified manner. Progress is already being made, such as the collaboration between **HSBC UK** and the **Alzheimer's Society** that is mentioned in this book, which relies heavily on educating bank staff, but also makes novel usage of already existing tech, such as chip technology as well as tweaking bank policy to make it easier for people suffering from dementia to seek out help from friends and family that they trust to help them with their banking.

Currently, banking for the aged in general is fixated on an image of the elderly with a fixed pension income and little spending power, where the appeal to the elderly might be reduced banking fees or a kinder rate for renting a safety deposit box for the over 65 clientele.

This is not to say that these are not things that are not helpful or wanted, and there are certainly seniors living on strict budgets. Too many in fact, and that is the reflection of a death obsessed rather than a Longevity empowered society, although one should keep in mind that ***globally the aged population represents a billion people***, whose aggregate spending power — as we have already touched — is staggering.

Seniors will become much more engaged and productive and will benefit from not losing their perceived relevance in society. The aged in a Longevity positive society will be even happier, healthier and wealthier than they are now.

As the Longevity Industry grows and rises to preeminence across all sectors, we will all enjoy not only longer lives, but more importantly a greater healthspan.

However, a more productive and better healthspan does not mean a life with no issues or limitations, especially earlier on in the evolution of the treatments and healthcare into P4 Medicine and beyond.

So how exactly can FinTech benefit and enable people as they grow older?

Before delving into this question, I should reiterate to those involved in the financial sector or even the financial sector oriented venture capital firms, that FinTech for the elderly is absolutely not simply a public outreach exercise, act of charity or some sort of regulatory burden, but rather an opportunity for astounding financial gain.

There is elder controlled money out there, in bank accounts, in home and property equity and stuffed under mattresses and into shoe boxes. It really is, as a first step, just a matter of engaging with that audience and appealing to them and accommodating them in a way that makes their economic engagement and the FinTech companies increased profits possible in the first place.

There are already some advances in place, as it is touched on in this book, but really it comes down to imagination and enabling people to overcome difficulties that would otherwise prevent or discourage them from using these services.

It is a case where the cliche "the person who makes the money is the one who sells umbrellas when it is raining" is correct.

Current efforts are largely focused on introducing an older generation of baby boomers and older to using FinTech solutions in the first place, and a lot of that is education and presenting ideas to them in their language, focusing on what is relevant to them.

This also allows seniors to stay active as investors as the advent of better and better AI will allow them to employ investment strategies appropriate to their needs and specific life situations.

Beyond that, current FinTech is focused on simplifying and automating a lot of the processes, not only eliminating a lot of remembering when to write and post which cheque, but also getting rid of a lot of hard-to-keep-track-of paper clutter.

There is also some focus on presenting FinTech to potential senior clients as a fraud resistant solution that protects both their finances and identity, as for instance it removes the age old trick of stealing personal information from people's rubbish bins and curbsides.

Much of this additional personal security will of course increasingly rely on the immutable distributed ledger technology of blockchain. Beyond that, there are some things that already exist but can be reimagined and repurposed for senior use, and some things that simply have yet to be imagined.

We can only guess what those things will be, but one can rest assured that they will come to be. This is because of the nature of the Longevity Industry in general in being liquidity intensive as well as providing a strong ROI. This self-perpetuating cycle will fuel and engender innovation in order to further grow and benefit the market, which will lead to even further innovations so that the sector can maintain a competitive edge over more traditional sectors, as well as between individual companies.

As for what is clearly ahead, just becomes a matter of looking at existing challenges for seniors such as gradual age-related loss of manual dexterity. Appropriate solutions here can involve hands free use combined with advanced vocal recognition, or just simply handheld devices and computer keyboards with more thoughtful ergonomic designs.

Automated teller machines already have audio jacks to allow the visually impaired to better access services and there is no reason that this can not also be the case with online financial activity.

Which perhaps is a good segue to touch briefly on what might be one of the most challenging areas for FinTech to address: the role that the simple act of going out to the bank plays in the lives of many seniors. For them a trip to the bank is not simply about completing financial transactions, but also social ones. It is a chance to chat with the tellers, and with the people in the line as well as people they might pass on the street. It, in short, becomes a way to get out and about. The same FinTech that

- **might make a younger person feel more independent,**
- **might have the opposite, isolating effect on a senior.**

Hybrid solutions, such as live video chats, an idea presented in this book, are helpful, but also clearly are just not quite hitting the mark.

The real solution, however, might not even come from the FinTech providers, but the seniors themselves. In a Longevity-focused world in which **P4 Medicine** and the **latest medical** and **technological advances** are in place, older people will simply be able to be more active for longer and longer periods of their life. The opportunities to interact socially by taking a trip out to the bank may shrink, but will be replaced by other activities, that previous, less affluent and less mobile seniors might have been forced to forego. The limits, as far as the tech is concerned, really comes down to the creativity and imagination of the FinTech companies, entrepreneurs and innovators.

- Maybe FinTech does not mean completely foregoing the brick and mortar bank altogether.
- Maybe the senior client can have wearable technology that logs them in and lets the teller know that they are there and even what they likely are there for, based on previous habits before they even reach the wicket.
- Maybe it is simply a matter of using a senior friendly mobile device to message ahead, so the bank can get a head start on any potentially complex transactions to limit the time the senior has to wait for service.

As with any new industry, there is also often a crossover period in which one technology or way of doing business displaces the other, and in some instances this happens more rapidly than in others.

The point here is that it is as ethically unsound as it is poor business judgement to ignore the needs of seniors and the potential profit and societal revitalization they represent. There is no doubt a "Silver Tsunami" is on the way, but if FinTech companies and innovators can mobilize correctly and intelligently, the Silver Tsunami will be a wave of prosperity and not destruction.

I would like to thank both of my esteemed colleagues Margaretta and Dmitry for graciously allowing me to contribute to this book and its amazing and important message.

Throw away a negative "aging" mindset

Replace it with a positive Longevity mindset

Introducing the Longevity Bank: Integrated AgeTech-WealthTech Solutions

Technological progress brings both challenges and opportunities. In 2014, UK non-cash payments exceeded cash payments by volume for the first time.

New technology holds out the promise of better, cheaper services – but only if a sufficient range of well-designed options are available for a consumer marketplace with a very diverse range of needs. The fast pace of change is difficult for many people to adjust to.

Bank branch closures, for example, can be particularly challenging for socially or digitally excluded older people. New technologies bring convenience, but also new opportunities for fraud and scams.

Today we can see the significant rise of FinTech banks, redefining the banking industry by connecting with a new generation of mobile-first consumers. The brightest examples of digital banks are Revolut, Monzo and Starling Bank in the UK, Curve and N26 in Europe, and BankMobile and GoBank in the USA.

FinTech banks are chasing income from the middle-age and younger generation, while missing 1 billion consumer or US$15 trillion market opportunity, developing technology only for a limited age category.

As the share of the population above 65 years old is increasing in every member state of the European Union, European banks are lagging behind in finding solutions for this age group, especially taking into account the fact that seniors are holding the lion's share of the savings. Traditional banks, as opposed to challenger banks, are making their first steps in AgeTech, adapting their infrastructure for the elderly; for example, HSBC has partnered with the Alzheimer's Society to create dementia-friendly products, while Barclays is actively developing software for seniors to make their customer experience more comfortable.

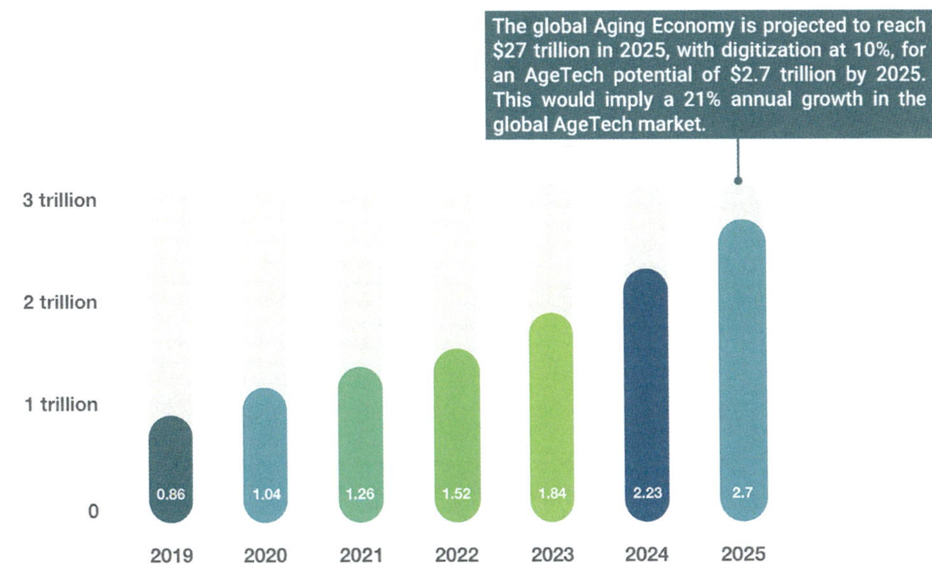

FinTech focused on financial wellness is just beginning to emerge. Aging baby boomers approaching retirement are interested in using tech and AI for financial planning. In a few years, financial start-ups targeting the mass market or focusing on the millennial generation will face consumer problems and convulsively begin to focus on the older market, while firms that target the senior segment of the population will have taken **70% of the market by this time**.

Financial companies, currently working with 55+ aged segment, are mainly focused on applying AgeTech for protecting older people's finances while ensuring that they do not surrender their independence.

An interesting point for the financial sector to note is that, according to doctors, the first easy sign to detect severe declines in cognitive abilities are the bad financial decisions that patients start to make.

For instance, paying the same bill twice, being an easy victim of scams, withdrawing money for people that are taking advantage of them, etc. **EverSafe** is a company focused on that issue, preventing financial exploitation of seniors, offering a detection and alert system designed to get in front of identity theft and other financial crimes.

In the near future, we are expecting the groundbreaking synergy between innovative

IT-technologies **Wealth Management**

Traditional Banking Services **Artificial Intelligence**

designed and adapted for retirees and seniors, which will lead to the creation of an AgeTech-Longevity banking trend.

Using progressive AgeTech technologies will make access to banking services easier, bringing new simply designed products at transparent costs. The fulfillment of typical and atypical needs will make banks old age-friendly, and establish trust and the much needed financial security among senior customers.

For a number of years, Deep Knowledge Ventures was specifically interested in this topic of bridging AgeTech and FinTech, and gathered significant expertise in this field.

In late 2020, we will launch a new substantial grand project, which will be focused on this field, leveraging AgeTech banking to a brand new level, targeting the market of 80-100 year old citizens, in some particular cases even up to 100-120 year old, and putting care for seniors at the heart of our technological, financial and business proposition.

FinTech Bubble: The End is Near

Why challenger banks failed to "challenge" the financial industry? Is it time for the challengers to be "challenged" in the very core of their business model?

Today we can see a significant raise of FinTech banks or so called **challenger banks**, which are "redefining" the banking industry by connecting with a new generation of mobile-first consumers. **As mentioned, the brightest examples of challenger banks are Revolut, Monzo and Starling Bank in the UK, Curve and N26 in Europe, and Chime, BankMobile and GoBank in the USA.**

A number of them (e.g. Revolut, N26) are considered by industry experts as overvalued, using technologies that in the present age of exponential innovation might also be considered actually outdated to some extent, or at least not innovative enough.

"Most challenger/neo banks are not banks at all. They are tech companies acting as introducing brokers to existing banks. To be considered a bank in very broad terms... the entity needs to be able to "take deposits", "issue cards" or "lend from balance sheet" and most challengers don't do any of those. So the real value they add is creative marketing. If the user base acquisition was achieved organically, it would be value, but when the trick is to use VC money to subsidise real costs then it's unsustainable."

Mushegh Tovmasyan, Chairman at Zenus Bank

The UK is home to the most challenger banks unicorns of any country: OakNorth (valued at US$2.8 billion), Monzo (US$2.5 billion) and Revolut (US$1.7 billion).

Furthermore, if analysts estimates are correct, Atom Bank (US$644 million) is closing in on the magic number of US$1 billion. Starling Bank, valued at US$161 million, may be a ways off from unicorn status, but isn't doing too bad for itself all the same.

If profitability is a key metric by which to measure how much these start-ups are actually worth, then we can argue that their valuation is inflated. In recent years, as FinTech has steadily disrupted and even occasionally menaced traditional financial services, venture capital has been pouring into the segment. So goes the FinTech bubble.

Monzo, for instance, faces mounting losses. In the 2018 fiscal year, it lost £47.2 million, 54% more than the previous year. Monzo's leadership says that the losses are necessary to grow quickly.

London-based Revolut — which has already raised almost US$340 million over 12 rounds — hopes to raise another US$500 million, which will give the company a valuation of more than US$5 billion. That's for a company that not only isn't making any profits, but also has been through a series of embarrassments and controversies in 2019, including having to admit that it had "mistakenly" switched off a system for flagging potential money-laundering for several months last year, and being investigated for false advertising.

At the same time CEO Nikolay Storonsky wants the firm to reach a valuation of between US$20 billion and US$40 billion before floating on the stock market.

German N26's valuation is at US$3.5 billion. N26 operates across the European continent and boasts 3.5 million customers, but it is not profitable, nor is it apparently concerned about reaching the black anytime soon.

"How can new firms that have yet to gain customers' main bank accounts — most of these new players are being used as secondary or even tertiary accounts by many people — be worth half of a Deutsche Bank, when you combine their current valuations?"

Chris Skinner, FinTech Expert

In the Tech community, a start-up's value is often linked to the size of its user base and the potential to scale rather than a proven business model.

There's good reason for that: *if investors insisted on profitability before investing, firms like Facebook, Twitter and Instagram could never have survived.* In fact, Twitter had its first profitable quarter in Q4 2017, more than 11 years after its founding. But what was relevant and normal for Social Media growth, and for many other network-related ecosystems (due in part to the synergetic effect of sharing economy business models), may not be implemented as easily for the FinTech Industry.

HypeTech vs. Real FinTech

Many modern challenger banks only look progressive in contrast to the overwhelming conservatism of traditional financial corporations and banks.

The real FinTech industry (built on AI and Data Science, willing and capable to on-board innovations as soon as they are created, constantly staying ahead of the technological curve) has been blurred and delayed by HypeTech, and by overvalued companies who care more about integrating the latest advances in superficial marketing to be on the first wave of hype, rather than the actual latest tech advances in Data Science technologies and their applications for FinTech and WealthTech.

80% of start-up banks will fail to raise still-larger rounds, and inevitably consolidation will begin to happen. Consolidation is definitely coming, not because the companies are overvalued, but because in order to deliver on their valuations they will have to become broader digital financial services companies (it will be hard to be an FX player worth US$10 billion, for example).

Entrepreneurs are raising bigger rounds, and more of them, because they can. Everything is fine. But raising larger and larger rounds is a lockstep. They have to exit some time. *The problem with start-ups raising more and more money in this way, and reaching such stratospheric valuations, is that they are setting themselves up with a Herculean task when it comes to actually trying to sell.* They might be buying time, but they are effectively mortgaging themselves.

European banks are a big buyer group of European FinTechs but cannot afford to buy heavily loss making FinTechs – many FinTechs regularly lose €5-10 million or more a year, and no bank can afford to pay more than €100 million and take on such losses.

However, not all modern FinTech companies are just introducing brokers. There are a number of players that are slicing off a service normally run by a bank and doing it much better.

TransferWise is using a smart approach to allow people to send and receive money safely from abroad without the high fees, Funding Circle is doing it in SME lending, Square in card payments, Zopa in peer-to-peer lending, to name just a few examples. That's the reason why in May 2019 BlackRock and other large investment funds have acquired a US$292 million stake in TransferWise. Audited financials for the fiscal year ending in March 2018 revealed a 77% revenue growth to £117 million and a net profit of £6.2 million after tax.

Challenger banks were aiming to compete with traditional banks, but in reality they are now competing with each other for a comparatively small slice of the entire user-base due to a lack of accelerated development, which lags behind the current pace of technological progress.

Longevity Bank: Where Real Tech Meets Profitability

"The one billion retired people globally are a multitrillion dollar opportunity for business."

Dmitry Kaminskiy interview in the Financial Times

"The global spending power of those who are aged 60 and over will reach US$15 trillion annually by 2020."

Merrill Lynch, Bank of America

Challenger banks are chasing income from the middle-age and younger generation, while missing 1 billion consumer or US$15 trillion market opportunity, developing technology only for a limited age category.

As the share of the population above 60 is increasing in every member state of the European Union, European banks are lagging behind in finding solutions for this age group, especially taking into account the fact that seniors are holding the lion's share of the savings. Traditional banks like UBS, HSBC, Credit Suisse, Barclays and Citi, as opposed to challenger banks, are making their first steps in AgeTech, adapting their infrastructure for the elderly. For example, HSBC has partnered with the Alzheimer's Society to create dementia-friendly products, as mentioned, while Barclays is actively developing software for seniors to make their customer experience more comfortable. UBS went so far as to create The Century Club among their clients expecting to live up to 100 years.

If traditional banks, with hundreds of years of history and nearly-unbreakable, guaranteed trust behind their brands and their long-standing reputations, were willing to on-board Data Science, **AI** and **advanced IT-solutions** and **technologies** to meet the needs of the untapped Silver Ocean (clients who are 60+ years old), they would stand in an almost unconquerable position to challenge and gain the multitrillion market opportunity that their younger, less experienced competitors failed to capture.

If they are able to do so, then the combination of their guaranteed brand stability and consumer/client trust and technology-driven AgeTech, WealthTech, InsurTech and HealthTech solutions would put them in an unstoppable position for growth, and enable them to transform a source of loss (the aging population) into an unprecedented source of growth, prosperity and stability.

As the 2020 decade begins, real FinTech companies should be fully capable of onboarding **AgeTech** and **HealthTech** (Health Longevity) into fully integrated financial products, services and solutions for the Silver Generation in order to seize the untapped and overwhelmingly neglected US$15 trillion market opportunity of 1 billion people in retirement.

Challenger banks are now making more to a low-margin wholesale marketplace, trying to scalp tiny slices of profit, rather than real financial products that are capable of making a profit for both banks and for their clients, in simultaneity and synergy. This is similar to several years ago when high frequency scalping, mechanic and robotic systems were taken over by progressive hedge funds, implementing sophisticated systems with strong AI.

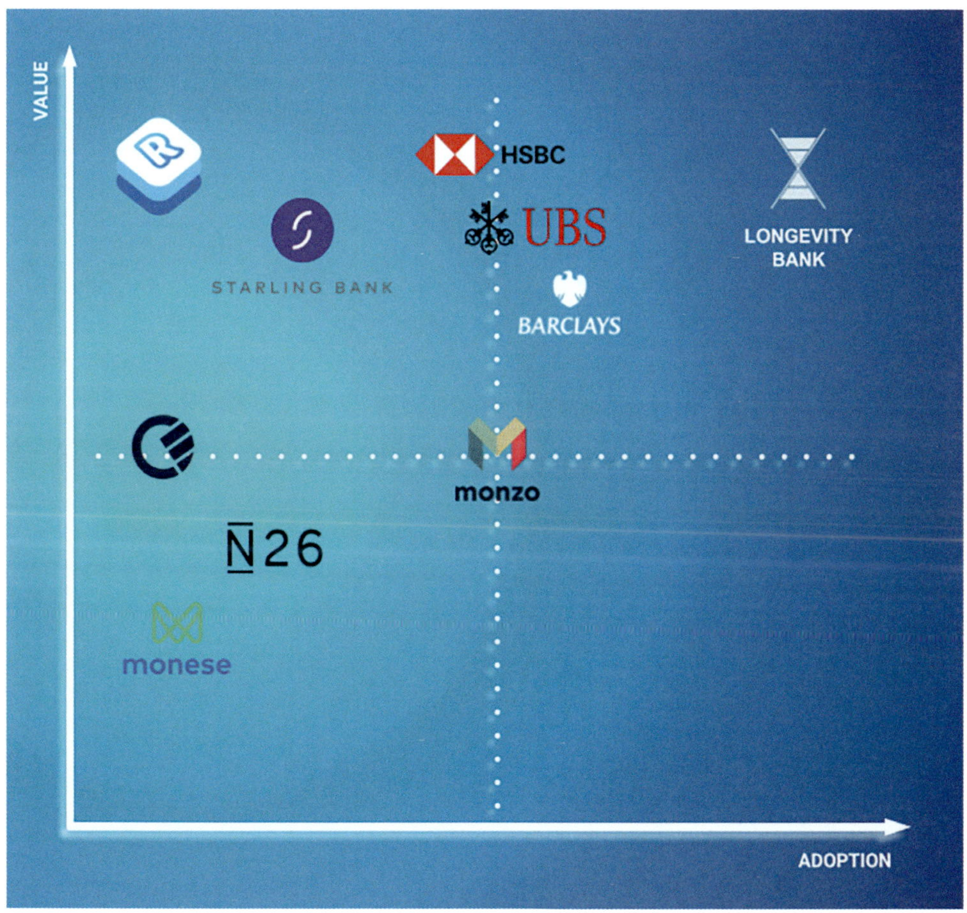

As increasing numbers of HNWIs and regular middle-class individuals age and begin to recognize Health as the New Wealth, the time has come for banks to offer fully-integrated, AI-empowered, Data Science-driven AgeTech, WealthTech and HealthTech solutions to create an ecosystem and infrastructure to secure the stability, sustainability and future of the Silver Generation, and to empower, enhance and extend their clients' healthspans and wealthspans in equal measure.

Chapter 17: Longevity Finance and the Shift from FinTech 1.0 to FinTech 2.0

Switzerland is home to a number of the world's biggest financial institutions, banks, asset management firms and insurance companies.

Switzerland is one of the most efficiently regulated and supervised financial centres in the world and has been leading transformative developments emerging from the digitalization of its banking and financial sector.

The country also probably has the most stable system in the world in terms of a combination of financial, social, economic and political frameworks and long-term stability. Also, its practical implementation framework of science and technology is quite developed. In fact, ETH Zurich is number 1 in terms of technology transfer in Europe, exceeding even Cambridge and Oxford by quantity of commercial spinoffs that succeeded to merge into advanced technological companies.

The digitization of finance, and a Novel Financial System which treats Longevity as a dividend, will play an integral role in the future Longevity Industry and economy.

Switzerland was recently recognized as the most AgeTech-friendly country by the United Nations. **However, Switzerland is not home to the most advanced FinTech industry; it is implementing some FinTech solutions, but the real hub of FinTech industry is London, as it is the nexus of the biggest quantity in a single town of FinTech and AI start-ups in the world.**

It is estimated that Switzerland is home to around **700 AI start-ups** and perhaps **1000 FinTech start-ups**.

In the next several years, FinTech is expected to merge into FinTech 2.0, when advances in **AI, InsurTech, MarTech, LegalTech, RegTech** will converge into a single integrated and advanced technology that will deliver the most sophisticated and robust results which were expected to be delivered over the last several years by the FinTech Industry, but which ultimately failed to occur.

$350 billion were exceeded in the last 10 years investments in the FinTech industry. The same amount of funding was received by industries like AI, Healthcare and AeroSpace and we saw a large number of technological breakthroughs in these fields, like self-driving cars, advanced deep learning AI, next-generation space aircrafts, significant achievements in the cancer research, etc.

Compared to these industries, modern FinTech remained stuck in the year 2015. As new technologies in Finance don't need FDA approval or many years of clinical trials to be implemented into banks, that creates unlimited opportunities and potential for driving innovation in this field. In our opinion, the amount of investments into FinTech and achieved results in practice compared to the current state of technological progress in other domains is illogically disproportionate.

The minimum threshold that FinTech should have achieved by 2020 is "FinTech 2.0" which shall fit into the formula:

FinTech 2.0 = AI + FinTech + LegalTech + RegTech + InsurTech + MarTech + HealthTech

The result is much greater than the sum of its parts. All these components will create a seamless user experience and modern approach for profit generation.

And yet, Switzerland, the UK and the entire FinTech and financial industries are missing a very big opportunity. The most valuable and capable client demographic in terms of purchasing power are the citizens of the 7th continent — the 7th continent is made up of 1 billion people around the world aged 50+.

The global spending power of people aged 50+ is expected to be US$15 trillion this year. Switzerland has the elements necessary to become a leading Longevity financial hub, including factors such as a lean political system that facilitates rapid implementation of integrated government programs, a strong research environment for geroscience, a strong research and business environment for digital health, and most importantly, international financial prowess.

Over the last 100 years, the Financial Industry was infected by ageism and financial exclusion of people in retirement.

The most bizarre thing is that tech entrepreneurs are working on the financial inclusion for underdeveloped countries and unbanked people, while ignoring the financial inclusion for **1 billion people in retirement**, the wealthiest part of the financial system. Governments should consider a legal framework for financial institutions to create an equal access to financial products for all age ranges, adjusting all technologies for each range.

In the next few years, a new generation of financial technology companies focused on WealthTech will create digital solutions to transform the investment and asset management industry. New companies have arrived on the scene offering advice based on AI and Big Data, micro-investment platforms, and trading solutions based on social networks. The growing aging population is one of the crucial drivers of innovation in WealthTech. Financial services innovators have an opportunity to enhance the financial lives of individuals over 50 by designing new solutions and adapting existing products and services for them. The depth and diversity of this group create an incredible opportunity to implement innovation and address financial health challenges head on.

As in P4 Medicine (Predictive, Preventive, Personalised and Participative Medicine), in the FinTech Industry should be created a P6 Finance Framework (Personalised, Participative, Predictive, Progressive, Protected and Precision).

The 7th Continent - 1 Billion People in Retirement Globally

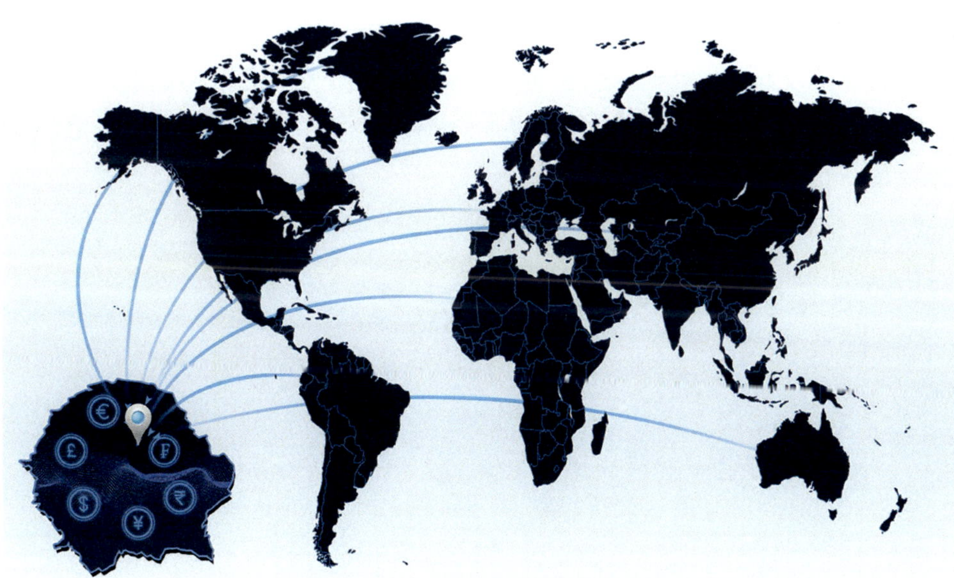

Clients 50+, and younger clients who are expecting to live 100 years and beyond, are a very diverse group in terms of their interests and desires. They can be segmented into different layers because the interests and desires of clients 50-60 years old are different from 60-70, and the interests of clients 70-80 years old may be different from other citizens of the 7th continent.

For example, AgeTech refers to advanced IT solutions for people 80+. Bankers and progressive FinTech executives should consider FinTech products designed specifically for clients who are 90 and even 100 years of age.

Based on these considerations, we can expect that:

- The most advanced FinTech 2.0 technology adjusted to the Longevity Industry will probably emerge in London.
- There is at least 1 company working exactly on that matter; it is Longevity FinTech Company, incorporated in London and managed by Sergey Balasanyan, (who is spearheading the company's subsidiary, Longevity Bank, spearheading its Longevity Card project and developing FinTech 2.0 tools and solutions for the framework of Longevity FinTech), with the help of Stefan Hascoet, who is working on the preparation of its subsidiary Longevity Bank in Switzerland.
- The first actual Longevity Bank will probably emerge in Switzerland, as there are a large number of corresponding pillars or cornerstones necessary for such a bank's success already present, including:
  - Progressive RegTech environment
  - Sufficient FinTech development
  - Sufficient development of its MedTech
  - HealthTech ecosystem
  - Significant base of individuals

  This will create the perfect ecosystem for Longevity Bank clients (wealthy people aged 50+ and younger people who are expecting to live 100 years and beyond, interested in maximizing their healthspans and wealthspans).

Chapter 18: FinTech 2.0 and the Rise of Longevity Banks: Where Healthspan Meets Wealthspan

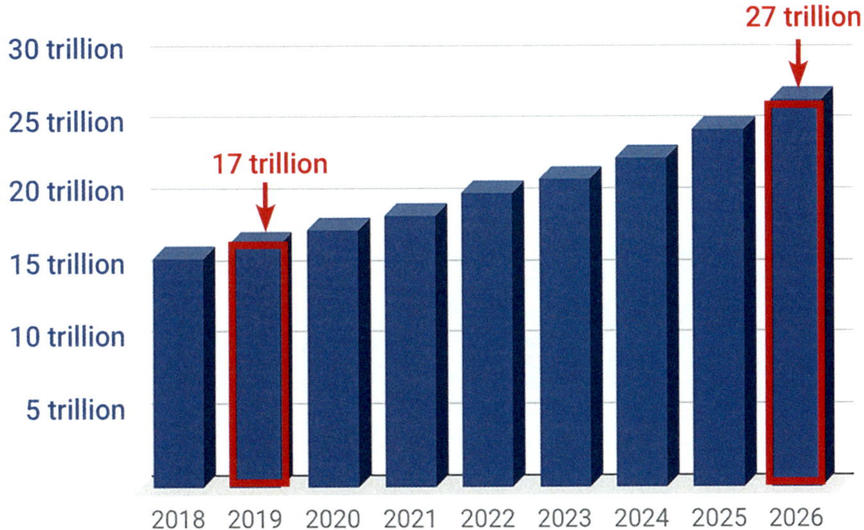

AI for Longevity has more potential to increase healthy Longevity in the short term than any other sector. **The application of AI for Longevity will bring the greatest real-world benefits and will be the main driver of progress in the widespread extension of healthy Longevity.** The global spending power of people aged 60 and over is anticipated to reach **US$15 trillion annually by 2020**.

The Longevity Industry will dwarf all other industries in both size and market capitalization, reshape the global financial system, and disrupt the business models of pension funds, insurance companies, investment banks, and entire national economies.

Longevity has become a recurring topic in analytical reports from leading financial institutions such as CitiBank, UBS Group, Julius Baer, and Barclays. At the recent AI for Longevity Summit in London, top executives from Prudential, HSBC, AXA Insurance, NVIDIA, Microsoft, Babylon Health, Insilico Medicine, Longevity.Capital, Longevity Vision

Fund, Juvenescence, and Deep Knowledge Ventures came together to discuss the Longevity Industry.

International policymakers and senior corporate executives shared learnings from Japan, Israel, Switzerland, the US and the UK, and exchanged ideas on beginning to work together in a new social contract to enhance global prosperity equitably. Switzerland is one of the most Longevity progressive countries in the world with both high investment in biotechnology and the capacity to integrate AI into its economic, financial and healthcare systems. Switzerland has the potential to be a world leader in both the Global Longevity Industry and the 4th Industrial Revolution.

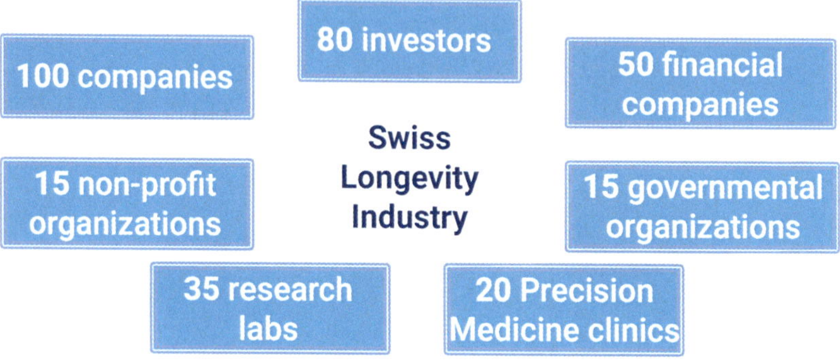

Switzerland is in an excellent position to retain its leadership by focusing on the optimal assembly of its existing resources to transform the challenge of demographic aging into a national asset.

The country has a large aging population and Swiss investment banks are acutely aware of the oncoming demographic challenge. Switzerland is one of the most efficiently regulated and supervised financial centres in the world and has been leading transformative developments emerging from the digitalization of its banking and financial sector.

Longevity-progressive countries typically have large aging populations, and aging populations have two longevity-progressive benefits: voting power and spending power.

The digitization of finance, and a Novel Financial System which treats Longevity as a dividend, will play an integral role in the Longevity economy. According to a recent report by Aging Analytics Agency, Switzerland has the elements necessary to become a leading Longevity financial hub, including, as was already stated, factors such as a lean political system that facilitates rapid implementation of integrated government programs, a strong research environment for geroscience, a strong research and business environment for digital health, and most importantly, international financial prowess.

Switzerland has the ability to develop several Longevity specific programs over the next several years.

One program is a Longevity progressive pension system and insurance company ecosystem that accounts for both population aging (which threatens to destabilize the current business models of insurance companies and pension funds) and the potential for widespread healthspan extension.

Another program is a national strategy for intensively developing Geroscience and FinTech to a state so advanced that it propels Switzerland into a central role in the international Longevity business ecosystem and as a global leader in Longevity Finance.

According to Aging Analytics Agency, 10% of all European FinTech enterprises are located in Switzerland.

Switzerland is leading the digitization of financial markets and establishing itself as a catalyst for financial innovation on a global level.

The country has a strong and productive geroscience community and has gained prominence among investors as a global

BioTech hub and hotbed of innovation. The Swiss Institute for Bioinformatics recently identified large numbers of genetic markers directly linked to human life expectancy.

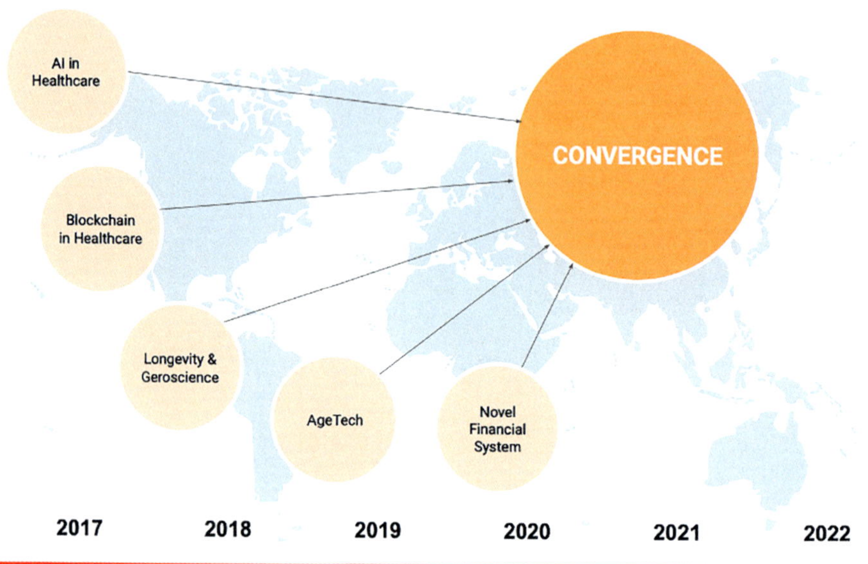

BioValley

Switzerland is situated at one end of the BioValley — one of the leading life sciences clusters in Europe. This cluster is unique in that it spans across three countries, Switzerland, Germany and France, and includes Basel, a global life sciences hub. BioValley brings together important ingredients for a successful BioTech cluster including a concentration of companies, rich availability of skills, experience within Life Sciences, and a world class research base.

The cluster in Switzerland has an excess of **50,000 people** working in the life sciences field including **15,000 scientists**. There are **600 companies** in the cluster developing therapeutic, diagnostic or medical devices to address a wide range of diseases in multiple therapeutic classes. There are **100,000 students** enrolled in **10 universities** and research institutions including the University of Basel, the Max Planck Institute and the Freiburg University.

The cluster has produced a number of spin-out companies supported by a financial network including both public and private financing initiatives as well as traditional venture capital and private equity.

Longevity AI Consortium Expands to Switzerland

In November 2019, Europe's first Longevity AI Consortium (LAIC) launched at King's College London. LAIC is currently developing collaborative research projects with Dynamics of Healthy Ageing (DynAge) and the Digital Society Initiative (DSI) at the University of Zurich. **The research will utilize AI technologies to predict the future cognitive ability of individuals using multimodal neuroimaging and risk factor data.**

Academics in Zurich will work in collaboration with colleagues at the Institute of Psychiatry, Psychology and Neuroscience at King's College London. LAIC plans to establish several collaborative projects with the University of Zurich and with other Swiss universities in 2020. The joint R&D between Ageing Research at Kings and Swiss universities forms the first phase of the global Longevity AI Consortium that will eventually be extended to Israel, Singapore, Japan and the US.

AgeTech

FinTech banks are redefining the banking industry by connecting with a new generation of mobile-first consumers.

However, as we are emphasizing in this book, FinTech banks are focusing on consumers who are middle-age and younger, not on the 1 billion people in retirement and the corresponding US$15 trillion market opportunity.

As the share of the population over 60 increases, Swiss banks are lagging behind in finding solutions for this age group. Traditional banks, as opposed to challenger banks, are taking their first steps in AgeTech and adapting their infrastructure for people over 60.

WealthTech

The WealthTech Industry refers to a new generation of financial technology companies that create digital solutions to transform the investment and asset management industry. New companies have arrived on the scene offering advice based on

- AI and Big Data,
- Micro-investment platforms,
- Trading solutions based on social networks.

A growing aging population is one of the main drivers of innovation in WealthTech. Financial services innovators have an opportunity to enhance the financial lives of individuals over 60 by designing new solutions and adapting existing products and services for them. This is an opportunity to implement innovations that address financial health challenges head on.

Financial Wellness

As a core component of its mission to develop Switzerland into a leading international Longevity Financial Industry hub, **Longevity Swiss**

Foundation plans on roadmapping the development of AI Centers for Financial Wellness.

Whereas the proposed AI Centers for Longevity would focus on optimizing health, these centres would focus on the application of AI to the creation of methods and technologies to promote wellness in other areas including financial wellness, continuing education, psychological well-being, neuroplasticity, and active social involvement.

The planned development of AI Centers for Financial Wellness will enable financial stability over extended periods of healthy Longevity for Swiss citizens.

Switzerland could become the centre of the Longevity financial industry. Given its geographic size and its reliance on international cooperation, its function in the Longevity Industry will be as a small but important node.

Due to its status as an international BioTech epicentre and its reputation as one of the most progressive countries in terms of its financial industry, the prospects for Switzerland to lead the world in the development of its Longevity financial industry are strong.

Today, change occurs at the intersection of two or more scientific and technological domains. We are at the beginning of a trend where the degree of complexity and the number of convergence points will increase exponentially.

The convergence of AI, advanced Data Science, and Longevity research will accelerate important medical breakthroughs that will benefit all humans.

During the 2020 decade, the Longevity Industry will impact many areas of our lives. Longevity policies enacted by governments and changes in the global financial industry will transform society.

Achieving small but practical results in Longevity distributed at scale will have enormous and multiplicative effects on society. Extending the functional lifespan of humans by just one year will decrease suffering for tens of millions of people and will improve the quality of life for billions of people.

The Rise of the Longevity Bank: Where Healthspan Meets Wealthspan

The "WealthTech industry" refers to a **new generation of financial technology companies** that create digital solutions to transform the investment and asset management industry. New companies have arrived on the scene offering advice based on artificial intelligence and Big Data, micro-investment platforms, or trading solutions based on social networks.

> **The global trend of aging population due to the increase in life expectancy and well-being is one of the crucial drivers of innovations in WealthTech.**

Financial services innovators have the opportunity to greatly enhance the financial lives of the **aged 60+ aiming to live up to 100 years** by designing new solutions, in addition to adapting existing products and services, and targeting them to this segment. The depth and diversity of this group creates an incredible opportunity to implement innovations on their behalf and address their financial health challenges head on.

WealthTech adjusted for clients aged 60+ aiming to live up to 100 years includes the following segments:

- **Investing tools:** products and services that provide comparison tools and access to consultancy on investments;
- **Robo-advisors:** AI-driven business and investment management advising tools;
- **Robo-retirement:** AI-driven advising tools on the subject of clients' retirement plans;
- **Micro-investing:** a technology that makes investing small amounts of money possible;
- **Financial services software:** applications directed at supporting wealth management and investment strategy;
- **Digital brokerage:** online services and applications directed at assisting access to assets and investment.

Longevity FinTech Company B2C Architecture

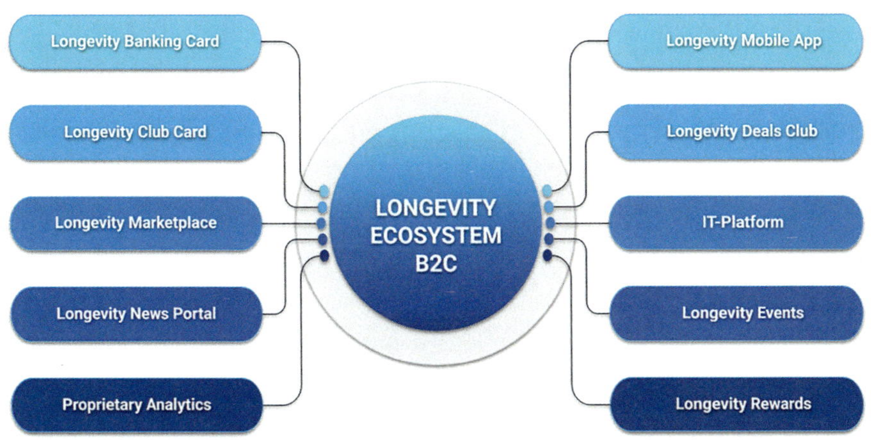

The Longevity Ecosystem is The World's First Fully-Integrated Platform enabling integrated end-to-end access to advanced Longevity Products, Services and Knowledge.

Longevity FinTech

The Longevity FinTech Company will provide high-end white label financial technology solutions for longevity-focused companies and start-ups.

Since more advanced financial technologies are appearing every day, our company will not be engaged in the development of its own technologies, but will take ready-made back-end systems from our partners' pool, and our front-end developers and the Longevity experts team will subsequently tune them to the longevity specifics and needs of the client.

Through the adaptation of complex financial technologies to the senior generation, our counterparties will get Plug & Play solutions for their business, including:

- **Customized design of interface;**
- **Implementation of AgeTech and WealthTech components;**
- **Payment gateway and escrow services;**
- **Longevity marketplace's partner pool;**
- **Analytics insights.**

Longevity LegalTech

Longevity Fintech Company's B2B LegalTech solution allows businesses to create contracts governed by business and compliance rules that can smartly and dynamically decide the clauses, metadata and templates to be used to generate a contract. It also offers an easy, intuitive user interface that encourages adoption by any front-line user.

Through the use of smart contracts, our counterparties will become faster and more flexible by:

- **Offering the ability to learn from past contracts.**
- **Providing an understanding of the risk-taking capacity of the organization.**
- **Creating adaptable contracts that change with underlying assets.**

All controversial issues will be brought to the London Court of International Arbitration, an international institution, generally regarded as the leading global forum for dispute resolution proceedings for all parties, irrespective of their location or system of law.

Longevity AgeTech and WealthTech

AgeTech and WealthTech for seniors, two rapidly developing sectors, provide new types of products and demonstrate the significant growth in the size of the market. WealthTech is providing innovative products, such as robo-financial advisors and digital brokers supervised and augmented by AI. AgeTech is designed to support the elderly and reduce the consequences of aging in everyday life.

Over the next few years, it is likely that both will come to be regarded as complementary functions within a single product or service. One example of this combination will be a new type of FinTech bank reconfigured for seniors.

Our WealthTech products will include:

- **Robo-advisors:** automated services that use machine-learning algorithms to provide users with advice based on the most profitable investment options, yield targets, user's risk aversion profile and other variables.

- **Robo-retirement:** another version of robo-advisors that is especially popular in the United States. Companies in this category specialize in managing retirement savings.
- **Digital brokers:** online platforms and software tools that put stock market information and the possibility of investing within anyone's reach.
- **Financial products** designed for investors expecting to live 100 years and beyond.

Making Banking Easier for Seniors

Voice Technology

Financial services are full of customer pain points, **especially for senior citizens**, that could be resolved with the help of **voice interaction technology**. Everyone has daily financial needs, but getting basic guidance can be difficult.

And even for those who already have a relationship with a bank, factors such as frustrating experiences with call centres, long wait times, and high fees are chipping away at customer loyalty.

Our voice technology will provide following features to the client:

- **Voice recognition** to strengthen account security;
- **Voice control** to make interaction and integration of mobile banking for the elderly more comfortable and easier.

The last feature includes access to all functions of mobile banking, including transferring money, opening accounts and getting help from AI-driven chatbot and others.

Biometric Identification

Biometric identification by fingertip can be an easy way to get into senior citizens' bank accounts, many of whom are suffering from age-related diseases, making them vulnerable in some cases. For this reason, the Longevity Fintech Company is using both fingertip and face identification to minimize fraud and financial abuse of the elderly.

Our **biometric facial recognition** technology authenticates customers based on who they are as opposed to what they know. This technology offers a second factor of authentication, with the first being possession of the device itself, and the second being a live facial image. Multi-factor authentication presents more barriers to fraudsters. **Facial biometrics** can also be used to access accounts from a computer via webcam. Every time our customer logs into his online account, he or she can use their facial biometrics as an additional security factor to login to their accounts and to request transactions.

Better Payment Gateways

> Aged people are looking into using digital payment methods for their monetary transactions. Their payments must be processed privately and safely (often in differing currencies), their credit cards must be run, their refunds issued and their coupons applied — all in compliance with local regulations.

A payment gateway facilitates a payment transaction by the transfer of information between a payment portal and the front-end processor or an acquiring bank.

For old customers, this service ensures that the payment process is safe and secure.

Besides its main function for authorizing transactions, a payment gateway actually offers a variety of additional features for optimum functionality and user experience:

- **Virtual POS:** a cloud-based service that processes credit card transactions without direct input of data by the customer, acting in the same way as a physical POS at any store or retail, but without the need for additional hardware or software.
- **White-Label Wallet:** gateways to implement digital wallet services for processing mobile payments, which is extremely useful for improving customer experience and managing all operations in one place.
- **PCI-DSS Vault:** gateways that usually allow to securely store information for recurring payments, avoiding the need to re-enter each time they want to make a purchase.

Escrow Services

As populations are getting older, aged people become suppliers of financial liquidity in financial markets.

As with investments, it is important for conservative older clients to consider the risk exposure of a particular financial transaction. Escrow agreements may be one of the best solutions to protect investments.

An escrow is a financial arrangement where a third party holds and regulates payment of the funds required for two parties involved in a given transaction.

It helps make transactions more secure by keeping the payment in a secure escrow account which is only released when all of the terms of an agreement are met as overseen by the escrow company.

Escrows are very useful in the case of a transaction where a large amount of money is involved and a certain number of obligations need to be fulfilled before a payment is released.

Facilitated by a trusted third-party, the escrow process acts as a personal tool to ensure a safe, secure and intuitive sale for both buyers and sellers.

We understand that escrows are not a "one size fits all" service.

Our services provide flexibility to the needs and wants of each individual escrow agreement.

Using licensed escrow services to buy and sell merchandise, services and more is the most convenient way to complete transactions online.

Longevity Bank - tapping into the multitrillion dollar opportunity of integrated AgeTech, WealthTech, financial products and services

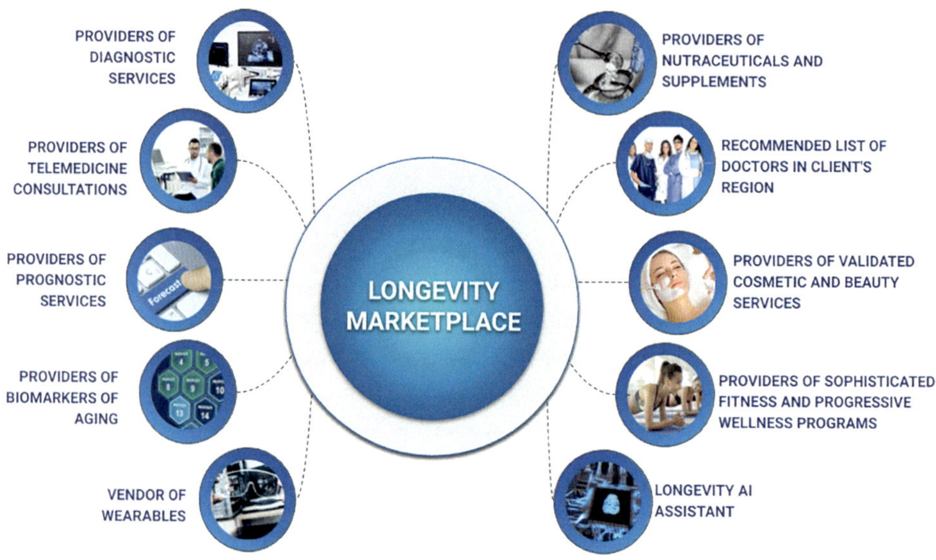

Standard banking products do not always meet the needs of older, especially low- and middle-income adults. **Effective banking products that are tailored to the needs of older adults are key to ensuring their ability to remain independent and financially secure.**

Multipurpose products

Longevity (AgeTech) Bank develops products for people of all ages

Accessibility

Attracts seniors by developing easy-to-use and accessible products

Fraud protection

It has tools for protection from financial exploitation

Special staff training

The staff in AgeTech Bank is trained to find special approach to seniors

Retirement Planning

Retirement planning is vital for older adults and has become a widely-offered service by financial institutions.

Assisting older adults in planning for Longevity and retirement as well as assisting families and caregivers with managing an elder's finances is essential for maintaining their financial wellness and independence.

Targeted Checking Accounts

Another innovation in financial services to help older adults manage their accounts and protect them from exploitation is the use of "View-Only" accounts.

Incorporating these products and services into financial institutions' product and service offerings gives older adults the ability to refrain from using alternative banking and be equipped with the necessary tools and support to remain financially stable and secure using traditional banking.

Training

Banks can also provide support for cognitive decline. Understanding the financial needs of older adults and the barriers they face in managing their finances is crucial for financial institutions to design products that ensure financial security for older adults.

Longevity Club

The Longevity Club is building an end-to-end ecosystem for Longevity commerce, offering a vast mobile and online marketplace where people can discover and save on health and wealth-related products, maximizing their **healthspan (healthy period of life) and wealthspan (period of financial stability)** using the optimal configurations of cutting edge personalised, preventive therapeutics, diagnostics and prognostics to achieve financial wellness over the course of extended healthy lifespans.

Longevity B2C Cards (*Banking + Membership*)

Our Members will have the unique opportunity to choose between a Membership Card, Banking Card or All-in-One Card with the full suit features, products and exclusive discounts.

Members will have access and discounts to the Longevity Marketplace, which offers the world's best products and services in the industry, exclusively featuring scientifically and technically validated vendors.

Longevity B2C Marketplace Architecture

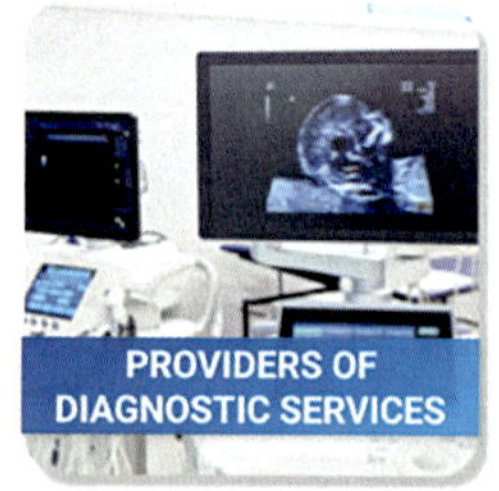

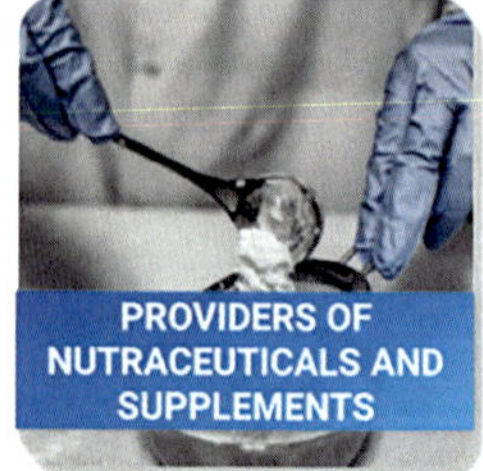

Longevity Club IT-Platform

Front-End User Interface & Mobile App

Mobile App

Longevity Ecosystem and Marketplace

Vendors of Wearables

Providers of Personalised Diagnostic Services

Providers of Personalised Prognostic Services

Providers of Telemedicine Consultations

Providers of Personalised Biomarkers of Aging

AI Assistant

LONGEVITY CARD HEALTHTECH

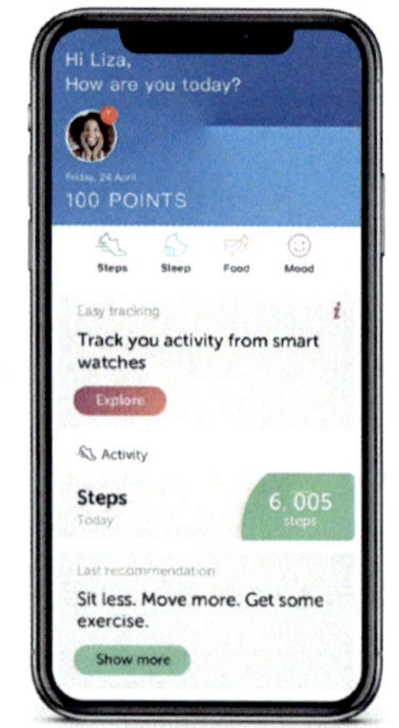

Marketing and Engagement Engine

- **Gamified Sharing and Engagement Economy**
- **Gamified Healthspan and Fitness Goals and Plans**
- **Longevity Reward Points**
- **Decentralized Vendor Ranking**
- **User Control of Persona BioData**

Innovative Back-End

- Advanced Cybersecurity, Big Data Analysis
- Cloud Data Storage

PART IV

Longevity Industry

Science, Technology & Biomedicine

- Global Industrialization of Longevity to Scale
- Most Developed Domains of Geroscience
- Precision Health and the Patient as CEO
- The Crucial Role of AI for Longevity
- AI, Data Science and Mathematical Technologies for Longevity Biomarker Development and R&D
- How AI-Driven Preventive Medicine and Novel InvestTech Solutions Will Disrupt BioTech and Healthcare Industries by 2025
- The Launch of the Longevity AI Consortium
- Longevity FemTech
- Biomarkers of Longevity 2.0: The Need for Maximally Actionable Biomarkers of Aging, Health and Longevity
- What if Geroscience Fails? - Pragmatic Optimism in the Longevity Industry

Chapter 19: The Birth and Rise of Geroscience (The Science of Longevity)

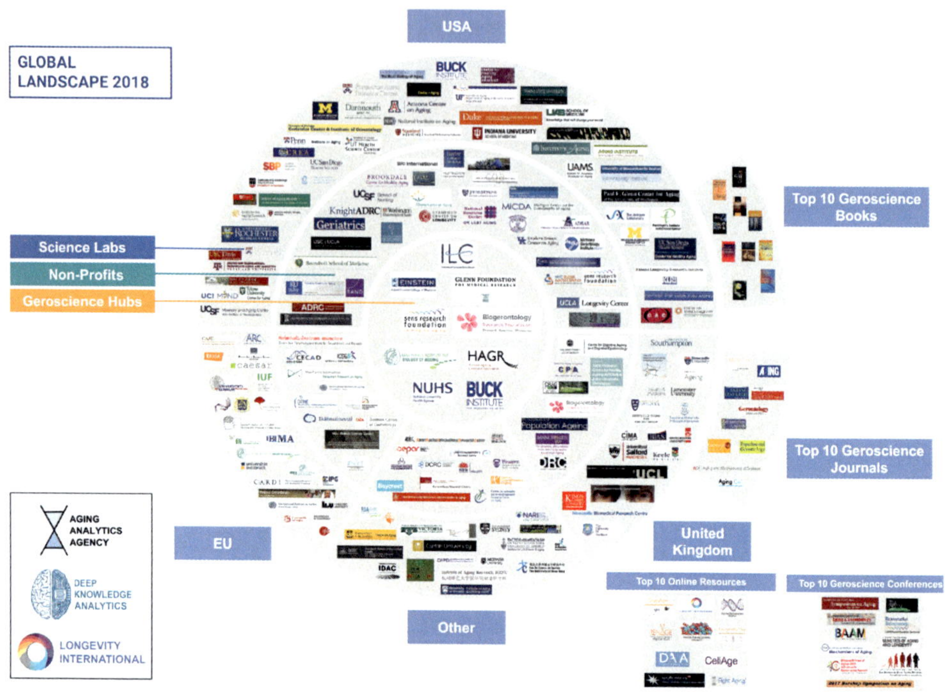

As it was already stated, the war on human illness has evolved from an invasion into a counter-insurgency operation. With infectious diseases now under biomedical control, the stubborn illnesses inflicted from within — cancer, Alzheimer's, arthritis, osteoporosis, not to mention more subtle defects such as progressive hearing loss and cognitive decline — are biomedicine's next and perhaps final challenges.

***Geriatric medicine**, the branch of medicine dealing with these individual diseases one by one, is fighting a losing battle.*

> By the end of the 20th century, biogerontology, the study of biological aging, and geroscience, the interdisciplinary field that aims to understand the relationship between aging and age-related diseases, had come into their own. Then, a wide range of theories on how aging happens emerged.

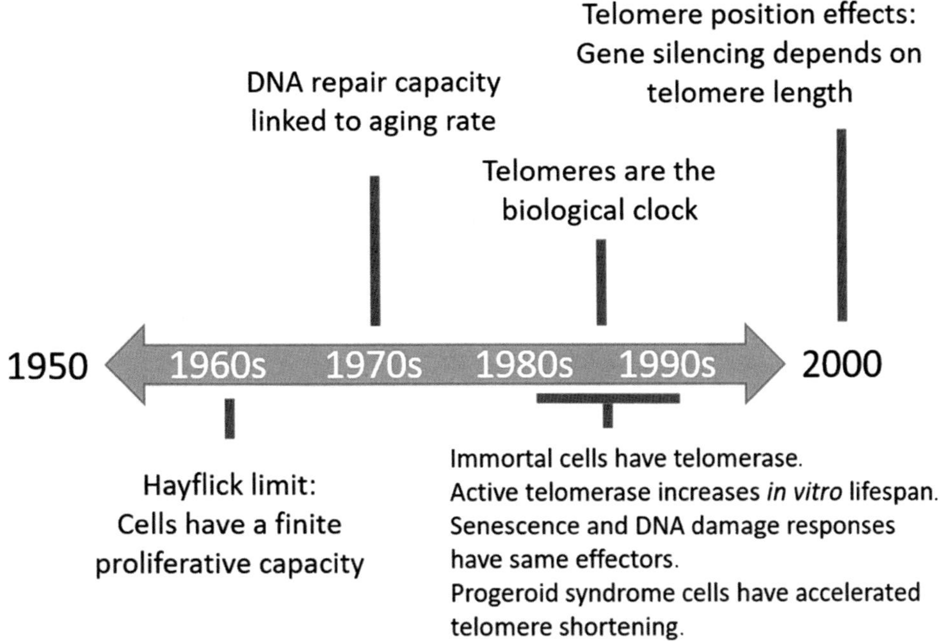

The first decade of the 21st century rapidly produced various proposals for biomedical intervention based on this theorizing and research. For example, basic research into the metabolism of organisms such as rats revealed that a sharp reduction in calorie intake considerably slowed down aging, and so lengthy calorie restriction trials on primates were commenced with a view of artificially "bottling", in the form of a drug, the effects of this dietary adjustment.

However, despite the undeniable promise of these attempts to extend life, as knowledge of human biology increased, the challenges of bringing aging under serious biomedical control grew clearer. One clear example is the "Hayflick Limit", named after its discoverer (Leonard Hayflick).

This is the point at which cells eventually stop dividing. This point is reached when telomeres, extra segments of DNA at the ends of chromosomes which get shorter with each cell division, eventually reach a critical length, and further division is halted.

This is just one of the many limitations one encounters in the science of aging. The human body is a very complex machine, and there are limits to how much any machine can be altered or even redesigned in order to last longer.

But as anyone with a car knows, we don't need to redesign a machine to improve its Longevity.

Just as we might like to be able to alter a car's inner workings so that they inflict less wear and tear on the metal parts, so too might we like to be able to somehow rearrange the systems of the human body so that they inflict less wear and tear on the tissues. Sadly this is not an option.

This brings us to the alternative approach to vehicle Longevity: repair and maintenance. Might there be some way we could allow aging to proceed as it normally does, while simultaneously clearing up the damage it leaves behind?

This approach originated with the Cambridge-based software engineer — turned biomedical gerontologist — Aubrey de Grey, who, having joined the ranks of aging science when he earned his PhD from Cambridge for his *Mitochondrial Free Radical Theory of Aging,* found himself part of what he regarded as a "pitifully small band of academics", who pursued a "curiosity-driven" basic research and had little contact with technological sectors which could assist with practical applications of the knowledge they gained.

At that time, all estimates about the feasibility of healthy life extension using biomedical interventions in aging were founded primarily on the assumption that interventions in aging must entail interventions in complex bodily processes such as metabolism, which can be rightly regarded as an unsolvable riddle.

De Grey, however, viewing the problem of aging through the eyes of his former occupation as an engineer, proposed turning our attention to the damage which is routinely inflicted on our cells and tissues by our bodily processes.

It is a shift to "age" rather than aging — to the "damage report" that emerges simply by enumerating the differences between old and young tissues, irrespective of how it is inflicted.

Specifically, he systematically organized existing knowledge of the differences between old and young tissue into a list of seven different types of tissue damage (or "Seven Deadly Things"), and proposed that it would be possible to devise biotechnological (artificial) regenerative therapies that can repair each, and thus significantly hinder degeneration and chronic disease.

These seven damage types were:

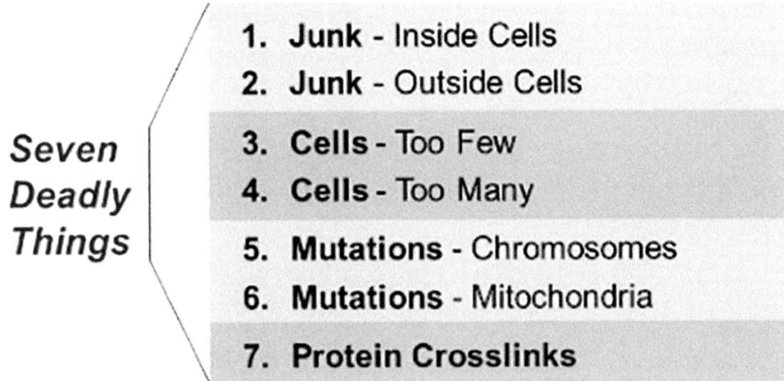

This produced a much simpler picture of what needs to be achieved, and changed the nature of the conversation overnight. Suddenly, the discussion was no longer about the vast sprawling unnavigable, unmanageable, uncharted systems of the human body, but rather about "too many or too few of this type of cell over here", or "too much junk between those cells over there", and so on.

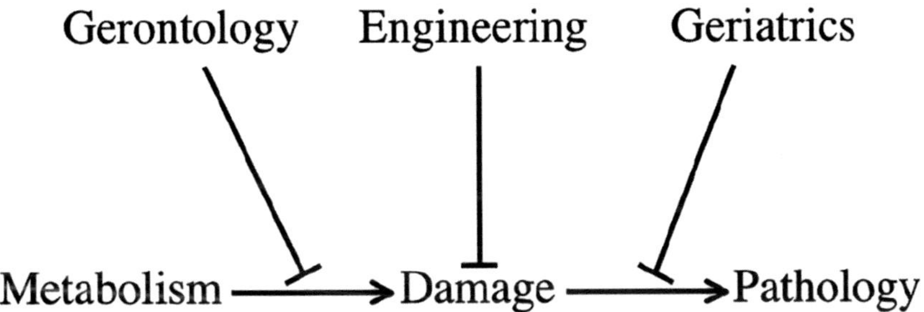

Above it is shown an early diagram identifying the emergence of advanced aging biomedicine in the form of the repair or "engineering" approach to aging. Whereas the oldest of these three sciences, geriatrics, addresses the miscellaneous diseases of aging, and the more recent science of biogerontology attempts to understand the causes and mechanisms of aging in order to alter them, the "engineering" or "repair" approach seeks to directly repair the damage as it accumulates, thus avoiding the need to intervene in complex systems.

De Grey is perhaps best known for his prediction that the first person to live to the age of 1000 had already been born, and would be the recurring beneficiary of exponentially improving regenerative medicine biotechnologies – a highly contestable claim, but as a comprehensive repair approach to aging was an unprecedented proposal at the time, there was no received wisdom one way or the other to call upon in response.

Although his views on the future of human Longevity are still not widely adopted, certainly not in official circles, de Grey has nonetheless come to be regarded as the father of "rejuvenation biotechnology", who successfully set in motion the **repair approach to aging which in the past ten years has gradually been adopted on an industrial scale.**

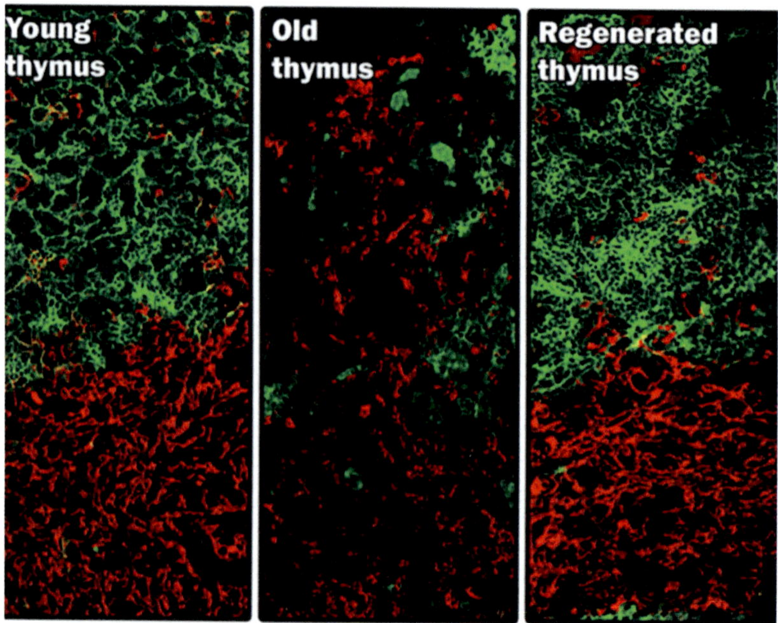

The thymus of an old mouse restored by scientists at Edinburgh University.

An early focal point for this part of the industry was the SENS Research Foundation (or SRF, "SENS" standing for "Strategies for Engineered Negligible Senescence") in Mountain View, California, the world's first biomedical research charity dedicated exclusively to the repair and restoration of aged tissues. SRF was co-founded in 2009 by de Grey in a pragmatic split from the Methuselah Foundation, an earlier biomedical research foundation with a broader remit, with initial capital from venture capitalist Peter Thiel.

At about this time, the think tank and business incubator Singularity University was established by Peter Diamandis and Ray Kurzweil at

NASA retail park, with a focus on "exponential technologies", of the life extending variety in particular. In 2013, Google and Arthur D. Levinson launched Calico with a mission statement echoing that of SRF, but a broader remit of "health, well-being and Longevity", and in partnership with a pharmaceutical company.

AbbVie, founded the same year, set up a R&D facility focused on aging and age-related infirmity such as neurodegeneration and cancer.

As the new sector took off, it drew interest and cooperation from luminaries in diverse fields. None of its scientific or industry conferences were complete without the presence of molecular geneticists such as George Church, regenerative medical technologists such as Tony Atala, molecular oncologists such as Maria Blasco, ethical philosophers such as Peter Singer or celebrity endorsers such as Edward James Olmos.

Around this Silicon Valley-based hub, an international community of institutions formed like spokes. The industry relied on the labour of research facilities throughout the West from the Wake Forest Institute for Regenerative Medicine (WFIRM), the Buck Institute for Research on Aging, Rice University, Albert Einstein College of Medicine, and Stanford University, to Britain's Oxford and Cambridge Universities.

In summary, over the past two decades we have seen multiple revolutionary shifts take place in the science of aging:

- The beginning of the "engineering approach", a sudden leap into the practical application of knowledge already gathered over decades.
- This is a key step toward the industrialization of aging. It represented the first major paradigm shift in the history of the industry, making Longevity a multi-sector industry for the first time and paving the way to the industry of almost innumerable sectors we see emerging today.

We have also seen a great many theoretical limits on the future of lifespan ceasing to apply, or thrown entirely into question. Most importantly, we have seen the first new bridges built between sectors, beginning a process of cross-sector community collaboration which has continued to this day.

Chapter 20: Most Well-Developed Domains of Longevity R&D and Top Longevity Scientists

Deep Knowledge Group and its Longevity-focused analytical subsidiary, Aging Analytics Agency, monitors each domain of geroscience closely. The present chapter lists some of the research areas, people and organizations to put on one's watchlist if one wishes to get an overview of which are progressing the fastest, along with commentary on the rate of progress in each domain, and the main bottlenecks, roadblocks and difficulties currently faced by each going forward.

It should be noted that Deep Knowledge Ventures, of which the authors are affiliated, is not an investor in any of the companies, nor a sponsor or strategic partner of the academic and/or non-profit research foundations listed in the present chapter, with select exceptions (e.g. Insilico Medicine, the Longevity AI Consortium, etc.).

Furthermore, the marker of

"Top Domains of Geroscience"

"Top Longevity Scientists"

should not be construed as the direct opinion of the authors about which Longevity Industry domains, companies or influencers are the "most promising" or have the greatest potentials to translate into the practical extension of Healthy Human Longevity, and instead represent our analysis of broader public and industry opinions and trends, i.e., those domains receiving the largest amount of development, attention and public and private investment.

Key points:

Indeed, as indicated in other chapters, Deep Knowledge Group feels that the current prevailing opinion of the public, Longevity scientists, academic groups and non-profit foundations, and the majority of Longevity investors is overvaluing some specific Longevity Industry sectors domains of Geroscience R&D and undervaluing others (often based on the erroneous assumption that promising results in model organisms will translate successfully to humans), and that this current state of disharmonization should be corrected in order to neutralize the risks of a Longevity Industry boom and bust, and to accelerate the practical implementation of extended **Healthy Human Longevity**.

There are many reasons for these disproportions, but two of the central factors are the fact that the majority of industry players are making their decisions not based on advanced, quantitative analytical frameworks based on a full-scope understanding of the Longevity Industry in all its multifarious dimensions (biomedical, technological, financial and governmental), and the misplaced confidence in the likelihood that results obtained in model organisms will successfully translate to humans.

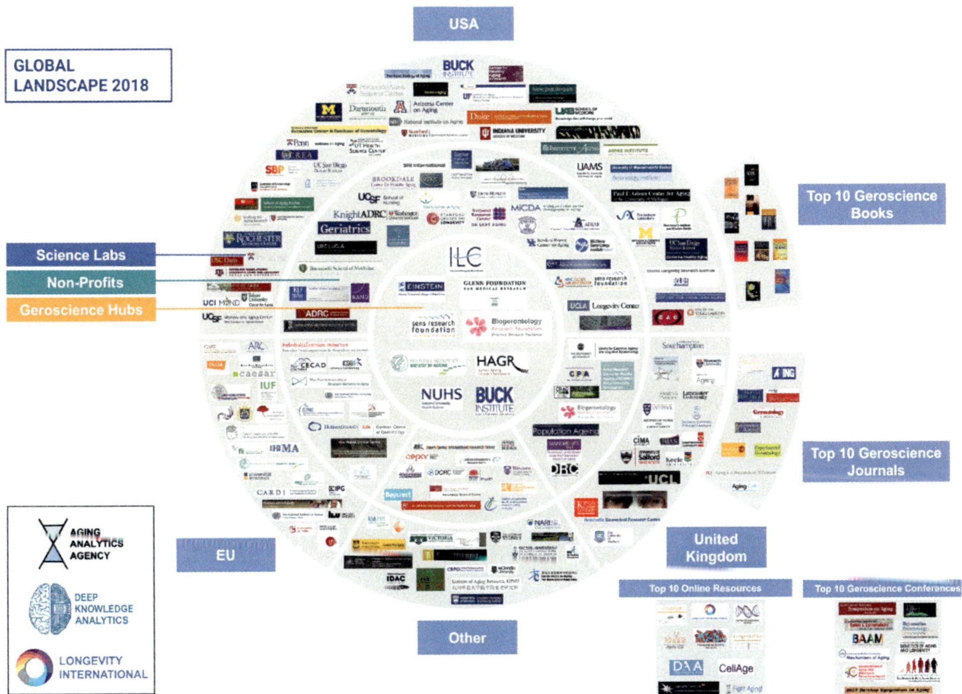

The sequel to this book, **"Longevity Industry 2.0"**, will provide a much deeper look into the actual, tangible opinions of the authors in terms of which domains and sectors of the Longevity science and industry are the overvalued and undervalued.

This sequel will also provide an overview of the methodologies required for the safe and effective testing and validation of Longevity therapeutics on humans, novel approaches to formulating new business models relevant for the challenges and opportunities of Longevity, new financial instruments, and the most advanced market-ready solutions and technology pipelines capable to be implemented in the most advanced Longevity clinics in the next 3-5 years horizon.

Senolytics

Senescent cells, also known as "zombies cells", are cells that refuse to die well after they are due to be replaced. Scientists believe that they speed up aging and create favourable conditions for pathologies when they build up in our body. A major interest of gerontologists is creating specific and low side-effect drugs that can induce death of senescent cells, referred to as senolytics.

The aim of senolytic research is to prevent or delay age-associated conditions, and many known potentially senolytic drugs are under intensive investigation. The main difficulty for finding remedies to this obstacle is that the science behind cellular senescence is not yet completely understood. The link between cellular senescence and aging needs to be further researched.

People to watch:

- Ned David
- Chris Gibson
- James Kirkland

Companies to watch:

- Senolytic Therapeutics
- Cleara Biotech
- Unity Biotechnology
- Oisín Biotechnologies
- Recursion Pharmaceuticals
- Mayo Clinic

Key Longevity Industry Influencers

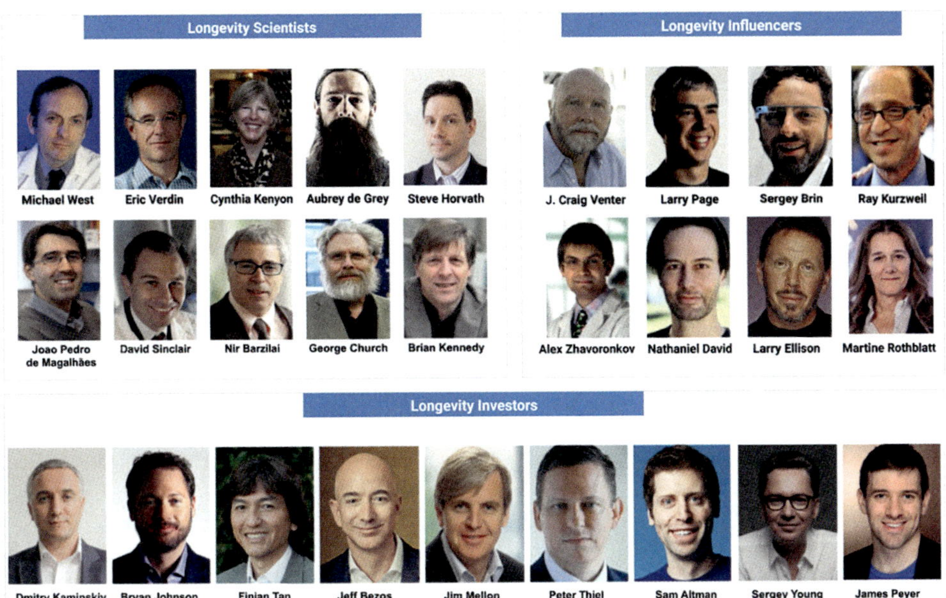

Influencer infographics are a staple of Aging Analytics Agency reports. It is important for purposes of relevant industry analytics to recognise the pivotal role of investors, scientists and influencers of popular opinions (the latter having ramifications for political will, another pivotal factor frequently discussed in this series of articles).

Geroprotectors

Geroprotectors are chemicals with the ability to slow down aging and age-related diseases. Usually, they achieve this through interplay with the key aging-associated signaling axes in cells. Two of the most well-known geroprotectors, **rapamycin** and **metformin**, have already been validated extensively in model organisms.

The challenge that remains is for gerontologists to find natural mimetics of validated synthetic drugs. The reason for this is that natural occurring mimetics should be less toxic and more bioavailable. This makes geroprotectors a very well-developed field of aging science and pharmacology industry.

People to watch:

- Alex Zhavoronkov
- Alexey Moskalev
- Vadim Gladyshev
- David Sinclair

Companies to watch:

- SENS Research Foundation
- resTORbio
- Insilico Medicine

Academic Writings & Meetings

Above is another format of infographic common in Aging Analytics Agency reports. The Agency has profiled and kept abreast of the great many academic events and publications touching on every aspect of the science.

Gene Therapy

Gene therapy is precision treatment for fixing deficient genes. It is achieved through editing genes by delivering replacement genetic code to cells packed inside viruses.

This can be done to germ cells as well as with adult organisms. Multiple systems of gene editing have been developed and the most recent – CRISPR – is a major subject of media hype and scrutiny.

The potential of gene therapy is vast and its possible uses innumerable. In particular, it is an eventual key component in rejuvenation biotechnology, mentioned below.

Anti-aging gene therapies have received a great deal of publicity in recent years and have made headlines with various lurches forward. Prominent Harvard geneticist George Church, via his company Rejuvenate Bio, has recently delivered 45 gene therapies to provide aging reversal and found the combined treatment effective against:

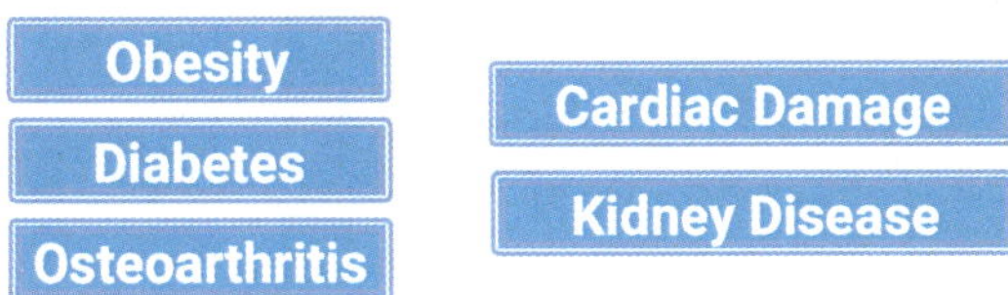

They expect to get the treatment in the hands of actual patients by around 2025.

People to watch:

- George Church
- James M. Wilson

Companies and organizations to watch:

- AVROBIO
- AveXis
- Bluebird Bio
- Homology Medicines
- Uniqure NV
- REGENXBIO Inc.
- MeiraGTx
- Voyager Therapeutics

Geroscience Institutes by Region

Since late 2017, Aging Analytics Agency has been painstakingly identifying geroscience institutes around the world, cataloging by region. Lists such as the one above first appeared in *Longevity Industry Landscape Overview Volume I: The Science of Longevity*.

Cell Therapies

Stem cell therapy is used to regenerate tissues and organs. There has already been some reported success in regenerating seriously damaged tissues and organs. Cellular therapies also include personalised cancer treatment by modified T-cells, also known as CAR T-cell therapies.

The field is now booming and in 2018 a Nobel Prize in relevant T-cell research was received by James P. Allison and Tasuku Honjo. Several CAR T-cell therapy products have been approved by the FDA already. Over 240 CAR-T clinical trials are running.

The field of immuno-oncology is attracting billions of dollars in investment and a great deal of interest from Pharma.

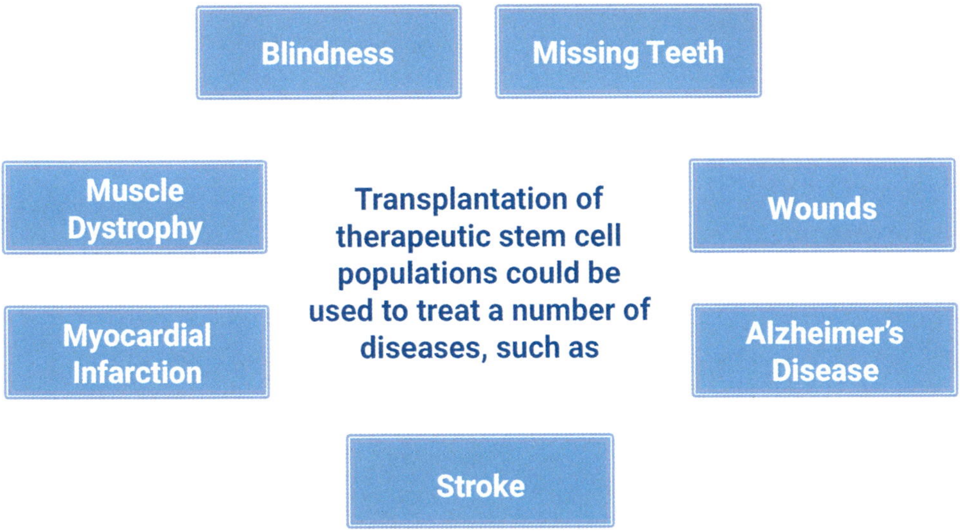

Transplantation of therapeutic stem cell populations could be used to treat a number of diseases, such as

- Blindness
- Missing Teeth
- Muscle Dystrophy
- Wounds
- Myocardial Infarction
- Alzheimer's Disease
- Stroke

There were 33 ongoing phase III clinical trials of cell therapies and 16 of gene-modified cell therapies, including CAR T-cell therapies, at the end of 2018.

People to watch:

- Michael West
- Robert Preti
- Chris Mason
- Emile Nuwaysir
- Daniel Kota

Companies and organizations to watch:

- BlueRock Therapeutics
- Celularity
- Hemostemix
- Aperion Biologics
- Celyad
- Kite Pharma

Aging Analytics Agency's recognition of the importance of politics and finance as pivotal to the future growth of the Longevity Industry necessitates the monitoring of events and publications outside the academic and scientific world.

Calorie Restriction Mimetics

Calorie restriction (CR) mimetics is a class of drug candidates that can mimic the anti-aging effects that occur naturally due to a decrease in calorie intake of 20-50%. This process happens without any harmful side-effects such as malnutrition. **It works by targeting key signaling pathways such as the rapamycin pathway.** Today, there are no validated CR mimetic drugs for human consumption, but this field is under intensive investigation. The explanation for the huge interest in this domain is that calorie restriction has already been shown to extend the lives of various laboratory organisms — from yeast and nematoda to rodents. CR mimetics is being thoroughly investigated, but the field holds limited promise in humans. It is perhaps implementable within a decade or so, but its benefits (the possible success of the mimicry itself) are an unknown quantity (even if the effects of actual calorie restriction are well documented).

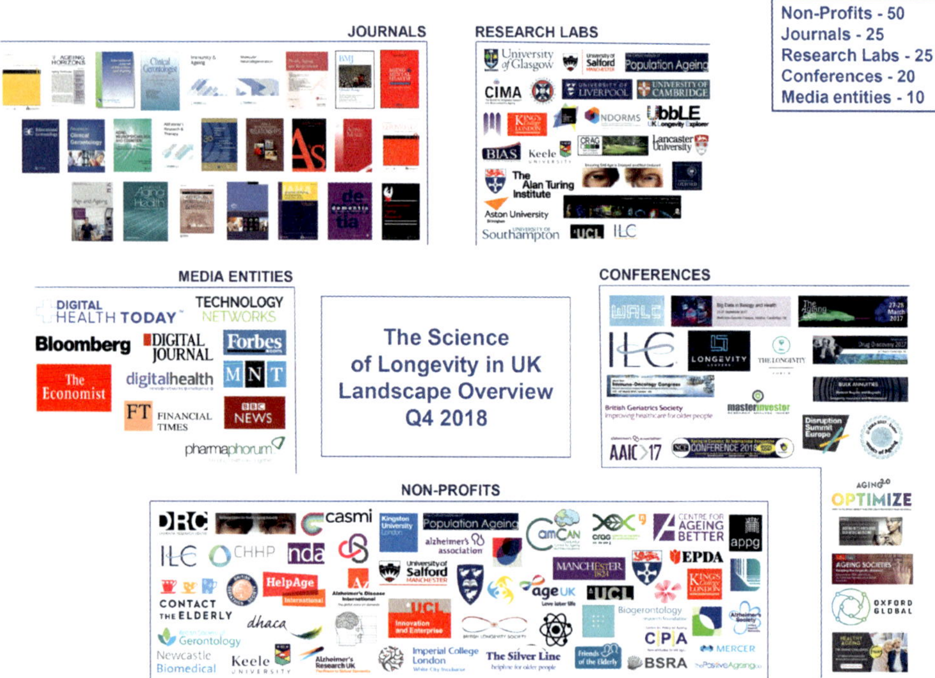

Above it is shown an infographic from Aging Analytics Agency's 2019 report *The Science of Longevity in the UK Landscape Overview Q4 2018*.

The United Kingdom is of special interest to Aging Analytics Agency due to its detailed industrial strategy which explicitly seeks to address the "Aging Society" as a major challenge. It is therefore a subject of multiple updated case studies per year.

People to watch

- David Sinclair
- Leonard Guarente
- Guido Kroemer
- Eric Ravussin

Company to watch

- Elysium

Regenerative Medicine

Regenerative medicine is the repair of damaged (or aged) tissues and organs, e.g. by regenerating human cells, artificially engineering tissues and organs to renew their functionality, and regrowing and repairing damaged, lost or aged cells, tissue or organs.

The application of regenerative medicine to aging is called "rejuvenation biotechnology", the most fully elaborated strategy for which is SENS (Strategies for Engineered Negligible Senescence), an action plan for repairing aged tissue based on a "damage report" consisting of a list of manifest differences between old and young cells and tissues.

A typical example of a problem of aging amenable to regenerative medicine solutions would be stem cell exhaustion.

This can:

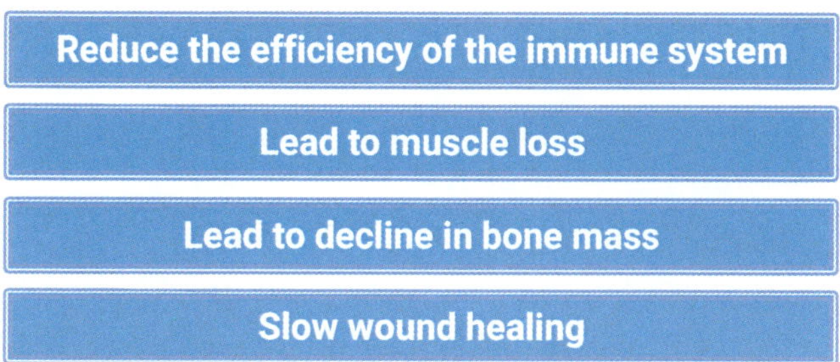

A solution to this obstacle, therefore, could significantly extend healthspan. A regenerative medical solution would be to find a way to enhance the activity of stem cells.

The difficulty with this approach is also typical of regenerative medical solutions: it can lead to unwanted side effects, as the stem cells can senesce at an accelerated rate, resulting in premature aging.

Slowing their activity, on the other hand, can cause premature aging as well. There's a clear need, therefore, for finding the "sweet spot" for stem cell activity and guiding the cells in that direction. We also need further development of effective tools to operate on stem cells in the tissues and either replace or rejuvenate them.

People to watch:

- Anthony Atala
- Aubrey de Grey
- Judith Campisi

Companies and organizations to watch:

- AgeX Therapeutics
- BioTime
- SENS Research Foundation
- Buck Institute for Research on Aging

Ovarian Rejuvenation

Menopause negatively affects women's lives as it leads to a hormone imbalance and a number of associated problems. Headaches, racing heart, urinary urgency, and weight gain are only some of those. However, women always have eggs inside their ovaries (even during postmenopause). A lot of eggs just stay dormant.

Ovarian rejuvenation is a new approach to re-awake egg maturation and development. It could lead to a more normal physical and mental state in 40+ women by removing menopause and postmenopause symptoms.

Also, it could slow down aging by keeping hormone balance typical for reproductive years. All-in-all it could decrease the number of women's disability-adjusted life years as it allows them to maintain health and well-being. Modern approaches to ovarian rejuvenation include PRP (Platelet Rich Plasma) injections, and injections of the patient's own fat stem cells directly into the ovaries.

People to watch:

- Judith Campisi
- John Jackson
- David Barad

Companies and organizations to watch:

- Inovium
- The Buck Institute for Research on Aging Center for Female Reproductive Longevity
- Center for Human Reproduction
- Robinson Research Institute
- New Hope Fertility Center

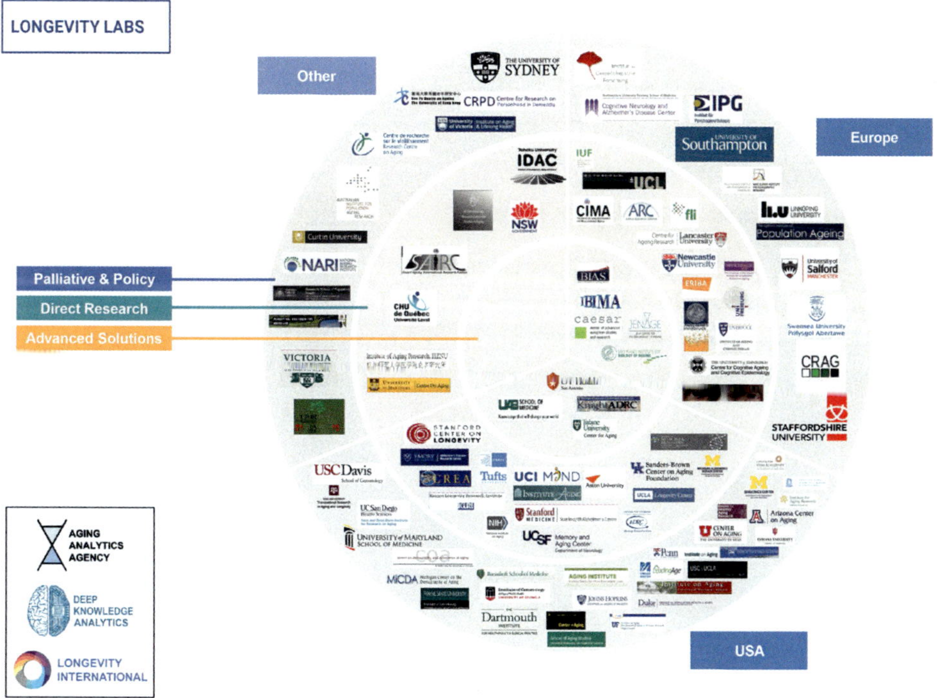

On the previous page there is another graphic from *Longevity Industry Landscape Overview Volume I, the Science of Longevity*. Here, laboratories themselves are identified rather than companies.

Note that the concentric circles represent increasing degrees of disruptiveness, with palliative technologies such as geriatrics represented by the outer ring and disruptive interventions in core aging processes at the centre.

Immune System Rejuvenation

People of advanced age frequently face immune dysfunction in their innate and adaptive immune systems. This type of age-related condition is known as **immunosenescence**.

This leads to:

Chronic inflammation

Chronic diseases

Higher rates of infection

> The task of the immune system rejuvenation is to stimulate and support the indigenous immune system to restore and maintain its optimal, youthful functionality.

Established rejuvenation practices include stem cells recovery, thymus rejuvenation, and modulation of hormone production.

Immune system rejuvenation is relatively far from practical implementation, but with some low hanging fruits – people are already experimenting with altering their own immune system through fasting, for example – there is a great deal of experimental data easily obtainable.

People to watch:

- Eric Verdin
- Joan Mannick
- Bobby Brooke
- Valter Longo

Companies and organizations to watch:

- resTORbio
- Serimmune
- Institute for Education, Research, and Scholarships (IFERS)

Top-30 Longevity Conferences 2019-2020: Regional Distribution

Aging Analytics Agency's report *Top-30 Longevity Conferences 2019-2020* presents the Top-30 conferences related to Longevity, as illustrated above, providing key facts and figures on each.

With the rapid development of the Longevity Industry, the number of events dedicated to this topic has increased proportionately. These events differ in a number of ways including target audience, central topics being covered, entrance fee range, location, venue, etc.

Potential participants need to be aware of such conferences details while planning which conferences to attend. This report aims to serve as a guide in this type of decision-making, which also includes a cost-benefit analysis of the conferences themselves.

The Top-30 Conferences chosen for this list, from 150 Longevity-themed conferences in total, satisfy the following criteria:

- They are well attended, with a large number of speakers as well as participants.

- They include at least one panel on the topic of Longevity.
- They feature speakers who are professionals in the industry.

Domain: Inflammaging

Aging impacts how cells communicate with each other, which can cause inflammaging: a constant state of low-level body-wide inflammation, which in turn brings about several age-related conditions. Countering inflammaging would improve the immune system's activity and could mitigate many age-related conditions.

Cells communicate with each other by sending chemical signals of various kinds. This ability is one respect in which aging can be a "contagious" process; for example, how senescent cells can urge other cells — even in other tissues — to undergo senescence themselves. Senescent cells release pro-inflammatory molecules that contribute to a general state of inflammation in the body.

This condition can hinder the function of adult stem cells, and is associated with aging and many age-related diseases including:

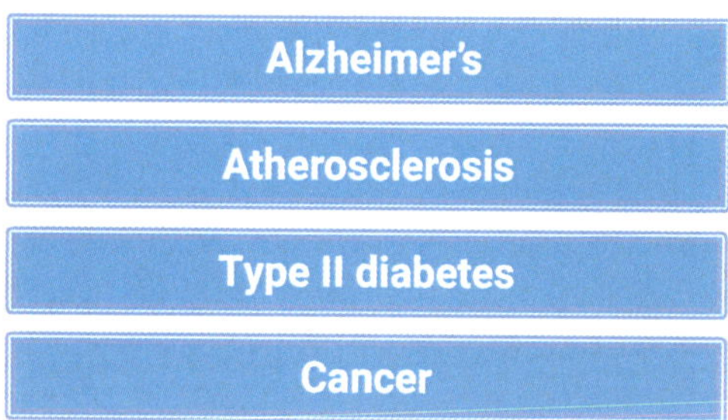

Constant inflammation can even accelerate telomere attrition, which then promotes cellular senescence.

People to watch:

- Philipp Leucht
- C. Franceschi
- Keith L. Kirkwood
- Anne Marie Josephson
- Judith Campisi
- Remi-Martin Laberge

Companies and organizations to watch:

- Buck Institute for Research on Aging
- NYU School of Medicine
- SENS Research Foundation
- National Institute of Arthritis and Musculoskeletal and Skin Diseases

Domain: Biogerontology

Biogerontology is the basic research into the biology of aging. Although those with a more utilitarian approach to geroscience would prefer to prioritize translational research rather than the pursuit of a fully comprehensive theory of how aging occurs, theoretical biogerontology still has much to achieve, and is likely to hold unforeseen promise. It was already proven to be essential to the kind of intelligence gathering which enables interventions in other domains listed here, such as senolytics and mimetics, and it is impossible to tell what new doors further research may uncover.

Biogerontology has in its sights the eventuality of a "robust theory of aging", a theory that ties together all the different mechanisms of aging and explains the relationship between them. The theory would predict how any change of the involved factors will affect the aging process. The development of such a theory would prove audacious but impactful, and a proof of concept is expected around the year 2030.

People to watch:

- Michael R. Rose
- Steven N. Austad
- Cynthia Kenyon
- Richard A. Miller

Companies and organizations to watch:

- Oxford University
- Cambridge University
- University College London
- University of Swansea
- Newcastle University

- Edinburgh University
- Stanford University
- Buck Institute for Aging Research
- Biogerontology Research Foundation

Domain: Biomarkers of Aging

The search for a reliable panel of biomarkers for aging opens up enough doors that it constitutes an entire domain of geroscience in itself. It is also unique among these domains as it approaches the intersection between the P4 and Geroscience quadrants of the industry, not to mention a major synergy between digital and BioTech sectors.

Success in this domain is a much lower hanging fruit than is commonly supposed, due to the overlooked possibility of a minimum viable panel of biomarkers.

People to watch:

- Richard Siow
- Alex Zhavoronkov
- Morten Scheibye-Knudsen
- Lee Uhn

Companies and organizations to watch:

- Longevity AI Consortium
- Insilico Medicine
- Exscientia
- bioAge
- Sophia Genetics
- Gachon University Gil Medical Center
- University of Copenhagen
- University of Alberta
- Biogerontology Research Foundation

Chapter 21: Current State of Longevity Clinical (Human) Trials

"Achieving small but practical results in Longevity distributed at scale will have enormous and multiplicative effects on society. Extending the functional lifespan of humans by just one year will decrease suffering for tens of millions of people and will improve the quality of life for billions of people."

Margaretta Colangelo in *Leveraging AI to Accelerate Precision Health For Longevity* (Forbes, November 2019)

Longevity drug development has evolved from a distant goal into an industry priority. A number of companies are working on developing drugs that target aging and some of these drugs are currently in clinical trials.

General Overview of Longevity Clinical Trials

Longevity Drugs Currently in Preclinical Development

Company	Drug	Company	Drug
JumpStart Fertility	Egg quality restoration drugs	UCSF	KLOTHO
cnio	Telomerase gene therapy	sens research foundation	MitoSens
AgeX Therapeutics	Combination of telomerase therapy and proprietary induced tissue regeneration technology	OISÍN Biotechnologies	SENSOlytics™
salk	OSKM	CLEARA	FOXO4-DRI
turn.bio NANOG	OSKMLN	ANTOXERENE	Small-molecule senolytics
ICHOR Therapeutics	Lysoclear		Ectopic replacement organs
	Cardizyme	Spotlight Biosciences	Machine learning platform to identify peptides (small proteins)
	Alzyme	Elevian	GDF11

Longevity Drugs in Phase III Clinical Trials

Company	Drug
samumed	lorecivivint (SM04690)
afar EINSTEIN	Targeting Aging with Metformin (TAME)

Longevity Drugs in Phase II Clinical Trials

Company	Drug
UNITY Biotechnology	UBX1967
	Quercetin and Dasatinib
MAYO CLINIC	Fisetin
CRATUS	Mesenchymal stem cell therapy
resTORbio	RTB101

Longevity Drugs in Phase I Clinical Trials

Company	Drug
	NPT088
Scholar Rock	SRK-015
salk	J147

This chapter is an overview of the current state of Longevity clinical trials. Although no Longevity drugs have received regulatory approval yet, a number of Longevity therapies have passed phase I and phase II clinical (human) trials, and a few are in phase III trials. In this chapter we review the progression of clinical trials and look at which hallmarks of aging are receiving the most pharmacological attention.

Currently in preclinical development

- GDF11, Elevian
- SENSOlytics™, Oisín Biotechnologies
- Ectopic replacement organs, Lygenesis
- MitoSens, SENS Research Foundation
- Egg quality restoration drugs, Jumpstart Fertility
- Telomerase gene therapy, Preclinical in vivo, CNIO
- Telomerase therapy & proprietary induced tissue regeneration (iTR) technology, AgeX Therapeutics
- OSKM - Oct4, Sox2, Klf4, and c-Myc, Salk
- OSKMLN - Oct4, Sox2, Klf4, and c-Myc LIN28, Nanog, Turn.Bio
- Lysoclear, Ichor Therapeutics
- Cardizyme, Covalent Bioscience
- Alzyme, Covalent Bioscience
- Klotho, UCSF
- FOXO4-DRI, Cleara Biotech
- Small-molecule senolytics, Antoxerene
- Machine learning platform to identify peptides (small proteins), Spotlight Biosciences

Completed preclinical development

- NMN (Nicotinamide mononucleotide), Sinclair Lab
- Gene therapy for restoration of short telomeres, Telocyte
- UBX1967, Unity Biotechnology
- Next Gen Apheresis, Conboy Lab

Longevity Drugs Currently in Preclinical Development

JumpStart Fertility	Egg quality restoration drugs
cnio Centro Nacional de Investigaciones Oncológicas	Telomerase gene therapy
AgeX Therapeutics	Combination of telomerase therapy and proprietary induced tissue regeneration technology
Salk. Where cures begin.	OSKM
turn.bio NANOG	OSKMLN
Ichor Therapeutics	Lysoclear
Covalent Bioscience, Inc	Cardizyme
Covalent Bioscience, Inc	Alzyme
UCSF	KLOTHO
sens research foundation reimagine aging	MitoSens
Oisín Biotechnologies	SENSOlytics™
Cleara	FOXO4-DRI
Antoxerene	Small-molecule senolytics
Lygenesis	Ectopic replacement organs
Spotlight Biosciences	Machine learning platform to identify peptides (small proteins)
Elevian	GDF11

Longevity Drugs that Finished Preclinical Development

SINCLAIR	NMN (Nicotinamide mononucleotide)
TELOCYTE	Gene therapy for short telomeres restoration
UNITY BIOTECHNOLOGY	UBX1967
Berkeley UNIVERSITY OF CALIFORNIA	Next Gen Apheresis

Phase I clinical trials

- NPT088, Proclara Bioscience and Michael J. Fox Foundation
- J147, Salk
- SRK-015, Scholar Rock

Longevity Drugs in Phase I Clinical Trials

THE MICHAEL J. FOX FOUNDATION FOR PARKINSON'S RESEARCH	NPT088
salk® Where cures begin.	J147
SCHOLAR ROCK	SRK-015

Phase II clinical trials

- UBX0101, Unity Biotechnology
- Quercetin and Dasatinib, The Scripps Research Institute
- Fisetin, Mayo Clinic
- Mesenchymal stem cell (MSC) therapy, Cratus
- RTB101, resTORbio

Longevity Drugs in Phase II Clinical Trials

UNITY BIOTECHNOLOGY	UBX0101
The Scripps Research Institute	Quercetin and Dasatinib
MAYO CLINIC	Fisetin
CRATUS	Mesenchymal stem cell therapy
resTORbio	RTB101

Phase III clinical trials

- Targeting Aging with Metformin (TAME), American Federation for Aging Research and Albert Einstein College of Medicine
- Lorecivivint (SM04690), Samumed

Longevity Drugs in Phase III Clinical Trials

 american federation for aging research  Albert Einstein College of Medicine	Metformin
samumed	Lorecivivint (SM04690)

Conclusions:

- Although no Longevity therapeutics have gained regulatory approval yet, promising potential drugs have passed phase I and II clinical trials and are in phase III. This indicates that interventions targeting the root causes of aging may not be very far from real-world implementation and clinical translation.
- The hallmarks that have received the most drug development attention are intercellular communication and cellular senescence.
- The hallmark receiving the least drug development attention is genomic instability, possibly due to the fact that the nature of the problem calls for a mainly non-pharmacological approach.
- The majority of drug candidates are still in a preclinical phase, but there are a number that have either finished or are currently in phase I and II clinical trials, and a small handful that have entered phase III trials.
- A snapshot such as this would not have been possible ten years ago. Interventions in the central aging processes are now a major focus of Longevity Industry drug development.

Chapter 22: Precision Medicine and Patient as CEO (Contributor: Robin Farmanfarmaian)

When you work in frontier fields that go against the current status quo, and strive to push forward new paradigm shifts in established domains as complex as biomedicine and healthcare, the majority of people you meet are resistant to change, and you have to expend a lot of effort to show them why your way is the way of the future.

This is why it was such a breath of fresh air when I first met Dmitry Kaminskiy, who completely got it. He had already read my book, ***The Patient as CEO***, and given that he was already pushing forward the agenda of a paradigm shift from treatment to prevention, increasing emphasis on Preventive Medicine for national healthcare systems and on the practical implementation of *Longevity technologies to increase Healthy Longevity not in ten years, but right now,* I had to say very little to get my point across. And, given that he was an entrepreneur and venture capitalist advancing the agenda of health as new wealth, the idea of the patient as the CEO, and the individual as the manager of their own wellness, was completely intuitive to him. When he and Margaretta invited me to contribute with a section introducing the rapidly-advancing realm of Precision Medicine, I was delighted to contribute, and I'm glad to do what I can to help a new book aiming to bring the major insights and near-future trajectory of the coming Longevity revolution to the public.

Personalised Medicine, also called Precision Medicine, will completely change the practice of medicine. It will:

- Start at the most fundamental level with your genetic profile.
- From there, your medical care will be personalised just for you.
- If you have a chronic condition, your care will be based on your individual case.
- You'll be able to track your health at a very detailed level.

- Every aspect of your preventative care, diagnosis, and treatment will be designed for you personally.

The days of one-size-fits-all medicine are rapidly receding into the past.

Key Points:

- Medicine will be tailored to the individual.
- Instead of trying out a drug on you to see if it works or if you'll have a bad side effect, you'll know in advance which drug is best for you, and at what dosage, based on your genetic makeup and by testing you in advance with very fast and easy lab work.
- You'll be tracked individually with telepresent medicine.
- You'll be pinged; if something isn't right, like a fever or a drug reaction, the problem will be caught earlier, when it's probably a lot easier to fix.

Personalised Medicine means targeting and completely individualizing the diagnosis, prevention, and treatment of disease.

Personalised Medicine means faster, easier access to care, ranging from labs on a chip at your local CVS to telepresence consultations with specialists thousands of miles away. It's medicine your way, completely tailored to you to the minute, accessed the way you want or need it.

Personalised Medicine will be very disruptive, with major impacts across the entire healthcare system. Let's say you're at home and start feeling really sick at two in the morning. You're nauseous and have severe pain in your lower right abdomen.

What do you do?

1. **You use an app on your smartphone to check your symptoms, or use an FDA approved point of care diagnostic device such as Omron's blood pressure monitoring watch, the Apple Watch EKG watch band, Continuous Glucose Monitors (CGMs) or read the data from the sensors embedded all over your body or in your clothes.**

2. **A virtual nurse using AI will talk to you, maybe diagnose you with appendicitis, and urge you to go to the closest ER at once.**

3. **An autonomous car or ambulance will come pick you up, courtesy of a platform company like Uber or Lyft, both of whom have healthcare departments that allow providers to order a car for a patient using a landline, categorized as NEMT, non-emergency medical transport.**

4. **When you get to the ER, you'll already be triaged, the right physicians or healthcare professionals will be waiting for you, with your complete electronic healthcare records already open.**

At the hospital, doctors determine your appendix needs to come out. Using laparoscopic surgery or a surgical robot, it's removed very quickly through tiny openings, leaving you with very little pain, little to no scarring, and a quick recovery.

If for some reason (say you have internal scarring from previous medical treatment) you need open surgery instead, advanced 3D imaging will help your surgeon know in advance where the problem areas are and come up with the best surgical approach. An exact replica of whatever part needs surgery can be 3D printed, and the doctors can either practice or refer to it during the surgery as an extra detailed representation.

Any drugs you need, ranging from pre-op meds to the anesthesia to post-op painkillers, will be selected with your genetic profile in mind. Each pill contain the exact dose you need, made by a 3D printer on the spot. In the recovery area, you'll be monitored by an AI robot.

When you go home within a day or so, a telepresent nurse will check in with you to make sure you're recovering smoothly. Your vitals signs will be monitored with small, inexpensive body sensors and transmitted to your healthcare team through the cloud. If a problem develops, a telepresence doctor will treat it. If all goes well, you'll be back to your normal life within a week.

You'll have not just Personalised Medicine, but a personalised experience. You'll get healthcare where you want, when you want, how you want, tailored just for you.

Personalised Medicine will also make a huge difference in treating cancer. We can already look at the genetic makeup of some tumours and use that to target the cancer-causing mutation with a drug designed to shut it down. Targeted therapy for cancer works by looking at the genetic event that's driving the cancer and matching the treatment to counteract it.

We can already do this with some types of cancer, like leukemia and lung cancer. This is an area where the research is moving ahead very rapidly. In the future, every cancer patient will be genetically tested and will receive targeted treatment that will simply switch off the mutation. Broad-spectrum chemotherapy, which kills off cancer cells, will become a thing of the past.

To discover if you have cancer, you'll have a liquid biopsy — basically a blood or urine test instead of an invasive surgical procedure. Eric Topol, M.D., the director of the Scripps Translational Science Institute in La Jolla, California, says liquid biopsies will soon become the stethoscope for the next two hundred years. Liquid biopsies will help detect and analyze molecular biomarkers in blood and other bodily fluids.

Companies like LifeNet are working on tissue engineering — growing tumours in the lab from the patient's actual tumour biopsy, which is then used to test a medication regimen on the tumour — before trying that treatment regimen on the patient. Expect this to be in use within a few years.

They can be used for early detection of cancer and for monitoring cancer patients.

They can also be used to determine what the best treatment will be for you and to detect drug resistance early on, before more time is wasted on an ineffective treatment. Imagine a world where you can frequently and easily get screened for cancer, more often than you do cholesterol or white blood count! Take it one step further. Converge this with sensors inside of blood vessels, and you'll be able to be monitored for cancer, 24/7, and catch it immediately.

One of the biggest opportunities in Longevity and Precision Medicine is replacement organs. Organ failure is the number one killer in the US, with over 730,000 annual US deaths attributable to end-stage organ disease. According to the World Health Organization, only 10% of the worldwide need for organ transplantation is being met. Imagine instead of having bypass surgery, just replace the whole heart. Imagine as you age, you replace your organs with new ones made from your own stem cells, extending your life.

That's the next frontier in 3D printing — biological 3D printing, also known as tissue engineering. Gabor Forgacs, one of the pioneers in biological printing, is the scientific founder of Organovo. One of their products is a 3D liver and kidney assay that can be used to test drug toxicity. A tiny patch of human liver or kidney cells are grown on a 3D scaffold inside a bioreactor. These cells react to drugs much as a liver inside you would.

This is a huge step forward for drug development. No longer do drugs have to be extensively tested on living animals and humans to see if they might be toxic to the liver. They can be quickly tested using a liver assay instead.

The next step from that would be to do something similar with an individual's liver cells. That way, if you need a drug that might cause liver or kidney damage, you can tell in advance if that will happen to you. Right now, all you can do is take the drug and hope for the best on a kidney or liver function test later on.

Big Pharma is very interested in what companies are doing with bioengineered tissues, because it could hugely disrupt the way drug trials are done.

At present, it takes on average between **US$1 billion** and **US$4 billion** and **10 years** of studies to bring a new drug to market.

If 3D bioengineering can make the clinical trials process much faster, it will save vast amounts of money and make valuable drugs available more quickly. We'll be able to learn right away what side effects and toxicities an experimental drug might have, without testing it on animals and humans first.

20% of drugs fail in last stage trials because they are toxic to the kidneys — and that's after spending hundreds of millions of dollars to get to that point.

A really exciting area for biological 3D printing is skin grafts. This will have an impact on patients with burns and hard-to-heal wounds. For skin grafts today, skin is taken from another part of the body and grafted to the damaged area. It's a slow and painful process. A lot of research on skin grafting has focused on ways to use less skin or make it grow in faster. With tissue engineering, the paradigm for skin grafts shifts.

Scans are used to determine exactly where the skin needs to go and at what depth — this is important because different layers of skin have different types of cells. The patient's own stem cells are used to grow the right sorts of skin cells in a hydrogel. A 3D printer lays down the hydrogel in the damaged area, just as an ink-jet printer lays down ink. The cells grow new skin exactly where it's needed.

The end result is faster healing with much less scarring and less contracture of the skin and underlying muscles. Right now we have printers that can lay down two layers of skin, deep enough to treat and to heal most burn wounds.

A number of researchers are working on engineering skin to improve wound healing, especially wounds caused by burns.

> Great strides have been made over the last 25 years in this area. Hohlfeld and his associates are responsible for some of the early breakthroughs in skin engineering. They used fetal skin constructs to help severe burns heal. Now, researchers are working to make bioengineered skin a better aid for wound care — one that can regenerate more completely and have a higher success rate.

The current technologies still have flaws such as cost and graft failure, but they are being used to help certain patients. **EPISKIN, a French company, is currently a leader in engineering skin.**

Tissue engineering to build organs could help reduce or even eliminate the need for transplanted organs. We already have a shortage of transplant organs that will only get worse in the future.

Nowadays, many organs come from people who die in car and motorcycle accidents. In the future, self-driving cars will mean far fewer fatal accidents, which in turn means even fewer organs for transplant.

An important advance in that regard is that in the lab is now possible to grow hollow organs such as bladders and some types of cartilage, such as ears and noses.

3D printed bladders have already been successfully used for some time.

> **In fact, one patient has now lived for 14 years with a 3D bioprinted bladder, which was created by Dr. Anthony Atala at Boston Children's Hospital. This patient, Luke Massella, has not needed additional surgery since he received his bioprinted organ. He is one of ten patients who have one of these bladders, which are grown from their own bladder cells and a scaffold created by the printer.**

A team at Indiana University led by Dr. Burcin Ekser is currently working to develop more transplantable organs using a US$9 million grant from Lung Biotechnology PBC.

Ekser and his research team are developing a process to print three-dimensional pig liver tissue so that they can ultimately develop models for transplanting animal organs into humans.

Vascular organs such as hearts, kidneys, and livers are much more complex. They need to have oxygen and nutrients delivered to every cell. One possible way to do this is to take an existing organ such as a liver and decellularize it (remove all the cells but leave behind the supporting structures and blood vessels as a scaffold); that's called a Ghost Organ.

Stem cells could be used to populate the scaffold and grow a new liver. **Another alternative is to 3D print the scaffolding (support structure) then tissue engineer the rest of the organ using stem cells extracted from the recipient patient's own adipose (fatty) tissue.**

One company to watch in this space is Lung Biotechnologies. They could be one of the first companies in animal trials with a tissue engineered, vascularized organ replacement — and in just a few years.

This is another area where 3D bioprinting has huge potential for breakthrough technology. **At the Wyss Institute for Biologically Inspired Engineering at Harvard University, Jennifer Lewis leads a team that has figured out how to print blood vessels in tissue using disappearing ink.**

The tissue is built up in layers with a 3D bioprinter. The "inks" are viscous gelatins that contain structural supports and living cells. To make the blood vessels, a different type of gelatin is used, one that is viscous at room temperature but liquid when it's cooled. This ink is used to print blood vessels within the cell layers. When the patch of tissue is cooled, the "invisible ink" of the blood vessels is gently sucked out, leaving the channels behind.

One of the greatest challenges in translating this work into practice is not just creating working tissues like vasculature, but making them work robustly enough to actually fill their natural role in the human body. And in the case of blood vessels, this means being able to transport oxygen, carbon dioxide and nutrients into and out of large, densely-packed and structurally-intricate organs. Feeding a finger with blood is one thing, but feeding a kidney or the lungs is something entirely else.

Epithelial stem cells, the kind that make the linings of blood vessels, are seeded into the channels, where they will grow into working capillaries.

Fortunately, the pace of progress in advancing the capabilities of these engineered tissues is also increasing at a rapid pace.

For example, in May 2019 researchers were able to bioprint complex vasculature grown around a lung-mimicking air sack, and demonstrated the capability to print biotissues with independent vasculature networks similar to the blood vessels and airways of lungs, and the bile ducts and blood vessels of the liver. The ability to create networks sufficiently inter-connected and entangled, physically and biochemically, to feed large organs with the blood they require is a major step forward.

Furthermore, this research is rapidly progressing from the level of tissues, like blood vessels, toward entire organs.

In April 2019, researchers in Tel Aviv created a tissue engineered heart the size of a cherry – which is about the size of a rabbit's heart – that was made from a patient's own cells and biological materials. The heart can contract already, and they are working on making it beat as well. They used a fatty tissue biopsy for 2 different types of cells: heart & endothelial. This marked the first time that a 3D heart containing a patient's own cells was ever created and validated. We can expect to see research extend into an increasing number of organs and tissues of increasing size, complexity and structural intricacy, and this area of research will continue to play a major role in the future of Precision Medicine.

An approach to bone grafting uses 3D printing with a biocompatible plastic called PEKK (polyetherketoneketone). It's similar to bone in density and strength, and it can withstand the high temperatures needed for sterilization. PEKK is being used now with 3D printing to make personalised facial and skull implants to replace damaged and missing bone.

The implant is printed with tiny perforations to allow the patient's own bone cells to grow in and attach to it. Because it's plastic, the patient can have MRI and CT scans, and it shows up on X-rays.

Medical professionals such as Dr. Gaurav Gupta, assistant professor of neurosurgery at Rutgers Robert Wood Johnson Medical School, have used 3D printing to replace pieces of the human skull. Sometimes doctors must take out a portion of a patient's skull to relieve pressure after a traumatic brain injury. On some occasions, that bone becomes unusable and cannot be used to close the skull. Dr. Gupta used a 3D printed bone made of polyetheretherketone (PEEK) to replace part of the patient's skull, fitted exactly to the patient.

In 2014, the top of an entire skull was printed using PEKK and implanted in a woman's head. The operation was successful — the surgeons were able to literally watch for blood clots and swelling in the brain after the surgery.

Titanium ribs have been a proven replacement for patients with rib deformities, but they have their limitations. They don't have the "give" of a natural rib, and they are also extremely expensive.

In January 2019, a patient in Bulgaria received one of the first 3D printed ribs. Created from a substance called Nylon 80, the rib took only 24 hours to print and can move much as a natural rib does. Creating the limb also costs less than 100 Euros — or slightly over US$100.

Developments in our ability to edit genes using CRISPR/Cas9 technology are really changing the face of Personalised Medicine. This is transforming tissue engineering, with possible results we can't even imagine yet. Right now, researchers are looking at 100,000 cancer cell specimens of the 50 most prevalent cancers, which means about 98 percent of all cancers, to find the driver mutations.

They've done about 5,000 so far. When that basic research on all the samples is done, a massive step forward will have been taken.

At that point, CRISPR/Cas9 technology will be able to edit the defective genes and find ways to stop them. It's all very dependent on massive amounts of computer power and AI.

Bill Gates and other investors have put US$120 million into Editas Medicine, a start-up using CRISPR/Cas9 gene editing in an effort to eliminate human diseases in previously impossible ways. Progress in this area of science is also progressing at a remarkable rate as well.

In October 2019, researchers at MIT and Harvard published a paper demonstrating an even more precise variant of CRISPR/Cas9 called "prime editing" that is able to directly overwrite existing genetic information in specific DNA sites with new information, which they claim opens up the doors to reversing 98% of genetic defects and diseases.

At Memorial Sloan Kettering Cancer Center in New York, researchers are finding new ways to do personalised drug treatment for lung cancer. To find out which of the many available drugs will work best for an individual patient, they're working on a tiny implantable device that will carry small doses of about 30 different drugs. The device is implanted in the tumour, where the drugs are released directly where they're needed.

The implant is a tiny tube that's only a few centimetres long. It delivers the drug dose molecule by molecule, and it can closely monitor the activity in the tumour. That means the cost of the treatment can really be cut, plus there are far fewer side effects for the patient.

What a lot of future Personalised Medicine comes down to is looking at the human body as a hardware system with a software system.

We want to use the hardware to go in and edit the human software — your genes. This will be the biggest thing to happen to Personalised Medicine, because there's nothing more personalised than editing your own genes.

We can now decode your DNA quickly and cheaply. Researchers are now working on decoding your microbiome as well. This is an area generating a lot of interest. Your microbiome is the ecological community of symbiotic and pathogenic microorganisms that literally share your body. They live in you and on you by the trillions, and are estimated to be a 1 to 1 ratio with human cells on your body.

Just as a rain forest is a balanced ecosystem because it's so varied, human beings with their integrated microbiomes are balanced ecosystems as well — and everyone's microbiome is unique to them. The balance naturally shifts and changes and, we're starting to learn, can have a powerful impact on our physical and even mental health. This will be the next big frontier in Personalised Medicine.

Once we understand the microbiome, we can find ways to alter it to solve health issues. And while this area of R&D is still one of the newer and younger domains of Precision Medicine research, the amount we are finding out about how the microbiome impacts health, and the levels of practical applications that are being developed, are increasing at an enormous pace.

We can expect this area of research to become one of the most impactful in the coming years.

The Future of Wellness

> **In the future, a huge amount of healthcare resources will be needed to treat people who have chronic diseases such as type 2 diabetes and high blood pressure. Treatment needs to go beyond drugs and 10-minute checkups every few months. Personalised programs for managing your health have been shown to be the most effective, especially for weight loss and chronic conditions. With the growth of AI, apps for this are now becoming a reality.**

Companies like **Omada Health and Fruit Street** offer digital health programs that help people prevent and manage chronic diseases through personalised programs that use technology to tackle the problems from every direction.

Personal health coaches, computerized scales, personal monitors, support groups, games and incentives, and other approaches are combined for maximum effectiveness. The outcomes are good: the average participant loses 10 or more pounds over 16 weeks and keeps them off.

More importantly, the behavioural changes Omada encourages can lead to healthcare cost savings of over **US$2,000 per participant** over two years. This is targeted, monitored, integrated, personalised treatment plans with daily feedback and minute-by-minute personalization of the program to fit the individual.

The approach to personal wellness and treating chronic conditions at a company called Arivale was to use cutting-edge science to translate your personal data into specific, actionable recommendations that would help you thrive.

Arivale, co-founded by the pioneering biologist Lee Hood, combined information from your genome, bodily fluids such as blood and saliva, gut microbiome, and lifestyle metrics to help you discover ways to improve your overall health, meet your personal goals, and minimize long-term problems.

All the baseline data was given to you and your personal health coach, who provided personal recommendations and helped you track your changes over time.

Conclusions:

- **As developments in biomedicine advance, and the state of science and knowledge of the human body,** wellness and disease progresses, it is only natural that treatments begin shifting towards the personal, taking into account the nuances of individual patients in order to deliver a more comprehensive and precise level of care.
- **And as the technologies for modifying and modulating one's own state of health and wellness become more extensive and less expensive,** it is also logical that individuals become active participants in the state of their own present and future health.
- **Precision Medicine**, despite its disruptive impact on medicine and healthcare, is not a fringe idea that needs great effort in order to fit within the established systems and frameworks for healthcare.
- Rather, it is the most natural and logical outcome of the continued advancement of science, technology and medicine, and something that will inevitably need to be embraced if society is to move forward, rather than backward, in its quest for better health and greater quality (and quantity) of life.

Chapter 23: AI for Longevity and Precision Health (Contributor: Richard Siow)

"AI holds enormous potential to rapidly accelerate the implementation of Longevity R&D. The nation is home to multiple centres of AI for Healthcare, but not a single Longevity AI Consortium. We are changing this through our unique academic-industry focus on preventive and personalised physical, mental and financial health, marking us out from other AI and Ageing centres around the world."

Richard Siow, Ph.D., at the *AI for Longevity Summit at King's College London* (November 2019)

"AI for Longevity is an underrepresented sector in the Longevity Industry despite having more potential to increase healthy Longevity in the short term than any other sector. It is our aim to change that with the launch of the Longevity AI Consortium at King's College London, which will work to facilitate the shift from treatment to prevention and from Preventive Medicine to real-world Precision Health."

Dmitry Kaminskiy at the *AI for Longevity Summit at King's College London* (November 2019)

I first met Dmitry via his activities related to the UK All-Party Parliamentary Group (APPG) Secretariat Longevity International UK, where during meetings and events hosted by the APPG, he was urging the need for leveraging the United Kingdom's specific strengths in the AI sphere to make rapid progress in translating Longevity technologies, diagnostics and therapeutics into practice.

As the director of Aging Research at King's (ARK), I am no stranger to the enormous disruptive and accelerative impact that AI is already having on aging research.

However, it is a much rarer thing to see someone like Dmitry, working in domains of practical implementation rather than strict scientific research, pressing so urgently and boldly for the application of AI toward the tangible translation of Healthy Longevity into practice via dedicated "AI for Longevity Centres" in the UK.

After hearing him out, I must say that I agreed with him – the application of AI to improving healthy human Longevity today, and not tomorrow, is a vastly underrepresented mission in the overall AI for Longevity sphere, and something must be done about it.

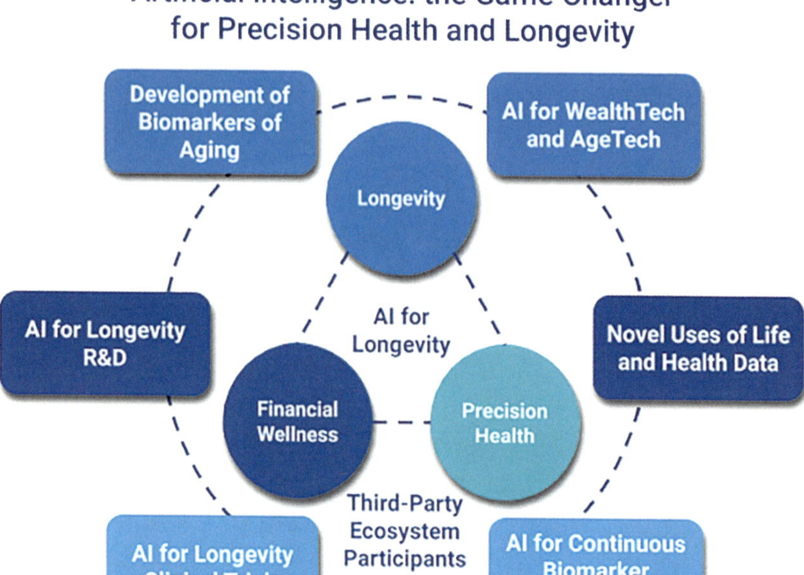

AI for Longevity is a vastly underrepresented sector within the broader Longevity Industry in comparison to the enormous potential it has to accelerate progress and industry development. Moreover, one could even make the point that much of the work going on in the AI for Longevity sphere is misdirected. I believe that there are a fairly clear set of domains and niches which need prioritized focus due to their large possible impact, including:

- Frontier applications of artificial intelligence in aging research, Longevity R&D and the development of biomarkers of health and Longevity, and the paradigm shift from disease treatment and sick care to Preventive Medicine, and from Preventive Medicine to Precision Health, utilizing nearly real-time assessment of biomarkers of aging to coordinate micro-dose interventions to continually rebalance biomarkers of health and Longevity and maintain an optimal state of precision health, and how AI will be necessary for the coordination of biomarker monitoring and interventions due to the sheer volume of data.

- The increasing shift toward actionable biomarkers of aging, including the identification of biomarkers of health, Longevity and aging that have the highest ratios of accuracy and precision vs. actionability, expense and ease-of-implementation, and the benchmarking of biomarkers that can be used in practice today.
- Emerging trends and novel paradigms relating to both the creation and application of life data collected on a massive scale from healthy individuals and used in scientifically-backed, quantifiable, tangible and precise ways to preserve and maintain an optimal state of health.
- The disruptive and accelerative impact that AI is having on Longevity R&D and the practical implementation and clinical translation of Longevity technologies and therapeutics.
- Frontier applications of AI for financial wellness over extended periods of Healthy Longevity, and the maintenance and optimization of "wealthspan" to complement advances in "healthspan", including the application of AI assistants and "robo-advisors" for personal financial management, and the utilization of novel forms of financial data to enable AI-empowered AgeTech and WealthTech services.
- Novel methods of using AI to optimize psychological wellness, social activity, promote neuroplasticity and combat loneliness and social isolation among the elderly.

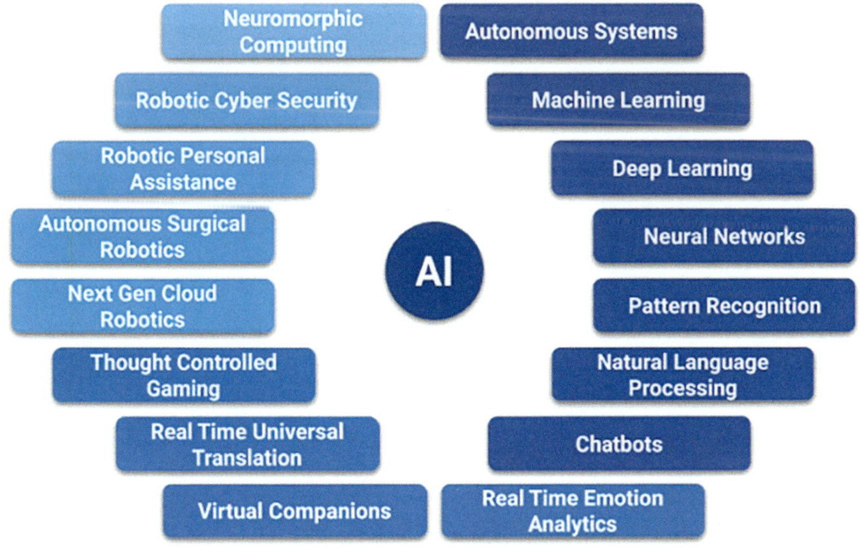

Thus, in late 2019, myself (on behalf of Aging Research at King's) and Dmitry (on behalf of Deep Knowledge Group), alongside other industry partners including Aging Analytics Agency, the Biogerontology Research Foundation and Insilico Medicine, decided to establish a dedicated hub at King's College specifically dedicated to the mission of rapidly translating Healthy Longevity into practice today. It is with this urgent mission in mind that the Longevity AI Consortium (LIAC) was born.

Modern deep learning techniques used to develop Longevity and aging predictors offer new possibilities for diverse data types. This will enable a holistic view to identify novel geroprotectors, biomarkers, drug discovery and biotechnology in the Longevity, healthcare and pharmaceutical industry.

With our partners, ARK and the LAIC are committed to bring together AI expertise across KCL and King's Health Partners to explore its utility and impact for Longevity and aging research. We will employ a variety of AI-based methods to explore patterns that have significant potential to impact Longevity, healthy aging, age-related diseases and targeted therapeutics from biomedicine to social and economic sciences.

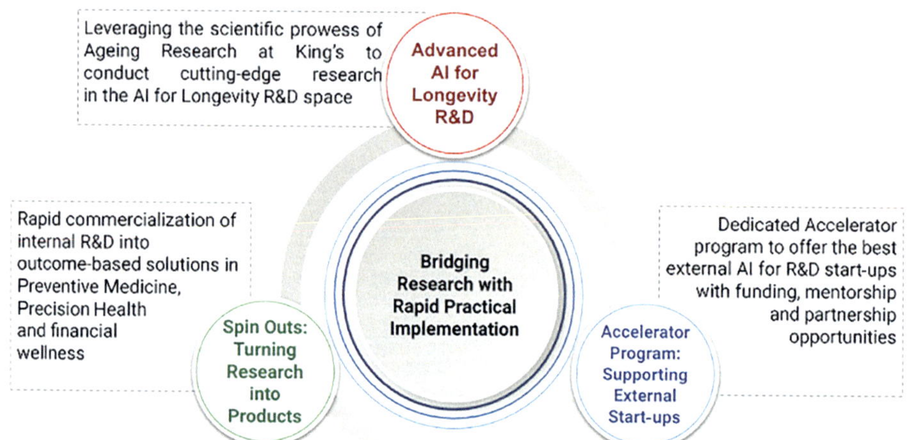

The core aims of the Longevity AI Consortium include:

- Identification of novel Longevity and healthy aging biomarkers.
- Accelerated diagnosis of age-related health decline, with increased accuracy.

- Refining demographic and clinical methods to facilitate recruitment, retention and ongoing reappraisal.
- Development of personalised health, Longevity and treatment practices.
- Promoting effective healthy lifestyles for Longevity, such as modifying patterns in sleep, nutrition, physical activity and environmental exposure.

Core Areas of R&D: Full Scope Research Across Biomedicine, Tech and Finance

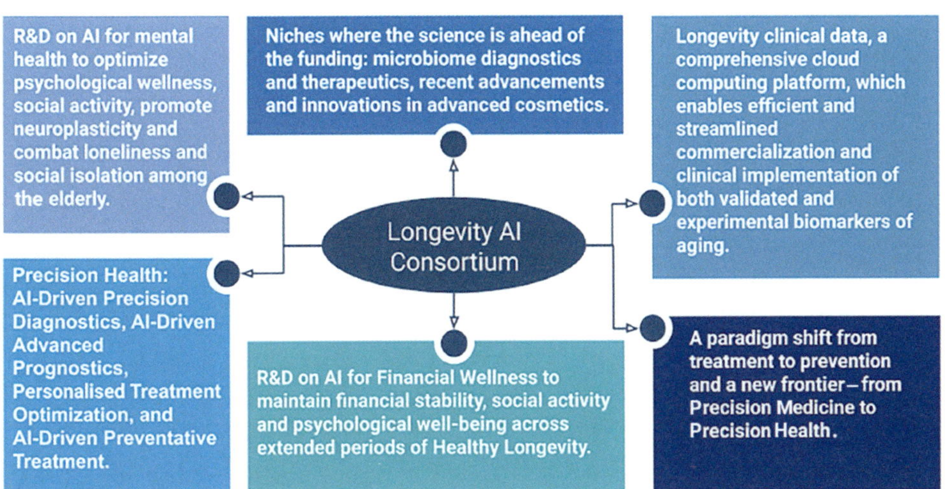

The Unmet Need for Dedicated Centers of AI for Longevity R&D and Practical Implementation

The number of companies, researchers, projects and technologies active in the P4 space from multiple sectors is significant and rapidly growing. Therefore, there is a demand for practical and sophisticated AI-driven approaches for improving and optimizing the products and services in this space.

It may be worth noting that a clear precedent for AI Longevity Centres already exists.

There are currently 4 major AI Centres for Healthcare in various major hubs in the UK, such as the new AI Centre for Value-Based Healthcare at King's College.

In order to satisfy this deficit, and help bring AI for Longevity technology transfer the attention and prioritization it deserves, we founded LIAC, which will focus first on AI for Longevity R&D and the creation and optimization of Precision Health technologies, techniques and protocols, and which will later expand its focus to include R&D and technology transfer of called "Lifetime Wellness": non-medical factors (including financial, psychological and social wellness) that impact quality of life and functionality for seniors, ranging from financial wellness, continuing education, happiness, psychological well-being, neuroplasticity and active social involvement.

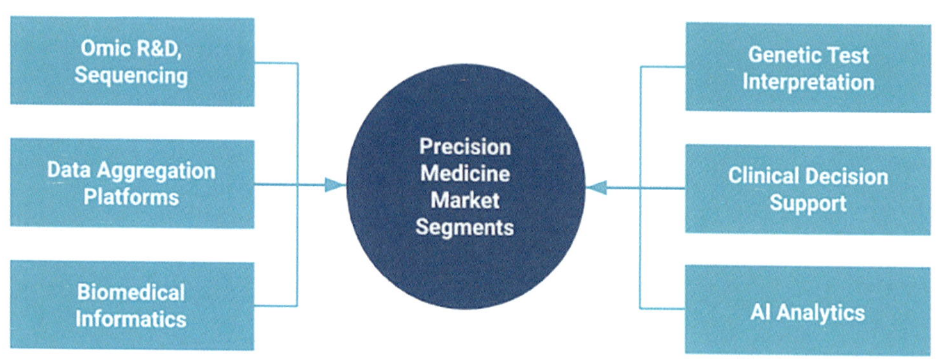

It is our hope that the work done by the LIAC will help in accelerating the paradigm shift from treatment to prevention and open up a new frontier of healthcare — from Precision Medicine to Precision Health — enabling the UK to become the number one global hub for the application of AI to Longevity and Precision Health, with a focus on a combination of AI-Driven Precision Diagnostics, AI-Driven Advanced Prognostics, Personalised Treatment Optimization, and AI-Driven Preventative Treatment.

Longevity AI Consortium: Agenda for 2020 and Beyond

The Longevity AI Consortium will serve as a leading R&D hub and industry-academic hotspot for advanced AI-driven personalised preventive diagnostics, prognostics and therapeutics.

It plans to dedicate resources to R&D in other niches where the science is ahead of the funding: e.g. microbiome diagnostics and therapeutics, and recent advancements and innovations in advanced cosmetics in particular.

The Consortium aims to identify novel Longevity and healthy aging biomarkers, accelerate diagnosis of age-related health decline, and develop personalised physical, mental and financial health to better implement and promote effective healthy lifestyles for Longevity, such as modifying patterns in sleep, nutrition, physical activity, environmental exposure and financial planning.

AI for Financial Wellness

Financial services innovators have an opportunity to greatly enhance the financial lives of the **aged 60+ aiming to live up to 100 years** individuals by designing new solutions, in addition to adapting existing products and services.

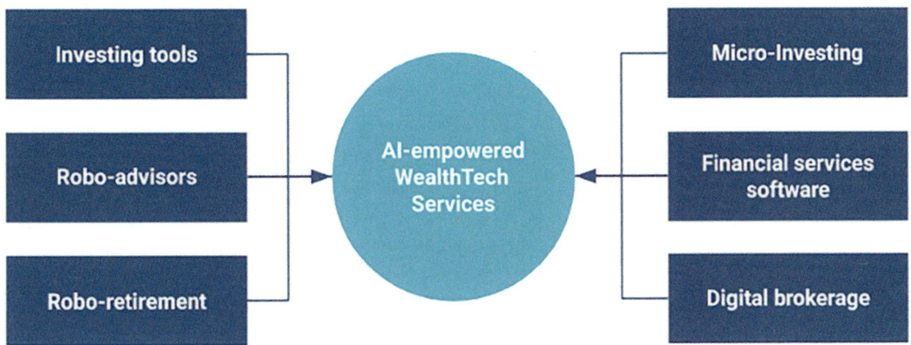

The Longevity AI Consortium will use sophisticated and multidimensional analytical frameworks developed by Aging Analytics Agency to perform industry benchmarking in Precision Health and Personalised Preventive Medicine clinics in order to construct the ideal diagnostic, prognostic and therapeutic pipeline using the most advanced market-ready methods and technologies.

The Consortium will develop a comprehensive cloud computing platform to enable the development of "minimum viable" and "most comprehensive" panels of biomarkers of aging, creating an ecosystem that incentivizes the participation of doctors, clinics, data providers, AI companies and corporate partners, and which will enable efficient and streamlined commercialization and clinical implementation of both validated and experimental biomarkers of aging as a framework for the extension of national Healthy Longevity in the UK.

King's College London is the logical choice of location for the first Longevity AI Consortium, due to their unique combination of resources, departments and technologies for both AI and Longevity. King's is also an ideal location for the AI Consortium because it has dedicated divisions and resources both for AI and for Longevity. Furthermore, being located in London, it is in an ideal physical location to engage in cross-sector and industry-academic collaboration.

The AI Longevity Consortium is currently designing a complementary AI Consortium for Financial Wellness which will utilize financial and behavioural data to develop products and services to enable UK citizens to maintain financial stability, social activity and psychological well-being across extended periods of Healthy Longevity.

Over the next few years, the Longevity AI Consortium plans to expand to include centres in Switzerland, Israel, Singapore and the US. This collaborative effort involves sophisticated methods for translating advanced AI for Longevity solutions, along with the development of advanced frameworks and technologies including novel applications of life data for insurance companies, pension funds, healthcare companies, and government bodies. These new technologies and instruments at the forefront of the rising Longevity Financial Industry provide practical applications of Preventive Medicine and Precision Health.

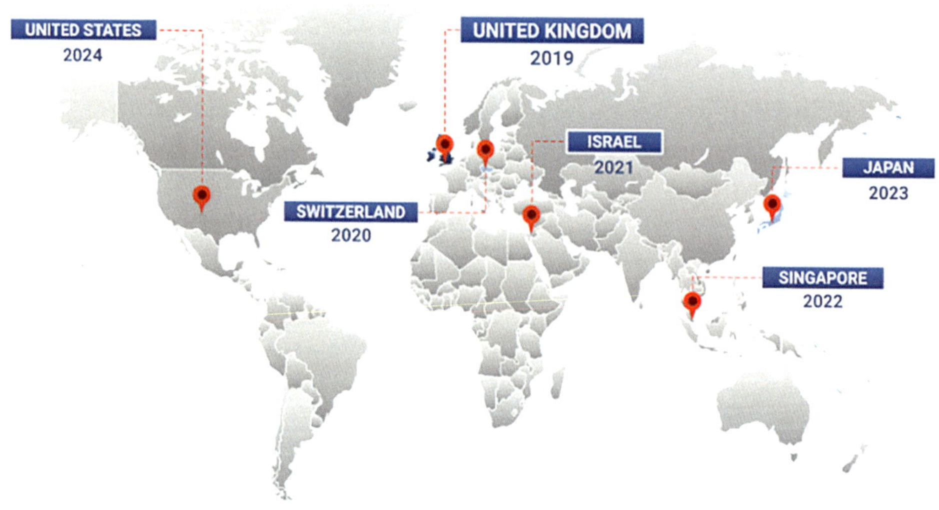

In 2020, following the completion of several key development milestones, the Longevity AI Consortium plans to launch an AI Longevity Accelerator Programme that will serve as a much-needed bridge between start-ups focusing on AI for Longevity research and drug development, and major UK investors.

The Longevity AI Accelerator

While the UK's AI and Longevity Industry ecosystems are very developed individually, the number of Longevity start-ups utilizing AI in a major way for their internal R&D is comparatively small compared to the overall disruptive impact, potential and promise that the synergy of these two sectors has.

All start-ups selected for inclusion into the accelerator will also receive mentorship and incubation resources, and will gain access to our global network of experts in the areas of scientific R&D, business development and investment relations, giving them the tools necessary to grow, expand and evolve following their time in the AI Longevity Accelerator, and to equip them with the skills required to develop further through later-stage venture capital and government grants.

Conclusions:

- AI holds more potential than any other technology vertical to rapidly accelerate Longevity research and development, and the practical implementation of technologies and solutions for extended healthspan, wealthspan and Precision Health.
- Although the UK is home to multiple centres of AI for Healthcare, there is not a single dedicated centre for AI for Longevity R&D.

- The Longevity AI Consortium (LAIC) is changing this through our unique academic-industry focus on the efficient validation and implementation of AI-driven technologies and solutions for Healthy Human Longevity, Preventive Medicine, and Precision Health and Financial Wellness over extended periods of healthy, productive and functional lifespans.
- In late 2020 the LAIC will also launch its AI Longevity Accelerator, which will provide investment, incubation and mentorship opportunities for the most promising UK-based AI for Longevity start-ups across the full scope of the Longevity Industry (biomedical, technological and financial), in order to serve as a much-needed bridge between start-ups focusing on AI for Longevity research/drug development and major UK investors.
- The LAIC, first established at King's College London, has plans to extend its reach into centres in Switzerland, Singapore, Israel, Japan and the United States.

Primary R&D Goals for 2020 - End-to-End Healthy Longevity Research

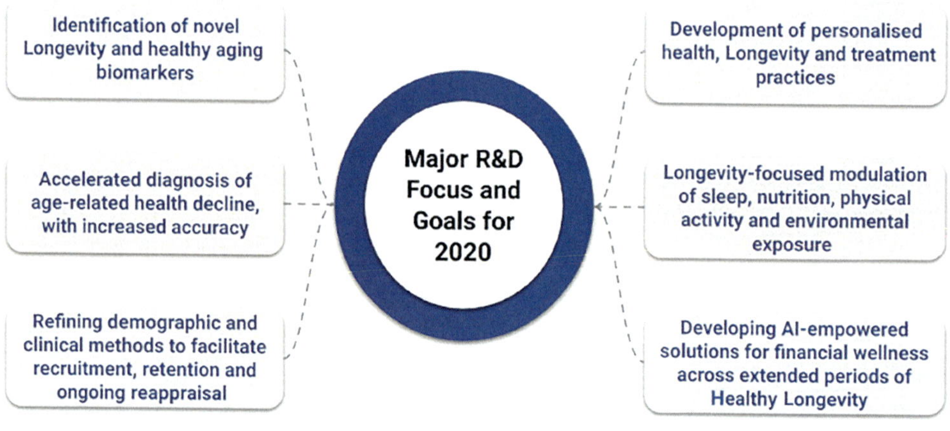

Chapter 24: The Effect of Diet and Exercise on Biological Aging: From Hype to Reality

It is widely accepted and common dogma that intensive sport is beneficial for Longevity and capable of delaying biological aging. And for people with absolutely ideal conditions (who are completely healthy, normal middle-aged individuals without any pathologies and living in an absolutely natural and clean environment) this is most likely the case. But how many people can really be considered to fit within that extremely idealistic case? In reality, the large majority of individuals seeking to extend their Healthy Longevity are older than 35 (and many beyond 50), living in dense metropolitan cities with high levels of pollution, and often having various minor (and in some cases major) pathological conditions. And therefore, the actual real impact of particular types of intensive sport and exercise is highly variable, and not very predictable. This issue is complicated even more when we consider traditional dogmas related to the so-called "Healthy Lifestyle" industry such as diets and supplements.

From a scientific and purely statistical point of view, there is not a sufficient volume of actual results and evidence to support a number of commonly-believed activities and behavioural interventions thought to affect biological aging or extend lifespan, including intensive exercise and sport, organic food, diets (such as vegetarian and vegan diets), vitamins and supplements, and others. The main issue revolves around the fact that most large-scale studies that appear to demonstrate the positive effects of these practices are not conducted in a sufficiently precise or personalized manner, taking into account the high degree of biological variability among their study participants, particularly in those that are in their later middle age, when the actual degree of variability increases exponentially due to the "entropic" nature of biological aging.

The sectors of fitness, diet, exercise, high-grade organic foods and other sectors within the so-called neo-wellness industry have become a kind of new religion, considered by large groups of people to be validated reality, but in practice built on hype and a serious lack of scientific validation. In reality, beginning from age 40, and especially for individuals aged 50-60, the exact practices and activities that on average will prove beneficial for younger adults (30-40 years old) may actually have negative effects on general health and biological aging, because the entire concept of "normal" or "average" health degrades beginning in the later stages of middle age. Biological aging can be considered as the highly variable disintegration of highly complex and interconnected biological systems, and the nature of aging (and how it affects individual health) varies incredibly from individual to individual. There may, indeed, only be 1% of individuals who in later middle age still fit into the concept of "normal", and the majority of people have specific issues with their immune systems, the presence of different pathologies and conditions, and highly variable microbiomes.

And, even more extremely, even very simple and "obvious" recommendations like "run and exercise regularly, drink lots of water, and eat organic food" are not applicable to people in their later middle age, due to high degrees of variability in the environmental conditions where they live. For individuals living in modern cities and metropolitan areas, the purity and quality of ambient air and their water systems may have so much pollution that increased intake of water and exercise actually increase the amount of contaminants they are absorbing in their bodies. Similarly with respect to food, diet, vitamins and supplements, what people can purchase in their local grocery or health food stores is extremely variable, and often contain high levels of impurities. For example, foods that are labelled organic are often highly processed, and when someone buys meat at a standard grocery store, they are likely buying meat that is highly saturated with antibiotics and growth hormones, as well as preservatives and other chemicals added after animals are slaughtered to extend their shelf-life.

Below, we will outline a number of common myths about the beneficial effects of some of the most popular fitness and neo-wellness fads.

- **Exercise and Intensive Sport:** In later middle age, long-distance running and high intensity sport can actually have quite significant negative effects, including damage to joints, up to 16x increased intake of pollutants, the generation of free-radicals, and damage to the vascular system for people with existing cardiac or vascular conditions, especially when the sport exercises including running are done with not right techniques.

- **High Water Intake:** While it is of course important to drink water, for the majority of individuals the water actually available to them is highly impure and contaminated, and one of the main sources of systematic chemical toxification, especially in individuals who are in their later middle age or older. Sophisticated methods of water detoxification must be applied in order to gain the beneficial effects of increased water intake (standard reverse osmosis is not enough for real water purification).
- **Organic Food:** Foods that are labelled organic very often contain hidden impurities. While it would be wise generally to eat foods that are labelled as organic over highly-processed foods, there is not enough regulation and validation over what constitutes "organic" to be reliably certain that it will have net-beneficial effects, or that it is sufficiently organic and free of impurities to have an effect on health and biological aging.
- **Diets:** It is also absolutely clear that, in the majority of cases, diets that seek to completely eliminate types of food that have been commonly ingested over the majority of human history have a net-negative effect for most individuals. And, interestingly, there is a good amount of evidence suggesting that specific positive and negative effects of diets are tied to how they affect the extremely sensitive and variable microbiome of individuals. Also, one of the most important considerations is specific factors impacting the way that food is ingested. Individuals seeking to gain health benefits from diet should follow the approach of food-as-medicine, and their decisions should be driven not by human opinion, but by tangible measurement of biomarkers integrated with modern bioinformatics and data-science techniques. These challenges, combined with the highly variable ways in which individuals react to specific nutrients, supplements and microelements based on age, gender, ethnicity, microbiome, current state of health and other factors, make any strong predictions nearly impossible.

However, even considering all the above, there are certainly ways in which these kinds of activities and practices (exercise, supplements, and specific dietary habits) can have an impact on biological aging and healthspan (the period in which people are healthy and free from major age-related diseases), if they are combined with very specific approaches involving extremely large-scale, highly precise and personalized studies (in which study participants are grouped into highly targeted groups based on shared factors including age, gender, ethnicity, location of residence and presence of existing conditions), analyzed via the coordination of data science and Artificial Intelligence rather than the personal assumptions and theories of wellness coaches and healthy lifestyle gurus.

The most effective method to do this would be to apply AI and data science to information collected from significant proportions of the general population via mHealth mobile applications and wearables which track (1) specific factors of users including age, sex, ethnicity, location and presence of existing conditions, (2) general state of biological health (and, ideally, their biological age as measured by various biomarkers of aging and Longevity), and (3) the specific dietary, supplement-based, exercise-based and behavioural interventions that they pursue, and the effects of those interventions on their biological age and general state of health. Naturally, the only way to coordinate, integrate and analyze this very large amount of data would be to use AI and data science techniques.

An ideal platform to facilitate this type of large-scale study would be a full-scope health and Longevity marketplace with millions of users, which gives access to a high volume of precisely-targeted health-focused products and services, combined with periodic measurement of the effects of those products on their general state of health and biological age. One of the good examples of such a platform may be Longevity Banking Card, which provides its cardholders and clients access to a specifically-adjusted retail Longevity Marketplace, giving them access to a highly-tailored full-scope marketplace of products and services designed to optimize health and Longevity, which will tend to include mHealth products aiming to track the effect of those products and services on their current state of health and Longevity (via periodic measurement of their Biomarkers of Longevity).

In the ideal (but not so far-future) scenario, the precision and frequency of this cycle of intervention application, monitoring and adjusting would be applied as close to real-time as possible, with AI-based systems applying micro-doses of interventions combined with immediate measurement of its effects on health and biological aging, and high-frequency dosage adjustment, in order to construct ideal precise and personalized regimens of medical and non-medical interventions tuned to the specific factors of each individual, and to adapt them over time as those factors change. This approach to healthy living (featuring integration of AI and data science-driven measurement of biomarkers coordinated with treatment and intervention adjustment and personalization) is not futurism, and there are projects and products falling within this approach that are either already on the market, or anticipated to be launched in the coming months and the next 1-2 year horizon.

Conclusions

- For the average person interested in living a longer, healthier and higher-quality life in their middle age, between the ages of 35-60, until the large-scale and highly precise and personalized studies necessary to really validate what works and what does not are conducted, our personal recommendations would include drinking extremely pure water, residing in low-pollution environments, ingesting extremely high-quality and validated organic foods, and conducting any specific behavioural interventions including diets, physical exercise and sport, and supplements in an very precise, targeted and personalized manner, adjusted to individuals' current age, gender, ethnicity, state of health, microbiome and presence of existing conditions.
- We would also recommend integrating and monitoring all of these health-optimization activities via the application of AI, data science, health tracking wearables and other related technologies, rather than the personal opinions of wellness industry professionals who cannot provide results tuned to the specifics of individual people.
- Finally, with regards to all these activities, the first principle that people should seek to follow is the very same as the core principle observed by doctors themselves: **first do no harm**. People seeking to optimize their health and Longevity should practice activities with the lowest likelihood of harming their bodies, and should prioritize the use of wellness, diet and exercise products, projects and techniques backed by AI and data science, tuned to the specifics of their own bodies via high-frequency testing, feedback and optimization.

Chapter 25: Longevity FemTech (Contributor: Robin Farmanfarmaian)

"Genetics, environment, and lifestyle all shape a woman's brain and body over the course of her lifetime. Research is finding that if women don't take control of their health in mid-life, it can negatively impact their standard of living, their families, and their long-term health."

Margaretta Colangelo in *Femtech Longevity Trailblazer Raises US$5.3M* (Official LinkedIn Longevity Newsletter, August 2019)

FemTech refers to the emerging range of digital technologies focused specifically on women's health. The majority of the market currently consists largely of wearable devices and smartphone interfaces, connected medical devices, and hygiene products.

The ultimate aim is to identify, within the broader FemTech Healthcare sector, those **companies and technologies related to Preventive Medicine, Longevity, and the extension of the healthy and active period of life, as it relates to female-specific biological functions.** Complex female health issues such as hormonal issues (PMS, contraception, menopause, fertility, side effects and mood, for example) have been historically neglected or underserved. Underserved areas can range anywhere from a lack of environmentally friendly menstrual products to female specific healthcare for skin health, depression, anxiety, libido and energy.

P4 medicine now allows for targeting the side effects of 140 different contraceptives that are generically offered to patients without attempt to personalise them to the individual. Pexxi company tests individuals for their own hormonal and genetic profile to recommend a contraceptive that will not give them side effects.

Products for dealing with menstrual flow, e.g. reusable absorbent underwear, the reusable cup, flushable pads, etc., are now competing to provide the safest, most convenient as well as affordable and environmentally friendly option to the hundreds of millions of people worldwide who are actively in need of them. Fertility into older years is another major area of research, and is at the core of AgeTech and Rejuvenation Biotechnologies.

A major focus of FemTech today is preventive care. Although nowadays many serious health threats can be detected in routine screenings, they still threaten the lives of thousands of individuals every year.

The risks are even higher in low-income communities and developing nations. Technology, however, could provide solutions – especially if it is properly promoted and summarily adopted among the mainstream.

The option of activating healthy eggs past patients' natural fertility will shift lifestyle priorities and open up the window of conception wider into middle age and beyond.

Achievements:

- Last year, Lehigh University announced that a team of engineers was able to create an artificial intelligence-based system able to screen for cervical cancer 10% more accurately than traditional methods. Moreover, the solution proved to be inexpensive enough to present a viable solution for reducing the threat of cervical cancer, particularly for the developing world.
- The Kilimanjaro Cervical Cancer Screening Project in Tanzania is utilizing smartphones and patient tracking apps to screen women for cervical cancer. In a process known as cervicography, non-physician health workers use their phones to transmit photographs of the cervix to a health centre to be reviewed by an expert. If cancerous areas are identified, treatment instructions are transmitted back to the healthcare worker. The entire review process takes mere minutes to complete; the quick diagnosis and treatment are especially useful for women in remote areas.
- Another FemTech approach to battling cervical cancer involves the development of drug therapeutics for treating the diseases caused by HPV.

Researchers have found that 91% of cervical cancer cases are caused by the human papillomavirus.

- FemTech treatments that target HPV thus help prevent cervical cancer, often making surgery unnecessary.

A tech sector focusing exclusively on female health will inevitably have some special significance for those areas of declining health which are inextricable from the aging process, such as the effects of menopause.

As such, FemTech has developed much more explicit links **with the Longevity Industry.** The identity of the FemTech sector was boosted by the creation of the Centre for Female Reproductive Longevity and Equality at the Buck Institute for Research on Aging – a centre for FemTech in all but name.

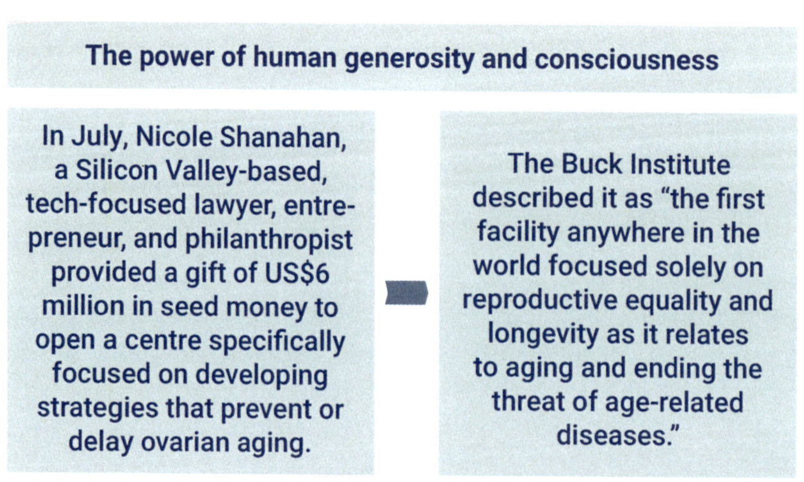

Buck's professor Judith Campisi, an expert in cellular senescence and a recurring name in our previous Longevity reports, will lead early recruitment efforts at the centre.

Campisi, therefore, stands at the intersection between FemTech and the Longevity Industry and hopes to bring the full power of the Buck Institute's 19 labs and research programs in stem cells, cellular stress and disease, mitochondria and bioenergetics, exercise, nutrition and metabolism for the centre.

What is the present state of ovarian rejuvenation?

A self-styled "fertility clinic of last resort", the Center for Human Reproduction is a leading fertility centre located in New York City. They currently specialise in “older” ovary rejuvenation, whether due to advanced female age or premature ovarian aging (POA), immunological problems affecting reproduction, repeated pregnancy loss, endometriosis, polycystic ovary syndrome (PCOS), tubal disease, male factor infertility, etc.

"Firsts" developed at CHR included the idea of vaginal egg retrieval, which was performed at CHR for the first time and published in the reputable medical journal The Lancet. CHR investigators also pioneered the concept of tubal catheterization to recanalize obstructed fallopian tubes, first published in the prestigious journal JAMA.

The most influential recent contribution of CHR research to infertility treatment was the introduction of supplementation with DHEA in women with poor ovarian reserve.

One already available technological mean of intervening directly in age-related declining female health is bioidentical hormone replacement therapy for women. Women are especially vulnerable to age-related hormonal imbalances such as thyroid disorder, premenstrual syndrome and low sexual desire.

Hormonal imbalance affects millions of women in the United States. Conditions such as menopause, thyroid dysfunction, and hypoactive sexual desire disorder (HSDD) are linked to out-of-balance hormones.

Women suffering from symptoms of hormone imbalance (e.g. mood swings, insomnia, weight gain and hair loss) can find relief in hormonal replacement therapies, which can be life-altering. Hormonal replacement offsets the effects of hormonal imbalance and allows women to experience better health and a higher quality of life when the balance is safely and effectively restored.

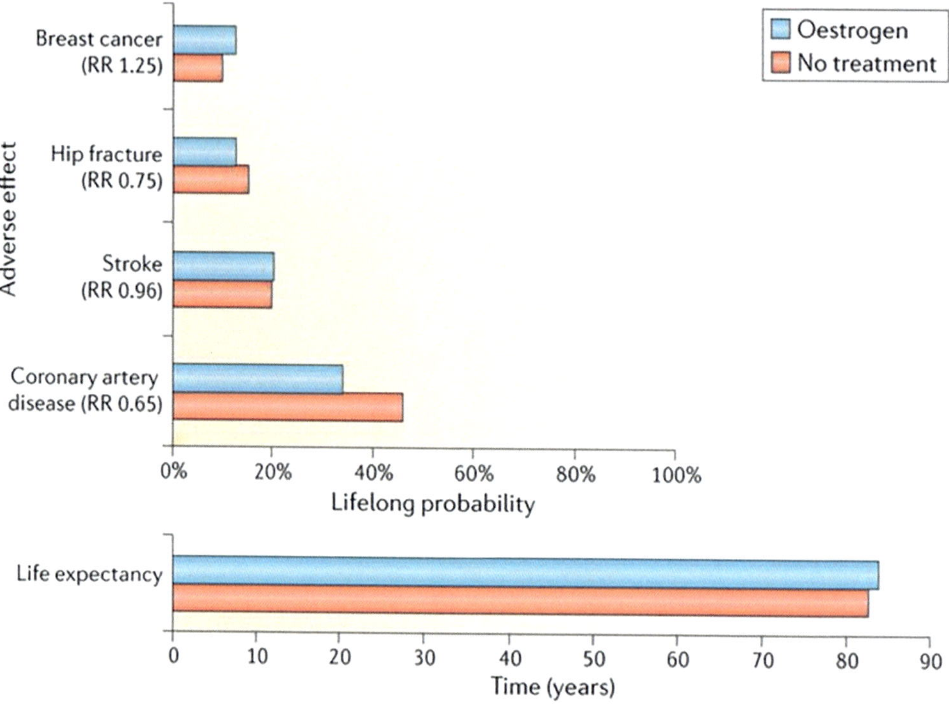

Since 2010, more than 10 major medical organizations have come forward to endorse menopausal hormone therapy, heralding it as the best treatment for menopause. Yet, many doctors still sidestep the therapy citing dangerous side effects and risk of disease.

This fear began in 2002 when the widely-publicized Women's Health Initiative (WHI) — the largest study ever conducted on the effects of hormone therapy was halted because female subjects were falling ill.

The study has since been reviewed and analyzed by experts nationwide (USA), finding that the study's design and methods were faulty and that the use of synthetic hormones – synthetic estrogen and progestin (synthetic progesterone) – were largely to blame.

Given the recent increase in the number of FemTech companies focused on a core Longevity component, we predict a rise in the number of FemTech companies focused on Longevity in particular.

But progress in biomedicine, especially in the use of gene therapies and stem cell therapies to reverse aging in entire biological systems such as the endocrine system, will bring an ever wider range of age-related issues under FemTech's purview.

We should also expect to see a female-centric healthspan extending sector emerge naturally in the course of the following pursuits:

- Finding geroprotectors that appear to have differential effects in men and women.
- Finding interventions (like geroprotectors and gene therapies) that upregulate genes associated with higher female life expectancy.

We have already, in previous sections, touched on a number of AI-reliant FemTech solutions, such as period-tracking apps and wearables.

However, the end product of a great deal of future FemTech will take the form of AI-powered software as a service (SaaS), courses of monitoring and advice particularly reliant on deep learning, such as that developed by Haut.AI.

Their product is a form of deep learning-powered SaaS for skincare. They help their clients:

- To develop new skincare strategies, selecting for them skin care treatments for their individual skin type, climate, health status, geography, and other parameters.
- To personalize the treatments for each individual, tracking and updating these parameters over the years.
- To help aging skin retain a youthful look.

But they also create an interaction between business and customer, facilitating R&D by feeding back data from 100,000 skin images to the company for further deep learning and consequently more accurate and efficient skin care regimes.

It is expected that information collected from individual users of such services will provide researchers with large databases of metrics, offering the potential for doctors to better understand diverse aspects of women's wellness as they age.

However, for serious kinds of female age-related diseases, such as breast cancer, these kinds of data analytics would need huge amounts of authentic patient data — possibly from patients in many different countries and diverse racial and genetic backgrounds — for deep analysis and creation of many different patterns for successful detection.

Will There Ever Be a MenTech Industry?

Despite there being much research and many solutions being produced specifically for male-focused Longevity, it is not as socially and politically popular for men to congregate to discuss them, the way women have started to do.

Men are more reluctant to consult their doctor about health issues, and do not have an accessible space to open up about personal issues around their physical and mental health.

Furthermore the specific issue of declining fertility does not affect men as early or as precipitously as women, and men are therefore less likely to feel prompted to seek solutions.

Therefore, from a marketing point of view, it is at present much easier to launch a FemTech Longevity fund than a MenTech one.

Chapter 26: Biomarkers of Longevity 2.0 – The Shift Toward Actionable, AI-Empowered Biomarkers of Aging, Health and Longevity (Contributor: Franco Cortese)

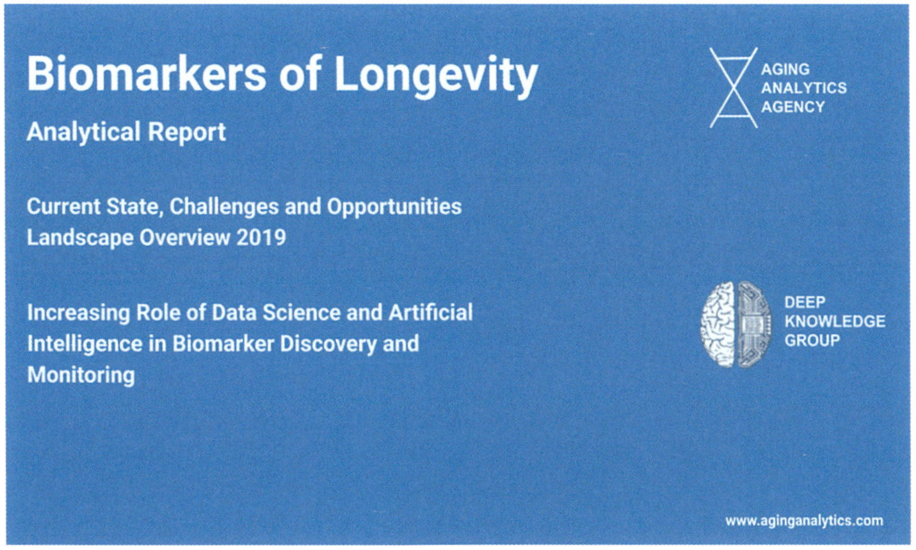

Key Points:

- The use of biomarkers is an indispensable component of Longevity Industry analytics and assessment. It is the foundation upon which measurement of Healthy Longevity and the effectiveness of Longevity therapeutics is built.
- Biomarkers are also the primary metric in P4 (Precision, Preventive, Personalised and Participatory) Medicine, which involves continuously monitoring of the progress of a disease state and recommending a series of corrective interventions in response, to keep patients' state of health in an optimal mode for as long as possible.
- Aggregating biomarkers of aging (rather than biomarkers of disease) is particularly difficult however, as by definition, they must

be sought in populations of healthy people rather than among the health data of the hospital populations.

- Furthermore, as the scope of P4 Medicine broadens, the number of biomarkers and technologies will increase rapidly to the thousands in the coming years. This makes the implementation of P4 Medicine impractical by current, manual means.
- Some possible solutions to these problems include the use of AI for the development of an optimal panel of biomarkers of aging, for the analysis of individual patients' biomarkers of aging, and for orchestrating therapeutic interventions in response to fluctuations in those biomarkers.
- As the number of data points increases, it becomes not only optimal, but strictly necessary, to use AI and Big Data analysis for these purposes.

I have worked with Dmitry Kaminskiy in a number of capacities over the past three years. Before working alongside him at Aging Analytics Agency, Deep Knowledge Group, and, more recently, its Longevity-focused hybrid investment fund Longevity.Capital, I served under him as Deputy Director of the Biogerontology Research Foundation, and a member of its Board of Trustees, from 2017 to 2018.

One of the projects I am most proud of during my tenure there was spearheading the Biogerontology Research Foundation's part of a multi-institution project to classify aging as a disease during the World Health Organization's most recent round of revisions to their International Classification of Diseases (ICD) — a framework that serves as the example followed by the majority of developed nations drug regulatory agencies.

The result of our proposal was the introduction by the World Health Organization of a new extension code for aging-related diseases — XT9T — that can be applied to both new and existing diseases.

While the addition of an extension code for "aging-related" via the ICD-11 does not amount to classifying aging as a disease, it is a step in the right direction.

It brings us one step closer to getting the World Health Organization to recognize aging as a pathological process with identifiable and quantifiable clinical indications, which can be intervened upon so as to enable human healthspan extension, compression of morbidity and prevention of age-related diseases, during subsequent ICD revision processes.

These efforts are about much more than theory or semantics.

Aubrey de Grey has remarked:

"The ICD is not just a taxonomy. It greatly influences how drugs are prescribed in most nations, because a physician's justification for writing a prescription must typically be documented in terms of an ICD code describing the diagnosis. As such, the addition of an extension code to denote aging may have a really huge impact on the financial rewards that drug developers can expect to reap if they bring treatments for age-related ill-health to the market."

One of the strongest conclusions I reached in working towards the classification of aging as a disease is the incredibly pressing need not just for biomarkers of aging and Longevity, but the need for actionable biomarkers that could be put into practice today to measure the effectiveness of healthspan-extending interventions.

It is biomarkers of aging and Longevity, which can serve as a proxy measure of the effectiveness of Longevity-focused therapies, that will pave the way to getting approval for drugs not on the basis of single, narrowly-classified diseases, but on their effects on aging itself, and will lay the necessary regulatory infrastructure needed for the rapid industrialization of Longevity to scale, as well as to allow governments to measure the effectiveness of their efforts to increase national Healthy Longevity, a goal that a number of Longevity-progressive governments are now keenly moving forward towards.

Now, through our work with Dr. Richard Siow and the Longevity AI Consortium at King's College London, we are:

- Striving to fill this unmet gap.
- Transforming this goal into reality, through the development of AI-empowered technologies and solutions to the development of actionable biomarkers of aging, health and Longevity to scale.

One special function of the Longevity AI Consortium will be the development of an optimal panel of biomarkers of aging – **a specific niche where the implementation is lagging behind the science.**

The present chapter aims to outline the need for actionable biomarkers of aging, health and Longevity, how AI will be the major driver for achieving them in the coming years, and Deep Knowledge Group's plans and activities focused on turning these potentials into concrete realities.

Artificial Intelligence will use Digital Biomarkers to reality-check the proposed Longevity therapies and filter out inappropriate or impractical biomarkers from those effective.

AI-Driven Development of Biomarker Panels of Aging

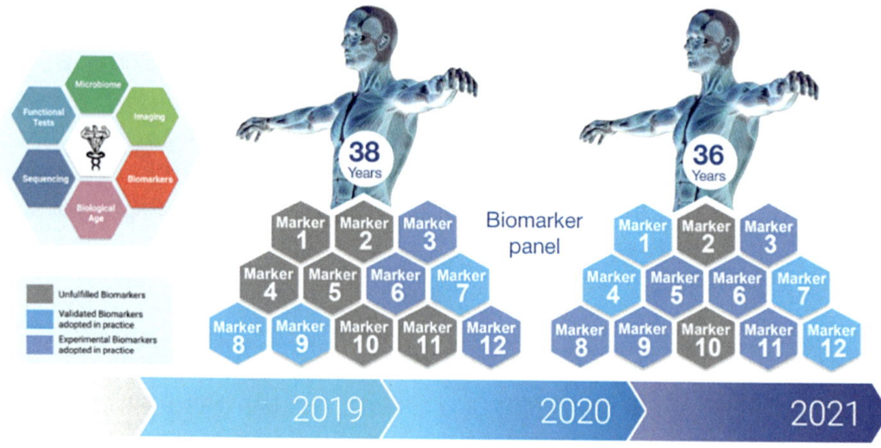

What are Biomarkers of Aging?

How do we know when a biomarker is a biomarker of aging? It depends on how it is sourced. The current approach to biomarkers is to take them from people at various stages of a disease's known progress, which in practice means sourcing them from hospital patients. Isolating biomarkers of aging, however, means collecting data which marks the difference between healthy people only, e.g. between the young and middle aged, with no traces of any officially recognised diseases.

This presents a challenge because whereas hospital patients remain in dedicated areas, and are available for analysis at the doctor's convenience, collecting biomarkers of aging means collecting vast amounts of data from the daily lives of people who have no reason to be in hospital. There are however options available for aggregating such data, such as the devices which come under the AgeTech umbrella, that will find their user base among those suffering from aging but not disease.

It is important in technology never to let the perfect be the enemy of good, especially when the technology is of great humanitarian significance.

For example, in the early 2000s, enthusiastic proponents of the application of regenerative medicine to aging were urging governments, entrepreneurs and thought-leaders to make this a priority.

They argued that technology was ahead of the science and the funding, and that while a great deal remains to be discovered about the mechanisms of aging, we already know enough to optimize the existing toolkit of regenerative medicine to address the damage of aging, which is already thoroughly researched.

And thus, out of the paradigm shift occurred from this, the field of rejuvenation biotechnology arose.

Now once again, the technology is ahead of the science and the funding. And, once again, a paradigm shift is due. Presently the necessary biotechnologies for the implementation of P4 Medicine technologies and therapies are already in place. What is needed now is Big Data analytics to develop optimal panels of biomarkers of aging and to determine how to optimize their implementation with maximum precision.

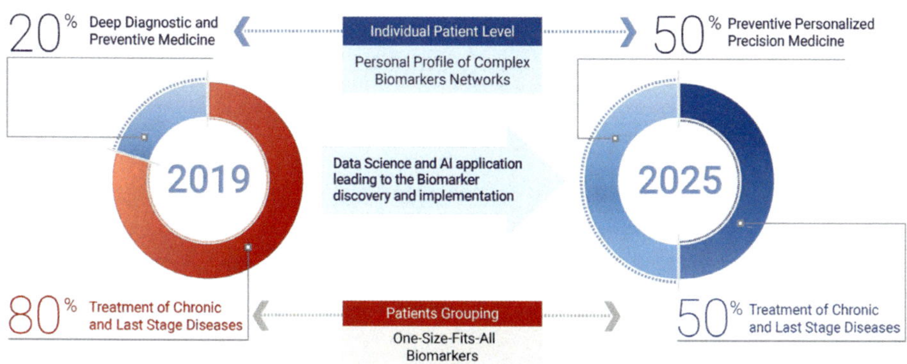

There is, however, a risk that governments and governmental or political strategic bodies may make one or both of the following errors:

- They might assume that the missing bridge on the road to HALE-extending P4 Medicine is still BioTech progress.
- They might assume that because the current scientific quest for ever more precise biomarkers is not slowing down, we don't yet have a set of biomarkers precise and sufficiently actionable to take immediate action.

As such, government strategic bodies risk limiting their strategic ambitions with regard to time frames.

For example, in the UK in 2019, Theresa May's government announced a commitment to adding 5 extra years on the nation's HALE by 2035, whereas Aging Analytics Agency subsequently advised the UK's newly formed APPG for Longevity that a much more relevant timeline would be 2025, provided **actionable biomarkers with sufficient accuracy are utilized**. This aspiration better reflects the real current rate and state of scientific and technological innovation.

It is therefore desirable that such bodies have access to a panel of biomarkers which are not only comprehensive but also actionable.

A panel of less precise but easily implementable biomarkers of aging would be much more useful much sooner than an extremely precise and comprehensive panel of biomarkers of aging that is too hard or expensive to translate easily into widespread practical use across nations.

Biomarkers for Paradigm Shift from P4 Medicine to Precision Health

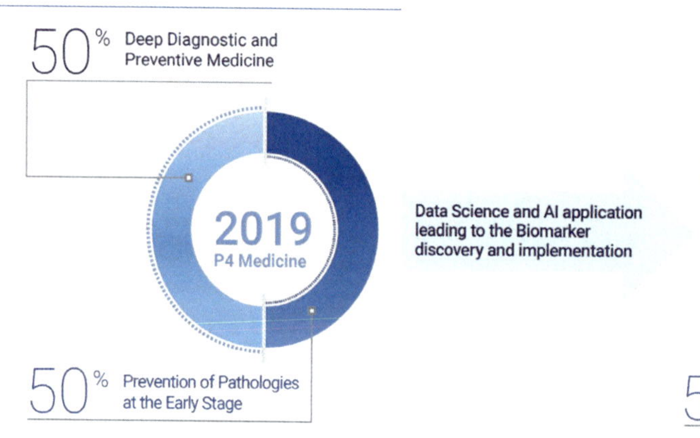

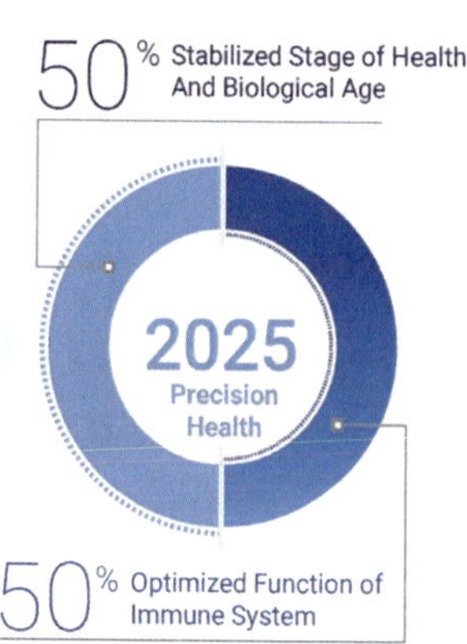

The Need for Actionable Biomarkers of Aging and Longevity

The development of precise and actionable biomarkers of aging is one of the most prevalent and important areas of Longevity research today, as well as an area where practical implementation is lagging behind the science.

This is one of the most important diagnostic services that could be offered, and yet it does not receive the attention it deserves when compared to the amount of tangible benefits it can deliver.

The current approach to biomarkers:

- Taking them from people at various stages of a disease's known progress, which in practice means sourcing them from hospital patients.
- Isolating biomarkers of aging, however, means collecting data which marks the difference between healthy people only, e.g. between the young and even younger, with no traces of any officially recognised diseases.
- This presents a challenge because whereas hospital patients remain in dedicated areas, and are available for analysis at the doctor's convenience, collecting biomarkers of aging means collecting vast amounts of data from the daily lives of people who have no reason to be in hospitals.

There are however options available for aggregating such data.

Also important is the degree of emphasis on achieving a panel of biomarkers which are not only comprehensive but also actionable. As it was mentioned, a panel of less precise but easily implementable biomarkers of aging would be much better than an extremely precise and comprehensive panel of biomarkers of aging that is too hard or expensive to translate easily into widespread practical use. For example, a panel of aging biomarkers was developed recently based on **Deep Learning analysis** of standard blood biomarkers.

This is less precise than the most precise available biomarkers of aging (DNA methylation clocks), but is nonetheless precise enough, and can be implemented by any researcher, doctor and clinician that has access to routine blood tests.

As a further example of actionability, consider that biomarkers of aging have been constructed using Deep Learning-based analysis of photographs of mice, which could quite easily be extended to humans. Their accuracy alone is not enough to make them a research priority, but the increasing video capabilities of smart-phones means that this rapid **development of photographic biomarkers of aging** (e.g. of the face or the eye) could now be a very actionable area of research whose practical level of precision and accuracy will develop quite rapidly in coming years.

Insilico Medicine is a leader in the application of AI for Longevity research, drug discovery and biomarker development.

However, the use of AI in R&D is lagging behind in its application to geroscience. While there is a small handful of companies that are working at this frontier, the overall proportion in comparison to the total size of the Longevity Industry is still quite small. Deep Knowledge Ventures has been identifying and supporting companies working on the frontlines of AI for Longevity since 2014, when it provided the seed funding for Insilico Medicine.

The Launch of the Longevity AI Consortium at King's College London

In late 2019, Europe's first Longevity AI Consortium (LAIC) launched at King's College London with strategic and financial support from Deep Knowledge Group and the Biogerontology Research Foundation.

AI for Longevity is an underrepresented sector in the Longevity Industry despite having more potential to increase Healthy Longevity in the short term than any other sector.

The Longevity AI Consortium will work to facilitate the shift from treatment to prevention and from Preventive Medicine to real-world Precision Health. The initial aim will be to identify novel Longevity and healthy aging biomarkers to accelerate diagnosis of age-related health decline.

Then researchers will develop personalised physical, mental and financial health to better implement and promote healthy lifestyles for Longevity, such as modifying patterns in sleep, nutrition, physical activity, environmental exposure and financial planning.

The initial focus will be on core Longevity academic-industry R&D, including the development of biomarkers of aging and novel implementation of life and health data analytics.

In 2020, after achieving several key scientific and funding milestones, AI-enabled solutions for physical, mental and financial wellness are expected to become a major focus, and an **AI Longevity Accelerator will be launched to serve as a much-needed bridge between start-ups and major UK investors**, creating for the first time a dedicated infrastructure for increased investments and developments in this important sector.

As part of its continuing development efforts over the next several years, the Consortium will expand to include centres in Switzerland, Israel, Singapore, United States and Japan.

The Consortium will serve as the leading R&D hub and industry-academic hotspot for advanced AI-driven personalised, preventive diagnostics, prognostics and therapeutics.

This represents a paradigm shift from treatment to prevention and a new frontier – from Precision Medicine to Precision Health, enabling the UK to become the number one global hub for the application of AI to Longevity and Precision Health. Precision Health through AI will be developed by a combination of AI-driven precision diagnostics, AI-driven advanced prognostics, personalised treatment optimization, and AI-driven preventative treatment.

Some of the major focus areas of the Consortium include:

- **Frontier applications of artificial intelligence in aging research, Longevity R&D and the development of biomarkers of health and Longevity**, and the paradigm shift from disease treatment and sick care to Preventive Medicine, and from Preventive Medicine to Precision Health.
- **The increasing shift toward actionable biomarkers of aging**, including the identification of biomarkers of health, Longevity and aging that have the highest ratios of accuracy and pre-

cision vs. actionability, expense and ease-of-implementation, and the benchmarking of biomarkers that can be used in practice today.

- Emerging trends and novel paradigms relating to both the **creation and application of life data** collected on a massive scale from healthy individuals and used in scientifically-backed, quantifiable, tangible and precise ways to preserve and maintain an optimal state of health.
- **The disruptive and accelerative impact that AI is having on Longevity R&D** and the practical implementation and clinical translation of Longevity technologies and therapeutics.
- **Frontier applications of AI for financial wellness over extended periods of healthy Longevity**, and the maintenance and optimization of "wealthspan" to complement advances in "healthspan", including the application of AI assistants and "robo-advisors" for personal financial management, and the utilization of novel forms of financial data to enable AI-empowered AgeTech and WealthTech services.
- **Novel methods of using AI** to optimize psychological wellness, social activity, promote neuroplasticity and combat loneliness and social isolation among the elderly.

Biomarkers of Longevity 2019: New Special Analytical Case Study by Aging Analytics Agency

Biomarkers of Longevity: Current State, Challenges and Opportunities Landscape Overview 2019 is an open-access special analytical case study published by Aging Analytics Agency that uses a comprehensive analytical framework to rank and benchmark existing panels of biomarkers of aging, health and Longevity according to their ratios of accuracy vs. actionability, identifying the panels of biomarkers that can have the greatest impact on increasing both individual and national Healthy Longevity in the next few years.

The report was officially launched and presented at the recent AI for Longevity Summit at King's College London, organized by the Longevity AI Consortium with the strategic support of Deep Knowledge Group, Aging Analytics Agency, the Biogerontology Research Foundation and others. The summit featured talks from top executives from Prudential, HSBC,

AXA Insurance, NVIDIA, Microsoft, Babylon Health, Insilico Medicine, Longevity.Capital, Longevity Vision Fund, Juvenescence, Deep Knowledge Ventures, and the UK All-Party Parliamentary Group for Longevity.

The use of biomarkers is an indispensable component of industry analytics and assessment. It is the foundation upon which measurement of Healthy Longevity and the effectiveness of **P4 (Precision, Preventive, Personalised and Participatory) Medicine and Longevity therapeutics** is built. The report is designed as an in-depth review of the state of the art in biomarkers of biological age to advise private and public sector participants effectively.

It was produced to offer a panoramic review of the global landscape of aging and Longevity biomarkers, containing selected lists, rankings and enhanced profiles of more than 50 Single Biomarkers directly correlated with the trajectories of age-related diseases and syndromes, and exceeding 100 diverse biomarker panels for analytical data-driven comparisons that allow an optimal integration of multiple biomarkers for practical use, achieving highly actionable monitoring systems for **healthcare, clinical practice, translational research and frontier developments** that exploit the current conditioning of the rising Longevity Industry, and the execution of public policies aiming to increase National Healthy Longevity that will result in a renaissance never seen before in economic and social dynamics.

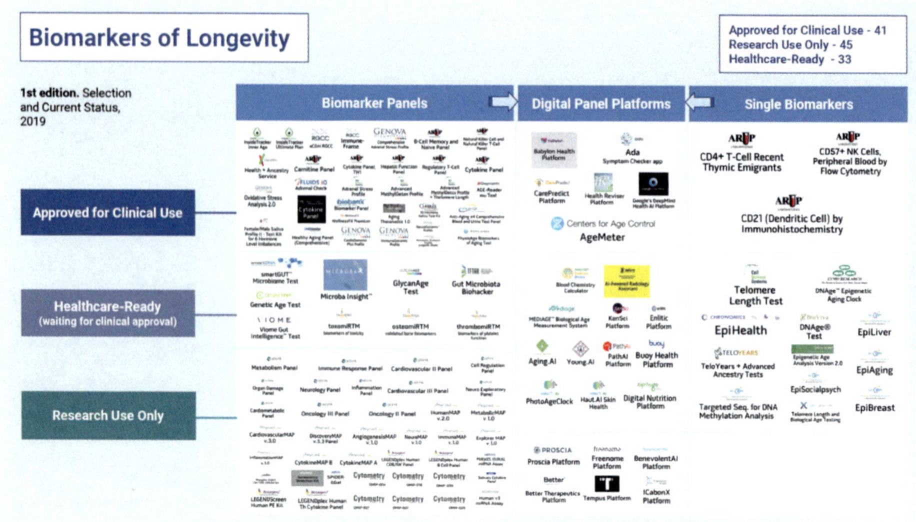

Biomarker Conventional Classification Frameworks

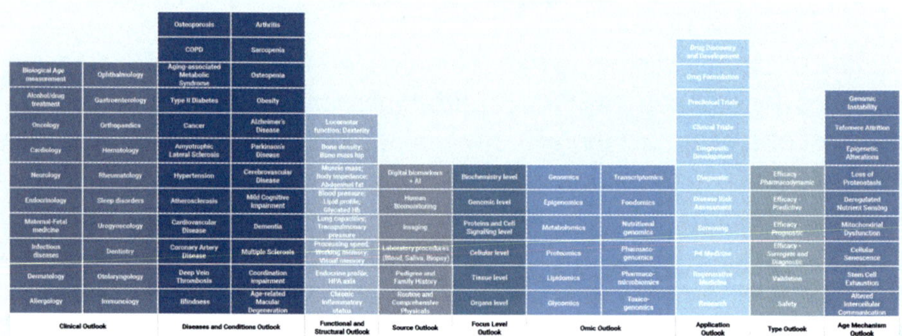

Special mention apart, biomarkers in pharmaceutical industry research and development are predominantly described based on a **Type Outlook** classification, the most widely used criterion; that is, as validation, safety and efficacy biomarkers, and likewise also as surrogate and diagnostic, prognostic, predictive, and pharmacodynamic biomarkers, all categories that are not mutually exclusive according to specific clinical setting can determine how the biomarker is used and interpreted. In the particular sphere of aging, age-related diseases and geriatric syndromes, biomarkers are usually classified according to an **Aging Mechanism Outlook**: by the root causes and the mechanisms or phenomena triggered by these causes; for instance, *loss of proteostasis* triggers *inflammaging* mechanisms, although this is not the single cause of age-related low grade inflammation.

In addition to their purely descriptive and analytical approaches, the report is designed to make key strategic recommendations, and to offer guidance regarding biomarker implementations, technologies and techniques within the reach of companies and nations today, in order to equip them with the tools necessary for optimizing their strategy and action plans, providing specialized guidelines for business, investment and policy decision-making.

Biomarker Conventional Classification Frameworks

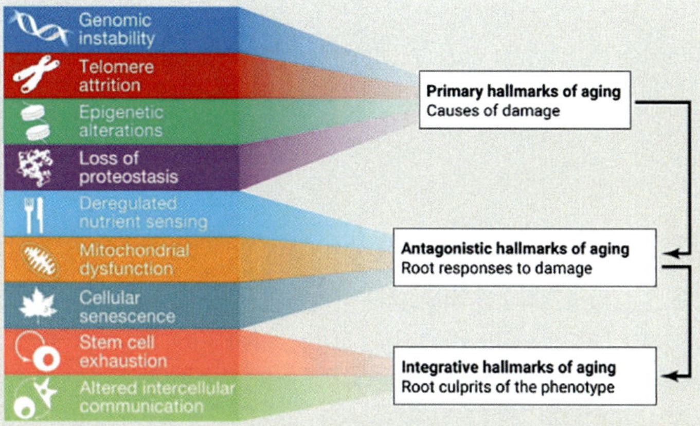

Aging Mechanism Outlook — The proposed nine hallmarks of aging are grouped into three categories: 1 - those hallmarks considered to be the primary causes of cellular damage; 2 - those considered to be part of compensatory or antagonistic responses to the damage (these responses initially mitigate the damage, but eventually, if chronic or exacerbated, they become deleterious themselves); 3 - integrative hallmarks that are the end result of the previous two groups of hallmarks and are ultimately responsible for the functional decline associated with aging. Source image: López-Otín C., et al. The hallmarks of aging. 2013.

The report delivers a most comprehensive list of single biomarkers and biomarker panels of biological age together with extensive and enhanced profiles: their advantages, disadvantages, future perspectives, challenges and opportunities, with a focus on technologies currently used for assessment; concrete analysis of routine, advanced and novel biomarkers of aging, emerging tools and platforms, and insights about the impact of these biomarkers on health systems and clinical practice.

Indexes Values for Single Aging Biomarkers and Aging Panels

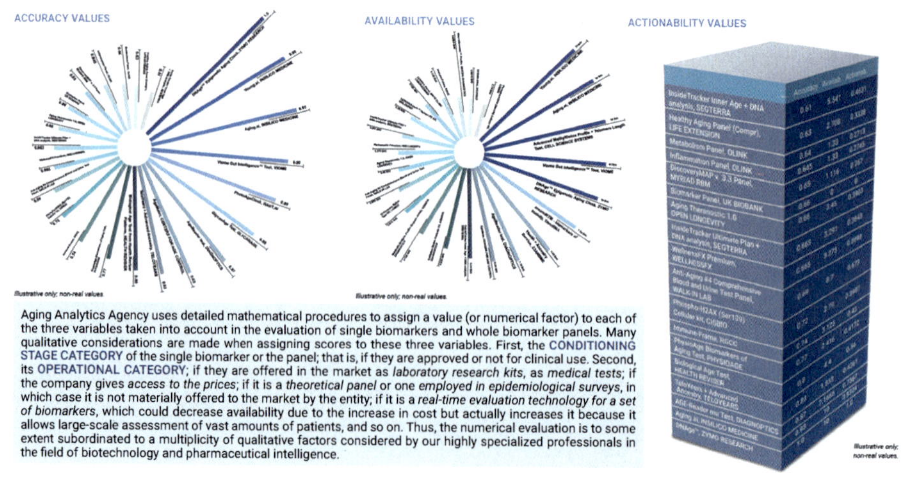

A special treatment tracing the role of Digital Biomarkers and AI platforms as necessary and indispensable components of the Longevity biomarker industry is also delivered, highlighting the fact that AI and Data Science are increasingly necessary to handle the increasing volume of biomarker, life and health data.

Digital Transformation of the Health and Longevity Industry

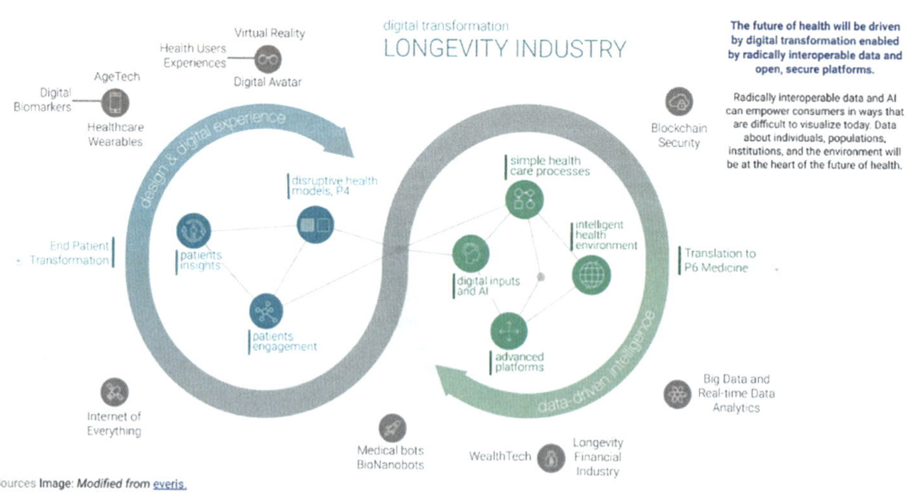

Sources Image: *Modified from* everis.

Conclusions:

- Deep Knowledge Group and the Biogerontology Research Foundation were pivotal in their strategic and financial support of the launch of the Longevity AI Consortium at King's College London, which is working to leverage the industry-academic strengths of the region and marshal them towards the intensive application of AI to leading-edge areas of Longevity R&D.
- A special focus for the Longevity AI Consortium will be using AI for the development of an optimal, actionable panel of biomarkers of aging, and devoting AI-driven R&D to neglected areas of research in Longevity and P4 Medicine.
- It is important in any domain of science or technology never to let the perfect be the enemy of good. It is desirable therefore to develop a minimum viable panel (MVP) of biomarkers: a panel of biomarkers which though not as precise as possible are precise enough and easily implementable. In order to kickstart a global discussion on the possibility of an MVP biomarker panel, Aging Analytics Agency has recently published a special analytical case study specifically on this topic, entitled *Biomarkers of Longevity: Current State, Challenges and Opportunities 2019 Landscape Overview*.
- Deep Knowledge Group will continue to support the development of AI-driven, actionable biomarkers of aging, health and Longevity through its involvement in the Longevity AI Consortium and its recently-announced AI Longevity Accelerator Program, and through the efforts of its Longevity-focused hybrid investment subsidiary fund, Longevity.Capital, which is heavily prioritizing the AI for Longevity and AI for Longevity FinTech, AgeTech and WealthTech sectors.

Chapter 27: The Crucial and Fundamental Role of AI in Longevity R&D and Practical Implementation

"In the near future, people will be able to monitor their health 24-7, with sensors attuned to various biomarkers that could indicate the onset of everything from the flu to diabetes. AI will be instrumental in not just ingesting the billions of data points required to develop such a system, but also what therapies, treatments, or micro-doses of a drug or supplement would be required to maintain homeostasis. Consider it like a Tesla with many, many detectors, analyzing the behaviour of the car in real time, and a cloud computing system monitoring those signals in real time with high frequency. So the same shall be applied for humans."

Dmitry Kaminskiy in *Why AI Will Be the Best Tool for Extending Our Longevity* (Singularity Hub, December 2019)

Key points:

- As with the state of geroscience 10 years ago, today the technology again is ahead of the policy, and the practical healthcare and medical frameworks of developed countries necessitate a paradigm shift toward greater prevention, personalization, precision and patient participation, utilizing all available tools and technologies that are market-ready today to optimize citizens' Healthy Longevity.
- The layering of paradigms, and the explosion of synergies that Data Aggregation in healthcare will produce within a short timeframe, means that by the normal methods of assessment, the science of Longevity will soon be comprised of tens of thousands of components, and to predict the effects of all of them on human health is already an incredibly complex challenge. The major tool for managing this will be AI.

- This is especially true of P4 Medicine itself. P4 is defined by the fact that its constituent leading-edge technologies have already achieved a state of market-readiness and clinical implementation.
- As such, when different strands of geroscience R&D reach a state of validation sufficient for their practical implementation, they cross over from R&D and into the scope of P4 Medicine.
- Given that P4 Medicine, by definition, consists of those Longevity-relevant technologies and techniques that are in practice today, what remains to be done in terms of actually applying them for the extension of Healthy Longevity is largely a matter of data mining, analysis and management, driven by advances in biomedicine, Data Science and Artificial Intelligence.
- For example, as AI for R&D in drug discovery becomes more sophisticated, drugs will become more customized to specific diseases and even specific patients.
- Drug development companies will transition from the current form of "blockbuster drugs" (standard drug formulations applicable to many millions of patients) to P4 Medicine, tailoring drugs to specific patient cases based on age, gender, ethnicity, state of health and genetics.
- As the scope of P4 Medicine grows, and the number of relevant biomedical interventions increases rapidly to the thousands in coming years, the number of associated biomarkers will increase to tens of thousands. Only AI is capable of handling and coordinating all this data.
- In order to effectively execute the paradigm shift from Precision Medicine to Precision Health, and enable citizens to become the CEOs of their own health through the combination of near-continuous monitoring of biomarkers of aging and high-frequency therapeutic micro-adjustments to normalize small deviations in those biomarkers long before the actual occurrence of disease, it will soon become necessary to utilize AI to manage, analyze and execute the monitoring and therapeutic adjustments.
- While today AI has an incredibly impactful role to play in terms of accelerating the rate of progress in P4 Medicine R&D, very soon it will become a strictly necessary component of its practical implementation due to the sheer volume of data involved.

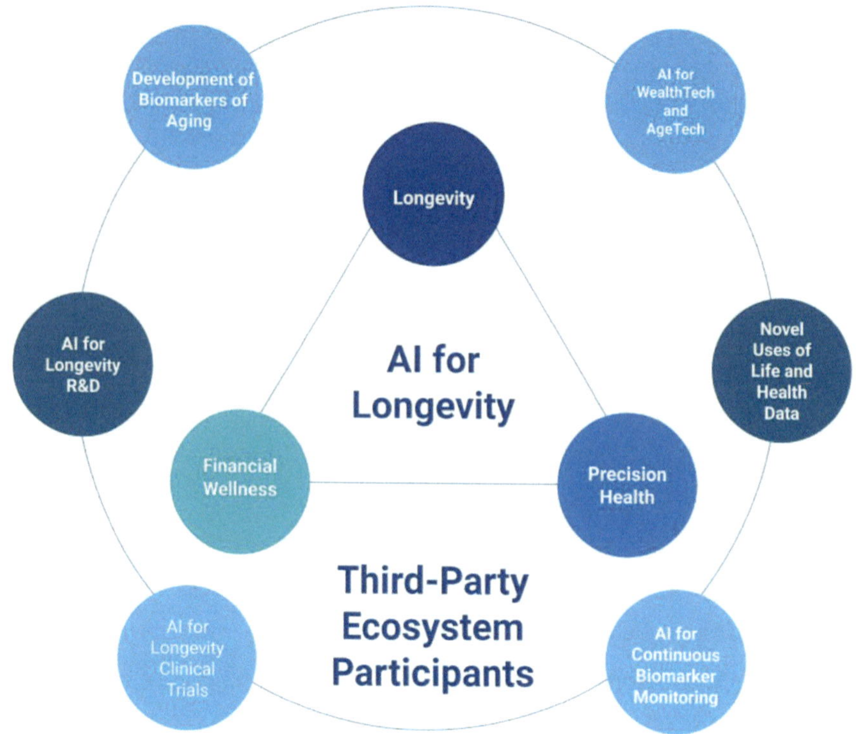

The science of Longevity, much like the broader Longevity Industry itself, is a field unprecedented in its levels of complexity, multidimensionality and intersectionality. The typical approaches for

- **Analysis,**
- **Benchmarking,**
- **Forecasting,**

developed for use in the BioTech and biomedical industries are not adequate when applied to the science of Longevity.

New methods and approaches for quantitative, tangible analysis, benchmarking and forecasting are necessitated by these unprecedented levels of complexity, and they need to be at least as sophisticated and multidimensional as the specific domain they are being applied to. This is the mission that Aging Analytics Agency and its parent company, Deep Knowledge Group, have been dedicated to for the past five years: the development and continuing refinement of novel analytical frameworks that are relevant in the face of the Longevity Industry's complexity.

Awareness of the importance of utilising Artificial Intelligence within aging and Longevity research is rapidly increasing in academia and industry. Modern deep learning techniques used to develop age predictors offer new possibilities for diverse data types.

This will enable a holistic view to identify novel biomarkers of health and Longevity; it will also bring novel geroprotectors and will become the core of drug discovery and healthcare in the biotechnological, pharmaceutical and health industries, integrating them like never before.

The role of AI in P4 Medicine is already remarkably apparent, especially in places such as the UK, USA, Switzerland and Singapore. For example, we have seen very proactive efforts by the UK government, both through their AI Industrial Grand Challenge and their aging Industrial Grand Challenge, to rapidly apply AI to Preventive Medicine, advanced biomedicine and digital health, and the recent establishment of the All-Party Parliamentary Group for Longevity.

Furthermore, its high degree of complexity necessitates innovative frameworks not only for general benchmarking and forecasting, but also for the general assessment of its technologies' and therapies' basic safety and efficacy. Take, for example, the common use of model organisms to assess the safety and efficacy of therapeutics.

While this works well enough for single diseases, it will become increasingly ineffective when applied to Longevity therapeutics due to the vast genetic difference between the aging processes in model organisms and humans.

This situation has created an urgent need for a shift away from model organisms and towards more human-centred approaches for safety and efficacy testing, utilizing comprehensive yet actionable panels of biomarkers of aging in patient populations. And only AI has the power to handle the volume of data necessary to put this into practice.

AI, Data Science and Mathematical Technologies for Longevity Biomarker Development

A large part of health information is digitized, which allows us to

- compile enormous amounts of data,
- access global servers,
- compare patient information,

sort of a dynamic repository of information that is constantly being updated. The massive advance in these databases facilitates doctors in their diagnostic process, their ability to measure, analyze, compare patients, and produce medical reports that are more accurate and personalised, that will, in turn, lead to the best available therapy or treatment of the time.

To shorten that translation delay from Research Use Only (RUO) and non-validated biomarkers and panels, to an Approved for Clinical Use (ACU) condition in the field of age-related diseases healthcare, and for a deep impact on applied health in a world of aging populations, it is an essential challenge to obtain a set of biomarkers already Approved for Clinical Use with high availability and actionability, and use it in conjunction with others, market- and healthcare-ready although less conventional biomarkers gathered in digital real-time monitoring environments.

That will enable a sufficiently accurate assessment of the overall process of aging, calculation of biological age, and analysis of the progression of particular elderly conditions nested by biomarker networks leading to the creation of a Most Viable Product, or the Minimum Required Panel.

Data Science for Biomarkers

Biomarker networks, which consist of the alignment between interactome and phenome levels, reveals new disease genes and connections between previously unrelated diseases or traits. Despite a great potential for novel discoveries, this approach is still rarely used in genomics and other omics. A biomarker network is a group of functionally related units of indicators, of any biological level, that contribute to the same phenotype — understanding by phenotype a

- molecular,
- metabolic,
- immune,
- physiological,
- physical,

trait and so on, pathological or not. The interactome (the whole set of molecular interactions for a trait, a condition, a disease, a cell or another biological unit) and the phenome (the set of all phenotypes expressed by that unit) are complexly connected at multiple levels.

At the root of these networks is the epigenome. Only AI-driven methods can efficiently address such complexity, those colossal bodies of data that can be currently entered into multiple and different digital platforms.

Precision Diagnostics

Only AI Can Handle Complex Multi-Omic Biomarker Analysis and Integration

Unlocking the value of epigenetic data for actionable insights will drive aging research, Precision Medicine, and ultimately population health. Fundamental questions should be addressed by integrative personal omics profiling with epigenomics at its centre, combining the

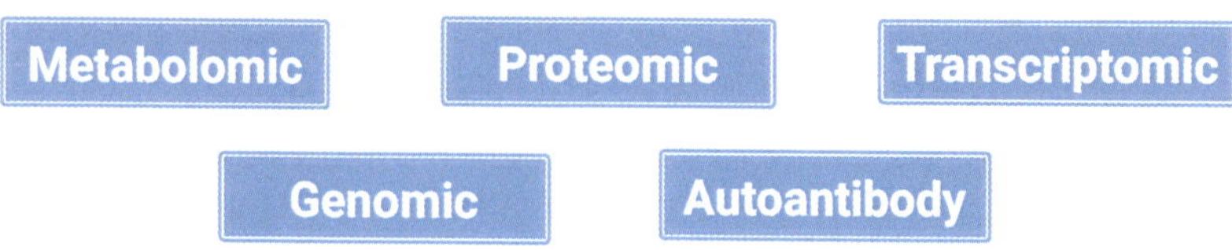

profiles from an individual to reveal dynamic molecular changes in health and disease.

With the evolution of better technologies and digital capacity, enormous amounts of omics data will be produced and stored in the digital space and researchers will need AI to be able to keep track of it. **AI is already transforming the world of medicine and will help healthcare providers make faster and more accurate diagnoses.** Based on epigenetic data, deep learning algorithms will predict the risk of a disease in time to prevent it and will help scientists understand how interindividual epigenetic variability leads to disease.

However, ensuring security and privacy in transmitting and storing personal epigenetic profiles will require building a new and open multi-omics data ecosystem. Blockchain, an open-source technology that uses a distributed database for secure transactions, has the potential to address many of the challenges related to security and privacy with personal health information. We are in the initial stages of a revolution in Precision Medicine enabled by advanced technologies such as epigenomics, AI, and blockchain.

Blockchain technology enables integrating data from a distributed network of participants in the healthcare value chain on a global scale.

The pioneering effort by early adopters from the research space is critical for putting these technologies within reach of the broader healthcare ecosystem.

Only AI Can Link Biomarker Aggregation, Monitoring and Analysis with Actual Preventive Treatment

Systems healthcare is a holistic approach to health premised on systems biology and medicine. The approach integrates data from:

Molecules	***Families***
Cells	***Communities***
Organs	***Natural Environment***
Individuals	***Man-made Environment***

Both extrinsic and intrinsic influences constantly challenge the biological networks associated with wellness. Such influences may dysregulate networks and allow pathobiology to evolve, resulting in early clinical presentation that requires astute assessment and timely intervention for successful mitigation.

The cornerstone of **P4 Medicine**, and of systems health, is the evaluation of dysfunctions of molecular or biomarker networks. The P4 Medicine paradigm involves a comprehensive understanding of the regulation and dysregulation of the complex molecular networks that forge the phenotype of an individual.

In this framework, disease is a consequence of aberrant reconstitution of cellular and molecular networks that lead to organ and organismal dysfunction (e.g. the patient's clinical presentation).

The interaction of the diseased organ within the person produces a cascade of dysregulated networks, resulting in associated comorbidities, some of which are evident, and others, asymptomatic (preclinical). In the state of wellness, networks are precisely regulated via complex homeostatic mechanisms.

Through one or a series of network (or sub-network) perturbations, wellness is driven toward altered nodal activity. Such nodal modulation constitutes the at-risk state, and although preclinical, it typically provides systemic signatures, which can be discerned and quantitated, and enable detection of dysregulation during a preclinical stage.

Therefore, the aim is to characterize specific nodal perturbations, some environmentally mediated, others rooted in the complexities of the intrinsic multidimensional networks only revealed via the aforementioned perturbations.

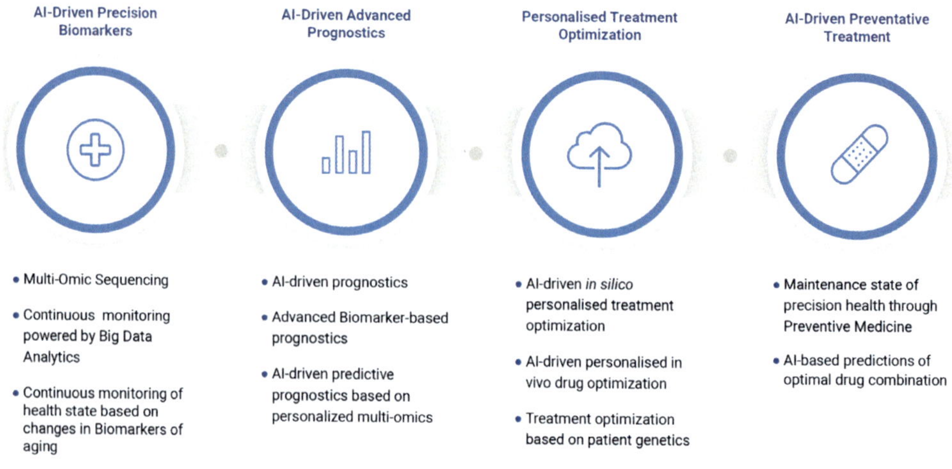

AI, Data Science, Machine Learning and Deep Learning Have Created a Golden Age of Biomarker Complexity

Machine and Deep Learning, systems health and multi-omics technologies revolutionize the way we acquire and process data. At their core, AI algorithms dissect the data to learn their structure and associations within, often without the need of specific knowledge on processes and models that generated them. The strength of AI techniques is proportional to the size and quality of the data amassed. At the same time, sequencing and molecular technologies can generate a vast amount of high quality data in an inexpensive, reproducible way and hence they allow an unprecedented system-level view of any organism.

Machine and Deep Learning analytics has been applied in biology to deal with the intrinsic complexity in omics data with a history of integration in recent years. The high-level overview of the Machine Learning analytic pipeline for integrated multiomics data consists of data preprocessing, modeling, and active learning.

Once a model is constructed and evaluated, active learning guides what experiments to perform next to minimize uncertainty in the model. Machine and Deep Learning analytics over integrated multi-omics data has the capacity to make far-reaching impacts across multiple industries. In biomedical applications, finding therapeutic targets and biomarkers is one of the major issues in human health, and such efforts are being more and more translated into the real world (e.g. BERG, Eagle Genomics).

These data sets, which can come from a variety of sources, equipment and experimental settings, are in their majority not ready to serve as training sets to computational models and Machine and Deep Learning methods, as they have not been created with that function in mind.

As such, there is a clear need for methods that process, normalize, integrate and transform the plethora of heterogeneous multi-omics data into cohesive compendia that can be used as training grounds for further analysis and learning.

Antibiotic resistance is of paramount importance as it is considered a global threat, and Machine Learning methods can be applied for predicting antibiotic resistance from the molecular signature of clinical isolates to select effective antibiotics. In food and nutrition science, optimizing nutrition treatment for individuals is enabled by **Machine Learning** over personal omics data accompanied with dietary information.

One prominent example of applying Deep Learning comes from gaming. In 2016, the program AlphaGo beat the world champion Lee Sedol in four out of five games of Go, a complex ancient Chinese board game.

It was a huge victory for AI that came decades earlier than most experts believed possible.

AlphaGo was developed by DeepMind, a subsidiary of Google that focuses on AI. Instead of relying on explicit programming, DeepMind applies general-purpose learning algorithms to large data set to make predictions. It is this type of advancement in Machine Learning that is delivering on the promise of real-time diagnostics and revolutionizing the future of Precision Medicine.

In the same year, the field of Machine Learning changed significantly because most of the major information and communication technology (ICT) companies have made their Deep Learning codes open source and available to anyone. Consequently, most major Machine Learning implementations are available for free to use and modify for everybody. This means it is possible for all researchers to set up a simple machine intelligence with nothing more than a laptop and a web connection. There already are over 50 different Deep Learning tool sets available and most are already open source.

As a key case study that cannot be omitted, some early approaches to merge epigenetics and Deep Learning exist already.

One of them is DeepCpG, which was designed to help scientists learn about the connections between genomic data and DNA methylation to make predictions about DNA methylation in single cells.

In particular, DeepCpG is trained to predict binary CpG methylation states from local DNA sequence windows and observed neighbouring methylation states.

The trained DeepCpG model can be used for different downstream analyses, including imputation low-coverage methylation profiles for sets of cells and discovery of DNA sequence motifs that are associated with methylation states and cell-to-cell variability. The long-term goal of using Deep Learning algorithms is to predict the effect of epigenetic drift and epimutations on a cell's regulatory landscape and how this, in turn, affects disease development, and aging itself.

Practical Longevity Developments from 2020 to 2025 Are Exclusively a Data Aggregation, Analysis and Management Challenge — Not a Biomedical Problem

Only the work of mass health data aggregation stands between us and a coming new age of precision diagnostics and prognostics based on aging biomarkers obtained from whole populations, in which AI analysis and automation using advanced mathematical tools and algorithms make predictions and recommendations based on thousands of data points for each person.

With each year, we will see increasingly precise and comprehensive diagnostics and prognostics, which, when combined with subsequent further advances in AI, will amount to a degree of predictive power which opens the doors to a whole new industry.

We predict that in the next few years a network of powerful tech hubs will spring up across the world's Longevity-progressive countries, who will compete with each other to establish the most favourable legal infrastructures and legislative ecosystems for advanced biomedical companies that, under the proper scrutiny, will test on humans rather than on model organisms.

These will not be traditional BioTech hubs like California's Silicon Valley or Switzerland's Health Valley. **They will be powerful ecosystems that utilize the full scope of P4 Medicine managed in real-time by AI, and will feature several distinct hallmarks, including:**

- AI data management, analysis and integration.

- High frequency biomarker monitoring and therapeutic micro-adjustments.
- Biomarkers-based P4 Medicine for maximizing Healthy Longevity.
- Full-scope ecosystems that synergistically integrate all sectors within the multidimensional Longevity Industry (Biomedicine, Technology and Finance).
- Integrated Longevity HealthTech, AgeTech, FinTech and WealthTech Hubs.
- More favourable legal frameworks for clinical trials on humans.

At the time of the Apollo 11 mission, the prerequisite sciences for space travel — rocketry, Newtonian physics, mathematics and basic astronomy — were already centuries old. It was the **added enhancements** of precision and predictiveness, brought about by digitization, with substantial government initiative, commitment and funding thrown in, which opened the door to another world.

Likewise, from this point on, advancing the Longevity Industry is less a matter of improving its constituent sciences and technologies and more a matter of enhancing their precision through data aggregation.

This is a fundamentally different approach from the one being taken by the majority of governments, investors and strategic decision-makers — namely, the one of investing in basic research into "frontier technologies" in the hope of remote future breakthroughs which, though potentially revolutionary, are still decades away from fruition.

Deep Knowledge Group prides itself in its early recognition of the expanded scope of the Longevity Industry beyond the core areas of geroscience R&D, and its active investment in the full spectrum of technologies that comprise the Longevity Industry, from short-term palliative solutions such as **AgeTech** and **Longevity FinTech/WealthTech**, that have achieved a state of market readiness and practical implementation literally today, to radical life extending rejuvenation biotechnologies which may not add a single year of healthy life for decades.

However, others are taking a more conservative and yet efficient approach that can go a long way toward establishing a bridge between Longevity start-ups in need of relevant amounts of investments, and conservative investors. It is the case of Longevity.Capital.

For example, only **10% of its investments** will be in start-ups pursuing technologies which are still years away from validation and practical implementation (and therefore still necessarily dragging along at the testing model organisms stage). **90% of its investments** will be in technologies that are either implementable in practice today or at a point of validation and Technology Readiness Level that indicates the feasibility of its practical implementation within the next 3-5 years.

Conclusions:

- As developments in the science of Longevity reach maturity and become implementable in practice, they fall under the domain of P4 Medicine, which consists of the entire scope of personalised, preventive, precision and participatory prognostics, diagnostics and therapeutics capable of maximizing citizens' Healthy Longevity, and maintaining an optimal state of health for as long as possible.

- One of the most important areas of Longevity scientific R&D is the development of biomarkers of aging – measurable indicators that can be used to estimate an individual's biological age, and test the effect of interventions on biological age.

  Biomarkers of aging lay the necessary groundwork to test the safety and effect of Longevity interventions.

- Even more important is the development of actionable biomarkers of aging, which can be thought of as the "minimum viable" panel of aging biomarkers: ones which have optimal levels of precision and accuracy vs. actionability (i.e. expense, ease of implementation, etc.), thus enabling their accelerated implementation into practical use.

  Also important are ongoing shifts in how biomarkers of aging are sourced and developed.

  Whereas historically the majority of such biomarkers came from persons of ill-health, there is an increasingly recognized need to begin sourcing them from healthy populations that differ from each other in terms of their age, state of health, ethnicity and sex.

  Moving forward, we will begin to see increasing levels of aging biomarker personalization, and the actual "minimum viable" panel of biomarkers used in practice by any given person will come to be highly tailored to their unique

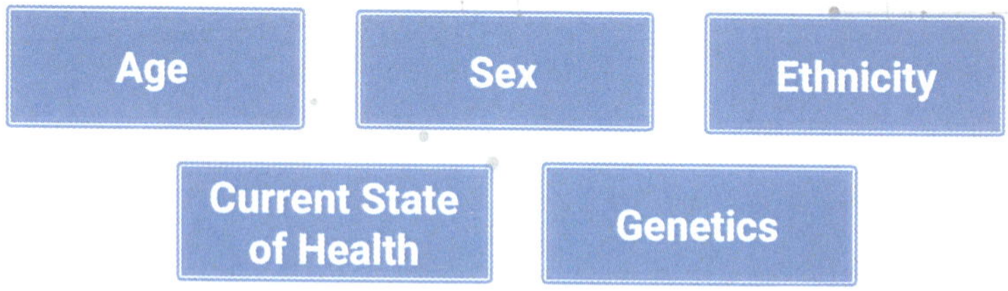

Age

Sex

Ethnicity

Current State of Health

Genetics

The continued development of implementable biomarkers of aging will quite rapidly lay the foundation for the paradigm shift from Precision Medicine to Precision Health, enabling citizens to become the CEOs of their own health via near-continuous monitoring of fluctuations in biomarkers of aging, and the application of therapeutic "micro-adjustments" to normalize those biomarkers when they deviate from their youthful optimum on an ongoing basis.

Health management on both the personal and national level today is operating in much the same way that financial trading operated 50 years ago, involving low-frequency transactions measured not in microseconds, but in days.

As P4 Medicine progresses, the entire healthcare, medical and health management paradigm will shift towards high-frequency diagnostics and therapeutics, enabling the normalization of deviations in biomarkers with very small adjustments in near real-time.

As both the number of biomarkers of aging and the number of practically-implementable interventions increases from tens or hundreds to thousands, the need for AI to manage and coordinate all those data points in order to formulate the most optimum ongoing therapeutic adjustments becomes increasingly necessary.

Whereas now AI's most pivotal role is in accelerating Longevity scientific R&D, its central role within Longevity and P4 Medicine will quickly come to be the management of citizen's everyday P4 diagnostic, prognostic and therapeutic regimens.

As the industry grows ever more elaborate, there is an increasing need for dedicated centres focusing on providing companies and researchers active in this space with advanced AI-driven support, to conduct cutting-edge R&D on the application of AI to the development of actionable and practically-realizable biomarkers of aging, in order to accelerate the coming paradigm shift from Precision Medicine to Precision Health, and enable citizens to take control of their own Healthy Longevity.

Chapter 28: What if Geroscience Fails? - Pragmatic Optimism in the Longevity Industry and Defining Hype vs. Reality

Back in 2014, Google promised us that it will solve the problem of death. Now, in the year 2020, we feel that progress in actual, practical life extension of humans is almost at the very same point as it was in 2014.

There is a great amount of positive hype, and many people (ranging from the public to scientists, entrepreneurs and investors) are confident that we are at the brink of actual human life extension techniques becoming real-world, accessible realities, but in this chapter we would like:

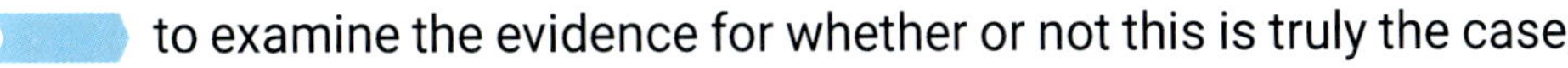

- to examine the evidence for whether or not this is truly the case;
- to provide a set of frameworks to separate hype from reality around this proposition in a concrete, logical, reasonable and tangible way.

Calico loses its second executive in 4 months as Daphne Koller quits

by Amirah Al Idrus | Mar 2, 2018 10:43am

Indeed, a number of Longevity scientists have achieved quite significant progress over the last decade in terms of stalling the aging process (and in some cases, progress in rejuvenation, i.e., restoring a young phenotype) in some model organisms, such as worms, yeast and flies, and in some select cases even mice.

For example, in January 2020, researchers at the MDI Biological Laboratory, in collaboration with scientists from the Buck Institute for Research on Aging and the Nanjing University in China, identified synergistic cellular pathways for Longevity that amplify lifespan fivefold in *C. elegans*, a nematode worm used as a model in aging research, which succeeded in extending their lifespan by 500%.

In another recent example, in October 2019, Maria Blasco and colleagues managed to extend the lifespan of mice by 24% by breeding a set of chimeric mice using embryonic stem cells with telomeres twice as long as usual. Headlines demonstrating substantial increases in both the lifespan and healthspans of model organisms have increased enormously in the past decade.

A 'Fountain Of Youth' Pill? Sure, If You're A Mouse.

he race for the cure to aging sparks hope and hype among top scientists — plus billions of dollar in investment.

By Marisa Taylor • FEBRUARY 11, 2019

A mouse in the pathology and geriatrics lab at the University of Michigan. (Melanie Maxwell for KHN)

However, in terms of practical human life extension and our understanding of human Longevity, we have been at a comparative standstill.

While there is significant progress in aging research as applied to model organisms (mice, flies, yeast, etc.), there has not yet been a single successful example of the successful translation of those results in humans.

While this area of research and practical implementation is by no means stagnating, progress has been much slower than it could have been compared to progress in model organisms.

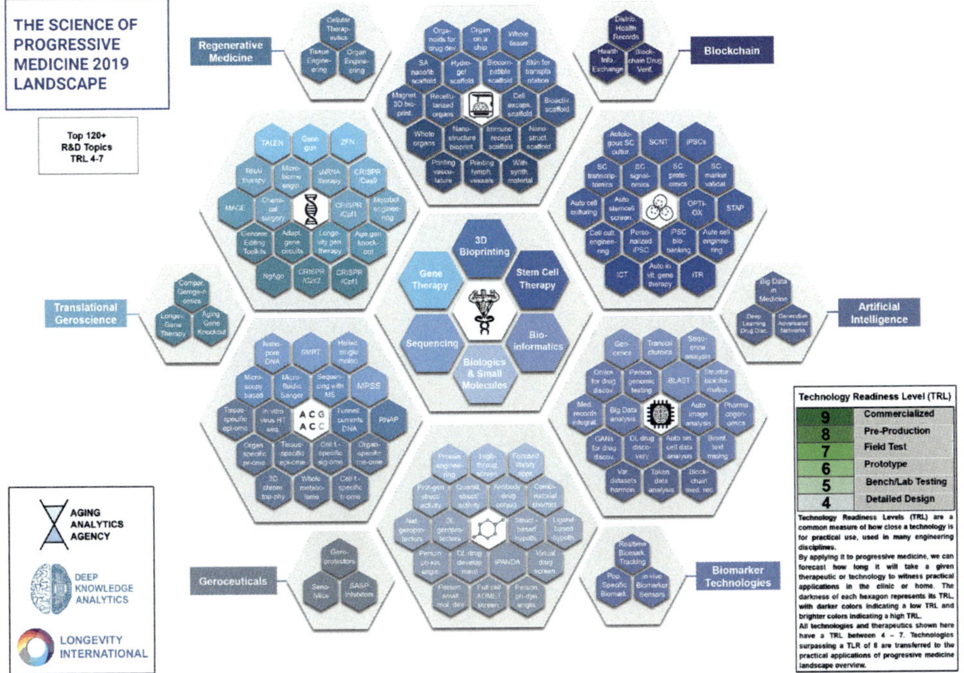

One factor behind this comparatively slower rate of progress is that aging research itself overvalues certain domains of research and undervalues others, and lacks a sufficiently safe degree of harmony, balance and diversification.

With the enormous volume of resources behind Tech giants like Google and Amazon, as well as many BioTech, biomedicine and healthcare companies, we should have seen much higher rates of practical, tangible developments in understanding the full technological pipeline necessary for human life and healthspan extension, and in understanding which specific sectors are overfinanced and which are underfinanced, but we have not.

Indeed, it is true that this prospect — of gaining a sufficient understanding of the nature of human aging and Longevity, and the necessary scope of technologies required for practical human life extension to the point of achieving the **Longevity Escape Velocity** (the point where more years are added onto the human lifespan than are taken away due to aging) — would require substantial resources. However, compared to the amount of money being spent even on general aging research, not to mention on the myriad of diseases that have their roots in aging, we are not dealing with unthinkable numbers.

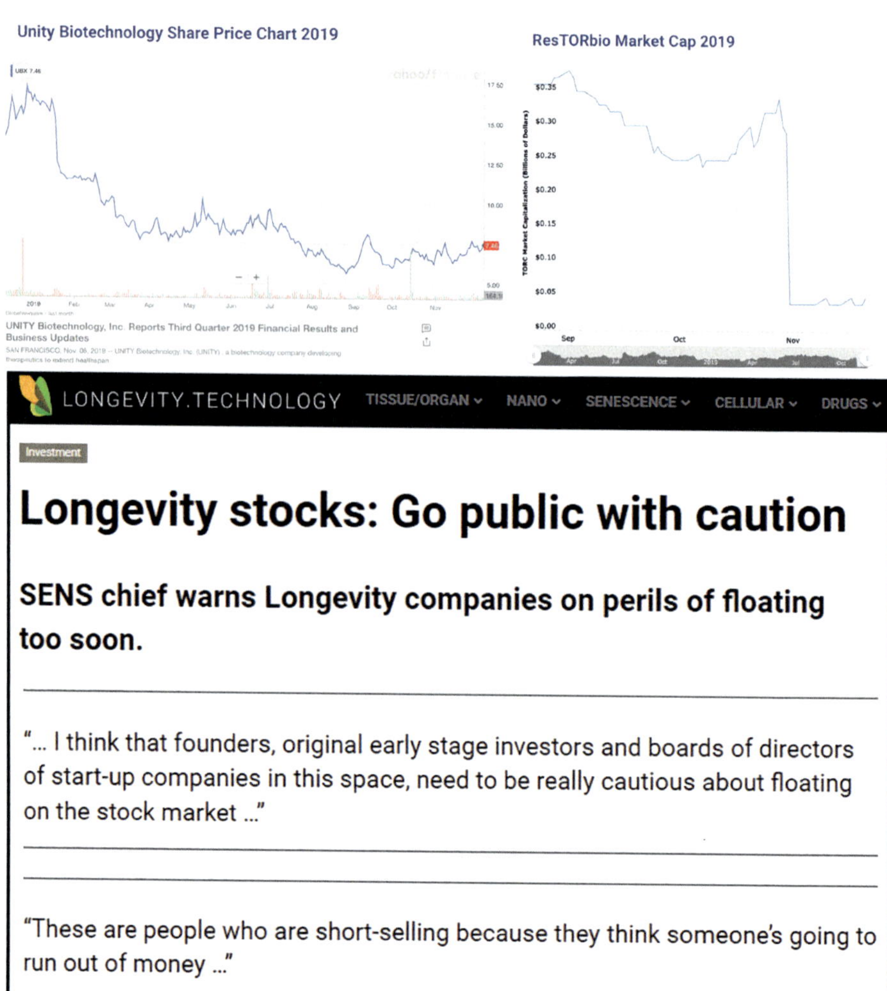

LONGEVITY.TECHNOLOGY TISSUE/ORGAN NANO SENESCENCE CELLULAR DRUGS

Investment

Longevity stocks: Go public with caution

SENS chief warns Longevity companies on perils of floating too soon.

"... I think that founders, original early stage investors and boards of directors of start-up companies in this space, need to be really cautious about floating on the stock market ..."

"These are people who are short-selling because they think someone's going to run out of money ..."

Furthermore, even if this level of money were indeed dedicated to this pursuit, we would still face the challenge of executing it in a sufficiently structured, harmonized and balanced way, which risks completing in 15-20 years what could have been accomplished in 10 years if it were executed in a maximally relevant and strategic manner in the first place.

The Longevity Industry, and its scientific and R&D communities, need to gain a consensus understanding of what roadblocks need to be overcome in order to achieve this critical inflection point (Longevity Escape Velocity) before the year 2030 (which we feel to be a very reasonable timeline, provided the necessary budget were available), rather than in the year 2035 or 2040, as well as what bottlenecks could be optimized to accelerate the process even more (i.e., to a timeframe of 7-8 years rather than 10).

In order to do this, we need to think about the problem not as doctors or BioTech scientists, but as aerospace engineers. In building a rocket, some parts (e.g. the navigation system, operating system, engine, etc.) require more R&D resources than others in order to meet the target deadline.

If we want to launch this Longevity rocket by the year 2030, more time and resources will need to be allocated to certain parts.

And if we wanted to achieve a pilot launch date 2-3 years sooner, what are the narrow components and fundamental bottlenecks that need to be prioritized?

Now, the same way as it was 10, if not 20, years ago, progress in human life extension research is comprised of several major paradigms or pillars.

The First Pillar: Experiments in Model Organisms

The first pillar in the field of aging research into human Longevity is the well-established but outdated practice of experimentation on model organisms with the expectation that their results will translate to humans.

This has been the common, consensus paradigm followed in the traditional BioPharma industry for the past 50 years, and has consistently shown that in the majority of cases drugs do, indeed, fail to translate to humans with sufficiently high effectiveness or sufficiently low adverse effects to make it to market.

Given the 90% failure rate of clinical translation into humans in the comparatively simpler biomedicine, BioPharma and BioTech industries, which deal with interventions with far fewer complex components (e.g. single molecules) targeting far simpler biological systems (e.g. individual disease targets), it is reasonable to expect higher failure rates for much more multidimensional therapies with more "moving parts" that target much more complex biological processes of aging and the treatments required for practical life extension in humans.

The source of this high anticipated failure rate is twofold. The first fundamental factor is the vast biological (physiological, genomic, epigenomic, etc.) differences between humans and model organisms, both in general and in terms of the actual nature of aging in particular.

The second is not so much a scientific (and, therefore, fundamental) problem, but one rooted in honest but flawed human nature and error — the fact that by current estimates as many as 70% of scientific experiments, studies and articles are not repeatable, due to either well-intentioned mistakes or intentional fraud. This phenomenon is often referred to as science's modern "replication crisis", and will pose even more problems for the expected success rate of human-focused Longevity therapeutics.

There is no evidence thus far of the ability to transfer any of the successes in model organisms in the field of aging research to humans, and in order to safeguard against the possibility that the transferability problem will indeed be insurmountable, it is our position that Longevity scientists and industry participants need to begin proactively prioritizing new methods of safely testing Longevity therapies in humans relevant for the 21st century, utilizing the full scope of sophisticated, precise AI-driven technologies available for that purpose.

The Second Pillar: BioHacking and Quantified Self

The second pillar is diametrically opposed to the first — the biohacking and quantified self movements, where individuals attempt to push the limits of the biomedical methods and technologies available to them to their extreme, utilizing the full arsenal of tools at their disposal (even those outside of the scope of FDA-approved treatments) in order to optimize their state of physical, biological and cognitive health and performance.

The Third Pillar: The Treatment and Neutralization of Age-Related Diseases

The third pillar has been around for much longer than the first two, and consists of the treatment of specific individual age-related diseases:

- **Cancer**
- **Diabetes**
- **Dementia**
- **Obesity**
- **Stroke**
- **Frailty**
- **Cardiovascular disease**
- **Cardiometabolic disease**
- **Cardiopulmonary disfunction**

While this, in theory, is the pillar with the least fundamental potential in terms of practical life extension, in the sense that it targets the end-products of aging, i.e. traditional diseases, without in any way modifying their source, it is perhaps surprisingly the pillar which so far has achieved the greatest level of actual, tangible real-world results in terms of human life expectancy, being abundantly financed by BioPharma corporations.

For example, due to recent progress in cancer therapy, breakthroughs that were still in the R&D phase **3-7** years ago (personalised, targeted chemotherapies and immunotherapies) are actually being used in practice, which has resulted in 2016-2017 being the largest ever single-year drop in the US cancer mortality rate, at 2.2%.

Whereas the majority of history saw researchers and companies focusing on treating these diseases, and minimizing their detrimental effects, in more recent years we have seen an increasingly prioritized emphasis on slowing down their progression, and on preventing them and delaying their occurrence, thus yielding success in not just treating them, but preventing them as well.

The fact that this pillar is the one with the highest rate of progress and real-world results in terms of what can be considered as practical human life extension, despite being the one with the least fundamental potential to increase either lifespan or healthspan, is due to two main factors. Firstly, **there are many distinct angles and approaches to treat individual diseases** (because they are at the top of the biological chain, rather than at the very centre or root in the way that biological aging is), and secondly, because of the enormous and unprecedented level of money and resources allocated by industry and government for their treatment.

The Fourth Pillar: AI, Data Science and Mathematical Technologies for Longevity

The fourth pillar, the one with the greatest potential to create real-world effects on human Longevity in short timeframes, and the one with the highest ratios of cost to effectiveness, is the application of AI and Data Science to Longevity.

Unfortunately, despite being the pillar with the greatest promise, it is also the pillar which is the most underrepresented and underfinanced within the global Longevity Industry.

The reasons for its enormous potential are numerous.

Firstly, Longevity is unprecedentedly multidimensional and complex, both as a science (dealing with the deepest levels of biology, health and disease) and as an industry (being composed of the intersection of many distinct, individually complex domains of frontier science and technology, as Artificial Intelligence, Data Science and mathematics).

These areas, specially AI, were precisely and literally invested in to manage complexity, and to do what is too voluminous and too complex for humans to do manually. They are the engine for not only neutralizing complexity, but for yielding its power to create new-positive effects.

Secondly, as the number of distinct data points on the nature of aging, the number of specific biomarkers of aging and Longevity, and the number of distinct Longevity therapies and technologies inevitably increase, AI is the only tool for managing the volume of data in a sensible manner, both in terms of P4 Medicine and Precision Health (real-world practical implementation of Longevity technologies) and in terms of core Longevity R&D (which will not reach the level of market-readiness for a number of years).

Thirdly, it is an industry vertical that is very well funded (with entire nations now competing to win the global AI race, develop and secure the most advanced AI technologies and IP, and capture the highest densities of AI specialists), and ongoing developments in core AI innovation are rapidly implementable (being a virtual, digital technology that can be replicated, transmitted near-instantaneously, and utilized at zero material cost once it is innovated), thus being capable of having immediate accelerative impacts on Longevity.

Fourthly, it is a self-evolving and self-accelerating technology, in the sense that the latest advances in AI make it easier to develop the next paradigm shift in AI, thus invoking an exponentializing effect on itself.

Fifthly, and perhaps most importantly, the technologies and techniques for extending Healthy Human Longevity, for Preventive Medicine and for maintaining an optimal state of Precision Health for as long as possible are already here, innovated and validated, ready for use, but lack an infrastructure for scaling them to the masses.

This is why we predict that the vast majority of practical, real-world effects in terms of extending personal and public healthspans in the next several years will come from existing, validated technologies, thus making it a data aggregation, analysis, management and optimization, rather than a biomedical or BioTech R&D problem.

AI for Longevity is the "smart money" sector of the industry, and can achieve enormous results and accelerated timelines in terms of progress in actual, tangible, real-world Healthy Human Longevity, even with comparatively tiny levels of financing compared to other sectors.

And this is exactly what the role of AI will be in the Longevity space from 2020-2025, i.e., the aggregation, development and deployment of:

- Biomarkers of Aging
- Health and Longevity
- Precision Health technologies and therapeutics
- Integrated wealthspan-extending AgeTech and WealthTech solutions to financial wellness across extended periods of Healthy Longevity

The apex of this case, and its most robust and advanced embodiment, consists of a digital avatar of the full human body, taking into account thousands, if not tens of thousands, of personalised biomarkers (with at least several hundreds of precise biomarkers of aging and Longevity), both biological and psychological/behavioural.

Longevity is Destined to Succeed, But the Timelines Are Up to Us

Once the logic makes itself apparent to all stakeholders, AI for Longevity will shift from one of the least-represented sectors to the most prioritized and emphasized sector within the global Longevity Industry, achieving enormous results in very short timeframes, considering that it has the potential to out-compete all three of the other pillars if given just a small fraction of the total amount of Longevity Industry financing.

Conclusions:

The progress in treating age-related diseases will progress almost automatically because the entire healthcare and BioTech industry is already treating these diseases and they will proceed to do this, because it is a very profitable business. Biohackers and quantified self-practitioners will progress because the number of techniques and technologies for optimization of health and performance reaching the level of practical implementation and market readiness are continually growing.

- This first pillar of aging research will continue to develop just based on its own momentum and the amount of energy and funding dedicated towards it, but there is nonetheless a distinct possibility that none of its successes will be transferrable to humans, and as a result, new methods of conducting safe clinical trials on humans are required.
- Thus, even if the first pillar fails due to the major roadblock of transferability to humans, it is entirely likely that we will see tangible, real-world progress in human Longevity given the progress of the second, third and fourth pillars, especially in the near-term, where progress in Longevity will come from existing, validated market-ready technologies, and not moonshot BioTech R&D.
- But, most importantly, if enough resources and priority are invested into the fourth pillar (AI for Longevity), it is entirely possible to achieve in 7-8 years what otherwise could only be done in 10 years. What the fourth pillar needs for this to become reality, however, is intelligent coordination and harmonization of experts and industry stakeholders (AI specialists, Longevity scientists and entrepreneurs, investors and governments, etc.) to achieve truly synergetic and self-accelerative effects.

Summary of *Longevity Industry 2.0 – DeepTech Engineering The Accelerated Trajectory of Human Longevity: The Blueprint and Pathway from 1.0 to 2.0*

In *Longevity Industry 1.0: Defining the Biggest and Most Complex Industry in Human History*, we have so far distilled the complex assembly of deep market intelligence and industry knowledge that we have developed over the past 5 years into a full-scope understanding of the global Longevity Industry, with the aim to show the public exactly how we managed to define the overwhelmingly complex and multidimensional Longevity Industry for the first time, and how we created tangible frameworks for its systematization and forecasting.

The book features first-of-its-kind coverage of entirely new segments and sectors of the rising Longevity Industry, including Longevity Politics and Governance, the Longevity Financial Industry (including coverage of AgeTech, WealthTech, FinTech, and the coming rise of new financial instruments and derivatives), the current state and forecasts on the global industrialization of Longevity to scale, and an overview of the near-future trajectory of the Longevity Industry's evolution between 2020 and 2025.

The completion of the book, however, does not bring you to the end of the Longevity story, but rather to its beginning. In Longevity Industry 1.0 we look at the factors involved in bringing us to the point we are today, at the Global Longevity Industry's current state of extremely promising growth, diversification and prosperity, while identifying the current challenges ahead. In our next book, Longevity Industry 2.0, we will:

Take a much deeper dive into tangible, pragmatic solutions and frameworks on how to solve those challenges and transform them into opportunities.

Outline the pathway to DeepTech proactively engineer the best and brightest future of the industry.

Longevity Industry 1.0 is a summary of the current state of affairs and the forces at work, the challenges and opportunities that have made the industrialization of Longevity a national priority for the world's most forward thinking and progressive governments.

Longevity Industry 2.0 will be focused on the state of the industry in the year 2025, and the transformation of the global Longevity Industry from 1.0 to 2.0, including the important role that Longevity-focused Mega-Hubs will play as well as painting a detailed and knowledge-rich picture of the full scope and scale of the global potential of the Longevity Industry, as BioTech and current healthcare models are disrupted by AI driven Preventive Medicine and novel InvestTech solutions.

If Longevity Industry 1.0 explains how we got to this point, 2.0 will give a detailed map of where we will be by the year 2025, and the hows and whys of the processes involved in every sector.

It will take a deeper analytical, more specified look at some of the mechanisms and practical techniques that would encompass a fully realized Longevity Industry. This sequel will explore in detail how today's Longevity start-up will become tomorrow's multitrillion dollar corporation, how AI will come into prominence as the critical and fundamental driver of progress in the industry, and much more.

It will cast an even deeper eye toward:

- The future of the Longevity financial industry and health as new wealth.
- The full maturation of the Longevity financial industry, including new forms of Longevity-focused banks, stock exchanges, financial derivatives and instruments, and Longevity FinTech products, services and ecosystems.
- The development of novel InvestTech solutions to de-risk and diversify investments in Longevity.
- The need not only for new methods of due diligence and analytics that can handle the Longevity mega-complexity, but also new approaches to cultivating the Longevity science and technology and guiding them from R&D to market readiness along accelerated timelines, new approaches to Longevity company financing, incubation and development.

- The evolution and natural selection of technocratic Longevity MegaHubs.
- The evolution of technologies to a sufficient state of market-readiness to be used by modern Preventive Medicine and Longevity clinics from 2020 to 2025.
- New methods of human Longevity therapy trials backed by modern AI and Data Science.
- The digitization and democratization of personalised, patient-driven and AI-empowered Precision Health and healthy Longevity technologies.

From the practical applications and processes of Precision Medicine to a more detailed analysis of de-risking strategies for Longevity investment, this book's sequel is designed to show you the future of Longevity.

In short, Longevity Industry 1.0 has brought us to the birth, of not just a new asset class, but also, in its novel approaches, a new knowledge class. In Longevity Industry 2.0, we will explore this deeper realm of knowledge to its fullest and deepest extent.

PART V

Longevity Industry Navigator

- Longevity Industry in the UK
- Longevity Industry in Singapore
- Longevity Industry in Israel
- FemTech Healthcare
- Longevity Industry in California
- Top-100 Longevity Leaders
- Top-50 Women Longevity Leaders
- Top-30 Longevity Conferences
- Advancing Financial Industry Longevity/AgeTech/WealthTech
- Longevity Industry in Switzerland
- Top-100 Supercentenarians Landscape Overview: 100 Longest-Lived, 100 Currently Living, 25 Socially and Professionally Active

Longevity Industry Navigator

Longevity Industry in UK Landscape Overview Q4 2018

Longevity Industry in UK Landscape Overview Q4 2018 is a 1000+ page follow-up regional case study to the first edition of Aging Analytics Agency's *Longevity Industry in UK Landscape Overview* released in early 2018, and features profiles of **260 companies**, **250 investors**, **50 non-profits** and **25 research centres**, as well as an updated list of **55 UK Longevity influencers** and **thought leaders**. It also features comprehensive infographics that enable the entire industry to be taken-in at a single glance, and an Executive Summary that provides a succinct summary of the report's scope and major insights, conclusions and forecasts.

One of the strongest conclusions of the report was that the UK has sufficient resources in each of the three most crucial sectors for Longevity — biotechnology, AI and the financial industry — to succeed. However, the nation must focus on cross-sector collaboration and synergetic convergence among disparate but related fields to become a leader in the global Longevity Industry. Q3 and Q4 of 2018 turned out to be periods of astonishingly accelerated industry development for this sector.

Given this exponential progress, it became relevant to reassess, update and extend the trends, insights and major conclusions of the original report. Furthermore, a re-evaluation allows us to closely tie new conclusions to progress made in Q4 2018, ensuring a more quantitative understanding of these new developments.

Longevity Industry in Singapore Landscape Overview 2019

Much of Singapore's progressive stance towards Longevity stems from its meritocratic governmental structure. As a city-state, the nation is highly adept at efficiently and effectively implementing sweeping industry development and progressive social policy initiatives and reforms.

This property makes it an ideal candidate to create a government-driven Longevity Industry national development plan, with potential of becoming a thriving international Longevity BioTech hub. Thus, Singapore is a natural subject for Aging Analytics Agency analyses.

Longevity Industry in Singapore: Landscape Overview 2019 seeks to document the factors that make this country a potential global Longevity Industry hub and how to further foster that potential, particularly at a political level.

In 2015, Singapore's ministerial committee for aging launched an action plan for successful aging, consisting of a multi-pronged approach that includes preventive and active aging programs that begin at the early age of 40. Singapore has also embraced the rising sector of AgeTech to help improve the quality of life and levels of social engagement of its elderly population.

AgeTech technologies, which encompass any digital technology that aid the elderly, are being rapidly adopted by medical institutions and nursing homes across the nation. As such, Aging Analytics Agency considers Singapore a natural subject of interest for their Longevity Industry report series.

Longevity Industry in Israel Landscape Overview 2019

Over 500 pages in length, *Longevity Industry in Israel Landscape Overview 2019* outlines the history, present state and future of the Longevity Industry in Israel, profiling **160 companies**, **180 investors**, **10 Longevity non-profit organizations**, **60 influencers**, **10 university research labs** and **10 conferences**.

Following systematic, data-driven analyses, the report concludes the following: although Israel has made solid initial steps over the past five years toward prioritizing aging as part of its national agenda, additional efforts are needed to continue to maintain and cultivate its existing strengths (which requires governmental support of the development of the Longevity Industry and a strong academic geroscience research

landscape) and to crystallize its national development strategy of placing healthspan extension at its centre, akin to the UK's successful decision of listing the problem of an aging population as the number two grand challenge in its industrial strategy. Also, Israel is a unique country with close academic and industrial ties to the United States and Europe.

Consequently, Israel's geroscience has matured at a pace that outstrips the rest of the geographical region, with at least one aging research centre or cluster already present or planned for every Israeli university. Israel is also an attractive technology and innovation hub: the amount of funding raised by high-tech start-ups in Israel continues to grow, reaching US$6.47 bln in 2018 through 623 deals.

Large IT and tech giants have also been opening locations in Israel. Google, for instance, established an R&D centre in Israel in 2016, where many of the company's most important products (including Google Suggest, Google Trends, and Google Live Results) were developed.

FemTech Healthcare Landscape Overview 2019

FemTech Landscape Overview Q1 2019 profiles **120 companies**, **335 investors**, **30 influencers**, **15 conferences** and **10 journalists active in the FemTech healthcare, Preventive Medicine and FemTech Longevity sectors**.

FemTech refers to the emerging range of digital technologies focused specifically on women's health. The majority of the market currently consists largely of wearable devices and smartphone interfaces, connected medical devices, and hygiene products. These products, platforms, and techniques are geared towards widening female access to healthcare on a global scale, empowering as well as educating women. FemTech is an offshoot of HealthTech, in the sense that it relies on preventive or analytic systems to monitor and maintain health, but represents a major departure from the traditional tech scene that has been dominated by male-oriented product designs and applications. It is a burgeoning, upstart industry with a rapidly increasing public profile, increasingly diverse applications, increasing investor attention, set to have an increasing share of the capital directed at healthcare.

The story of FemTech is apparent from an examination of the sectors of the industry – Healthcare, Preventive, and Longevity – in that order. In fact, these three categories mark the stages of the same paradigm shift that this report series has sought to document for years now: the shift toward increased disruption, away from palliative solutions and toward comprehensive, Preventive Medicine solutions, made possible by a series of synergies. The main body of the report begins by charting how FemTech has emerged from current synergies between the traditional decades-old solutions to female health, and more recent digital and biomedical advances. It continues into an overview of Preventive FemTech, illustrating how FemTech, in lockstep with the other technologies described in this report series, has undergone a shift from treatment to prevention through advanced prognostics.

Longevity Industry in California Landscape Overview 2019

Longevity Industry in California: Landscape Overview 2019 delivers a comprehensive overview of the history, present state and near-future trajectory of the Californian Longevity Industry, profiling its key players including **220 leading companies**, **255 investors**, **80 influencers**, **40 research labs**, **40 non-profits** and **15 governmental organizations active in the Golden State's Longevity sphere**.

The choice of California as the subject of Aging Analytics Agency's regional Longevity Industry report series is justified for a number of reasons. The Golden State plays an important role on the global Longevity scene. It is the world's fifth-largest economy and, at almost 40 million people, is the most populous US state. It is home to a plethora of top-ranked universities and research institutions which lead this nation in biomedical research grants from NIH and drive innovation.

California's decades-long public policy supports a life sciences ecosystem through tax incentives as well as state-sponsored initiatives promoting the use of advanced technology to better understand and treat diseases.

Due to the state's healthy business climate as well as a strong success record of its life sciences companies, the state has long been a magnet for BioTech investment — it consistently leads the nation in attracting venture capital funding and boasts four BioTech mega-clusters in San Francisco Bay Area, Los Angeles, Orange and San Diego counties.

The report is structured so as to introduce readers to the key developments in the Longevity field in California and offers a global perspective on the topic. By utilizing a variety of infographic mind maps, the report first enables the audience to quickly identify its core analytical findings and conclusions.

Top-100 Longevity Leaders

Top-100 Longevity Leaders identifies and categorizes 100 public and private-sector professionals working to grow the Longevity landscape through their efforts in business, science, policy and media outreach, and features infographics that classify these Longevity Leaders by industry, region, sector, and primary activity. The report presents its list of the Top 100 Longevity Leaders as categorized according to several core subcategories: Investors and Donors, Research and Academia, Entrepreneurs, Politics, Policy and Governance, and Media Influencers. These leaders are additionally classified by the type of activity in which each spends the majority of their time and efforts: Entrepreneurship, Research and Academia, or Publicity. The report aims to provide readers with a clearer understanding of the types of private and public-sector professionals directing the rapidly rising Longevity Industry as a whole, listing the top 100 individuals influencing the direction of the entire multifaceted industry, and measuring the leadership impact of each individual in their respective field.

The overall purpose of the report is to understand where the Longevity Industry's sources of influence lie, to help promote establishing efficient links between sectors in order to achieve a healthy and mature global Longevity Industry. To achieve this, it is crucial to analyze the existing examples of accomplished leaders in this area, their backgrounds, skill-sets, strengths, competencies, and types of im-

pact they have on the industry in general. The report reveals that the Longevity Industry sources its expertise from a variety of disparate sectors, and that the industry is driven by a disproportionately high number of people with direct involvement in more than one sector. It also reveals that while there has been a large publicity-seeking component of the industry, there is an important public sector involvement also, as the industry begins to be embraced by politicians and parliamentarians.

Top-100 Journalists Covering Advanced Biomedicine and Longevity

Top-100 Journalists Covering Advanced Biomedicine and Longevity focuses on the media and journalism landscape that covers Longevity as a mainstream topic. Its objective is to illustrate how the Longevity Industry is perceived by the world's top media, and how media coverage, in turn, influences public perception of the industry. The report profiles the top 100 journalists and associated media entities covering the topic of Longevity, as classified according to the following subcategories: The Science of Longevity, The Business of Longevity, Aging and Society, the Financial Industry, Artificial Intelligence and AgeTech. Longevity is an industry with many different sides, an intersection between many technologies.

The past few years have seen a rapidly increasing number of objective, conservative, clear portraits of the industry in the world's top media, and an overall increase in coverage by highly-reputable media outlets like TIME, The Economist, Bloomberg, Financial Times and others. The report offers an overview of the Longevity media and journalism landscape, and illustrates how the topic of Longevity has gone from fringe to mainstream in the past five years, being embraced by the world's top business and tech media entities, and features in-depth profiles of the 100 most active journalists writing on the topic of Longevity, and infographic MindMaps that chart the top 60 media entities that have published articles on Longevity.

Fortunately, recent years have seen a notable increase in the number of clear and comprehensive portraits of the industry in the world's top media. The purpose of this report is to distill the complex Longevity media industry and its trends into a set of comprehensive infographics and profiles that allow the entire ecosystem to be viewed and comprehended in a single glance.

Top-50 Women Longevity Leaders

Top-50 Women Longevity Leaders identifies 50 leading female professionals influencing the direction and development of the Global Longevity Industry, giving readers greater insight into what types of public and private-sector professionals are driving and directing this multi-sector, rapidly rising industry as a whole, where its major sources of influence lie, and where to begin in terms of building strategic alliances to promote a more synergetic trajectory of industry development.

In tandem with an increase in the number of female professionals in the broader tech, BioTech and biomedical industries, we are also seeing an increasing number of prominent female leaders in the rising Longevity Sphere. Just a few illustrative examples include Carol Greider, the only Longevity scientist to win a Nobel Prize, Daria Khaltourina, who led the task force that succeeded in having the World Health Organization add an extension code (XT9T) for "age-related" during the ICD-11 revisions, and Laura Deming, a prominent Longevity investor who began her activities in the Longevity Industry working in Cynthia Kenyon's lab at the age of 11.

This report follows Aging Analytics Agency's "Top-100 Longevity Leaders" report, which offered an overview of the 100 most active and influential public and private sector professionals working to grow the global Longevity landscape through their efforts in business, science, policy and media outreach.

Some readers may have noticed the relative underrepresentation of women in the list presented in that report. In its composition of the Top-100 Longevity Leaders, Aging Analytics Agency used a method which was gender-blind, aiming to include as many of the most representative individuals in each core front of the expanding Longevity sphere as possible.

Top-30 Longevity Conferences

Top-30 Longevity Conferences 2019-2020 uses cost-benefit analysis to identify the Top-30 Longevity Conferences globally taking place in 2019-2020, including detailed analysis and infographics on their regional distribution, cost and focus. With the rapid development of the Longevity Industry in recent years, the number of events dedicated to this topic has increased proportionately. These events differ from one another in a number of ways including target audience, scope of featured topics, entrance fee range, region and venue, etc. Potential participants need to be aware of such details while planning which conferences to attend.

This report aims to serve as a guide in this type of decision-making, which also includes a cost-benefit analysis of the conferences themselves. Since the turn of the century, a number of conferences have proven to have a seminal role, often acting as centres of gravity for the industry or any of its constituent technologies.

In many cases, however, their full significance does not become apparent without the benefit of hindsight. It is for these reasons that the report contains a section on the influential past conferences (with an emphasis on the rapid succession of Longevity conferences hosted by prominent financial institutions and media brands in the past few years) that helped to solidify Longevity as the prominent, mainstream topic that it is today.

The rapid succession of finance-centred conferences that occurred in 2016-2018 marked a turning point for the maturation of the industry. The Business of Longevity panel discussion at the 2017 Financial

Times' Global Pharmaceutical and Biotechnology Conference, for example, followed close on the heels of The Economist's Business of Longevity Conference in Hong Kong on October 27th, 2017.

Advancing Financial Industry Longevity / AgeTech / WealthTech

Advancing Financial Industry – Longevity / AgeTech / WealthTech delivers a broad overview of the emerging Longevity Financial Industry. Aging and the Silver Tsunami should be considered as one of the most acute problems of our time, whereas progress in biomedicine and increasing Healthy Longevity as one of the most promising opportunities in human history. And the upcoming collision of these opposed MegaTrends has created a massive multitrillion market for AgeTech, Longevity WealthTech and novel financial products targeted toward the 1 billion people in retirement globally. The market size of the global Longevity economy reached US$17 trillion in 2019, and is expected to grow to US$27 trillion by 2026.

Volume I delivers a broad overview of the industry's various sectors, major participants and overall trajectory, profiling the Longevity activities and prospects of 150 large financial institutions including banks, pension funds, insurance and reinsurance companies and asset management firms. The report establishes a general framework and delivers relevant information about the Longevity trends shaping the financial industry, as well as the Longevity risks, challenges and opportunities it currently faces, providing knowledge, expertise and conclusions that will be of interest not just for financial industry professionals and investors, but also for the broader public, government representatives, media, scientists, entrepreneurs and others. Financial institutions can either utilize the opportunity of Healthy Longevity and thrive, or stagnate and decline when hit by the oncoming Silver Tsunami. Whether they succeed at riding the wave or drown under it will depend not only on their willingness to deploy new business models adapted to the aging population, but also on the quality of the analytics and forecasting methods underlying them.

Longevity Industry in Switzerland Landscape Overview 2019

Longevity Industry in Switzerland: Landscape Overview 2019 delivers a comprehensive overview of the history, present state and near-future trajectory of the Switzerland Longevity Industry, profiling its key players, including **100 leading companies**, **80 investors**, **50 financial corporations**, **15 influencers**, **35 research labs**, **20 P4 clinics**, **15 non-profits**, **15 governmental organizations**, **10 journals**, **15 scientists** and **15 journalists active in the Swiss Longevity sphere**. Switzerland is thought to be second only to Japan in terms of the number of people who have reached 100 (Switzerland has the highest life expectancy in Europe at 83.7 years, according to Eurostat). According to the study conducted by the Institute for Social and Preventive Medicine, about 40 out of every 10,000 people born in 1900 in Switzerland made it to their 100th birthday. Life expectancy has increased by 98 per cent for men and 96 per cent for women in the past century and a half.

Switzerland has been leading transformative developments emerging from the digitalization of its banking and financial sector. Switzerland is also one of the most efficiently regulated and supervised financial centres in the world today. Switzerland is known to be one of the most longevity-progressive countries, which means it is not simply a country with high investment in biotechnology, but also one of the most capable of integrating AI into its economic, financial, and healthcare systems. By utilizing a variety of infographic mindmaps, the report first enables the audience to quickly identify its core analytical findings and conclusions. Its chapter sequence then introduces readers to specific areas of the Longevity Industry in Switzerland by highlighting pertinent scientific and technological trends, providing an overview of underlying demographic and economic data and analyzing existing and projected governmental policies.

Top-100 Supercentenarians Landscape Overview: 100 Longest-Lived, 100 Currently Living, 25 Socially and Professionally Active

Supercentenarians Landscape Overview delivers a comprehensive analysis and overview of the **top-100 longest-lived supercentenarians** of all time, the **top-100 currently living supercentenarians**, as well as the **top-25 most socially and professionally active centenarians**. The report delivers not just an overview of the history and data concerning the supercentenarian population, but also provides a more intimate look at the individuals who are possible supercentenarians, both those verified and recognized by the Gerontology Research Group and those still under investigation, providing valuable trends, such as gender and geographic distribution of supercentenarians, and first-hand accounts on how they live their lives.

Throughout history there have always been human beings who have lived well beyond normal life expectancy, these "supercentenarians" who lived past 110 years of age. What did not exist was a codified system of tracking and verifying these claims and separating fact from human error and false claims. In 1990, however, L. Stephen Coles, MD PhD, created the Gerontology Research Group (GRG), which for the first time could verify and catalogue these claims. This was as part of the GRG's mission statement to "slow and ultimately reverse age-related decline for more healthy years of life".

A number of interesting trends and conclusions were also derived from the analysis behind the special case study. For example, across all continents, the gender distribution of supercentenarians tilts heavily towards females, typically by a factor of 10. Even when the overall numbers are low — as is the case in Africa and Australia — the disparity remains. In fact, the trend cuts across cultures and disparate environmental factors. Even within the supercentenarian group, those at the highest age ranges tend to be exclusively women.

1000 Longevity Leaders IT-Platform

Longevity.International's 1000 Longevity Leaders Interactive IT-Platform aims to serve as the largest and most comprehensive interactive database of Longevity Industry professionals developed to date. The platform profiles 1000 public and private-sector professionals working to grow the Longevity landscape through their efforts in business, science, policy, philanthropy and thought-leadership, categorizing them by region and by their sector of focus. The 1000 Longevity Leaders interactive IT-platform was created by Aging Analytics Agency, using their sophisticated, multidimensional Longevity Industry analytical frameworks, as a pro-bono project at the request of Longevity.International. The platform is in a continuous state of development, expansion and enhancement, and future iterations will include advanced filtering and search functions, an expanded scope of data visualization capabilities, and quantitative, multidimensional Longevity Leaders rankings.

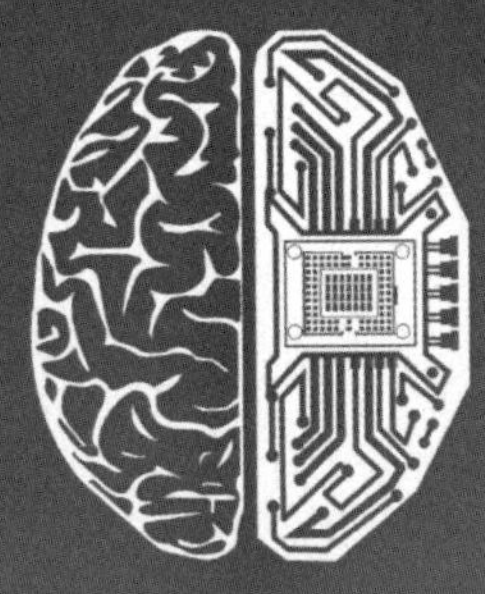

DEEP KNOWLEDGE GROUP OVERVIEW

Knowledge is Power

Deep Knowledge is Transcending Power

Deep Knowledge Group Overview

Deep Knowledge Group is a consortium of commercial and non-profit organizations active on many fronts in the realm of DeepTech and Frontier Technologies (AI, Longevity, FinTech, GovTech, InvestTech), ranging from scientific research to investment, entrepreneurship, analytics, media, philanthropy and more.

Its subsidiaries include Deep Knowledge Ventures, Longevity.Capital, AI-Pharma.Capital, Longevity FinTech Company, Deep Knowledge Analytics, Aging Analytics Agency, NeuroTech Analytics, Biogerontology Research Foundation, Longevity Swiss Foundation, AI-Longevity Consortium at King's College London, and Longevity International UK — Secretariat for the UK All-Party Parliamentary Group on Longevity.

The consortium's major projects and initiatives grew out of the initial activities of Deep Knowledge Ventures, which was active on so many fronts of high technology- and science-driven domains that it made the decision to form dedicated subsidiaries for each of the specific domains it was involved in.

Deep Knowledge Ventures was founded in 2014 as a data-driven investment fund focused on the synergetic convergence of DeepTech and frontier technologies, and it is renowned for the use of sophisticated analytical systems for investment target identification and due-diligence.

Major investment sectors include AI, Precision Medicine, Longevity, FinTech and InvestTech.

Major short-term interests include AI and DeepTech, with a long term strategic focus on Longevity and Precision Health.

Deep Knowledge Group values knowledge above profit — a vision embedded in its very name and brand.

Deep Knowledge Ventures fund considers its analytical subsidiaries among its most precious assets, marshalling the fund toward a long-term strategic vision.

Analytical subsidiaries are the knowledge engines driving the investment strategy of Deep Knowledge Group, producing open-source and proprietary analytics and advanced Big Data visualization solutions.

Our analytical and non-profit activities are powerful tools for efficient and productive engagement with governments, progressive top-tier corporations, industry influencers, media and a wide range of other strategically relevant people and organizations.

Deep Knowledge Group Structure

Investment Funds

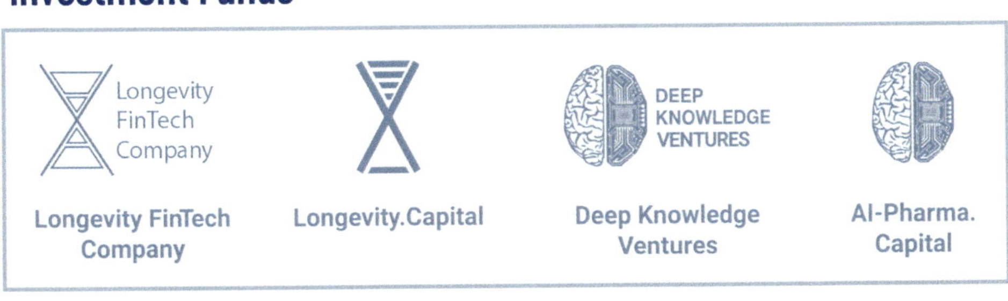

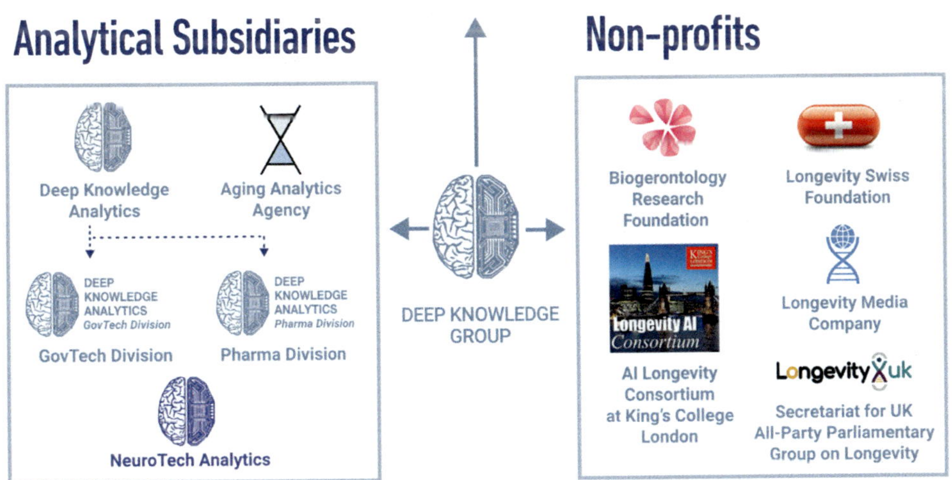

Deep Knowledge Group Geography

Deep Knowledge Group Analytical Subsidiaries

Deep Knowledge Analytics is a DeepTech analytical agency using multidimensional algorithms to produce advanced industrial reports on DeepTech and frontier technologies. An online analytics platform with interactive visuals updated in real-time was released early this year.

The Pharma Division of Deep Knowledge Analytics specializes in the production of the most comprehensive analytical reports on the topics of Artificial Intelligence, drug discovery, Data Science and digital health within the broader Pharma healthcare industry and intersection of AI and Pharma.

The GovTech Division of Deep Knowledge Analytics focuses on producing sophisticated open-access and proprietary analytics to reveal the factors driving the ongoing transformation of the global GovTech industry, the main sectors to be changed, the barriers to this process, and the ways to overcome them.

Aging Analytics Agency began producing reports before the industry emerged and it is exclusively focused on Longevity, Geroscience, AgeTech and Preventive Medicine. The company has been developing its methodology since 2015 and is the main source of market intelligence in the field.

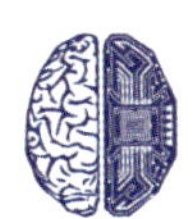

NeuroTech Analytics specializes in the production of open-access and commercial comparative analytics on the full scope of the global NeuroTech industry, ranging from brain-computer interfaces to implant technologies, neurostimulation and neuromodulation, and neuroplasticity-increasing apps.

Deep Knowledge Group Investment Funds

Deep Knowledge Ventures is a leading data-driven investment fund focused on the synergetic convergence of DeepTech, frontier technologies and technological megatrends, renowned for its use of sophisticated analytical systems for investment target identification and due diligence. While its major short term interests are AI and DeepTech, its long term vision is focused on Longevity and Precision Health. The fund has offices in London, Zurich, Geneva, San Francisco, Toronto, Hawaii, Edinburgh and Hong Kong.

Longevity.Capital is a hybrid investment fund specifically focused on the Longevity Industry, backed by seasoned professionals who have been active in both the investment banking and Longevity industries for 25+ years, long before the sector was recognized as a serious prospect by the overwhelming majority of investors. The fund structures its portfolio based on sophisticated industry intelligence and comparative analytics provided by the world-leading Longevity analytics entity Aging Analytics Agency.

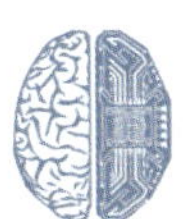

AI-Pharma.Capital is a hybrid investment fund focused on the AI in Pharma and drug discovery sectors, backed by seasoned professionals who have been active in both the investment banking and AI for drug discovery industries for years, long before the sector was recognized as a serious prospect by the overwhelming majority of investors, and some of whom made their first investments into the sector in 2014. The fund structures its portfolio based on industry intelligence and analytics by the Pharma Division of Deep Knowledge Analytics.

Deep Knowledge Group Non-profits

BIOGERONTOLOGY RESEARCH FOUNDATION

Biogerontology Research Foundation is a non-profit focused on Longevity, disease treatment and precision prevention. It is actively involved in UK Longevity policy, politics and government initiatives. Its aim is to neutralize the economic burden of an aging population.

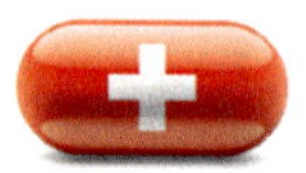

LONGEVITY SWISS FOUNDATION

Longevity Swiss Foundation engaged with members of the Swiss government in establishing a National Swiss Longevity Development Plan to extend life expectancy through the application of AI, working alongside Swiss financial institutions, making Switzerland a leader in Longevity, Precision Health and biomedicine.

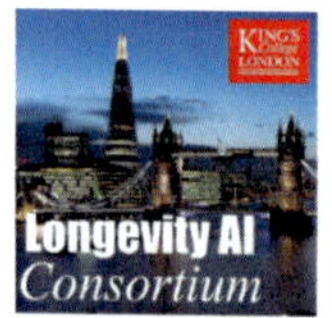

AI-LONGEVITY CONSORTIUM AT KING'S COLLEGE LONDON

The Longevity AI Consortium will serve as a leading R&D hub and industry-academic hotspot for advanced AI-driven personalised preventive diagnostics, prognostics and therapeutics. The main concept of Precision Medicine is providing healthcare which is individually tailored to a person's genes, lifestyle and environment.

LONGEVITY MEDIA COMPANY

Longevity Media Company is a source of the latest Longevity news, from science to lifestyle and investment. Its aim is to expand through curating relevant news to the public and hosting conferences. It also offers partnership opportunities and consulting services tuned to the needs of investors and HNWIs.

Our non-profit activities are powerful tools for ethical and productive engagement with governments, progressive top-tier corporations, industry influencers, journalists and a wide range of other relevant people and organizations.

Deep Knowledge Group in Social Media

Series of articles **officially authorized by LinkedIn**.

Weekly newsletters on the topic of **DeepTech** by Dmitry Kaminskiy and Margaretta Colangelo.

DeepTech Official Linkedin Newsletter:
Where advanced engineering meets DeepTech science.

The synergetic convergence of AI, science, advanced engineering and DeepTech.

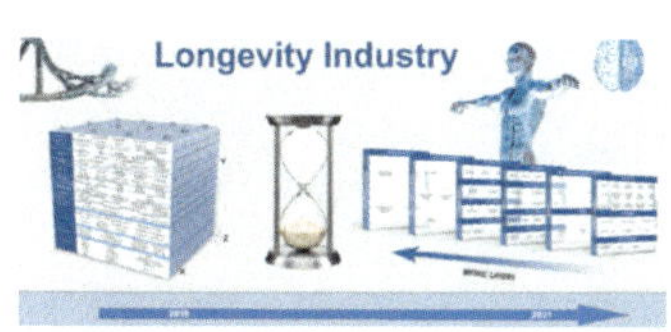

Series of articles **officially authorized by LinkedIn**.

Weekly newsletters on the topic of **Longevity** by Dmitry Kaminskiy and Margaretta Colangelo.

Longevity Official LinkedIn Newsletter:
Where technology meets Precision Health.

Biomedicine scientific breakthroughs, frontier technologies & Novel Financial System in the new era of Longevity.

Deep Knowledge Group in Publishing

"Deep Knowledge Ventures, a Hong Kong based venture capital fund that invests in life sciences, cancer research, age-related diseases and regenerative medicine has appointed an artificial intelligence algorithm called VITAL (Validating Investment Tool for Advancing Life Sciences) to its board of directors.

Klaus Schwab
The Fourth Industrial Revolution, page 149

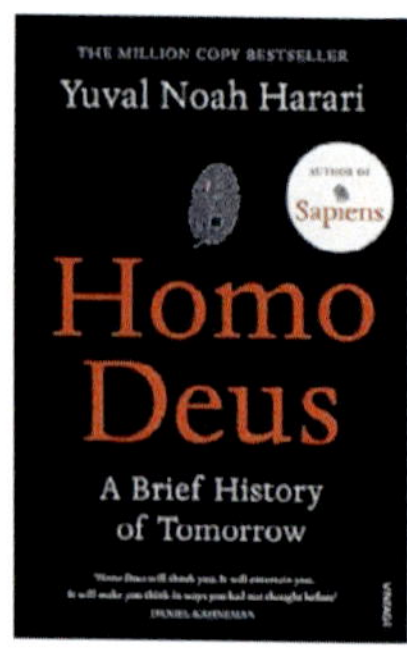

"In May 2014 Deep Knowledge Ventures – a Hong Kong venture-capital firm specialising in regenerative medicine – broke new ground by appointing an algorithm called VITAL to its board. VITAL makes investment recommendations by analysing huge amounts of data on the financial situation, clinical trials and intellectual property of prospective companies. Like the other five board members, the algorithm gets to vote on whether the firm makes an investment in a specific company or not."

Yuval Noah Harari
Homo Deus: A Brief History of Tomorrow, page 437

Deep Knowledge Group in the Media

The Telegraph

"A report published on Wednesday by the All-Party Parliamentary Group for AI claimed that the UK has all of the basic elements necessary to compete effectively in a global race to develop AI technology. The Big Innovation Centre and Deep Knowledge Analytics collected and produced the report. Dmitry Kaminskiy, who was one of the authors of the report and co-founder of Deep Knowledge Analytics, said: 'It should be noted that Chinese companies have been proactive and even aggressive in their investments, especially compared to that of the activity of US firms.'"

FORTUNE

"Hong Kong-based investment firm Deep Knowledge Ventures made headlines in 2014 by appointing a computer algorithm to its corporate board. The firm, which has about 100 million euros under management, wanted a way to enforce a data-driven approach to investing, rather than relying on human intuition and personal interactions with founders. Managing partner Dmitry Kaminskiy says the algorithm served mostly as a veto mechanism – if it spotted red flags, Deep Knowledge wouldn't invest."

Daily Mail

"In a world first, Japanese venture capital firm Deep Knowledge recently named an artificial intelligence (AI) to its board of directors. The robot, named Vital, was chosen for its ability to pick up on market trends 'not immediately obvious to humans.'"

The Guardian

"For Deep Knowledge Ventures, the Hong Kong-based venture firm that added a machine learning algorithm named VITAL to its board in 2014, it was about adding a tool to analyse market data around investment."

CNN

"The firm, Deep Knowledge Ventures (DKV), which invests in companies researching treatments for age-related diseases and analyze financing trends to make investment recommendations in the life sciences sector (...)"

BBC

"A venture capital firm has appointed a computer algorithm to its board of directors. According to Deep Knowledge Ventures, Vital has already approved two investment decisions. The software was developed by UK-based Aging Analytics."

NIKKEI ASIAN REVIEW

"Artificial intelligence gets a seat in the boardroom. Hong Kong venture capitalist sees AI running Asian companies within 5 years."

"The One Billion Retired People Globally are a Multi-Trillion Dolar Opportunity for Business" - Dmitry Kaminskiy for Financial Times.

Forbes

"An Insight Of AI's Penetration In Drug Development Market. Thanks to Deep Knowledge Ventures, which a couple of days ago updated their research data, we took the opportunity to delve into the latest developments of this market."

HUFFPOST

"Deep Knowledge Ventures said that the AI would help make financial and business decisions, help lead its research into biotechnology and regenerative medicine, and would act as an 'equal member of the board.'"

FierceBiotech
THE BIOTECH INDUSTRY'S DAILY MONITOR

"AI-based drug designer Insilico Medicine has raised US$37 million to help commercialize its technology, on the heels of a landmark paper for the company that showed its computer networks were able to generate, synthesize and preclinically validate a series of promising compounds from scratch in less than 50 days. Another of the company's investors — Deep Knowledge Ventures, which has backed Insilico since its 2014 seed round — described its work as one of the fund's most promising, and a central player among its companies focused on AI-based drug discovery and longevity."

"Dmitry Kaminskiy, a senior partner at Deep Knowledge Ventures, and Alex Zhavoronkov, Ph.D., the CEO of the anti-aging drug company Insilico Medicine Inc., signed a wager last month at a large anti-aging science conference stating that the one who died first owed the other a million dollars in stock or cash."

Deep Knowledge Group COVID-19 Analytics

Deep Knowledge Group's COVID-19 analytical frameworks and methodology have been designed to rapidly account for the new and ongoing actions of regions as they strive to mitigate the health and economic consequences of COVID-19 within their own borders. By applying Big Data Analysis to a large scope of quantified and relevant parameters, and comparing them in tangible practical ways, they are able to serve as the ideal tools for responsible governments and relevant decision makers to derive actionable data and insights on their own specific situation over time on the effectiveness of their counter-infection measures and how to adapt the best-case examples (and avoid the mistakes) of other regions in a way that is tuned to the specifics of their own regional, healthcare and economic circumstance. These frameworks are designed to identify positive cases such as these, and enable relevant decision makers to get a tangible understanding of how they can apply them to their own situations in an efficient, cost-effective and actionable manner.

Big Data Analysis for Tangible Insights
COVID-19 is a complex system impacted by the intersection and interaction of many different factors and entities. Big Data Analysis can rapidly help identify hidden patterns and correlations.

Gaining a Dynamic Lens on regions' COVID Efforts
The frameworks are periodically updated, and analyzing changes in specific ranking frameworks over time can help measure the effectiveness of regions' efforts, and adjust them over time.

Region-Specific Metrics for Precise Ranking
The frameworks are designed to be both generally applicable across many different regions, and to include region-specific metrics to account for the inevitable specifics of various regions.

Applying Best Case Examples from Other regions
By analyzing the specific metrics that certain regions rank well in, decision makers can identify the exact factors behind positive region rankings in specific categories.

Avoiding the Mistakes of Other regions
The frameworks account for both positive and negative factors impacting regions' effectiveness at combating COVID-19, identifying critical mistakes to avoid.

Actionable Data-Driven Answers to Key Questions
Above all else, the frameworks have been formulated to enable the identification of *tangible action-oriented insights* on how regions should adjust their policies and efforts to maximize beneficial outcomes for their citizens and national economies.

Deep Knowledge Group COVID-19 MedTech Analytics IT-Platform

Deep Knowledge Group's new **COVID-19 MedTech Analytics IT-Platform** is designed to serve as a comprehensive database of the most relevant entities, technologies, and developments in the COVID-19

MedTech ecosystem, aggregating, profiling and visualizing the companies, organizations, scientists and technologies at the forefront of neutralizing the COVID-19 pandemic and ensuring the health and safety of individuals and nations during this time of unprecedented crisis. The platform aims to cover all major sectors and relevant activities in the global COVID-19 MedTech landscape from science to technology, R&D, treatment, diagnostic and vaccine development, and practical applications occurring globally, providing data on particular scientific and technological sectors and geographical regions.

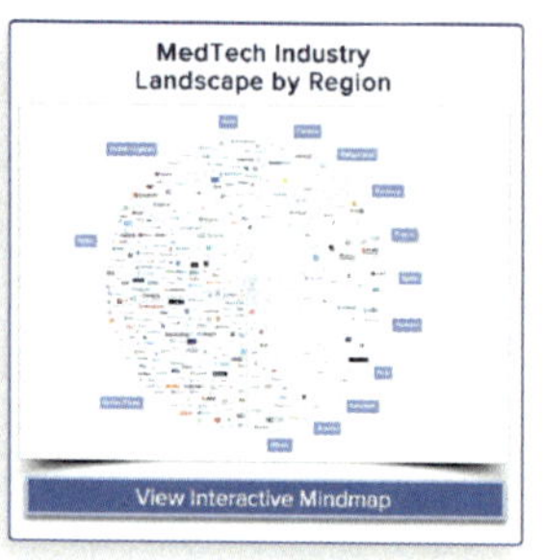

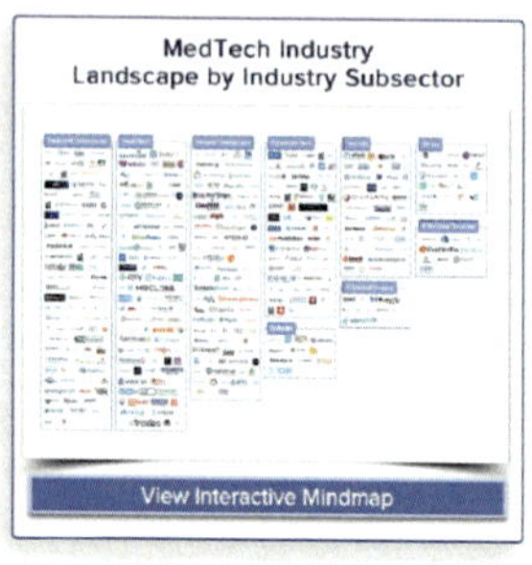

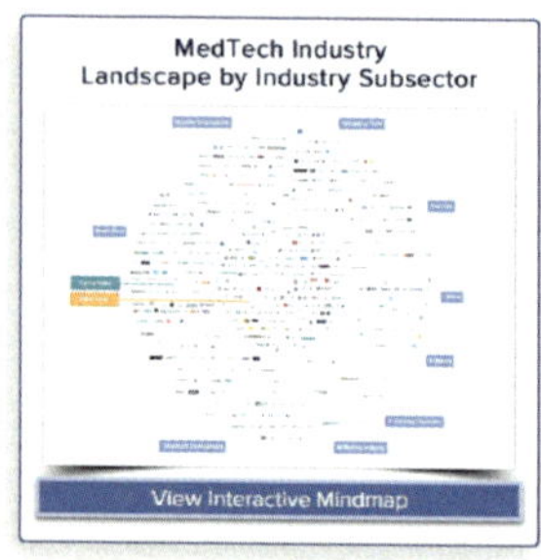

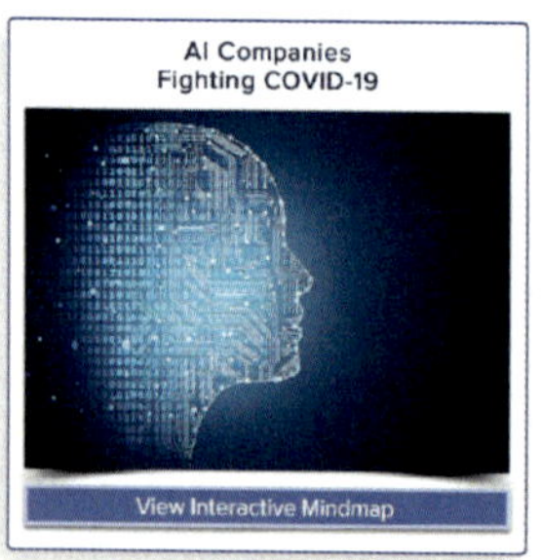

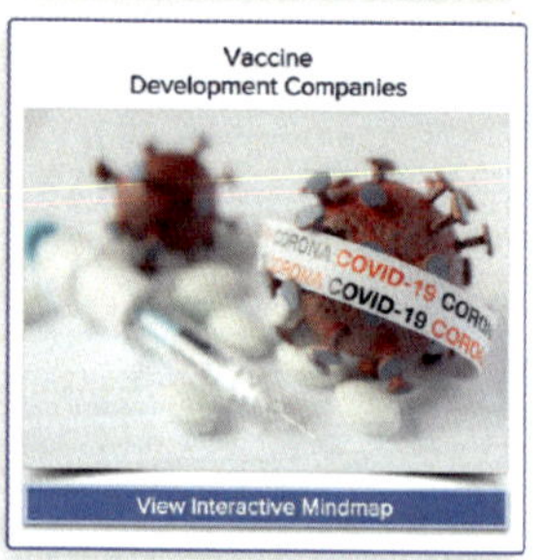

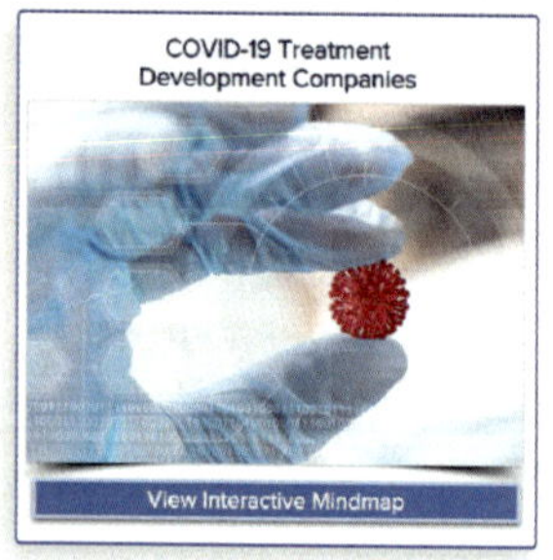

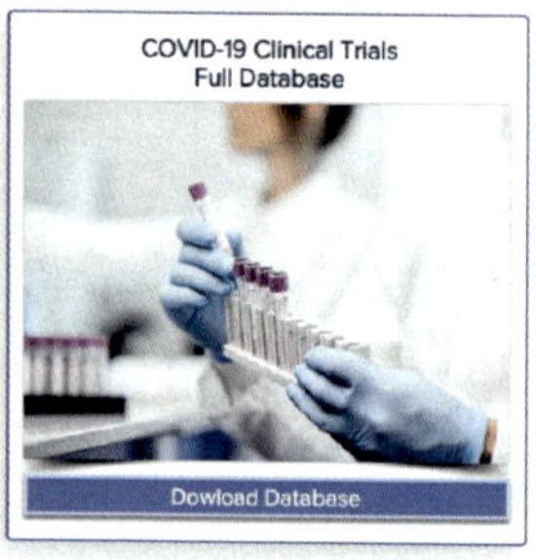

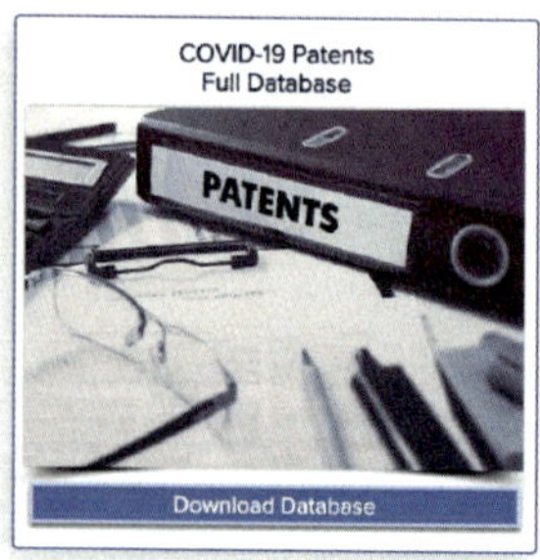

The platform was created by **Deep Knowledge Analytics** utilizing the sophisticated IT-solutions and **Interactive MindMap and Data Visualization** capabilities that the DeepTech analytics subsidiary of the group has developed over the past several years. Its ultimate aim is to serve as a comprehensive database and one-stop informational resource designed to keep both the public and relevant decision makers informed on the latest developments in the COVID-19 MedTech landscape, profiling 95 Treatment Candidates, 85 Vaccine Candidates, 60 Preventative Tech, 40 Test Kits, 220 Scientists, 380 Companies, 535 Investors, 50 Funding Agencies, 1500+ Clinical Trials and 180 Universities, Labs and R&D Hubs working at the frontier of neutralizing the pandemic and promoting beneficial outcomes for those already infected.

420 Companies	240 Scientists	50 Funding Agencies
535 Investors	190 Labs and R&D Hubs	40 Test Kits
45 Preventive Technologies	85 Vaccine Candidates	95 Treatment Candidates
1,500+ Clinical Trials	7,000+ Patents	10,000+ Scientific Papers

Deep Knowledge Group's **UK COVID-19 MedTech Analytics IT-Platform** is designed to serve as a comprehensive database of the most relevant entities, technologies, and developments in the UK COVID-19 MedTech ecosystem, showcasing, profiling and visualizing 800 companies, labs, R&D hubs, investors and funding and support bodies (governmental, non-governmental which could be providing funding to COVID-19 solutions but are not) leading the fight against COVID-19, and was developed in an open-access manner to provide proactive government representatives, companies, labs and scientists with the full scope of information required to accelerate the neutralization of negative post-pandemic outcomes within the UK.

Deep Knowledge Group's **UK COVID-19 MedTech Analytics IT-Platform** and its sister platform, the **Global COVID-19 MedTech Analytics IT-Platform**, profile the full scope of the international and UK-specific COVID-19 MedTech landscape from science to technology, R&D,

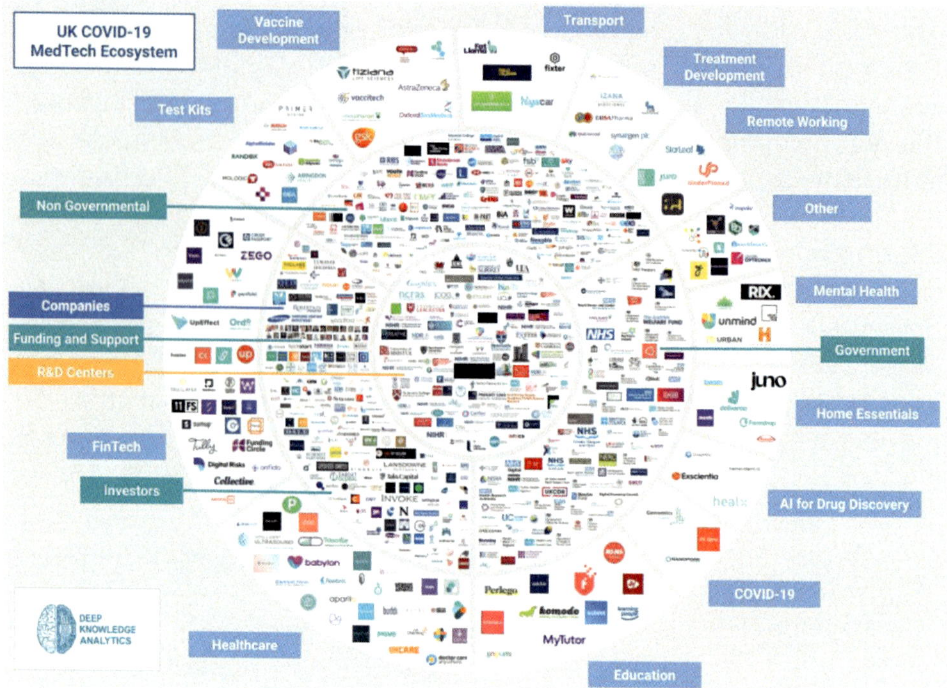

treatment, diagnostic and vaccine development, and practical applications occurring globally.

In addition to compiling and visualizing data on the full scope of the UK AgeTech Ecosystem, the upcoming platform also places particular emphasis on AgeTech solutions that can help protect and treat COVID-19 in the UK's elderly population, including COVID-19 as a specific industry subsector, and highlighting significant intersections between the distinct national challenges of ageing population and the coronavirus pandemic.

These platforms and other recent Deep Knowledge Group's COVID-19 Analytics, have received widespread media coverage and notable government acknowledgements since their release, including **Alain Berset, Former President of Switzerland**, several **Israeli embassies**, the **Saudi Arabian Ministry of Media**, the **Official Georgian Government Office and Ministry of Foreign Affairs**, and many others).

COVID-19 Regional Safety Assessment 250 Countries, Regions & Territories

Based on the data collected up until August 23rd 2020

As vaccine research advances it is becoming more crucial to have in place a more thorough analysis of the spread of virus and various levels of success at prevention and recovery, as well as up to date information on emerging threats in some specific areas, and where they might appear (white spots). In order to be assured that countries, regions and international organizations have all the necessary data, there must be tight collaboration between the statisticians, data scientists, medics and other involved parties.

140+ Parameters	**250+ Countries and Regions**	**35000+ Data Points**

At any rate, the coronavirus pandemic is a critical challenge that must be faced in order to plan the best strategic measures to reduce and neutralize negative repercussions, until the final solution of a vaccine is within the reach of the scientific and medical community. With this in mind, Deep Knowledge Group's new COVID-19 special analytical case study is designed to classify, analyze and rank the economic, social and health stability achieved by each of the 250 countries and regions included in its analysis, as well as the strengths, weaknesses, opportunities, and threats or risks that they present in the battle against the global health and economic crisis triggered by COVID-19.

It is Deep Knowledge Group's aim that, regardless of whether the conclusions and recommendations presented in this special analytical case study are adopted wholesale, the present analysis can serve as a starting point for discussion and a resource for governments to optimize current and post-pandemic safety and stability, and as a toolset for establishing the best possible action plans for each particular region, in order to maintain the health and economic well-being of their populations and reverse the collateral damage caused by COVID-19.

This framework comprises 6 top-level categories (Quarantine Efficiency, Government Efficiency of Risk Management, Monitoring and Detection, Health Readiness, Regional Resilience and Emergency Preparedness). Each category consists of a matrix of sub-parameters (referred to here as Indicators), whereas each indicator itself consists of a matrix of 2-10 quantitative

COVID-19 Regional Safety Assessment (250 Regions)

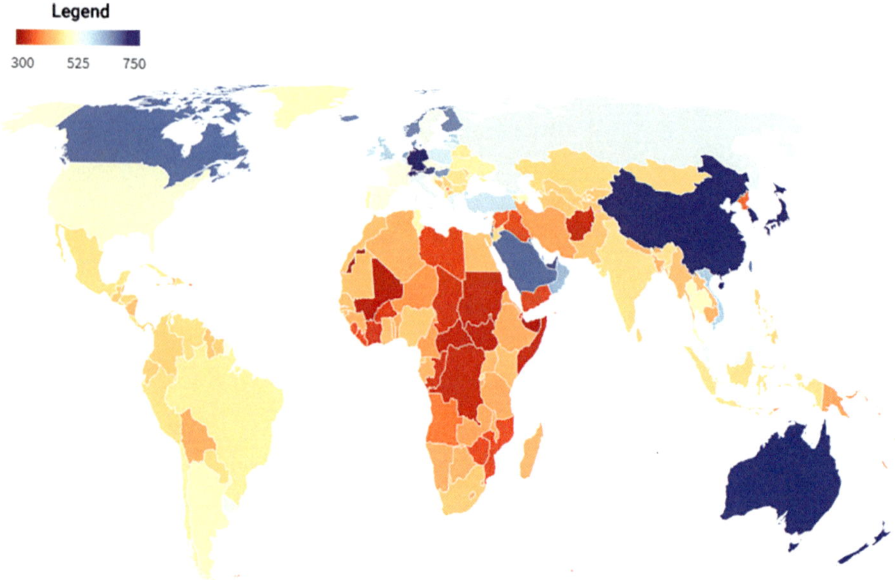

or qualitative sub-parameters, relating to the specific topic and composed from available databases. They relate to specific important factors impacting the stability of current regional circumstances and the effectiveness of various regions' emergency response efforts, and these variables will also address post-pandemic planning measures in future studies.

We are only just now emerging from a period of a spontaneous and widespread cessation or reduction of economic activity. Not all devastation brought on the health and wealth of the global population are seen yet. As behavioural scientists have advised governments worldwide, a population will tolerate a total lockdown for about three months before they come to regard a citizen's responsibility to hygiene as a matter of public behaviour rather than public seclusion. This is evident in the extent to which even the later, looser lockdown regulations were flaunted in the latter stages of lockdown while public behaviour remained more precautious than ever, with social distancing and mask wearing practiced almost ubiquitously even where voluntary. Furthermore, being housebound for months takes a mental, physical and financial toll on people of all age groups.

As such, the peoples and economies of the world simply cannot abide another lockdown any time soon. And yet the health systems of the world cannot withstand a return to normal for as long as the risk of a future spike remains.

As with many historical predicaments, the best route out is technological innovation.

Many nations are locked in a race to develop a coronavirus vaccine before the end of the year. Britain, Germany, the USA, Japan, Israel and China all claim some measure of success, while Russia is claiming to have already approved mass vaccinations for October, bringing things to an alleged state of completion so swiftly that competitors suspect them of cutting corners. International development institutions and inter-governmental bodies and public persons already have made speeches addressed to policymakers warning them to avoid "supply nationalism". Discrepancies in political matters between nations were put aside in order to concentrate on more collaborative actions aimed to provide treatment and vaccination. The European Commission, which is one of the most active players at the forefront of fighting COVID-19 has committed to bring about cooperation in order to enable not only members of the EU but also the rest of the world, especially less developed countries, to have access to vaccination and supply of other necessary equipment.

In any event, the main hindrance in the race for a vaccine for a novel pandemic is lack of data, which must be sampled from the wild as the crisis progresses and utilised as efficiently as possible in order that the crisis need not proceed a minute longer than is necessary. Much of this data is hard to come by. For example many statistically significant regions, such as the African islands, are hard to sample and the data is slow to arrive.

Metrics indicate that positive indicators of healthcare system efficiency do not necessarily correlate with a positive effect on mortality rates. On the contrary, the correlation is 0.1-0.3, which would mean that more health expenditures coincide with a higher ratio of fatal cases.

COVID-19 Analytics International Acknowledgements

Deep Knowledge Group's recent "**COVID-19 regions Health Safety Ranking**" attracted significant public interest. Since their initial publication, the rankings have received widespread media attention in **Der Spiegel**, **NIKKEI Asian Review**, **Deutsche Welle**, **Esquire**, **Forbes** and others, and was acknowledged by Israel's **Prime Minister Office**, **Ministry of Foreign Affairs of Israel** and personally by Israel's Prime Minister, **Benjamin Netanyahu**. The Group was also mentioned on i24 TV Channel. The Full Media Coverage can be found here: **https://www.dkv.global/media-news**

Benjamin Netanyahu

Prime Minister of Israel

Prime Minister of Israel, Benjamin Netanyahu several times tweeted about Deep Knowledge Group's COVID-19 Rankings published both on 31st of March 2020 and 14th of April 2020.

Alain Berset

Former President of Switzerland

Alain Berset is Federal Councillor, Head of the Federal Department of Home Affairs (DFI) and former President of the Swiss Confederation. Alain Berset mentioned Deep Knowledge Group's COVID-19 Safety Ranking published on 4th of June 2020 on his Twitter account.

DubaiTourism

Government Office

Dubai's Department of Tourism and Commerce Marketing tweeted about Deep Knowledge Group's COVID-19 Safety Ranking published on 4th of June 2020.

#UAE ranks first in the Arab region and 11th globally in @Forbes' list "The 100 Safest Countries In The World For COVID-19" bit.ly/2XHHamx

Karin Prien

German Minister

German Minister of Minister of Education, Science and Culture, Karin Prien, tweeted Der Spiegel Article about Deep Knowledge Group's COVID-19 Rankings published on 14th of April 2020.

Im Ländervergleich liegt Deutschland sehr weit vorn:

"Deutschland hat im Vergleich zu den anderen Ländern derzeit das beste Sicherheits- und Stabilitätsranking in Europa und gehört auch weltweit zu den führenden Nationen in Sachen Krisenmanagement."

Hong Nam-ki

Deputy Prime Minister of South Korea

Hong Nam-ki posted about Deep Knowledge Group's COVID-19 Safety Ranking published on 26th of August 2020.

'한국이 코로나19 100대 안전국가중 3위로 선정'되었다고 미국 포브스紙(Forbes) 보도

▷ 미국 경제전문지 포브스紙(Forbes, 9.3일)는 홍콩 기반의 씽크탱크 DKG(Deep Knowledge Group)의 연구보고서를 인용하여 '한국이 코로나19 100대 안전국가중 3위'라고 보도했습니다.

동 보고서는 전 세계 250개국을 대상으로 코로나19와 관련된 경제, 정치, 보건 · 의료의 안전성을 평가하였습니다. 이는 방역효율성, 위기대응능력 등 6개 카테고리, 30개 지표, 140개 변수에 대해 빅데이터 기법을 활용, 분석 · 평가하여 각국의 안전점수를 산출한 것입니다. ...

한국 코로나19 안전국가 3위 선정 (포브스지 보도)

* Deep Knowledge Group : 홍콩 DK Ventures의 기업 및 비영리단체 컨소시엄

1 (개요) 한국은 전세계 코로나19 안전국가 3위로 최상위권

Top Tier Media About Deep Knowledge Group's COVID-19 Rankings

KBS WORLD

"Finance Minister Hong Nam-ki posted a Forbes article that ranked South Korea as the third safest out of 100 countries around the world during the COVID-19 pandemic. The ranking is based on an updated report by the Hong Kong-based Deep Knowledge Group, which assesses the economy, politics, health care and safety of 250 countries in relation to COVID-19."

Forbes

"The Deep Knowledge Group first released a ranking of the safest countries in the world for COVID-19 back in June. Now the think tank has updated its data and methodology and re-issued a report on the safest countries and regions."

ARAB NEWS

"Saudi Arabia has been ranked 17th among the top 20 safest countries in the world during the COVID-19 pandemic, according to a regional safety assessment analysis conducted by Hong Kong-based consortium, Deep Knowledge Group."

The Washington Post

"Israel had been ranked in March as having the world's top covid-19 safety rating by Deep Knowledge Group, which describes itself as a consortium of commercial and non-profit organizations. But now with infections spiking anew, Israel has been consigned to the "Red List" of covid-19 pariah countries barred from entry into European Union nations, along with the United States, Russia and Brazil."

NIKKEI ASIAN REVIEW

"To prevent the initial spread of the pandemic, it was not rocket science," said Dmitry Kaminskiy, founder of Deep Knowledge Ventures, a Hong Kong-based investment fund analyzing the global impact of COVID-19. "It was quite an easy task if governments reacted quickly."

"The Palestinians benefit from the Israeli assistance, since Israel was just ranked the safest country in the world during the pandemic by the Deep Knowledge Group."

THE STRAITS TIMES

"Strong monitoring and detection, a meritocratic government and a 'high degree' of technological sophistication helped make Singapore one of the safest places to live during the Covid-19 pandemic. Those qualities helped Singapore execute effective quarantines as well as social distancing and mandatory mask-wearing, the Deep Knowledge Group survey of 200 countries and territories said."

SWI swissinfo.ch

"Switzerland ranks first for its economic resilience and its careful approach towards relaxing 'lockdown and economic freezing mandates in a fact- and science-based manner, without sacrificing public health and safety', states Deep Knowledge Group in its Covid-19 Regional Safety Assessment."

"According to the survey, the safest country is Switzerland, while the most dangerous is South Sudan. As for Greece, which is also opening its tourism, it is in the 34th place of the list which consists of the 100 countries."

DER SPIEGEL

"According to a ranking, the Federal Republic is currently the safest and most stable country in Europe and even the second safest in the world. Only Israel manages the crisis better, according to the country comparison of the London Deep Knowledge Group (DKG) , which is exclusively available to SPIEGEL."

Esquire

"Deep Knowledge Ventures, which is focused on health care and longevity technology, ranked 20 countries in Asia Pacific on these parameters: lowest likelihood of infection, lowest chance of mortality, and highest likelihood of recovery based on efficiency of quarantine and government management, monitoring and detection, and emergency treatment readiness."

euronews.

"According to research by Deep Knowledge Group, the COVID-19 crisis is best managed by Israel on a global scale. Germany is the second and South Korea in the third. Deep Knowledge Group is a London-based artificial intelligence and data company."

Aging Analytics Agency Scope, History, Agenda

Aging Analytics Agency has been developing enhanced iterations of its proprietary methodology and analytics system since 2015, and serves as the main source of market intelligence for the specialized hybrid index hedge fund Longevity.Capital, helping to establish pragmatic portfolio company valuation and efficient due diligence procedures, and to structure an advanced investment strategy in the overly-complex Longevity Industry.

The agency's ongoing proprietary analytics has consistently been accompanied by the production of dozens of vast open-access landscape overview reports on the Longevity Industry of particular geographic regions, and on specific technological domains, that are tens of thousands of pages in combined length.

Today, these analytical methodologies have evolved to the level of 3D and 6D frameworks where metrics and submetrics can be visualized simultaneously, and the implementation of "timeline machines" that allow to analyze the changing state of industry players' strengths in specific areas ranging from scientific validation to business development, R&D, technological prowess, IP, etc. to be visualized over time, and projected into the future based on the statistical properties of the past behaviour using Machine Learning, Big Data analysis and other advanced statistical tools. Aging Analytics Agency is a subsidiary of Deep Knowledge Ventures. It works closely with a consortium of non-profit and for-profit organizations including Longevity.Capital, Longevity.International and Deep Knowledge Analytics.

Major Topics of the Reports		
Science of Aging	Precision Health	Artificial Intelligence
Advanced Biomedicine	Preventive Medicine	Data-Driven Medicine

Types of Analytics		
Open Source Analytics	Special Case Studies	Proprietary Analytical Reports

Aging Analytics Agency is the main source of data and analytics for the UK-based **All-Party Parliamentary Group for Longevity**, it is also an official member organization of the **United Nations NGO Committee on Ageing**, and regularly and systematically submits policy and strategy proposals to the **World Health Organization**, **World Economic Forum**, the **UK House of Lords** and other Longevity policy and governance organizations.

Developing Advanced Industry Analytics Since 2013 for Longevity Industry Benchmarking, SWOT, and Competitive Analytics

Aging Analytics Agency has, since its inception in 2013, been applying systematic methodologies to create various types of analytical frameworks that clearly define and classify distinct scientific domains, technologies and applications in a way that allows them to be quantitatively compared, continually refining them to maintain their relevance against the changing dynamics of the industry sectors they are applied to. Since then, the company has continued to improve these comparative analysis systems, both in terms of the specific metrics used to conduct its market studies and the mathematical formulas used to combine them as well as created advanced visualization techniques for making forecasts, rankings and determinations maximally understandable.

This ongoing proprietary analytics has consistently been accompanied by the production of open-access landscape overviews covering the Longevity Industry in certain geographic regions as well as specific technological domains, with corresponding reports often exceeding more than 1,000 pages in length. The purpose of producing such broad landscape overviews is to widely disseminate ongoing developments in innovation-driven industries in order to promote its continued growth, expansion and refinement.

However, the reports also serve an important secondary purpose — laying the groundwork for a comprehensive understanding of the entire

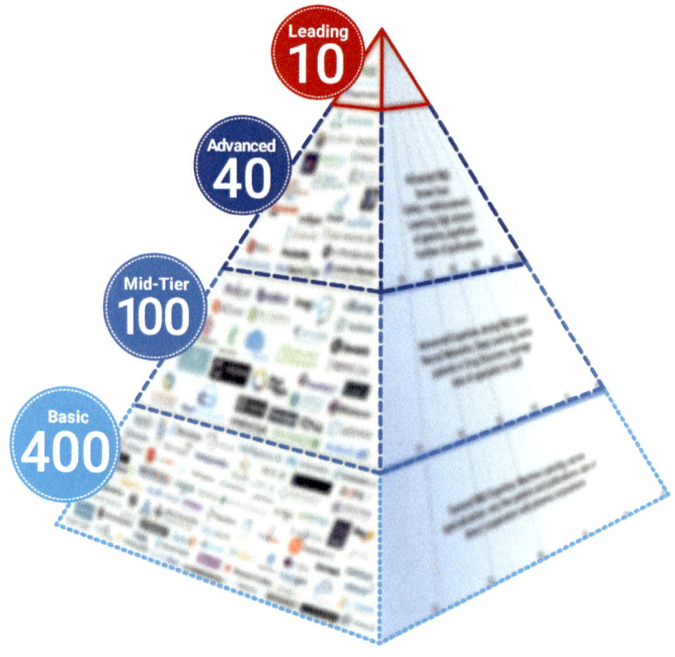

scope of the Longevity Industry across the globe and facilitating a greater comprehension of the specific industry players, their activities, and their interconnections. In other words, these reports establish the necessary foundation upon which more targeted, relevant and complex analyses can be implemented.

Strategic Consulting and Analytics for Longevity Governance, Policy, Politics and Industrial Strategies

In early 2019, Aging Analytics Agency began shifting increasingly large proportions of its resources away from open-source landscape overviews and special case studies of the Longevity industries of various nations and towards benchmarking and ranking of the strength, relevance and proactivity of various entities including companies, investors, financial institutions and government initiatives within the Longevity sphere, leveraging the very broad and deep understanding of the global Longevity Industry created through the production of tens of thousands of pages of global and regional landscape overviews from 2013 to 2018 in order to begin conducting deeper, more targeted analytics.

In Q2 2019, following the appointment of Eric Kihlstrom (former Director of the government-led £98 million Healthy Ageing Industrial Strategy Challenge Fund) as its new Director, and becoming the main source of data and analytics for the UK All-Party Parliamentary Group for Longevity, Aging Analytics Agency also began expanding the scope and focus of its efforts relating to deep industry analytics on the emerging front of the Longevity Financial Industry, and on benchmarking and strategic consulting services relating to government-led Longevity Industry development and national policy efforts of various countries.

Aging Analytics Agency is currently cooperating with a number of government departments and public sector bodies and authorities in the UK, Singapore, Switzerland, Israel and the US to create advanced IT solutions, deep analytics, special case studies and composite sets of tangible recommendations and development plans for national industrial strategies, science and technology policy, modernization and reforms in healthcare, frontier-technology sectors including Longevity, AI and Precision Health, and financial reforms relating to pension systems and insurance companies looking to transform the problem of an aging population into the opportunity of Healthy Longevity.

More specifically, many of these efforts are currently focused on the topics of Longevity policy, politics and governance, the formulation and development of National Longevity Development Plans, and targeted recommendations regarding decreasing the gap between life expectancy and health-adjusted life expectancy (HALE), developing various nation's Longevity Industries to scale, and fostering sophisticated innovation ecosystems around the convergence of Longevity, AI, Precision Health and the Longevity Financial Industry.

Longevity Governance		
Recommendation Packs	Industrial Strategies	Precision Health
Advanced IT Solutions	Analytics & Benchmarking	Modernization & Reform

Longevity Financial Industry		
Pension Systems	Insurance Companies	Novel Financial Derivatives

Aging Analytics Agency Proprietary and Public Longevity Industry Analytics

AGING ANALYTICS AGENCY UPCOMING PROPRIETARY ANALYTICS Q3 & 04 2019

Enhanced Analysis of Leading Longevity Companies as Prospective Investment Targets for Longevity.Capital

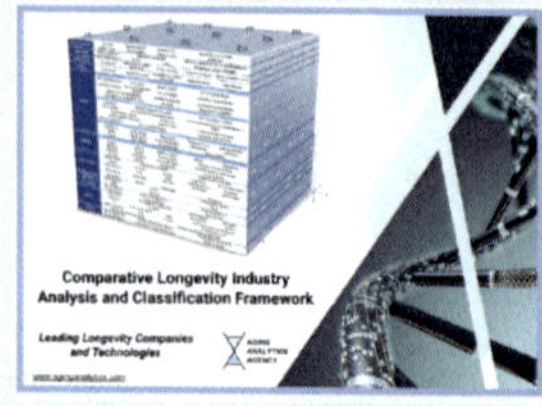

Comparative Longevity Industry Analysis and Classification Framework

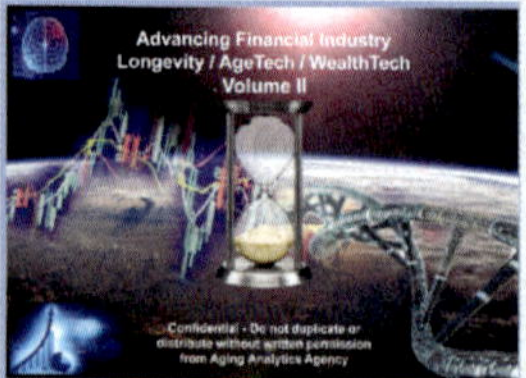

Advancing Financial Industry Longevity / Age Tech / Wealth Tech Volume II

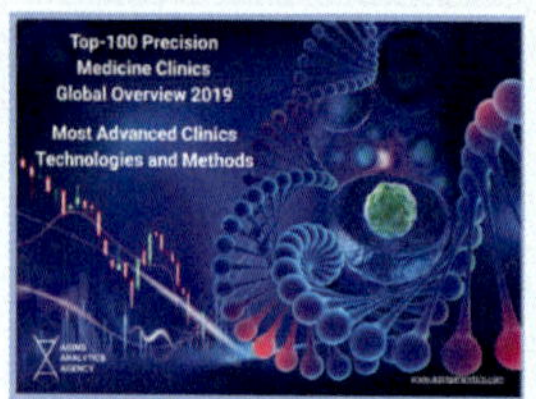

Precision Medicine Clinics Landscape Overview 2019 - Most Advanced Clinics Technologies and Methods

Top-20 Leading Longevity Investors Comparative Analysis

Defining Hype vs. Reality in the Longevity Industry

UPCOMING ANALYTICAL REPORTS BY AGING ANALYTICS AGENCY

Global Longevity Governance Landscape

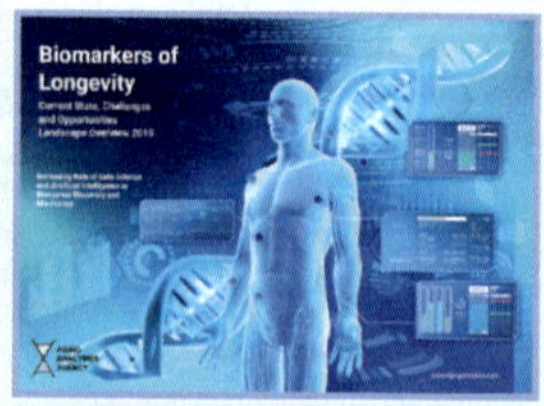

Biomarkers of Longevity: Most Comprehensive and Minimum Required Panels of Biomarkers of Aging

Supercentenarians Landscape Overview Top-100 Living, Top-100 Longest-Lived, Top-25 Socially and Professionally Active

Longevity Industry in Hong Kong Landscape Overview 2019

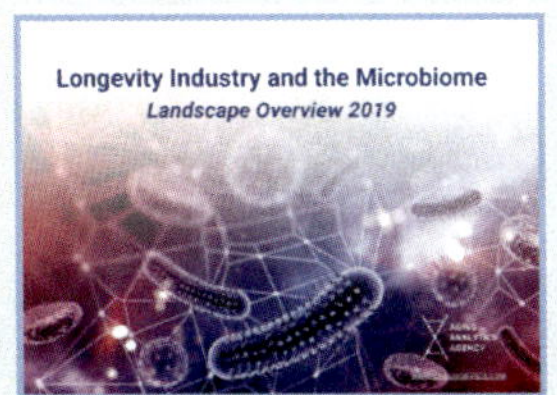

Longevity Industry & the Microbiome Landscape Overview 2019

Longevity Industry in Japan Landscape Overview 2019

Aging Analytics Agency Proprietary and Public Longevity Industry Analytics

PUBLISHED 01 - 02 2019

Longevity Industry in UK Landscape Overview 2019

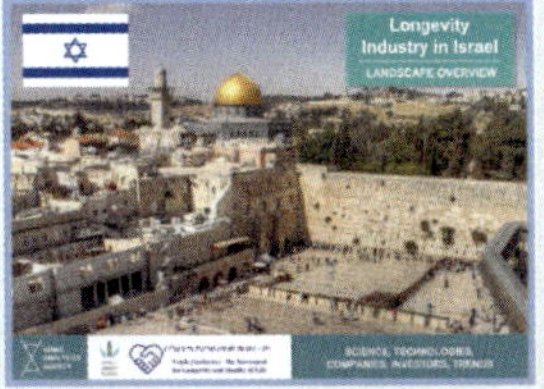

Longevity Industry in Israel Landscape Overview 2019

Longevity Industry in Singapore Landscape Overview 2019

Top-100 Journalists Covering Advanced Biomedicine and Longevity

FemTech Healthcare Landscape Overview Q1 2019

Top-100 Longevity Leaders

PUBLISHED 02 - 03 2019

National Longevity Development Plans: Global Overview 2019

Advancing Financial Industry Longevity / Age Tech / Wealth Tech

Metabesity and Longevity: USA Special Case Study

Top-50 Women Longevity Leaders

Longevity Industry in Switzerland: Landscape Overview 2019

Top-30 Longevity Conferences 2019-2020

Aging Analytics Agency is the world's premier provider of industry analytics on the topics of Longevity, Precision Preventive Medicine and economics

of aging, and the convergence of technologies such as AI and Digital Health and their impact on healthcare.

It currently serves as the primary source of data and analytics to the UK All-Party Parliamentary Group for Longevity, it is an Official Member Organization of the United Nations NGO Committee on Ageing, and routinely submits Longevity policy, governance and strategy proposals to a number of national and international policy organizations.

Aging Analytics Agency also has a number of upcoming proposals currently in production, to be submitted to the United Nations, the United States Congress, and relevant policy organizations in Switzerland. In addition to its official policy proposals and Longevity Governance-themed analytical reports, Aging Analytics Agency supported the International Longevity Policy and Governance Summit, organized by Longevity International UK at King's College, in London on November 12th 2019, in an effort to support and promote a greater degree of international synergy and cooperation on the expanding frontier of Longevity policy and governance.

The inaugural summit looked at the international response to harnessing the opportunities of an aging demographic, and what lessons could be learned and shared across countries from a policy perspective, with high-profile representatives and government officials of healthcare departments from the top-5 Longevity-progressive countries attending.

LONGEVITY POLICY ACTIVITIES

National Longevity Development Plans Global Overview 2019 - analytical report presented in UK Parliament; *Global Longevity Governance* - special case study published in November 2019.

Two chapters forthcoming in the United Nations Encyclopedia of Gerontology and Population Aging (Springer Nature, 2021) edited by Dr. Danan Gu of the United Nations Population Division.

Official Member Organization of the United Nations NGO Committee on Ageing, systematically submitting policy proposals to the World Health Organization, UK House of Lords and APPG for Longevity.

Supporting the inaugural International Longevity Policy and Governance Summit, organized by Longevity International UK, held at King's College London in November 2019.

UK HOUSE OF LORDS SCIENCE AND TECHNOLOGY COMMITTEE

Proposal to the UK House of Lords Science and Technology Committee's "Ageing: Science, Technology and Healthy Living" Evidence Inquiry

WORLD HEALTH ORGANIZATION

Response to the World Health Organization's "Decade of Healthy Aging: 2020 - 2030 Draft Zero Action Plan"

UK ALL-PARTY PARLIAMENTARY GROUP FOR LONGEVITY

Proposal to the APPG for Longevity's "National Strategy for Five More Years of Healthy Life Expectancy While Closing the Social Gap by 2035: Call for Evidence and Solutions"

UNITED STATES

Metabesity and Longevity: USA Special Case Study (Joint Project with Targeting Metabesity)

UNITED NATIONS

Proposal to the United Nations on Optimization of International Longevity Policy and Governance

SWITZERLAND

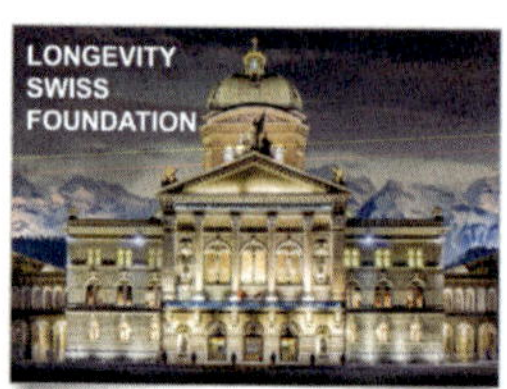

Longevity Policy and Governance in Switzerland (Joint Project with Longevity Swiss Foundation)

www.aginganalytics.com

policy@aginganalytics.com

Longevity Policy and Strategy Proposals Submitted to the World Health Organization, the UK House of Lords and the UK All-Party Parliamentary Group for Longevity

As interest in the topic of Longevity continues to mount around the world, an increasing number of progressive countries and government bodies are beginning to actively solicit consultation on Longevity policy, strategy and development plans. In response to this growing megatrend, Aging Analytics Agency has correspondingly increased the scope of its activities in the realm of Longevity policy, and during September 2019, submitted three proposals to a number of national and international governance and policy-structuring organizations concerned with the issues of aging population and the opportunities of Healthy Longevity, including the UK All-Party Parliamentary Group for Longevity, the World Health Organization, and the UK House of Lords Science and Technology Committee.

Aging Analytics Agency's activities in this specific sphere began with the appointment of Eric Kihlstrom (former Interim Director of the UK Government led Healthy Ageing Industrial Strategy Challenge Fund) as its new Director in Q1 2019, and has continued with the publication of its 315-page open-access analytical report *National Longevity Development Plans: Global Overview 2019 (First Edition)*, and the production of the follow-up analytical case study *Global Longevity Governance: 50 Countries Big Data Comparative Analysis of Longevity Progressiveness*

(which utilizes Big Data analysis to identify the major factors impacting the levels of Healthy Longevity in 50 countries and make practical policy recommendations for Health-Adjusted Life Expectancy development and optimization).

Aging Analytics Agency is an official partner of the UK All-Party Parliamentary Group for Longevity, and also serves as its main source of data and analytics. The company is also an official member organization of the United Nations NGO Committee on Ageing. Aging Analytics Agency believes that Longevity Policy and Governance is the next great frontier of the emerging Longevity sphere, and remains committed to provide strategy and policy proposals and recommendations to relevant national and international policy and governance organizations interested in transforming the problem of an aging population into the opportunity of Healthy Longevity, and is open to discussions on tailored policy proposals.

Aging Analytics Agency Pipeline of Products

In 2018, Deep Knowledge Ventures injected additional financing to support Aging Analytics Agency's ongoing and future projects. This enabled Aging Analytics Agency to extend the size of its analytics team by 10-fold.

This growth in brain power allowed it to proportionally increase the rate of production of its reports. Just in 2018, Aging Analytics Agency has doubled the number of high-quality reports compared to previous years, which include:

- Global Longevity Industry Overview, totaling over 1200 pages, which offers in-depth profiles of the top 100 companies, investors, non-profits and research labs active in the sphere;
- 850-page specialized case study on the Longevity Industry Landscape in the United Kingdom.

In line with this expansion, it is on track for publishing a greater number of diverse and in-depth reports throughout 2020, with some reports expanding further in their prior scope whereas others will be targeting particular topics and niches within the Longevity Industry.

Proprietary Reports

- Enhanced Analysis of Leading Longevity Companies as Prospective Investment Targets for Longevity.Capital
- Comparative Longevity Industry Analysis and Classification Framework
- Precision Medicine Clinics Landscape Overview
- Advancing Financial Longevity Industry / AgeTech / WealthTech Volume II
- Top-20 Leading Longevity Investors Comparative Analysis
- Defining Hype vs. Reality in the Longevity Industry

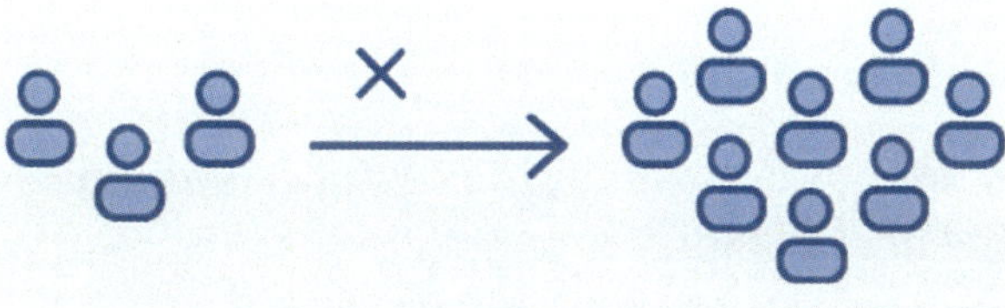

Open-Access Reports

- Longevity Industry Landscape Overview
- Longevity Industry in UK Landscape Overview
- Longevity Industry in Singapore Landscape Overview
- Longevity Industry in Israel Landscape Overview
- FemTech Healthcare Landscape Overview

- National Longevity Development Plans: Global Overview
- Top-100 Journalists Covering Advanced Biomedicine and Longevity
- Longevity Industry in California Landscape Overview
- Top-100 Longevity Leaders
- Top-50 Women Longevity Leaders
- Top-30 Longevity Conferences 2019 - 2020
- Advancing Financial Longevity Industry / AgeTech / WealthTech Volume I
- Longevity Industry in Switzerland Landscape Overview
- Longevity and Metabesity: USA Special Case Study
- Supercentenarians Landscape Overview
- Biomarkers of Longevity: Most Comprehensive and Minimum Required Panels of Biomarkers

Cooperation

Aging Analytics Agency is primarily interested in strategic collaboration with international corporations, organisations and governments of progressive countries on projects and initiatives related to Longevity.

www.aginganalytics.com
info@aginganalytics.com

Aging Analytics Agency utilizes sophisticated comparative analytical frameworks to provide end-to-end Longevity Industry analytics services and tangible, tailored, organization-specific recommendations to relevant counterparties including Longevity companies, investment funds and governance-related entities on ways that they can optimize their business models, product and service offerings, and strategic decision-making to maintain maximum relevance in the face of the overwhelmingly complex global Longevity Industry.

Aging Analytics Agency is open to engage with strategic clients via a variety of approaches, including:

- Conducting customised case studies, research and analytics for internal (organizational) use, tailored to the precise needs of specific clients;
- Producing open-access analytical reports;
- Offering customised analysis using specialised interactive industry and technology databases and IT-platforms.

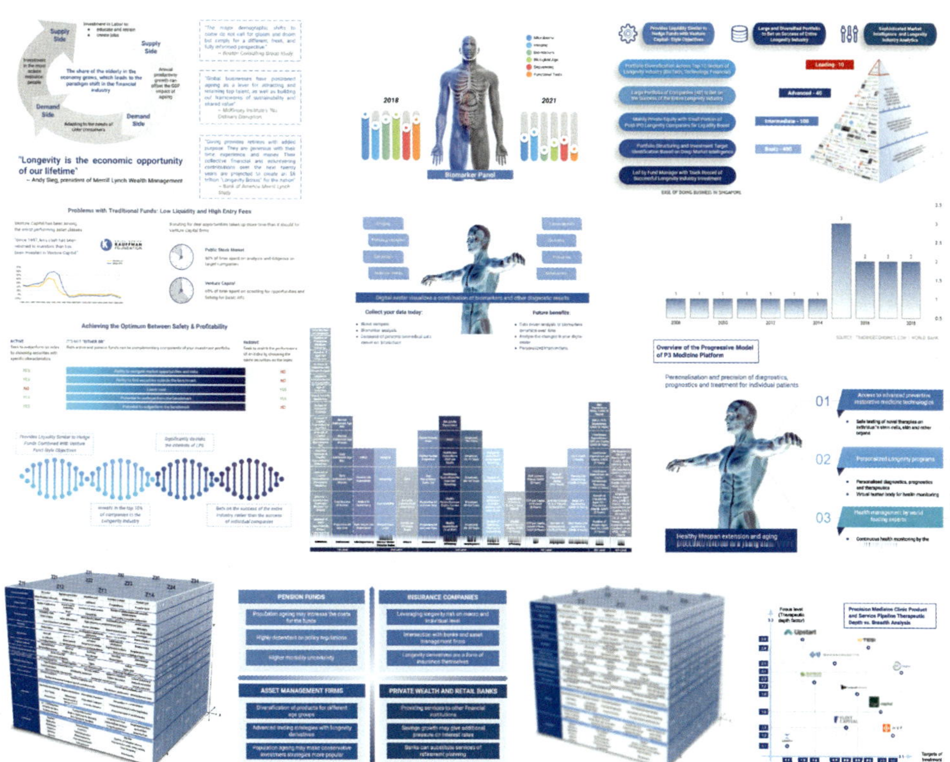

Key Analytical and Consulting Services

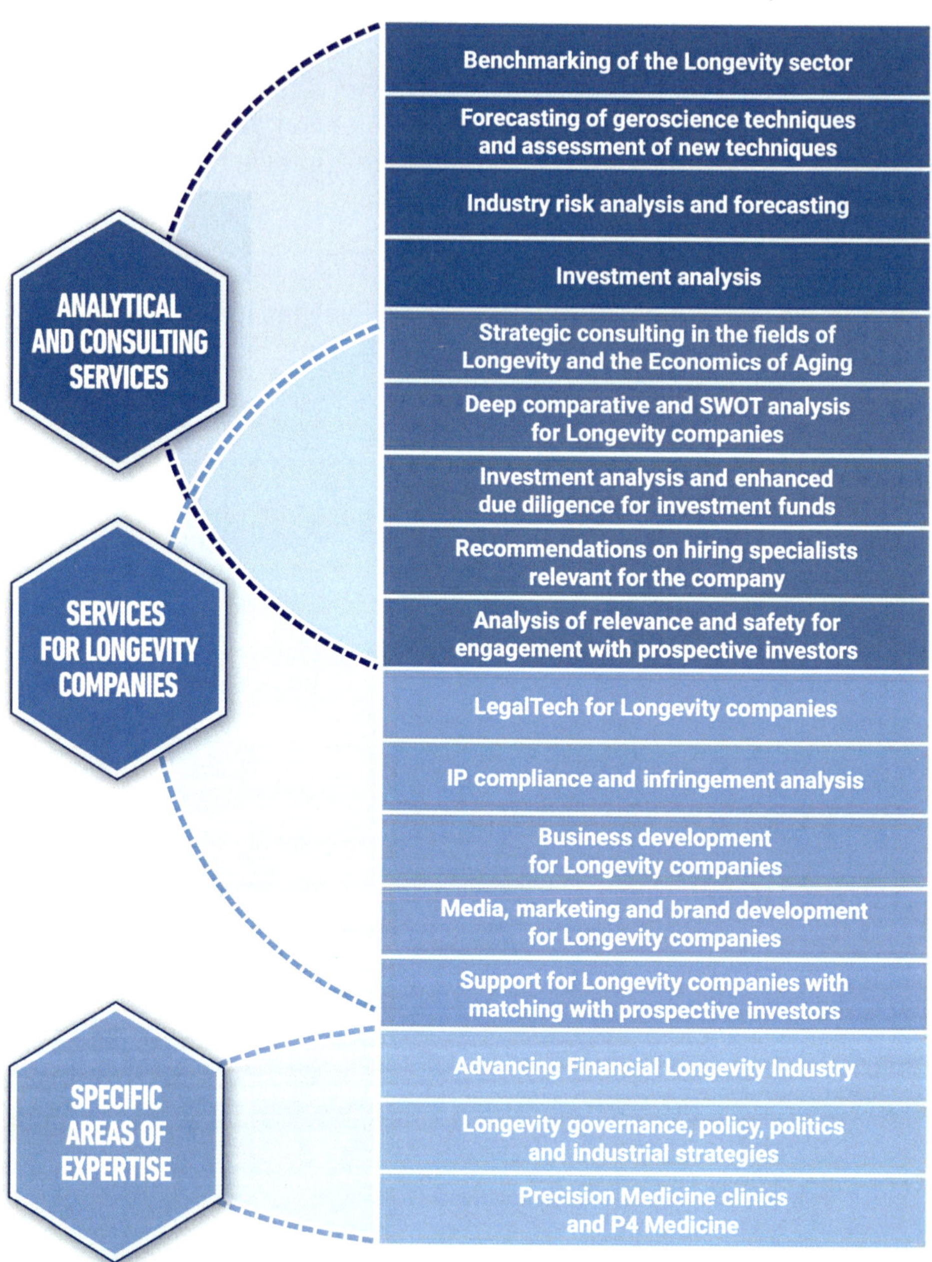

Benchmarking of the Global Longevity Industry

Aging Analytics Agency has been continually developing sophisticated and quantitative analytical frameworks for Longevity Industry analysis, benchmarking, competitive landscaping and forecasting for over 5 years, which enable Longevity companies to be evaluated and analyzed in a validated and tangible manner for the first time.

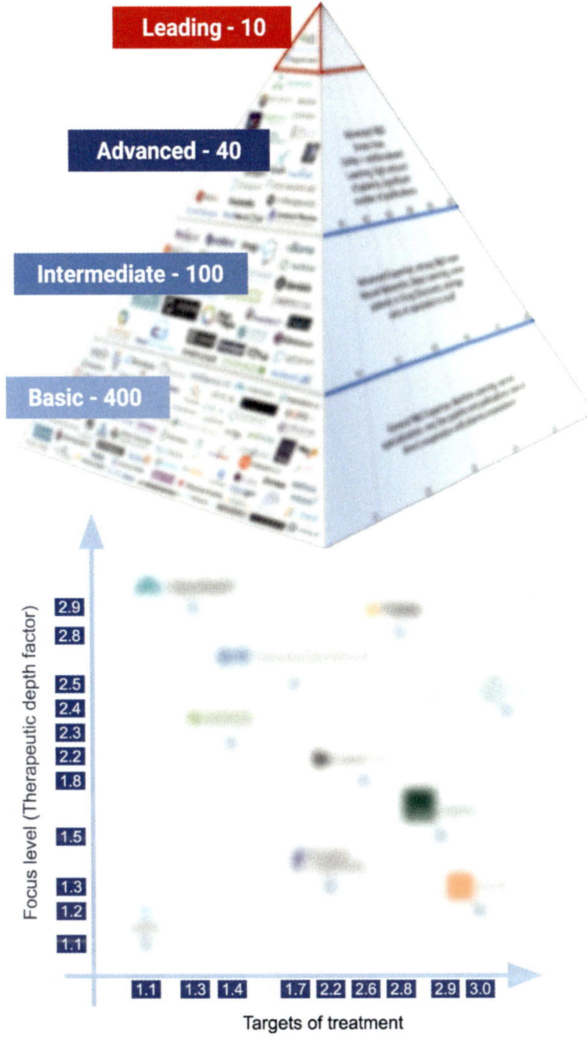

In contrast to traditional BioTech, the Longevity Industry is an extremely advanced domain of science and technology, and can be considered as the very cutting edge of advanced biomedicine.

This poses unique challenges to standard approaches for forecasting, investment target identification and due diligence. In an industry marked by extreme levels of complexity and multidimensionality, the old approaches which proved successful in BioTech break down and become ineffective.

Being situated at the intersection of many frontier technologies and domains of science, Longevity Industry benchmarking and analysis need to be as complex and multidimensional as the sectors they are applied to in order to be relevant.

Specific Areas of Expertise: Precision Medicine Clinics and P4 Medicine

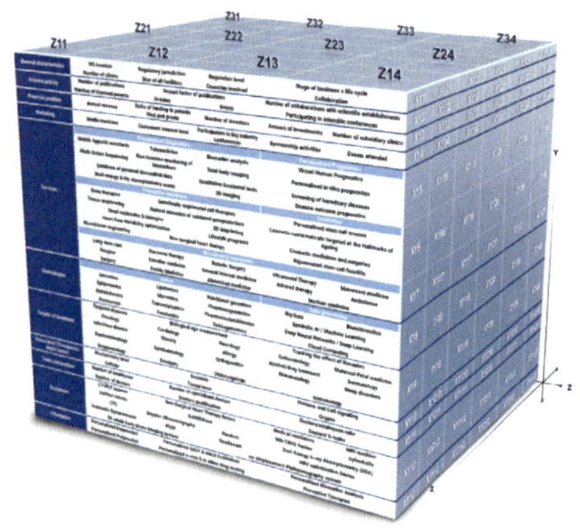

Aging Analytics Agency has produced a comprehensive proprietary report on the Precision Medicine clinics industry landscape, *Precision Medicine Clinics Landscape Overview 2019: Most Advanced Clinics, Technologies and Methods*, profiling the top 100 Precision Medicine clinics globally, as chosen according to a comprehensive, multidimensional analytical framework that uses tangible, quantitative metrics to rank the level of clinics' scientific validation, technological sophistication, level of business development, and level of personalised, preventive care they are able to offer to their clients.

Aging Analytics Agency has developed a sophisticated multidimensional analytical framework to benchmark the full scope of clinics focused on Precision, Preventive, Personalised and Participatory Medicine, to identify the top-100 Precision Medicine clinics.

We believe that the effective analysis of as complex and multidimensional an industry as Precision Medicine clinics requires the application of an equally multidimensional framework. This sophisticated sector-specific analytical framework includes metrics for identifying the breadth of the industry, identifying the degree of technological development, staff professionalism, range of provided services, financial position and scientific activity.

Our analysts use detailed mathematical procedures to assign a weighting (or importance factor) to each of the dozens of metrics they applied to Precision Medicine clinics, and combine them into a single calculated percentage, by dividing the final score of a company by the maximal score (sum of all weight factors), wherein each metric is taken into account in proportion to its overall level of importance, in order to arrive at a single adjusted company ranking that takes into account all relevant variables.

Aging Analytics Agency proposes the full scope of analytical and consulting services to Precision Medicine clinics. Its clients can expect the most advanced services based on a deep expertise in the industry.

Deep Comparative and SWOT Analysis for Longevity Companies

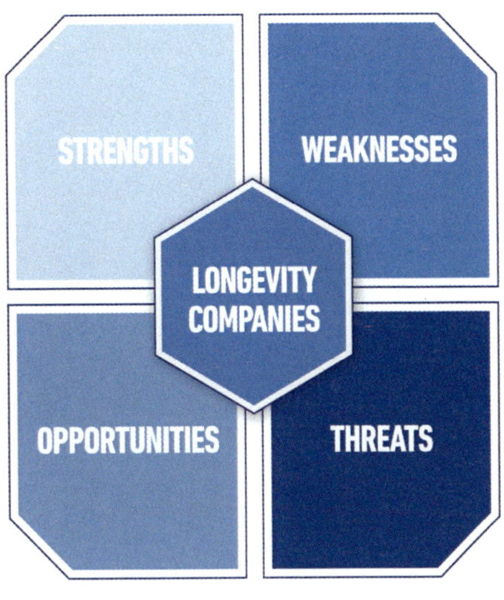

Aging Analytics Agency has, since its inception in 2013, been applying systematic methodologies to create various types of analytical frameworks that clearly define and classify distinct scientific domains, technologies and applications in a way that allows them to be quantitatively compared, continually refining them to maintain their relevance against the changing dynamics of the industry sectors they are applied to. Since then, the company has continued to improve these comparative analysis systems, both in terms of the specific metrics used to conduct its market studies and the mathematical formulas used to combine them as well as created advanced visualization techniques for making forecasts, rankings and determinations maximally understandable. Aging Analytics Agency offers comprehensive research on the Longevity companies. It has gathered a multidisciplinary team of consultants and analysts which can perform technology evaluation and overall company due diligence to understand the key strengths, weaknesses, opportunities and threats ("SWOT").

LONGEVITY INDUSTRY ANALYTICAL FRAMEWORK: COMPANY HARMONIZATION ANALYSIS

The service includes the following:

- Identifying the key strengths and weaknesses of the company compared to the overall competitive landscape;
- Describing the ways to improve weaknesses;
- Key areas in which companies are already strong, and recommendations on how to use them;
- Specific recommendations on how to improve company's overall, composite rank and standing in the industry.

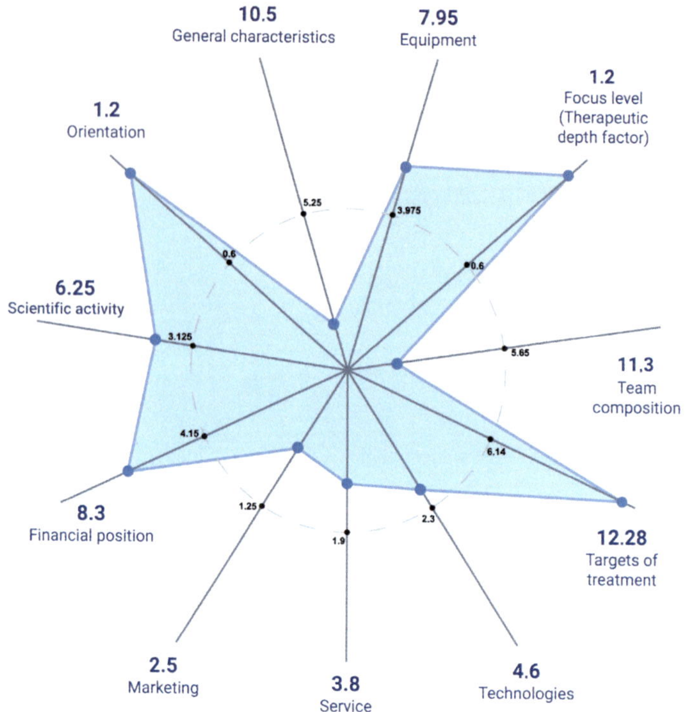

Specific Areas of Expertise: Advancing Financial Longevity Industry

Aging Analytics Agency has produced the *Advancing Financial Industry - Longevity / AgeTech / WealthTech Volume I* open-access report and the proprietary Volume II version. The main goal of the report is to deliver practical answers to specific questions concerning the influence of aging on financial institutions' activity in order to optimize their short and long-term strategies, with a new updated edition being released each financial quarter, incrementally increasing the precision, relevance and actionability of its industry analysis.

The value of this series of reports is explained by the fact that it answers three main questions which are extremely important for all financial institutions under modern conditions: What are the major threats and opportunities facing financial institutions regarding population aging? What are the tools to deal with Longevity risk? How exactly can and should they be applied? How can financial institutions benefit from the collision of Longevity megatrends?

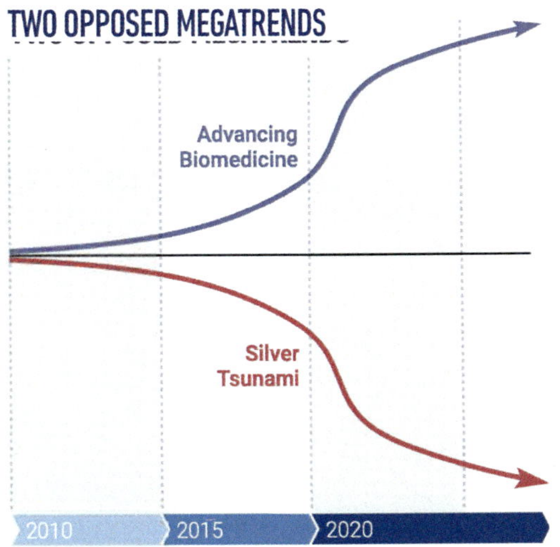

The acceleration of biomedicine has been mainly spurred by advances in the collection, gathering and analysis of data. The industry is poised to witness a quantum leap in the near future, particularly because of the impact of Artificial Intelligence in biomedicine R&D, and in light of the upcoming paradigm shift from treatment to prevention.

At the same time, the inevitable Silver Tsunami (demographic aging) poses major economic burdens not just for the healthcare systems of developing nations, but also for the major financial institutions including pension funds, insurance companies, asset management firms and retail/private wealth banks. An increase in the costs associated with old age is expected.

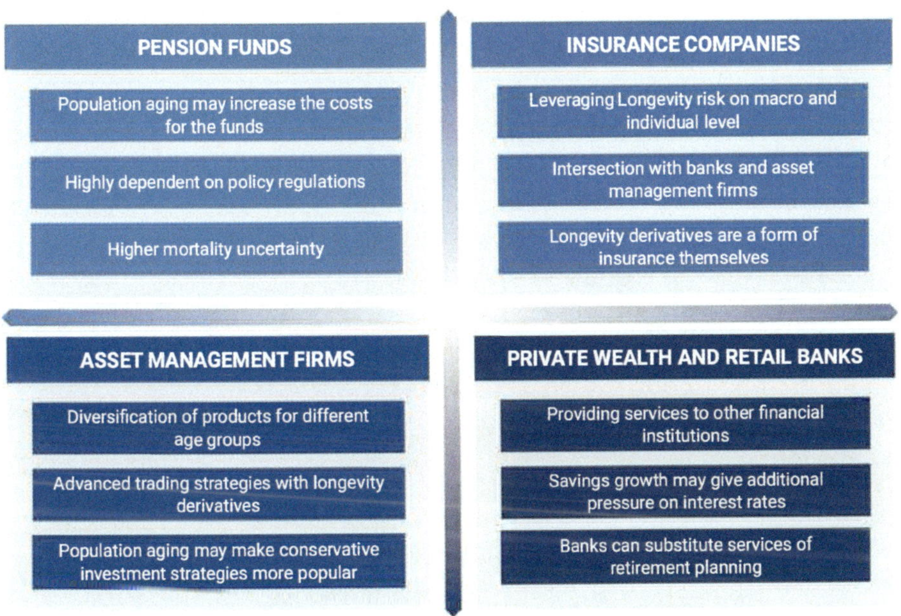

Specific Areas of Expertise: Longevity Governance

Aging Analytics Agency has published the *National Longevity Development Plans: Global Landscape Overview 2019* report providing comprehensive international overview of the projects, initiatives and efforts that different countries across the globe are making in order to combat the issues associated with aging populations and to promote the extension and maintenance of their citizens' Healthy Longevity. The report also charts how nations can most successfully build upon previous efforts in this direction, such as the UK naming the Aging Population as one of its four core Industrial Grand Challenges, and their allocation of £300 million to promote industry efforts focused on securing the nation's position as the world leader in Healthy Longevity. Furthermore, the report describes important next steps that the governments can execute in order to translate their efforts into tangible deliverables like increased healthy life expectancy and a thriving Longevity Financial Industry.

Moreover, Aging Analytics Agency produced the *Global Longevity Governance Landscape: 50 Countries Big Data Comparative Analysis of Longevity Progressiveness* report. It uses a complex analytic framework of metrics to provide a comprehensive overview of the factors involved with Health-Adjusted Life Expectancy (HALE), and its causes and effects globally, and what steps each country would need to take to maximize their HALE and minimize the gap between HALE and life expectancy. The focus of this study was primarily on 6 levels of analysis and aimed at perceptions of actual changes of interconnections between the nearly 200 parameters. Quantitative data analysis in this report include approximately 10,000 numerical values to indicate trends in Longevity. The report delivers not only deep analysis of Healthy Longevity in the countries, their advancements and drawbacks, but also provides tangible recommendations for each of 50 countries' governments.

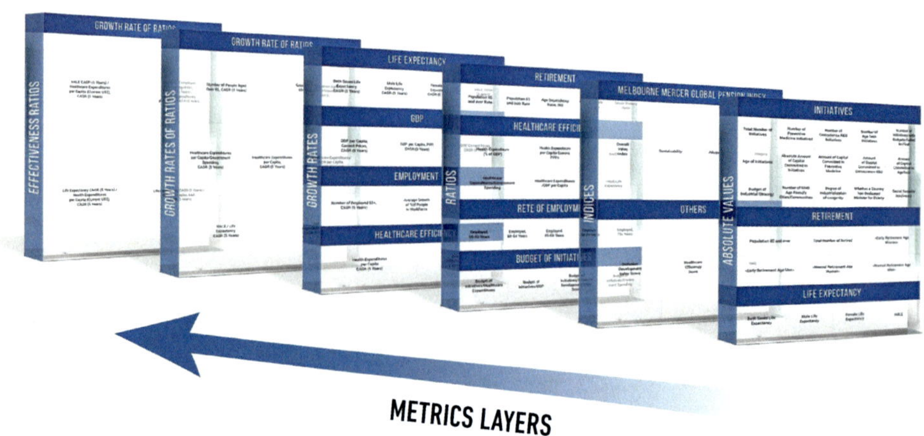

Strategic Consulting: Longevity Governance and Longevity Financial Industry

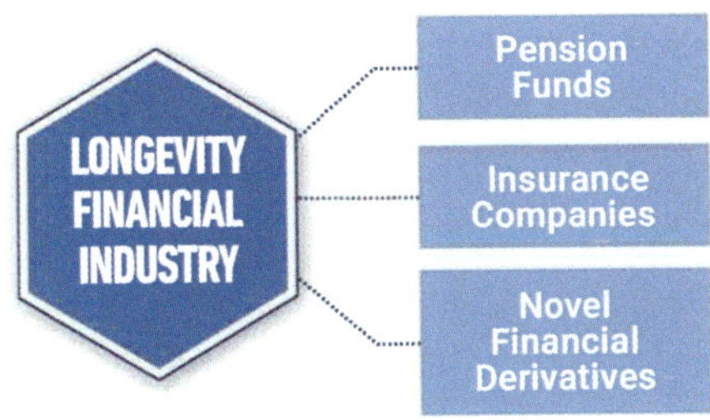

In Q2 2019, following the appointment of Eric Kihlstrom (former Director of the government-led £98 million Healthy Aging Industrial Strategy Challenge Fund) as its new Director, and becoming the main source of data and analytics for the UK All-Party Parliamentary Group for Longevity, Aging Analytics Agency also began expanding the scope and focus of its efforts relating to deep industry analytics on the emerging front of the Longevity Financial Industry, and on benchmarking and strategic consulting services relating to government-led Longevity Industry development and national policy efforts of various countries.

As mentioned, in early 2019, Aging Analytics Agency began shifting increasingly large proportions of its resources away from open-source landscape overviews and special case studies of the Longevity industries of various nations and towards benchmarking and ranking of the strength, relevance and proactivity of various entities including companies, investors, financial institutions and government initiatives within the Longevity sphere, leveraging the very broad and deep understanding of the global Longevity Industry created through the production of tens of thousands of pages of global and regional landscape overviews from 2013 to 2018 in order to begin conducting deeper, more targeted analytics. Aging Analytics Agency is currently cooperating with a number of government departments and public sector bodies and authorities in the UK, Singapore, Switzerland, Israel and the US to create advanced IT solutions, deep analytics, special case studies and composite sets of tangible recommendations and development plans for national industrial strategies, science and technology policy, modernization and reforms in healthcare, frontier-technology sectors including Longevity, AI and Precision Health, and financial reforms relating to pension systems and insurance companies looking to transform the problem of aging population into the opportunity of Healthy Longevity.

Benchmarking of the Longevity Sector

In sum, Aging Analytics Agency has been continually developing sophisticated and quantitative analytical frameworks for Longevity Industry analysis, benchmarking, competitive landscaping and forecasting for over 5 years, which enables Longevity companies to be evaluated and analyzed in a validated and tangible manner for the first time. In contrast to traditional BioTech, the Longevity Industry is an extremely advanced domain of science and technology, and can be considered as the very cutting edge of advanced biomedicine. This poses unique challenges to standard approaches for forecasting, investment target identification and due diligence.

In an industry marked by extreme levels of complexity and multidimensionality, the old approaches which proved successful in BioTech break down and become ineffective. Being situated at the intersection of many frontier technologies and domains of science, Longevity Industry benchmarking and analysis needs to be as complex and multidimensional as the sectors they are applied to in order to be relevant.

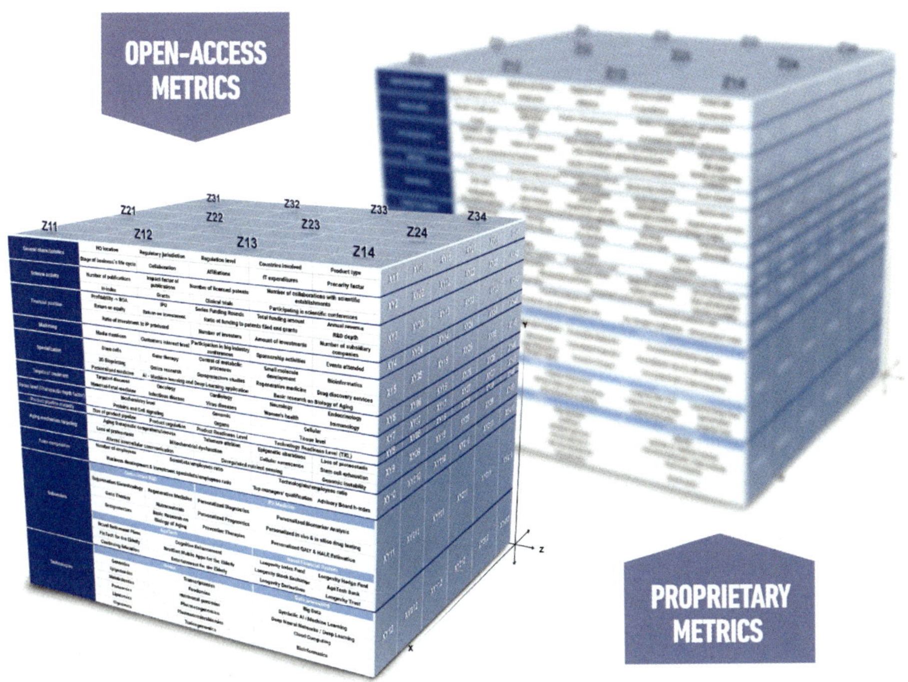

In order to develop a robust strategy to grow your business in a technological and scientifically complex market, it is essential to have a clear overall picture of the sector, with all its key players, their competitive positions, deals, relations, and relative strengths and weaknesses. To address this need, Aging Analytics Agency offers a service of benchmarking the entire scope of key players in the Longevity Industry, including deep analysis and ranking based on multiple parameters.

About the Authors

Dmitry Kaminskiy is an innovative entrepreneur and investor active in the fields of Longevity, Precision Medicine, and Artificial Intelligence. He is co-founder and managing partner at Deep Knowledge Ventures, a leading investment fund focused on DeepTech, renowned for its use of sophisticated analytical systems for investment target identification and due diligence. He is a frequent speaker on AI and Longevity including events organized in London by The Economist ("Aging Societies and The Business of Longevity") and organized by the Financial Times ("Smart Machines vs. Smart People" and "Global Pharmaceutical and Biotechnology Conference"), as well as the "Precision Medicine World Conference" in Silicon Valley, and other events at Oxford and Cambridge universities. He is actively involved in the work of the initiative group and was instrumental at the initial stage of the launch of the All-Party Parliamentary Group for Longevity in the UK Parliament. He now serves as co-director of the secretariat, overseeing the APPG's international Longevity cooperation development division.

Margaretta Colangelo is Co-founder and Managing Director of Deep Knowledge Group, an international consortium of commercial and non-profit organizations focused on the synergetic convergence of DeepTech and Frontier Technologies. Margaretta is a native San Franciscan with over 30 years of experience in working in software companies in the Silicon Valley. She has a deep and multifaceted understanding of business, science, and technology and is highly adept at tracking and forecasting innovation in technology. Margaretta has been at the forefront of emerging technologies throughout her entire career. In the 1990s she was a core member of the team that developed the first Java-based secure messaging software for stock trading platforms that is still used today by the world's top multinational banks. She's been a core member of teams that have influenced important technical specifications and standards, including JDBC (Java Database Connectivity) and JMS (Java Messaging Service) that have helped advance the technology industry. She has published over 100 articles on DeepTech and AI and publishes weekly newsletters on DeepTech, FinTech, and the Longevity Industry with over 40,000 subscribers. She has appeared multiple times in Forbes, MIT Technology Review Italia, Fierce Biotech, Health Management Journal, Outsourced Pharma, Pharmaceutical Executive, Healthcare IT News, Asian Robotics Review, and Bahrain Entrepreneur. Margaretta serves on the Advisory Boards of the AI Precision Health Institute at the University of Hawai'i Cancer Center and the Longevity AI Consortium at King's College London. She has an extensive network in the technology and venture capital communities and has over 35,000 followers on LinkedIn.

About the Contributors

Eric Kihlstrom

Eric Kihlstrom is the Strategic Director of Aging Analytics Agency and the former Interim Director of the £98 million Healthy Ageing Industrial Strategy Challenge Fund. He serves as Head of Industry Collaboration for Longevity International UK, the All-Party Parliamentary Group for Longevity Secretariat.

Franco Cortese

Franco Cortese is Director of Aging Analytics Agency, and has been a member of the company's executive management team since its inception. He is one of the co-creators of the Longevity Industry Framework behind many of the company's Longevity Industry analytics, benchmarking and forecasting.

Robin Farmanfarmaian

Robin Farmanfarmaian is a professional speaker, entrepreneur, and angel investor working with cutting-edge Artificial Intelligence software, device and pharma companies poised to impact 100M patients. She is the author of "The Patient as CEO" and "The Thought Leader Formula".

Kate Batz

Kate Batz is Managing Partner of Longevity.Capital and Director of Strategic Business Development at Deep Knowledge Ventures. She has 15+ years of experience as a corporate attorney and leads the legal framework development of Deep Knowledge Group.

Sergey Balasanyan

Sergey Balasanyan is Partner at Deep Knowledge Ventures and Co-Founder of Longevity Bank. He is leading the Longevity FinTech department of Longevity.Capital, as well as the activities of the Longevity FinTech division of Aging Analytics Agency, leveraging his significant experience in the broader FinTech industry.

Stefan Hascoet

Stefan Hascoet is a Partner at Deep Knowledge Ventures and head of its Switzerland headquarters, with 15 years of experience in investment banking. He leads the development of InvestTech progressive solutions of Deep Knowledge Group.

Richard Siow

Richard Siow is Director of Ageing Research at King's College University in London (ARK) and the Longevity AI Consortium, and is the leading scientific advisor of the AI Longevity activities of Deep Knowledge Group.

Online Resources

Advancing Financial Industry Longevity / AgeTech / WealthTech
https://www.aginganalytics.com/financial-longevity-industry

Aging Analytics Agency
https://www.aginganalytics.com/

AI-Pharma.Capital Fund
https://www.ai-pharma.capital/

All-Party Parliamentary Group for Longevity
https://appg-longevity.org/

Biogerontology Research Foundation
http://bg-rf.org.uk/

Biomarkers of Longevity
https://www.aginganalytics.com/biomarkers-of-longevity

Deep Knowledge Analytics
https://dka.global/

Deep Knowledge Analytics Pharma Division
https://ai-pharma.dka.global/

Deep Knowledge Group
https://www.dkv.global/

FemTech Healthcare Landscape Overview Q1 2019
https://www.aginganalytics.com/femtech-healthcare-q1-2019

Global Longevity Governance Landscape Overview 2019
https://www.aginganalytics.com/global-longevity-governance

Longevity AI Consortium at King's College London
https://www.ai-longevity.center/

Longevity.Capital
https://www.longevity.capital/

Longevity FinTech Company
https://www.longevity.finance/

Longevity Industry in California
https://www.aginganalytics.com/longevity-california

Longevity Industry in Israel
https://www.aginganalytics.com/longevity-in-israel

Longevity Industry in Singapore
https://www.aginganalytics.com/longevity-in-singapore

Longevity Industry in Switzerland
https://www.aginganalytics.com/longevity-switzerland

Longevity Industry in United Kingdom
https://www.aginganalytics.com/longevity-in-uk-2-edition

Longevity Industry Landscape Overview 2018 Volume I
https://www.aginganalytics.com/longevity-industry-2018-vol-1

Longevity Swiss Foundation
https://www.longevitysuisse.org/

Metabesity and Longevity: USA Special Case Study
https://www.aginganalytics.com/longevity-usa

National Longevity Development Plans: Global Overview 2019
https://www.aginganalytics.com/longevity-development-plans

NeuroTech Analytics
https://www.neurotech.com/

Policy Governance
https://www.aginganalytics.com/policy-governance

Proprietary Analytics
https://www.aginganalytics.com/proprietary-analytics

Made in the USA
Columbia, SC
13 November 2020